M000201289

THE HISTORY OF THE CHURCH

By EUSEBIUS

Translated by
ARTHUR CUSHMAN McGIFFERT

The History of the Church
By Eusebius
Translated by Arthur Cushman McGiffert

Print ISBN 13: 978-1-4209-5721-1
eBook ISBN 13: 978-1-4209-5722-8

This edition copyright © 2018. Digireads.com Publishing.

All rights reserved. No part of this publication may be reproduced, distributed, or transmitted in any form or by any means, including photocopying, recording, or other electronic or mechanical methods, without the prior written permission of the publisher, except in the case of brief quotations embodied in critical reviews and certain other noncommercial uses permitted by copyright law.

Cover Image: a detail of "Christ Giving the Keys to St. Peter" by Pietro Perugino, c. 1481-1482, fresco, Sistine Chapel, Rome.

Please visit *www.digireads.com*

CONTENTS

BOOK I.

BOOK II.

BOOK III.

BOOK IV.

BOOK V.

BOOK VI.

BOOK VII.

SUPPLEMENT TO BOOK VIII.

The Martyrs of Palestine.

BOOK IX.

BOOK X.

Book I.

Chapter I.

THE PLAN OF THE WORK.

1. It is my purpose to write an account of the successions of the holy apostles, as well as of the times which have elapsed from the days of our Saviour to our own; and to relate the many important events which are said to have occurred in the history of the Church; and to mention those who have governed and presided over the Church in the most prominent parishes, and those who in each generation have proclaimed the divine word either orally or in writing.

2. It is my purpose also to give the names and number and times of those who through love of innovation have run into the greatest errors, and, proclaiming themselves discoverers of knowledge falsely so-called, have like fierce wolves unmercifully devastated the flock of Christ.

3. It is my intention, moreover, to recount the misfortunes which immediately came upon the whole Jewish nation in consequence of their plots against our Saviour, and to record the ways and the times in which the divine word has been attacked by the Gentiles, and to describe the character of those who at various periods have contended for it in the face of blood and of tortures, as well as the confessions which have been made in our own days, and finally the gracious and kindly succor which our Saviour has afforded them all. Since I propose to write of all these things I shall commence my work with the beginning of the dispensation of our Saviour and Lord Jesus Christ.

4. But at the outset I must crave for my work the indulgence of the wise, for I confess that it is beyond my power to produce a perfect and complete history, and since I am the first to enter upon the subject, I am attempting to traverse as it were a lonely and untrodden path. I pray that I may have God as my guide and the power of the Lord as my aid, since I am unable to find even the bare footsteps of those who have traveled the way before me, except in brief fragments, in which some in one way, others in another, have transmitted to us particular accounts of the times in which they lived. From afar they raise their voices like torches, and they cry out, as from some lofty and conspicuous watch-tower, admonishing us where to walk and how to direct the course of our work steadily and safely.

5. Having gathered therefore from the matters mentioned here and there by them whatever we consider important for the present work, and having plucked like flowers from a meadow the appropriate passages from ancient writers, we shall endeavor to embody the whole

in an historical narrative, content if we preserve the memory of the successions of the apostles of our Saviour; if not indeed of all, yet of the most renowned of them in those churches which are the most noted, and which even to the present time are held in honor.

6. This work seems to me of especial importance because I know of no ecclesiastical writer who has devoted himself to this subject; and I hope that it will appear most useful to those who are fond of historical research.

7. I have already given an epitome of these things in the Chronological Canons which I have composed, but notwithstanding that, I have undertaken in the present work to write as full an account of them as I am able.

8. My work will begin, as I have said, with the dispensation of the Saviour Christ,—which is loftier and greater than human conception,— and with a discussion of his divinity;

9. for it is necessary, inasmuch as we derive even our name from Christ, for one who proposes to write a history of the Church to begin with the very origin of Christ's dispensation, a dispensation more divine than many think.

Chapter II.

SUMMARY VIEW OF THE PRE-EXISTENCE AND DIVINITY
OF OUR SAVIOUR AND LORD JESUS CHRIST.

1. Since in Christ there is a twofold nature, and the one—in so far as he is thought of as God—resembles the head of the body, while the other may be compared with the feet,—in so far as he, for the sake of our salvation, put on human nature with the same passions as our own,—the following work will be complete only if we begin with the chief and lordliest events of all his history. In this way will the antiquity and divinity of Christianity be shown to those who suppose it of recent and foreign origin, and imagine that it appeared only yesterday.

2. No language is sufficient to express the origin and the worth, the being and the nature of Christ. Wherefore also the divine Spirit says in the prophecies, "Who shall declare his generation?"

3. For none knoweth the Father except the Son, neither can any one know the Son adequately except the Father alone who hath begotten him. For alone who beside the Father could clearly understand the Light which was before the world, the intellectual and essential Wisdom which existed before the ages, the living Word which was in the beginning with the Father and which was God, the first and only begotten of God which was before every creature and creation visible and invisible, the commander-in-chief of the rational and immortal host

of heaven, the messenger of the great counsel, the executor of the Father's unspoken will, the creator, with the Father, of all things, the second cause of the universe after the Father, the true and only-begotten Son of God, the Lord and God and King of all created things, the one who has received dominion and power, with divinity itself, and with might and honor from the Father; as it is said in regard to him in the mystical passages of Scripture which speak of his divinity: "In the beginning was the Word, and the Word was with God, and the Word was God." "All things were made by him; and without him was not anything made."

4. This, too, the great Moses teaches, when, as the most ancient of all the prophets, he describes under the influence of the divine Spirit the creation and arrangement of the universe. He declares that the maker of the world and the creator of all things yielded to Christ himself, and to none other than his own clearly divine and first-born Word, the making of inferior things, and communed with him respecting the creation of man. Says he: "For God said, Let us make man in our image and in our likeness."

5. And another of the prophets confirms this, speaking of God in his hymns as follows: "He spake and they were made; he commanded and they were created." He here introduces the Father and Maker as Ruler of all, commanding with a kingly nod, and second to him the divine Word, none other than the one who is proclaimed by us, as carrying out the Father's commands.

6. All that are said to have excelled in righteousness and piety since the creation of man, the great servant Moses and before him in the first place Abraham and his children, and as many righteous men and prophets as afterward appeared, have contemplated him with the pure eyes of the mind, and have recognized him and offered to him the worship which is due him as Son of God.

7. But he, by no means neglectful of the reverence due to the Father, was appointed to teach the knowledge of the Father to them all. For instance, the Lord God, it is said, appeared as a common man to Abraham while he was sitting at the oak of Mambre. And he, immediately failing down, although he saw a man with his eyes, nevertheless worshiped him as God, and sacrificed to him as Lord, and confessed that he was not ignorant of his identity when he uttered the words, "Lord, the judge of all the earth, wilt thou not execute righteous judgment?"

8. For if it is unreasonable to suppose that the unbegotten and immutable essence of the almighty God was changed into the form of man or that it deceived the eyes of the beholders with the appearance of some created thing, and if it is unreasonable to suppose, on the other hand, that the Scripture should falsely invent such things, when the God and Lord who judgeth all the earth and executeth judgment is seen

in the form of a man, who else can be called, if it be not lawful to call him the first cause of all things, than his only pre-existent Word? Concerning whom it is said in the Psalms, "He sent his Word and healed them, and delivered them from their destructions."

9. Moses most clearly proclaims him second Lord after the Father, when he says, "The Lord rained upon Sodom and Gomorrah brimstone and fire from the Lord." The divine Scripture also calls him God, when he appeared again to Jacob in the form of a man, and said to Jacob, "Thy name shall be called no more Jacob, but Israel shall be thy name, because thou hast prevailed with God." Wherefore also Jacob called the name of that place "Vision of God," saying, "For I have seen God face to face, and my life is preserved."

10. Nor is it admissible to suppose that the theophanies recorded were appearances of subordinate angels and ministers of God, for whenever any of these appeared to men, the Scripture does not conceal the fact, but calls them by name not God nor Lord, but angels, as it is easy to prove by numberless testimonies.

11. Joshua, also, the successor of Moses, calls him, as leader of the heavenly angels and archangels and of the supramundane powers, and as lieutenant of the Father, entrusted with the second rank of sovereignty and rule over all, "captain of the host of the Lords" although he saw him not otherwise than again in the form and appearance of a man.

12. For it is written: "And it came to pass when Joshua was at Jericho that he looked and saw a man standing over against him with his sword drawn in his hand, and Joshua went unto him and said, Art thou for us or for our adversaries? And he said unto him, As captain of the host of the Lord am I now come. And Joshua fell on his face to the earth and said unto him, Lord, what dost thou command thy servant? and the captain of the Lord said unto Joshua, Loose thy shoe from off thy feet, for the place whereon thou standest is holy."

13. You will perceive also from the same words that this was no other than he who talked with Moses. For the Scripture says in the same words and with reference to the same one, "When the Lord saw that he drew near to see, the Lord called to him out of the bush and said, Moses, Moses. And he said, What is it? And he said, Draw not nigh hither; loose thy shoe from off thy feet, for the place whereon thou standest is holy ground. And he said unto him, I am the God of thy fathers, the God of Abraham, and the God of Isaac, and the God of Jacob."

14. And that there is a certain substance which lived and subsisted before the world, and which ministered unto the Father and God of the universe for the formation of all created things, and which, is called the Word of God and Wisdom, we may learn, to quote other proofs in addition to those already cited, from the mouth of Wisdom herself, who

reveals most clearly through Solomon the following mysteries concerning herself: "I, Wisdom, have dwelt with prudence and knowledge, and I have invoked understanding. Through me kings reign, and princes ordain righteousness. Through me the great are magnified, and through me sovereigns rule the earth."

15. To which she adds: "The Lord created me in the beginning of his ways, for his works; before the world he established me, in the beginning, before he made the earth, before he made the depths, before the mountains were settled, before all hills he begat me. When he prepared the heavens I was present with him, and when he established the fountains of the region under heaven I was with him, disposing. I was the one in whom he delighted; daily I rejoiced before him at all times when he was rejoicing at having completed the world."

16. That the divine Word, therefore, pre-existed and appeared to some, if not to all, has thus been briefly shown by us.

17. But why the Gospel was not preached in ancient times to all men and to all nations, as it is now, will appear from the following considerations. The life of the ancients was not of such a kind as to permit them to receive the all-wise and all-virtuous teaching of Christ.

18. For immediately in the beginning, after his original life of blessedness, the first man despised the command of God, and fell into this mortal and perishable state, and exchanged his former divinely inspired luxury for this curse-laden earth. His descendants having filled our earth, showed themselves much worse, with the exception of one here and there, and entered upon a certain brutal and insupportable mode of life.

19. They thought neither of city nor state, neither of arts nor sciences. They were ignorant even of the name of laws and of justice, of virtue and of philosophy. As nomads, they passed their lives in deserts, like wild and fierce beasts, destroying, by an excess of voluntary wickedness, the natural reason of man, and the seeds of thought and of culture implanted in the human soul. They gave themselves wholly over to all kinds of profanity, now seducing one another, now slaying one another, now eating human flesh, and now daring to wage war with the Gods and to undertake those battles of the giants celebrated by all; now planning to fortify earth against heaven, and in the madness of ungoverned pride to prepare an attack upon the very God of all.

20. On account of these things, when they conducted themselves thus, the all-seeing God sent down upon them floods and conflagrations as upon a wild forest spread over the whole earth. He cut them down with continuous famines and plagues, with wars, and with thunderbolts from heaven, as if to check some terrible and obstinate disease of souls with more severe punishments.

21. Then, when the excess of wickedness had overwhelmed nearly

all the race, like a deep fit of drunkenness, beclouding and darkening the minds of men, the first-born and first-created wisdom of God, the pre-existent Word himself, induced by his exceeding love for man, appeared to his servants, now in the form of angels, and again to one and another of those ancients who enjoyed the favor of God, in his own person as the saving power of God, not otherwise, however, than in the shape of man, because it was impossible to appear in any other way.

22. And as by them the seeds of piety were sown among a multitude of men and the whole nation, descended from the Hebrews, devoted themselves persistently to the worship of God, he imparted to them through the prophet Moses, as to multitudes still corrupted by their ancient practices, images and symbols of a certain mystic Sabbath and of circumcision, and elements of other spiritual principles, but he did not grant them a complete knowledge of the mysteries themselves.

23. But when their law became celebrated, and, like a sweet odor, was diffused among all men, as a result of their influence the dispositions of the majority of the heathen were softened by the lawgivers and philosophers who arose on every side, and their wild and savage brutality was changed into mildness, so that they enjoyed deep peace, friendship, and social intercourse. Then, finally, at the time of the origin of the Roman Empire, there appeared again to all men and nations throughout the world, who had been, as it were, previously assisted, and were now fitted to receive the knowledge of the Father, that same teacher of virtue, the minister of the Father in all good things, the divine and heavenly Word of God, in a human body not at all differing in substance from our own. He did and suffered the things which had been prophesied. For it had been foretold that one who was at the same time man and God should come and dwell in the world, should per form wonderful works, and should show himself a teacher to all nations of the piety of the Father. The marvelous nature of his birth, and his new teaching, and his wonderful works had also been foretold; so likewise the manner of his death, his resurrection from the dead, and, finally, his divine ascension into heaven.

24. For instance, Daniel the prophet, under the influence of the divine Spirit, seeing his kingdom at the end of time, was inspired thus to describe the divine vision in language fitted to human comprehension: "For I beheld," he says, "until thrones were placed, and the Ancient of Days did sit, whose garment was white as snow and the hair of his head like pure wool; his throne was a flame of fire and his wheels burning fire. A river of fire flowed before him. Thousand thousands ministered unto him, and ten thousand times ten thousand stood before him.

25. He appointed judgment, and the books were opened." And again, "I saw," says he, "and behold, one like the Son of man came with the clouds of heaven, and he hastened unto the Ancient of Days

and was brought into his presence, and there was given him the dominion and the glory and the kingdom; and all peoples, tribes, and tongues serve him. His dominion is an everlasting dominion which shall not pass away, and his kingdom shall not be destroyed."

26. It is clear that these words can refer to no one else than to our Saviour, the God Word who was in the beginning with God, and who was called the Son of man because of his final appearance in the flesh.

27. But since we have collected in separate books as the selections from the prophets which relate to our Saviour Jesus Christ, and have arranged in a more logical form those things which have been revealed concerning him, what has been said will suffice for the present.

Chapter III.

THE NAME JESUS AND ALSO THE NAME CHRIST WERE
KNOWN FROM THE BEGINNING, AND WERE HONORED BY
THE INSPIRED PROPHETS.

1. It is now the proper place to show that the very name Jesus and also the name Christ were honored by the ancient prophets beloved of God.

2. Moses was the first to make known the name of Christ as a name especially august and glorious. When he delivered types and symbols of heavenly things, and mysterious images, in accordance with the oracle which said to him, "Look that thou make all things according to the pattern which was shown thee in the mount," he consecrated a man high priest of God, in so far as that was possible, and him he called Christ. And thus to this dignity of the high priesthood, which in his opinion surpassed the most honorable position among men, he attached for the sake of honor and glory the name of Christ.

3. He knew so well that in Christ was something divine. And the same one foreseeing, under the influence of the divine Spirit, the name Jesus, dignified it also with a certain distinguished privilege. For the name of Jesus, which had never been uttered among men before the time of Moses, he applied first and only to the one who he knew would receive after his death, again as a type and symbol, the supreme command.

4. His successor, therefore, who had not hitherto borne the name Jesus, but had been called by another name, Auses, which had been given him by his parents, he now called Jesus, bestowing the name upon him as a gift of honor, far greater than any kingly diadem. For Jesus himself, the son of Nave, bore a resemblance to our Saviour in the fact that he alone, after Moses and after the completion of the symbolical worship which had been transmitted by him, succeeded to the government of the true and pure religion.

5. Thus Moses bestowed the name of our Saviour, Jesus Christ, as a mark of the highest honor, upon the two men who in his time surpassed all the rest of the people in virtue and glory; namely, upon the high priest and upon his own successor in the government.

6. And the prophets that came after also clearly foretold Christ by name, predicting at the same time the plots which the Jewish people would form against him, and the calling of the nations through him. Jeremiah, for instance, speaks as follows: "The Spirit before our face, Christ the Lord, was taken in their destructions; of whom we said, under his shadow we shall live among the nations." And David, in perplexity, says, "Why did the nations rage and the people imagine vain things? The kings of the earth set themselves in array, and the rulers were gathered together against the Lord and against his Christ"; to which he adds, in the person of Christ himself, "The Lord said unto me, Thou art my Son, this day have I begotten thee. Ask of me, and I will give thee the nations for thine inheritance, and the uttermost parts of the earth for thy possession."

7. And not only those who were honored with the high priesthood, and who for the sake of the symbol were anointed with especially prepared oil, were adorned with the name of Christ among the Hebrews, but also the kings whom the prophets anointed under the influence of the divine Spirit, and thus constituted, as it were, typical Christs. For they also bore in their own persons types of the royal and sovereign power of the true and only Christ, the divine Word who ruleth over all.

8. And we have been told also that certain of the prophets themselves became, by the act of anointing, Christs in type, so that all these have reference to the true Christ, the divinely inspired and heavenly Word, who is the only high priest of all, and the only King of every creature, and the Father's only supreme prophet of prophets.

9. And a proof of this is that no one of those who were of old symbolically anointed, whether priests, or kings, or prophets, possessed so great a power of inspired virtue as was exhibited by our Saviour and Lord Jesus, the true and only Christ.

10. None of them at least, however superior in dignity and honor they may have been for many generations among their own people, ever gave to their followers the name of Christians from their own typical name of Christ. Neither was divine honor ever rendered to any one of them by their subjects; nor after their death was the disposition of their followers such that they were ready to die for the one whom they honored. And never did so great a commotion arise among all the nations of the earth in respect to any one of that age; for the mere symbol could not act with such power among them as the truth itself which was exhibited by our Saviour.

11. He, although he received no symbols and types of high

priesthood from any one, although he was not born of a race of priests, although he was not elevated to a kingdom by military guards, although he was not a prophet like those of old, although he obtained no honor nor pre-eminence among the Jews, nevertheless was adorned by the Father with all, if not with the symbols, yet with the truth itself.

12. And therefore, although he did not possess like honors with those whom we have mentioned, he is called Christ more than all of them. And as himself the true and only Christ of God, he has filled the whole earth with the truly august and sacred name of Christians, committing to his followers no longer types and images, but the uncovered virtues themselves, and a heavenly life in the very doctrines of truth.

13. And he was not anointed with oil prepared from material substances, but, as befits divinity, with the divine Spirit himself, by participation in the unbegotten deity of the Father. And this is taught also again by Isaiah, who exclaims, as if in the person of Christ himself, "The Spirit of the Lord is upon me; therefore hath he anointed me. He hath sent me to preach the Gospel to the poor, to proclaim deliverance to captives, and recovery of sight to the blind."

14. And not only Isaiah, but also David addresses him, saying, "Thy throne, O God, is forever and ever. A scepter of equity is the scepter of thy kingdom. Thou hast loved righteousness and hast hated iniquity. Therefore God, thy God, hath anointed thee with the oil of gladness above thy fellows." Here the Scripture calls him God in the first verse, in the second it honors him with a royal scepter.

15. Then a little farther on, after the divine and royal power, it represents him in the third place as having become Christ, being anointed not with oil made of material substances, but with the divine oil of gladness. It thus indicates his especial honor, far superior to and different from that of those who, as types, were of old anointed in a more material way.

16. And elsewhere the same writer speaks of him as follows: "The Lord said unto my Lord, Sit thou at my right hand until I make thine enemies thy footstool"; and, "Out of the womb, before the morning star, have I begotten thee. The Lord hath sworn and he will not repent. Thou art a priest forever after the order of Melchizedec."

17. But this Melchizedec is introduced in the Holy Scriptures as a priest of the most high God, not consecrated by any anointing oil, especially prepared, and not even belonging by descent to the priesthood of the Jews. Wherefore after his order, but not after the order of the others, who received symbols and types, was our Saviour proclaimed, with an appeal to an oath, Christ and priest.

18. History, therefore, does not relate that he was anointed corporeally by the Jews, nor that he belonged to the lineage of priests, but that he came into existence from God himself before the morning

star, that is before the organization of the world, and that he obtained an immortal and undecaying priesthood for eternal ages.

19. But it is a great and convincing proof of his incorporeal and divine unction that he alone of all those who have ever existed is even to the present day called Christ by all men throughout the world, and is confessed and witnessed to under this name, and is commemorated both by Greeks and Barbarians and even to this day is honored as a King by his followers throughout the world, and is admired as more than a prophet, and is glorified as the true and only high priest of God. And besides all this, as the pre-existent Word of God, called into being before all ages, he has received august honor from the Father, and is worshiped as God.

20. But most wonderful of all is the fact that we who have consecrated ourselves to him, honor him not only with our voices and with the sound of words, but also with complete elevation of soul, so that we choose to give testimony unto him rather than to preserve our own lives.

21. I have of necessity prefaced my history with these matters in order that no one, judging from the date of his incarnation, may think that our Saviour and Lord Jesus, the Christ, has but recently come into being.

Chapter IV.

THE RELIGION PROCLAIMED BY HIM TO ALL NATIONS WAS NEITHER NEW NOR STRANGE.

1. But that no one may suppose that his doctrine is new and strange, as if it were framed by a man of recent origin, differing in no respect from other men, let us now briefly consider this point also.

2. It is admitted that when in recent times the appearance of our Saviour Jesus Christ had become known to all men there immediately made its appearance a new nation; a nation confessedly not small, and not dwelling in some corner of the earth, but the most numerous and pious of all nations, indestructible and unconquerable, because it always receives assistance from God. This nation, thus suddenly appearing at the time appointed by the inscrutable counsel of God, is the one which has been honored by all with the name of Christ.

3. One of the prophets, when he saw beforehand with the eye of the Divine Spirit that which was to be, was so astonished at it that he cried out, "Who hath heard of such things, and who hath spoken thus? Hath the earth brought forth in one day, and hath a nation been born at once?" And the same prophet gives a hint also of the name by which the nation was to be called, when he says, "Those that serve me shall be called by a new name, which shall be blessed upon the earth."

4. But although it is clear that we are new and that this new name of Christians has really but recently been known among all nations, nevertheless our life and our conduct, with our doctrines of religion, have not been lately invented by us, but from the first creation of man, so to speak, have been established by the natural understanding of divinely favored men of old. That this is so we shall show in the following way.

5. That the Hebrew nation is not new, but is universally honored on account of its antiquity, is known to all. The books and writings of this people contain accounts of ancient men, rare indeed and few in number, but nevertheless distinguished for piety and righteousness and every other virtue. Of these, some excellent men lived before the flood, others of the sons and descendants of Noah lived after it, among them Abraham, whom the Hebrews celebrate as their own founder and forefather.

6. If any one should assert that all those who have enjoyed the testimony of righteousness, from Abraham himself back to the first man, were Christians in fact if not in name, he would not go beyond the truth.

7. For that which the name indicates, that the Christian man, through the knowledge and the teaching of Christ, is distinguished for temperance and righteousness, for patience in life and manly virtue, and for a profession of piety toward the one and only God over all—all that was zealously practiced by them not less than by us.

8. They did not care about circumcision of the body, neither do we. They did not care about observing Sabbaths, nor do we. They did not avoid certain kinds of food, neither did they regard the other distinctions which Moses first delivered to their posterity to be observed as symbols; nor do Christians of the present day do such things. But they also clearly knew the very Christ of God; for it has already been shown that he appeared unto Abraham, that he imparted revelations to Isaac, that he talked with Jacob, that he held converse with Moses and with the prophets that came after.

9. Hence you will find those divinely favored men honored with the name of Christ, according to the passage which says of them, "Touch not my Christs, and do my prophets no harm."

10. So that it is clearly necessary to consider that religion, which has lately been preached to all nations through the teaching of Christ, the first and most ancient of all religions, and the one discovered by those divinely favored men in the age of Abraham.

11. If it is said that Abraham, a long time afterward, was given the command of circumcision, we reply that nevertheless before this it was declared that he had received the testimony of righteousness through faith; as the divine word says, "Abraham believed in God, and it was counted unto him for righteousness."

12. And indeed unto Abraham, who was thus before his circumcision a justified man, there was given by God, who revealed himself unto him (but this was Christ himself, the word of God), a prophecy in regard to those who in coming ages should be justified in the same way as he. The prophecy was in the following words: "And in thee shall all the tribes of the earth be blessed." And again, "He shall become a nation great and numerous; and in him shall all the nations of the earth be blessed."

13. It is permissible to understand this as fulfilled in us. For he, having renounced the superstition of his fathers, and the former error of his life, and having confessed the one God over all, and having worshiped him with deeds of virtue, and not with the service of the law which was afterward given by Moses, was justified by faith in Christ, the Word of God, who appeared unto him. To him, then, who was a man of this character, it was said that all the tribes and all the nations of the earth should be blessed in him.

14. But that very religion of Abraham has reappeared at the present time, practiced in deeds, more efficacious than words, by Christians alone throughout the world.

15. What then should prevent the confession that we who are of Christ practice one and the same mode of life and have one and the same religion as those divinely favored men of old? Whence it is evident that the perfect religion committed to us by the teaching of Christ is not new and strange, but, if the truth must be spoken, it is the first and the true religion. This may suffice for this subject.

Chapter V.

THE TIME OF HIS APPEARANCE AMONG MEN.

1. And now, after this necessary introduction to our proposed history of the Church, we can enter, so to speak, upon our journey, beginning with the appearance of our Saviour in the flesh. And we invoke God, the Father of the Word, and him, of whom we have been speaking, Jesus Christ himself our Saviour and Lord, the heavenly Word of God, as our aid and fellow-laborer in the narration of the truth.

2. It was in the forty-second year of the reign of Augustus and the twenty-eighth after the subjugation of Egypt and the death of Antony and Cleopatra, with whom the dynasty of the Ptolemies in Egypt came to an end, that our Saviour and Lord Jesus Christ was born in Bethlehem of Judea, according to the prophecies which had been uttered concerning him. His birth took place during the first census, while Cyrenius was governor of Syria.

3. Flavius Josephus, the most celebrated of Hebrew historians, also mentions this census, which was taken during Cyrenius' term of office.

In the same connection he gives an account of the uprising of the Galileans, which took place at that time, of which also Luke, among our writers, has made mention in the Acts, in the following words: "After this man rose up Judas of Galilee in the days of the taxing, and drew away a multitude after him: he also perished; and all, even as many as obeyed him, were dispersed."

4. The above-mentioned author, in the eighteenth book of his Antiquities, in agreement with these words, adds the following, which we quote exactly: "Cyrenius, a member of the senate, one who had held other offices and had passed through them all to the consulship, a man also of great dignity in other respects, came to Syria with a small retinue, being sent by Cæsar to be a judge of the nation and to make an assessment of their property."

5. And after a little he says: "But Judas, a Gaulonite, from a city called Gamala, taking with him Sadduchus, a Pharisee, urged the people to revolt, both of them saying that the taxation meant nothing else than downright slavery, and exhorting the nation to defend their liberty."

6. And in the second book of his History of the Jewish War, he writes as follows concerning the same man: "At this time a certain Galilean, whose name was Judas, persuaded his countrymen to revolt, declaring that they were cowards if they submitted to pay tribute to the Romans, and if they endured, besides God, masters who were mortal." These things are recorded by Josephus.

Chapter VI.

ABOUT THE TIME OF CHRIST, IN ACCORDANCE WITH PROPHECY, THE RULERS WHO HAD GOVERNED THE JEWISH NATION IN REGULAR SUCCESSION FROM THE DAYS OF ANTIQUITY CAME TO AN END, AND HEROD, THE FIRST FOREIGNER, BECAME KING.

1. When Herod, the first ruler of foreign blood, became King, the prophecy of Moses received its fulfillment, according to which there should "not be wanting a prince of Judah, nor a ruler from his loins, until he come for whom it is reserved." The latter, he also shows, was to be the expectation of the nations.

2. This prediction remained unfulfilled so long as it was permitted them to live under rulers from their own nation, that is, from the time of Moses to the reign of Augustus. Under the latter, Herod, the first foreigner, was given the Kingdom of the Jews by the Romans. As Josephus relates, he was an Idumean on his father's side and an Arabian on his mother's. But Africanus, who was also no common writer, says that they who were more accurately informed about him

report that he was a son of Antipater, and that the latter was the son of a certain Herod of Ascalon, one of the so-called servants of the temple of Apollo.

3. This Antipater, having been taken a prisoner while a boy by Idumean robbers, lived with them, because his father, being a poor man, was unable to pay a ransom for him. Growing up in their practices he was afterward befriended by Hyrcanus, the high priest of the Jews. A son of his was that Herod who lived in the, times of our Saviour.

4. When the Kingdom of the Jews had devolved upon such a man the expectation of the nations was, according to prophecy, already at the door. For with him their princes and governors, who had ruled in regular succession from the time of Moses came to an end.

5. Before their captivity and their transportation to Babylon they were ruled by Saul first and then by David, and before the kings leaders governed them who were called Judges, and who came after Moses and his successor Jesus.

6. After their return from Babylon they continued to have without interruption an aristocratic form of government, with an oligarchy. For the priests had the direction of affairs until Pompey, the Roman general, took Jerusalem by force, and defiled the holy places by entering the very innermost sanctuary of the temple. Aristobulus, who, by the right of ancient succession, had been up to that time both king and high priest, he sent with his children in chains to Rome; and gave to Hyrcanus, brother of Aristobulus, the high priesthood, while the whole nation of the Jews was made tributary to the Romans from that time.

7. But Hyrcanus, who was the last of the regular line of high priests, was, very soon afterward taken prisoner by the Parthians, and Herod, the first foreigner, as I have already said, was made King of the Jewish nation by the Roman senate and by Augustus.

8. Under him Christ appeared in bodily shape, and the expected Salvation of the nations and their calling followed in accordance with prophecy. From this time the princes and rulers of Judah, I mean of the Jewish nation, came to an end, and as a natural consequence the order of the high priesthood, which from ancient times had proceeded regularly in closest succession from generation to generation, was immediately thrown into confusion,

9. Of these things Josephus is also a witness, who shows that when Herod was made King by the Romans he no longer appointed the high priests from the ancient line, but gave the honor to certain obscure persons. A course similar to that of Herod in the appointment of the priests was pursued by his son Archelaus, and after him by the Romans, who took the government into their own hands.

10. The same writer shows that Herod was the first that locked up the sacred garment of the high priest under his own seal and refused to

permit the high priests to keep it for themselves. The same course was followed by Archelaus after him, and after Archelaus by the Romans.

11. These things have been recorded by us in order to show that another prophecy has been fulfilled in the appearance of our Saviour Jesus Christ. For the Scripture, in the book of Daniel, having expressly mentioned a certain number of weeks until the coming of Christ, of which we have treated in other books, most clearly prophesies, that after the completion of those weeks the unction among the Jews should totally perish. And this, it has been clearly shown, was fulfilled at the time of the birth of our Saviour Jesus Christ. This has been necessarily premised by us as a proof of the correctness of the time.

Chapter VII.

THE ALLEGED DISCREPANCY IN THE GOSPELS IN REGARD TO THE GENEALOGY OF CHRIST.

1. Matthew and Luke in their gospels have given us the genealogy of Christ differently, and many suppose that they are at variance with one another. Since as a consequence every believer, in ignorance of the truth, has been zealous to invent some explanation which shall harmonize the two passages, permit us to subjoin the account of the matter which has come down to us, and which is given by Africanus, who was mentioned by us just above, in his epistle to Aristides, where he discusses the harmony of the gospel genealogies. After refuting the opinions of others as forced and deceptive, he give the account which he had received from tradition in these words:

2. "For whereas the names of the generations were reckoned in Israel either according to nature or according to law;—according to nature by the succession of legitimate offspring, and according to law whenever another raised up a child to the name of a brother dying childless; for because a clear hope of resurrection was not yet given they had a representation of the future promise by a kind of mortal resurrection, in order that the name of the one deceased might be perpetuated;—

3. whereas then some of those who are inserted in this genealogical table succeeded by natural descent, the son to the father, while others, though born of one father, were ascribed by name to another, mention was made of both of those who were progenitors in fact and of those who were so only in name.

4. Thus neither of the gospels is in error, for one reckons by nature, the other by law. For the line of descent from Solomon and that from Nathan were so involved, the one with the other, by the raising up of children to the childless and by second marriages, that the same persons are justly considered to belong at one time to one, at another time to

another; that is, at one time to the reputed fathers, at another to the actual fathers. So that both these accounts are strictly true and come down to Joseph with considerable intricacy indeed, yet quite accurately.

5. But in order that what I have said may be made clear I shall explain the interchange of the generations. If we reckon the generations from David through Solomon, the third from the end is found to be Matthan, who begat Jacob the father of Joseph. But if, with Luke, we reckon them from Nathan the son of David, in like manner the third from the end is Melchi, whose son Eli was the father of Joseph. For Joseph was the son of Eli, the son of Melchi.

6. Joseph therefore being the object proposed to us, it must be shown how it is that each is recorded to be his father, both Jacob, who derived his descent from Solomon, and Eli, who derived his from Nathan; first how it is that these two, Jacob and Eli, were brothers, and then how it is that their fathers, Matthan and Melchi, although of different families, are declared to be grandfathers of Joseph.

7. Matthan and Melchi having married in succession the same woman, begat children who were uterine brothers, for the law did not prohibit a widow, whether such by divorce or by the death of her husband, from marrying another.

8. By Estha then (for this was the woman's name according to tradition) Matthan, a descendant of Solomon, first begat Jacob. And when Matthan was dead, Melchi, who traced his descent back to Nathan, being of the same tribe but of another family, married her as before said, and begat a son Eli.

9. Thus we shall find the two, Jacob and Eli, although belonging to different families, yet brethren by the same mother. Of these the one, Jacob, when his brother Eli had died childless, took the latter's wife and begat by her a son Joseph, his own son by nature and in accordance with reason. Wherefore also it is written: 'Jacob begat Joseph.' But according to law he was the son of Eli, for Jacob, being the brother of the latter, raised up seed to him.

10. Hence the genealogy traced through him will not be rendered void, which the evangelist Matthew in his enumeration gives thus: 'Jacob begat Joseph.' But Luke, on the other hand, says: 'Who was the son, as was supposed' (for this he also adds), 'of Joseph, the son of Eli, the son of Melchi'; for he could not more clearly express the generation according to law. And the expression 'he begat' he has omitted in his genealogical table up to the end, tracing the genealogy back to Adam the son of God. This interpretation is neither incapable of proof nor is it an idle conjecture.

11. For the relatives of our Lord according to the flesh, whether with the desire of boasting or simply wishing to state the fact, in either case truly, have banded down the following account: Some Idumean robbers, having attacked Ascalon, a city of Palestine, carried away from

a temple of Apollo which stood near the walls, in addition to other booty, Antipater, son of a certain temple slave named Herod. And since the priest was not able to pay the ransom for his son, Antipater was brought up in the customs of the Idumeans, and afterward was befriended by Hyrcanus, the high priest of the Jews.

12 And having, been sent by Hyrcanus on an embassy to Pompey, and having restored to him the kingdom which had been invaded by his brother Aristobulus, he had the good fortune to be named procurator of Palestine. But Antipater having been slain by those who were envious of his great good fortune was succeeded by his son Herod, who was afterward, by a decree of the senate, made King of the Jews under Antony and Augustus. His sons were Herod and the other tetrarchs. These accounts agree also with those of the Greeks.

13. But as there had been kept in the archives up to that time the genealogies of the Hebrews as well as of those who traced their lineage back to proselytes, such as Achior the Ammonite and Ruth the Moabitess, and to those who were mingled with the Israelites and came out of Egypt with them, Herod, inasmuch as the lineage of the Israelites contributed nothing to his advantage, and since he was goaded with the consciousness of his own ignoble extraction, burned all the genealogical records, thinking that he might appear of noble origin if no one else were able, from the public registers, to trace back his lineage to the patriarchs or proselytes and to those mingled with them, who were called Georae.

14. A few of the careful, however, having obtained private records of their own, either by remembering the names or by getting them in some other way from the registers, pride themselves on preserving the memory of their noble extraction. Among these are those already mentioned, called Desposyni, on account of their connection with the family of the Saviour. Coming from Nazara and Cochaba, villages of Judea, into other parts of the world, they drew the aforesaid genealogy from memory and from the book of daily records as faithfully as possible.

15. Whether then the case stand thus or not no one could find a clearer explanation, according to my own opinion and that of every candid person. And let this suffice us, for, although we can urge no testimony in its support, we have nothing. better or truer to offer. In any case the Gospel states the truth." And at the end of the same epistle he adds these words: "Matthan, who was descended from Solomon, begat Jacob. And when Matthan was dead, Melchi, who was descended from Nathan begat Eli by the same woman. Eli and Jacob were thus uterine brothers. Eli having died childless, Jacob raised up seed to him, begetting Joseph, his own son by nature, but by law the son of Eli. Thus Joseph was the son of both."

16. Thus far Africanus. And the lineage of Joseph being thus

traced, Mary also is virtually shown to be of the same tribe with him, since, according to the law of Moses, inter-marriages between different tribes were not permitted. For the command is to marry one of the same family and lineage, so that the inheritance may not pass from tribe to tribe. This may suffice here.

Chapter VIII.

THE CRUELTY OF HEROD TOWARD THE INFANTS, AND THE MANNER OF HIS DEATH.

1. When Christ was born, according to the prophecies, in Bethlehem of Judea, at the time indicated, Herod was not a little disturbed by the enquiry of the magi who came from the east, asking where he who was born King of the Jews was to be found,—for they had seen his star, and this was their reason for taking so long a journey; for they earnestly desired to worship the infant as God,—for he imagined that his kingdom might be endangered; and he enquired therefore of the doctors of the law, who belonged to the Jewish nation, where they expected Christ to be born. When he learned that the prophecy of Micah announced that Bethlehem was to be his birthplace he commanded, in a single edict, all the male infants in Bethlehem, and all its borders, that were two years of age or less, according to the time which he had accurately ascertained from the magi, to be slain, supposing that Jesus, as was indeed likely, would share the same fate as the others of his own age.

2. But the child anticipated the snare, being carried into Egypt by his parents, who had learned from an angel that appeared unto them what was about to happen, These things are recorded by the Holy Scriptures in the Gospel.

3. It is worth while, in addition to this, to observe the reward which Herod received for his daring crime against Christ and those of the same age. For immediately, without the least delay, the divine vengeance overtook him while he was still alive, and gave him a foretaste of what he was to receive after death.

4. It is not possible to relate here how he tarnished the supposed felicity of his reign by successive calamities in his family, by the murder of wife and children, and others of his nearest relatives and dearest friends. The account, which casts every other tragic drama into the shade, is detailed at length in the histories of Josephus.

5. How, immediately after his crime against our Saviour and the other infants, the punishment sent by God drove him on to his death, we can best learn from the words of that historian who, in the seventeenth book of his Antiquities of the Jews, writes as follows concerning his end:

6. "But the disease of Herod grew more severe, God inflicting punishment for his crimes. For a slow fire burned in him which was not so apparent to those who touched him, but augmented his internal distress; for he had a terrible desire for food which it was not possible to resist. He was affected also with ulceration of the intestines, and with especially severe pains in the colon, while a watery and transparent humor settled about his feet.

7. He suffered also from a similar trouble in his abdomen. Nay more, his privy member was putrefied and produced worms. He found also excessive difficulty in breathing, and it was particularly disagreeable because of the offensiveness of the odor and the rapidity of respiration.

8. He had convulsions also in every limb, which gave him uncontrollable strength. It was said, indeed, by those who possessed the power of divination and wisdom to explain such events, that God had inflicted this punishment upon the King on account of his great impiety."

9. The writer mentioned above recounts these things in the work referred to. And in the second book of his History he gives a similar account of the same Herod, which runs as follows: "The disease then seized upon his whole body and distracted it by various torments. For he had a slow fever, and the itching of the skin of his whole body was insupportable. He suffered also from continuous pains in his colon, and there were swellings on his feet like those of a person suffering from dropsy, while his abdomen was inflamed and his privy member so putrefied as to produce worms. Besides this he could breathe only in an upright posture, and then only with difficulty, and he had convulsions in all his limbs, so that the diviners said that his diseases were a punishment.

10. But he, although wrestling with such sufferings, nevertheless clung to life and hoped for safety, and devised methods of cure. For instance, crossing over Jordan he used the warm baths at Callirhoë, which flow into the Lake Asphaltites, but are themselves sweet enough to drink.

11. His physicians here thought that they could warm his whole body again by means of heated oil. But when they had let him down into a tub filled with oil, his eyes became weak and turned up like the eyes of a dead person. But when his attendants raised an outcry, he recovered at the noise; but finally, despairing of a cure, he commanded about fifty drachms to be distributed among the soldiers, and great sums to be given to his generals 12 and friends.

12. Then returning he came to Jericho, where, being seized with melancholy, he planned to commit an impious deed, as if challenging death itself. For, collecting from every town the most illustrious men of all Judea, he commanded that they be shut up in the so-called

hippodrome.

13. And having summoned Salome, his sister, and her husband, Alexander, he said: 'I know that the Jews will rejoice at my death. But I may be lamented by others and have a splendid funeral if you are willing to perform my commands. When I shall expire surround these men, who are now under guard, as quickly as possible with soldiers, and slay them, in order that all Judea and every house may weep for me even against their will.'"

14. And after a little Josephus says, "And again he was so tortured by want of food and by a convulsive cough that, overcome by his pains, he planned to anticipate his fate. Taking an apple he asked also for a knife, for he was accustomed to cut apples and eat them. Then looking round to see that there was no one to hinder, he raised his right hand as if to stab himself."

15. In addition to these things the same writer records that he slew another of his own sons before his death, the third one slain by his command, and that immediately afterward he breathed his last, not without excessive pain.

16. Such was the end of Herod, who suffered a just punishment for his slaughter of the children of Bethlehem, which was the result of his plots against our Saviour.

17. After this an angel appeared in a dream to Joseph in Egypt and commanded him to go to Judea with the child and its mother, revealing to him that those who had sought the life of the child were dead. To this the evangelist adds, "But when he heard that Archelaus did reign in the room of his father Herod he was afraid to go thither; notwithstanding being warned of God in a dream he turned aside into the parts of Galilee."

Chapter IX.

THE TIMES OF PILATE.

1. The historian already mentioned agrees with the evangelist in regard to the fact that Archelaus succeeded to the government after Herod. He records the manner in which he received the kingdom of the Jews by the will of his father Herod and by the decree of Cæsar Augustus, and how, after he had reigned ten years, he lost his kingdom, and his brothers Philip and Herod the younger, with Lysanias, still ruled their own tetrarchies. The same writer, in the eighteenth book of his Antiquities, says that about the twelfth year of the reign of Tiberius, who had succeeded to the empire after Augustus had ruled fifty-seven years, Pontius Pilate was entrusted with the government of Judea, and that he remained there ten full years, almost until the death of Tiberius.

2. Accordingly the forgery of those who have recently given

currency to acts against our Saviour is clearly proved. For the very date given in them shows the falsehood of their fabricators.

3. For the things which they have dared to say concerning the passion of the Saviour are put into the fourth consulship of Tiberius, which occurred in the seventh year of his reign; at which time it is plain that Pilate was not yet ruling in Judea, if the testimony of Josephus is to be believed, who clearly shows in the above-mentioned work that Pilate was made procurator of Judea by Tiberius in the twelfth year of his reign.

Chapter X.

THE HIGH PRIESTS OF THE JEWS UNDER WHOM CHRIST TAUGHT.

1. It was in the fifteenth year of the reign of Tiberius, according to the evangelist, and in the fourth year of the governorship of Pontius Pilate, while Herod and Lysanias and Philip were ruling the rest of Judea, that our Saviour and Lord, Jesus the Christ of God, being about thirty years of age, came to John for baptism and began the promulgation of the Gospel.

2. The Divine Scripture says, moreover, that he passed the entire time of his ministry under the high priests Annas and Caiaphas, showing that in the time which belonged to the priesthood of those two men the whole period of his teaching was completed. Since he began his work during the high priesthood of Annas and taught until Caiaphas held the office, the entire time does not comprise quite four years.

3. For the rites of the law having been already abolished since that time, the customary usages in connection with the worship of God, according to which the high priest acquired his office by hereditary descent and held it for life, were also annulled and there were appointed to the high priesthood by the Roman governors now one and now another person who continued in office not more than one year.

4. Josephus relates that there were four high priests in succession from Annas to Caiaphas. Thus in the same book of the Antiquities he writes as follows: "Valerius Graters having put an end to the priesthood of Ananus appoints Ishmael, the son of Fabi, high priest. And having removed him after a little he appoints Eleazer, the son of Ananus the high priest, to the same office. And having removed him also at the end of a year he gives the high priesthood to Simon, the son of Camithus. But he likewise held the honor no more than a year, when Josephus, called also Caiaphas, succeeded him." Accordingly the whole time of our Saviour's ministry is shown to have been not quite four full years, four high priests, from Annas to the accession of Caiaphas, having held office a year each. The Gospel therefore has rightly indicated Caiaphas

as the high priest under whom the Saviour suffered. From which also we can see that the time of our Saviour's ministry does not disagree with the foregoing investigation.

5. Our Saviour and Lord, not long after the beginning of his ministry, called the twelve apostles, and these alone of all his disciples he named apostles, as an especial honor. And again he appointed seventy others whom he sent out two by two before his face into every place and city whither he himself was about to come.

Chapter XI.

TESTIMONIES IN REGARD TO JOHN THE BAPTIST AND CHRIST.

1. Not long after this John the Baptist was beheaded by the younger Herod, as is stated in the Gospels. Josephus also records the same fact, making mention of Herodias by name, and stating that, although she was the wife of his brother, Herod made her his own wife after divorcing his former lawful wife, who was the daughter of Aretas, king of Petra, and separating Herodias from her husband while he was still alive.

2. It was on her account also that he slew John, and waged war with Aretas, because of the disgrace inflicted on the daughter of the latter. Josephus relates that in this war, when they came to battle, Herod's entire army was destroyed, and that he suffered this calamity on account of his crime against John.

3. The same Josephus confesses in this account that John the Baptist was an exceedingly righteous man, and thus agrees with the things written of him in the Gospels. He records also that Herod lost his kingdom on account of the same Herodias, and that he was driven into banishment with her, and condemned to live at Vienne in Gaul.

4. He relates these things in the eighteenth book of the Antiquities, where he writes of John in the following words: "It seemed to some of the Jews that the army of Herod was destroyed by God, who most justly avenged John called the Baptist.

5. For Herod slew him, a good man and one who exhorted the Jews to come and receive baptism, practicing virtue and exercising righteousness toward each other and toward God; for baptism would appear acceptable unto Him when they employed it, not for the remission of certain sins, but for the purification of the body, as the soul had been already purified in righteousness.

6. And when others gathered about him (for they found much pleasure in listening to his words), Herod feared that his great influence might lead to some sedition, for they appeared ready to do whatever he might advise. He therefore considered it much better, before any new

thing should be done under John's influence, to anticipate it by slaying him, than to repent after revolution had come, and when he found himself in the midst of difficulties. On account of Herod's suspicion John was sent in bonds to the above-mentioned citadel of Machæra, and there slain."

7. After relating these things concerning John, he makes mention of our Saviour in the same work, in the following words: "And there lived at that time Jesus, a wise man, if indeed it be proper to call him a man. For he was a doer of wonderful works, and a teacher of such men as receive the truth in gladness. And he attached to himself many of the Jews, and many also of the Greeks. He was the Christ.

8. When Pilate, on the accusation of our principal men, condemned him to the cross, those who had loved him in the beginning did not cease loving him. For he appeared unto them again alive on the third day, the divine prophets having told these and countless other wonderful things concerning him. Moreover, the race of Christians, named after him, continues down to the present day."

9. Since an historian, who is one of the Hebrews themselves, has recorded in his work these things concerning John the Baptist and our Saviour, what excuse is there left for not convicting them of being destitute of all shame, who have forged the acts against them? But let this suffice here.

Chapter XII.

THE DISCIPLES OF OUR SAVIOUR.

1. The names of the apostles of our Saviour are known to every one from the Gospels. But there exists no catalogue of the seventy disciples. Barnabas, indeed, is said to have been one of them, of whom the Acts of the apostles makes mention in various places, and especially Paul in his Epistle to the Galatians. They say that Sosthenes also, who wrote to the Corinthians with Paul, was one of them.

2. This is the account of Clement in the fifth book of his Hypotyposes, in which he also says that Cephas was one of the seventy disciples, a man who bore the same name as the apostle Peter, and the one concerning whom Paul says, "When Cephas came to Antioch I withstood him to his face."

3. Matthias, also, who was numbered with the apostles in the place of Judas, and the one who was honored by being made a candidate with him, are like-wise said to have been deemed worthy of the same calling with the seventy. They say that Thaddeus also was one of them, concerning whom I shall presently relate an account which has come down to us. And upon examination you will find that our Saviour had more than seventy disciples, according to the testimony of Paul, who

says that after his resurrection from the dead he appeared first to Cephas, then to the twelve, and after them to above five hundred brethren at once, of whom some had fallen asleep; but the majority were still living 4 at the time he wrote.

4. Afterwards he says he appeared unto James, who was one of the so-called brethren of the Saviour. But, since in addition to these, there were many others who were called apostles, in imitation of the Twelve, as was Paul himself, he adds: "Afterward he appeared to all the apostles." So much in regard to these persons. But the story concerning Thaddeus is as follows.

Chapter XIII.

NARRATIVE CONCERNING THE PRINCE OF THE EDESSENES.

1. The divinity of our Lord and Saviour Jesus Christ being noised abroad among all men on account of his wonder-working power, he attracted countless numbers from foreign countries lying far away from Judea, who had the opening of being cured of their diseases and of all kinds of sufferings.

2. For instance the King Abgarus, who ruled with great glory the nations beyond the Euphrates, being afflicted with a terrible disease which it was beyond the power of human skill to cure, when he heard of the name of Jesus, and of his miracles, which were attested by all with one accord sent a message to him by a courier and begged him to heal his disease.

3. But he did not at that time comply with his request; yet he deemed him worthy of a personal letter in which he said that he would send one of his disciples to cure his disease, and at the same time promised salvation to himself and all his house.

4. Not long afterward his promise was fulfilled. For after his resurrection from the dead and his ascent into heaven, Thomas, one of the twelve apostles, under divine impulse sent Thaddeus, who was also numbered among the seventy disciples of Christ, to Edessa, as a preacher and evangelist of the teaching of Christ. And all that our Saviour had promised received through him its fulfillment.

5. You have written evidence of these things taken from the archives of Edessa, which was at that time a royal city. For in the public registers there, which contain accounts of ancient times and the acts of Abgarus, these things have been found preserved down to the present time. But there is no better way than to hear the epistles themselves which we have taken from the archives and have literally translated from the Syriac language in the following manner.

6. *Copy of an epistle written by Abgarus the ruler to Jesus tend sent to him at Jerusalem by Ananias the swift courier.* "Abgarus, ruler

Of Edessa, to Jesus the 6 excellent Saviour who has appeared in the country of Jerusalem, greeting. I have heard the reports of thee and of thy cures as performed by thee without medicines or herbs. For it is said that thou makest the blind to see and the lame to walk, that thou cleansest lepers and castest out impure spirits and demons, and that thou healest those afflicted with lingering disease, and raisest the dead.

7. And having heard all these things concerning thee, I have concluded that one of two things must be true: either thou art God, and having come down from heaven thou doest these things, or else thou, who doest these things, art the Son of God.

8. I have therefore written to thee to ask thee that thou wouldest take the trouble to come to me and heal the disease which I have. For I have heard that the Jews are murmuring against thee and are plotting to injure thee. But I have a very small yet noble city which is great enough for us both."

9. *The answer of Jesus to the ruler Abgarus by the courier Ananias.* "Blessed art thou who hast believed in me without having seen me. For it is written concerning me, that they who have seen me will not believe in me, and that they who have not seen me will believe and be saved. But in regard to what thou hast written me, that I should come to thee, it is necessary for me to fulfill all things here for which I have been sent, and after I have fulfilled them thus to be taken up again to him that sent me. But after I have been taken up I will send to thee one of my disciples, that he may heal thy disease and give life to thee and thine."

10. To these epistles there was added the following account in the Syriac language. "After the ascension of Jesus, Judas, who was also called Thomas, sent to him Thaddeus, an apostle, one of the Seventy. When he was come he lodged with Tobias, the son of Tobias. When the report of him got abroad, it was told Abgarus that an apostle of Jesus was come, as he had written him.

11. Thaddeus began then in the power of God to heal every disease and infirmity, insomuch that all wondered. And when Abgarus heard of the great and wonderful things which he did and of the cures which he performed, he began to suspect that he was the one of whom Jesus had written him, saying, 'After I have been taken up I will send to thee one of my disciples who will heal thee.'

12. Therefore, summoning Tobias, with whom Thaddeus lodged, he said, I have heard that a certain man of power has come and is lodging in thy house. Bring him to me. And Tobias coming to Thaddeus said to him, The ruler Abgarus summoned me and told me to bring thee to him that thou mightest heal him. And Thaddeus said, I will go, for I have been sent to him with power.

13. Tobias therefore arose early on the following day, and taking Thaddeus came to Abgarus. And when he came, the nobles were

present and stood about Abgarus. And immediately upon his entrance a great vision appeared to Abgarus in the countenance of the apostle Thaddeus. When Abgarus saw it he prostrated himself before Thaddeus, while all those who stood about were astonished; for they did not see the vision, which appeared to Abgarus alone.

14. He then asked Thaddeus if he were in truth a disciple of Jesus the Son of God, who had said to him, 'I will send thee one of my disciples, who shall heal thee and give thee life.' And Thaddeus said, Because thou hast mightily believed in him that sent me, therefore have I been sent unto thee. And still further, if thou believest in him, the petitions of thy heart shall be granted thee as thou believest.

15. And Abgarus said to him, So much have I believed in him that I wished to take an army and destroy those Jews who crucified him, had I not been deterred from it by reason of the dominion of the Romans. And Thaddeus said, Our Lord has fulfilled the will of his Father, and having fulfilled it has been taken up to his Father. And Abgarus said to him, I too have believed in him and in his Father.

16. And Thaddeus said to him, Therefore I place my hand upon thee in his name. And when he had done it, immediately Abgarus was cured of the disease and of the suffering which he had.

17. And Abgarus marvelled, that as he had heard concerning Jesus, so he had received in very deed through his disciple Thaddeus, who healed him without medicines and herbs, and not only him, but also Abdus the son of Abdus, who was afflicted with the gout; for he too came to him and fell at his feet, and having received a benediction by the imposition of his hands, he was healed. The same Thaddeus cured also many other inhabitants of the city, and did wonders and marvelous works, and preached the word of God.

18. And afterward Abgarus said, Thou, O Thaddeus, doest these things with the power of God, and we marvel. But, in addition to these things, I pray thee to inform me in regard to the coming of Jesus, how he was born; and in regard to his power, by what power he performed those deeds of which I have heard.

19. And Thaddeus said, Now indeed will I keep silence, since I have been sent to proclaim the word publicly. But tomorrow assemble for me all thy citizens, and I will preach in their presence and sow among them the word of God, concerning the coming of Jesus, how he was born; and concerning his mission, for what purpose he was sent by the Father; and concerning the power of his works, and the mysteries which he proclaimed in the world, and by what power he did these things; and concerning his new preaching, and his abasement and humiliation, and how he humbled himself, and died and debased his divinity and was crucified, and descended into Hades, and burst the bars which from eternity had not been broken, and raised the dead; for he descended alone, but rose with many, and thus ascended to his

Father.

20. Abgarus therefore commanded the citizens to assemble early in the morning to hear the preaching of Thaddeus, and afterward he ordered gold and silver to be given him. But he refused to take it, saying, If we have forsaken that which was our own, how shall we take that which is another's? These things were done in the three hundred and fortieth year."

I have inserted them here in their proper place, translated from the Syriac literally, and I hope to good purpose.

Book II.

Introduction.

1. We have discussed in the preceding book those subjects in ecclesiastical history which it was necessary to treat by way of introduction, and have accompanied them with brief proofs. Such were the divinity of the saving Word, and the antiquity of the doctrines which we teach, as well as of that evangelical life which is led by Christians, together with the events which have taken place in connection with Christ's recent appearance, and in connection with his passion and with the choice of the apostles.

2. In the present book let us examine the events which took place after his ascension, confirming some of them from the divine Scriptures, and others from such writings as we shall refer to from time to time.

Chapter I.

THE COURSE PURSUED BY THE APOSTLES AFTER THE ASCENSION OF CHRIST.

1. First, then, in the place of Judas, the betrayer, Matthias, who, as has been shown was also one of the Seventy, was chosen to the apostolate. And there were appointed to the diaconate, for the service of the congregation, by prayer and the laying on of the hands of the apostles, approved men, seven in number, of whom Stephen was one. He first, after the Lord, was stoned to death at the time of his ordination by the slayers of the Lord, as if he had been promoted for this very purpose. And thus he was the first to receive the crown, corresponding to his name, which belongs to the martyrs of Christ, who are worthy of the meed of victory.

2. Then James, whom the ancients surnamed the Just on account of the excellence of his virtue, is recorded to have been the first to be made bishop of the church of Jerusalem. This James was called the

brother of the Lord because he was known as a son of Joseph, and Joseph was supposed to be the father of Christ, because the Virgin, being betrothed to him, "was found with child by the Holy Ghost before they came together," as the account of the holy Gospels shows.

3. But Clement in the sixth book of his Hypotyposes writes thus: "For they say that Peter and James and John after the ascension of our Saviour, as if also preferred by our Lord, strove not after honor, but chose James the Just bishop of Jerusalem."

4. But the same writer, in the seventh book of the same work, relates also the following things concerning him: "The Lord after his resurrection imparted knowledge to James the Just and to John and Peter, and they imparted it to the rest of the apostles, and the rest of the apostles to the seventy, of whom Barnabas was one. But there were two Jameses: one called the Just, who was thrown from the pinnacle of the temple and was beaten to death with a club by a fuller, and another who was beheaded." Paul also makes mention of the same James the Just, where he writes, "Other of the apostles saw I none, save James the Lord's brother."

5. At that time also the promise of our Saviour to the king of the Osrhœnians was fulfilled. For Thomas, under a divine impulse, sent Thaddeus to Edessa as a preacher and evangelist of the religion of Christ, as we have shown a little above from the document found there?

6. When he came to that place he healed Abgarus by the word of Christ; and after bringing all the people there into the right attitude of mind by means of his works, and leading them to adore the power of Christ, he made them disciples of the Saviour's teaching. And from that time down to the present the whole city of the Edessenes has been devoted to the name of Christ, offering no common proof of the beneficence of our Saviour toward them also.

7. These things have been drawn from ancient accounts; but let us now turn again to the divine Scripture. When the first and greatest persecution was instigated by the Jews against the church of Jerusalem in connection with the martyrdom of Stephen, and when all the disciples, except the Twelve, were scattered throughout Judea and Samaria, some, as the divine Scripture says, went as far as Phœnicia and Cyprus and Antioch, but could not yet venture to impart the word of faith to the nations, and therefore preached it to the Jews alone.

8. During this time Paul was still persecuting the church, and entering the houses of believers was dragging men and women away and committing them to prison.

9. Philip also, one of those who with Stephen had been entrusted with the diaconate, being among those who were scattered abroad, went down to Samaria, and being filled with the divine power, he first preached the word to the inhabitants of that country. And divine grace worked so mightily with him that even Simon Magus with many others

was attracted by his words.

10. Simon was at that time so celebrated, and had acquired, by his jugglery, such influence over those who were deceived by him, that he was thought to be the great power of God. But at this time, being amazed at the wonderful deeds wrought by Philip through the divine power, he reigned and counterfeited faith in Christ, even going so far as to receive baptism.

11. And what is surprising, the same thing is done even to this day by those who follow his most impure heresy. For they, after the manner of their forefather, slipping into the Church, like a pestilential and leprous disease greatly afflict those into whom they are able to infuse the deadly and terrible poison concealed in themselves. The most of these have been expelled as soon as they have been caught in their wickedness, as Simon himself, when detected by Peter, received the merited punishment.

12. But as the preaching of the Saviour's Gospel was daily advancing, a certain providence led from the land of the Ethiopians an officer of the queen of that country, for Ethiopia even to the present day is ruled, according to ancestral custom, by a woman. He, first among the Gentiles, received of the mysteries of the divine word from Philip in consequence of a revelation, and having become the first-fruits of believers throughout the world, he is said to have been the first on returning to his country to proclaim the knowledge of the God of the universe and the life-giving sojourn of our Saviour among men; so that through him in truth the prophecy obtained its fulfillment, which declares that "Ethiopia stretcheth out her hand unto God."

13. In addition to these, Paul, that "chosen vessel," "not of men neither through men, but by the revelation of Jesus Christ himself and of God the Father who raised him from the dead," was appointed an apostle, being made worthy of the call by a vision and by a voice which was uttered in a revelation from heaven.

Chapter II.

HOW TIBERIUS WAS AFFECTED WHEN INFORMED
BY PILATE CONCERNING CHRIST.

1. And when the wonderful resurrection and ascension of our Saviour were already noised abroad, in accordance with an ancient custom which prevailed among the rulers of the provinces, of reporting to the emperor the novel occurrences which took place in them, in order that nothing might escape him, Pontius Pilate informed Tiberius of the reports which were noised abroad through all Palestine concerning the resurrection of our Saviour Jesus from the dead.

2. He gave an account also of other wonders which he had learned

of him, and how, after his death, having risen from the dead, he was now believed by many to be a God. They say that Tiberius referred the matter to the Senate, but that they rejected it, ostensibly because they had not first examined into the matter (for an ancient law prevailed that no one should be made a God by the Romans except by a vote and decree of the senate), but in reality because the saving teaching of the divine Gospel did not need the confirmation and recommendation of men.

3. But although the Senate of the Romans rejected the proposition made in regard to our Saviour, Tiberius still retained the opinion which he had held at first, and contrived no hostile measures against Christ.

4. These things are recorded by Tertullian, a man well versed in the laws of the Romans, and in other respects of high repute, and one of those especially distinguished in Rome. In his apology for the Christians, which was written by him in the Latin language, and has been translated into Greek, he writes as follows:

5. "But in order that we may give an account of these laws from their origin, it was an ancient decree that no one should be consecrated a God by the emperor until the Senate had expressed its approval. Marcus Aurelius did thus concerning a certain idol, Alburnus. And this is a point in favor of our doctrine, that among you divine dignity is conferred by human decree. If a God does not please a man he is not made a God. Thus, according to this custom, it is necessary for man to be gracious to God.

6. Tiberius, therefore, under whom the name of Christ made its entry into the world, when this doctrine was reported to him from Palestine, where it first began, communicated with the Senate, making it clear to them that he was pleased with the doctrine. But the Senate, since it had not itself proved the matter, rejected it. But Tiberius continued to hold his own opinion, and threatened death to the accusers of the Christians." Heavenly providence had wisely instilled this into his mind in order that the doctrine of the Gospel, unhindered at its beginning, might spread in all directions throughout the world.

Chapter III.

THE DOCTRINE OF CHRIST SOON SPREAD THROUGHOUT ALL THE WORLD.

1. Thus, under the influence of heavenly power, and with the divine co-operation, the doctrine of the Saviour, like the rays of the sun, quickly illumined the whole world; and straightway, in accordance with the divine Scriptures, the voice of the inspired evangelists and apostles went forth through all the earth, and their words to the end of the world.

2. In every city and village, churches were quickly established,

filled with multitudes of people like a replenished threshing-floor. And those whose minds, in consequence of errors which had descended to them from their forefathers, were fettered by the ancient disease of idolatrous superstition, were, by the power of Christ operating through the teaching and the wonderful works of his disciples, set free, as it were, from terrible masters, and found a release from the most cruel bondage. They renounced with abhorrence every species of demoniacal polytheism, and confessed that there was only one God, the creator of all things, and him they honored with the rites of true piety, through the inspired and rational worship which has been planted by our Saviour among men.

3. But the divine grace being now poured out upon the rest of the nations Cornelius, of Cæsarea in Palestine, with his whole house, through a divine revelation and the agency of Peter, first received faith in Christ; and after him a multitude of other Greeks in Antioch, to whom those who were scattered by the persecution of Stephen had preached the Gospel. When the church of Antioch was now increasing and abounding, and a multitude of prophets from Jerusalem were on the ground, among them Barnabas and Paul and in addition many other brethren, the name of Christians first sprang up there, as from a fresh and life-giving fountain.

4. And Agabus, one of the prophets who was with them, uttered a prophecy concerning the famine which was about to take place, and Paul and Barnabas were sent to relieve the necessities of the brethren.

Chapter IV.

AFTER THE DEATH OF TIBERIUS, CAIUS APPOINTED AGRIPPA KING OF THE JEWS, HAVING PUNISHED HEROD WITH PERPETUAL EXILE.

1. Tiberius died, after having reigned about twenty-two years, and Caius succeeded him in the empire. He immediately gave the government of the Jews to Agrippa, making him king over the tetrarchies of Philip and of Lysanias; in addition to which he bestowed upon him, not long afterward, the tetrarchy of Herod, having punished Herod (the one under whom the Saviour suffered) and his wife Herodias with perpetual exile on account of numerous crimes. Josephus is a witness to these facts.

2. Under this emperor, Philo became known; a man most celebrated not only among many of our own, but also among many scholars without the Church. He was a Hebrew by birth, but was inferior to none of those who held high dignities in Alexandria. How exceedingly he labored in the Scriptures and in the studies of his nation is plain to all from the work which he has done. How familiar he was

with philosophy and with the liberal studies of foreign nations, it is not necessary to say, since he is reported to have surpassed all his contemporaries in the study of Platonic and Pythagorean. philosophy, to which he particularly devoted his attention.

Chapter V.

PHILO'S EMBASSY TO CAIUS IN BEHALF OF THE JEWS.

1. Philo has given us an account, in five books, of the misfortunes of the Jews under Caius. He recounts at the same time the madness of Caius: how he called himself a god, and performed as emperor innumerable acts of tyranny; and he describes further the miseries of the Jews under him, and gives a report of the embassy upon which he himself was sent to Rome in behalf of his fellow-countrymen in Alexandria; how when he appeared before Caius in behalf of the laws of his fathers he received nothing but laughter and ridicule, and almost incurred the risk of his life.

2. Josephus also makes mention of these things in the eighteenth book of his Antiquities, in the following words: a "A sedition having arisen in Alexandria between the Jews that dwell there and the Greeks, three deputies were chosen from each faction and went to Caius.

3. One of the Alexandrian deputies was Apion, who uttered many slanders against the Jews; among other things saying that they neglected the honors due to Cæsar. For while all other subjects of Rome erected altars and temples to Caius, and in all other respects treated him just as they did the gods, they alone considered it disgraceful to honor him with statues and to swear by his name.

4. And when Apion had uttered many severe charges by which he hoped that Caius would be aroused, as indeed was likely, Philo, the chief of the Jewish embassy, a man celebrated in every respect, a brother of Alexander the Alabarch, and not unskilled in philosophy, was prepared to enter upon a defense in reply to his accusations.

5. But Caius prevented him and ordered him to leave, and being very angry, it was plain that he meditated some severe measure against them. And Philo departed covered with insult and told the Jews that were with him to be of good courage; for while Caius was raging against them he was in fact already contending with God."

6. Thus far Josephus. And Philo himself, in the work *On the Embassy* which he wrote, describes accurately and in detail the things which were done by him at that time. But I shall omit the most of them and record only those things which will make clearly evident to the reader that the misfortunes of the Jews came upon them not long after their daring deeds against Christ and on account of the same.

7. And in the first place he relates that at Rome in the reign of

Tiberius, Sejanus, who at that time enjoyed great influence with the emperor, made every effort to destroy the Jewish nation utterly; and that in Judea, Pilate, under whom the crimes against the Saviour were committed, attempted something contrary to the Jewish law in respect to the temple, which was at that time still standing in Jerusalem, and excited them to the greatest tumults.

Chapter VI.

THE MISFORTUNES WHICH OVERWHELMED THE JEWS AFTER THEIR PRESUMPTION AGAINST CHRIST.

1. After the death of Tiberius, Caius received the empire, and, besides innumerable other acts of tyranny against many people, he greatly afflicted especially the whole nation of the Jews These things we may learn briefly from the words of Philo, who writes as follows:

2. "So great was the caprice of Caius in his conduct toward all, and especially toward the nation of the Jews. The latter he so bitterly hated that he appropriated to himself their places of worship in the other cities, and beginning with Alexandria he filled them with images and statues of himself. The temple in the holy city, which had hitherto been left untouched, and had been regarded as an inviolable asylum, he altered and transformed into a temple of his own, that it might be called the temple of the visible Jupiter, the younger Caius."

3. Innumerable other terrible and almost indescribable calamities which came upon the Jews in Alexandria during the reign of the same emperor, are recorded by the same author in a second work, to which he gave the title, *On the Virtues*. With him agrees also Josephus, who likewise indicates that the misfortunes of the whole nation began with the time of Pilate, and with their daring crimes against the Saviour.

4. Hear what he says in the second book of his Jewish War, where he writes as follows: "Pilate being sent to Judea as procurator by Tiberius, secretly carried veiled images of the emperor, called ensigns, to Jerusalem by night. The following day this caused the greatest disturbance among the Jews. For those who were near were confounded at the sight, beholding their laws, as it were, trampled under foot. For they allow no image to be set up in their city."

5. Comparing these things with the writings of the evangelists, you will see that it was not long before there came upon them the penalty for the exclamation which they had uttered under the same Pilate, when they cried out that they had no other king than Cæsar.

6. The same writer further records that after this another calamity overtook them. He writes as follows: "After this he. stirred up another tumult by snaking use of the holy treasure, which is called Corban, in the construction of an aqueduct three hundred stadia in length.

7. The multitude were greatly displeased at it, and when Pilate was in Jerusalem they surrounded his tribunal and gave utterance to loud complaints. But he, anticipating the tumult, had distributed through the crowd armed soldiers disguised in citizen's clothing, forbidding them to use the sword, but commanding them to strike with clubs those who should make an outcry. To them he now gave the preconcerted signal from the tribunal. And the Jews being beaten, many of them perished in consequence of the blows, while many others were trampled under foot by their own countrymen in their flight, and thus lost their lives. But the multitude, overawed by the fate of those who were slain, held their peace."

8. In addition to these the same author records many other tumults which were stirred up in Jerusalem itself, and shows that from that time seditions and wars and mischievous plots followed each other in quick succession, and never ceased in the city and in all Judea until finally the siege of Vespasian overwhelmed them. Thus the divine vengeance overtook the Jews for the crimes which they dared to commit against Christ.

Chapter VII.

PILATE'S SUICIDE.

1. It is worthy of note that Pilate himself, who was governor in the time of our Saviour, is reported to have fallen into such misfortunes under Caius, whose times we are recording, that he was forced to become his own murderer and executioner; and thus divine vengeance, as it seems, was not long in overtaking him. This is stated by those Greek historians who have recorded the Olympiads, together with the respective events which have taken place in each period.

Chapter VIII.

THE FAMINE WHICH TOOK PLACE IN
THE REIGN OF CLAUDIUS.

1. Caius had held the power not quite four years, when he was succeeded by the emperor Claudius. Under him the world was visited with a famine, which writers that are entire strangers to our religion have recorded in their histories. And thus the prediction of Agabus recorded in the Acts of the Apostles, according to which the whole world was to be visited by a famine, received its fulfillment.

2. And Luke, in the Acts, after mentioning the famine in the time of Claudius, and stating that the brethren of Antioch, each according to his ability, sent to the brethren of Judea by the hands of Paul and

Barnabas, adds the following account.

Chapter IX.

THE MARTYRDOM OF JAMES THE APOSTLE.

1. "Now about that time" (it is clear that he means the time of Claudius) "Herod the King stretched forth his hands to vex certain of the Church. And he killed James the brother of John with the sword."

2. And concerning this James, Clement, in the seventh book of his Hypotyposes, relates a story which is worthy of mention; telling it as he received it from those who had lived before him. He says that the one who led James to the judgment-seat, when he saw him bearing his testimony, was moved, and confessed that he was himself also a Christian.

3. They were both therefore, he says, led away together; and on the way he begged James to forgive him. And he, after considering a little, said, "Peace be with thee," and kissed him. And thus they were both beheaded at the same time.

4. And then, as the divine Scripture says, Herod, upon the death of James, seeing that the deed pleased the Jews, attacked Peter also and committed him to prison, and would have slain him if he had not, by the divine appearance of an angel who came to him by night, been wonderfully released from his bonds, and thus liberated for the service of the Gospel. Such was the providence of God in respect to Peter.

Chapter X.

AGRIPPA, WHO WAS ALSO CALLED HEROD, HAVING PERSECUTED THE APOSTLES, IMMEDIATELY EXPERIENCED THE DIVINE VENGEANCE.

1. The consequences of the king's undertaking against the apostles were no, long deferred, but the avenging minister of divine justice overtook him immediately after his plots against them, as the Book of Acts records. For when he had journeyed to Cæsarea, on a notable feast-day, clothed in a splendid and royal garment, he delivered an address to the people from a lofty throne in front of the tribunal. And when all the multitude applauded the speech, as if it were the voice of a god and not of a man, the Scripture relates that an angel of the Lord smote him, and being eaten of worms he gave up the ghost.

2. We must admire the account of Josephus for its agreement with the divine Scriptures in regard to this wonderful event; for he clearly bears witness to the truth in the nineteenth book of his Antiquities, where he relates the wonder in the following words:

3. "He had completed the third year of his reign over all Judea when he came to Cæsarea, which was formerly called Strato's Tower. There he held games in honor of Cæsar, learning that this was a festival observed in behalf of Cæsar's safety. At this festival was collected a great multitude of the highest and most honorable men in the province.

4. And on the second day of the games he proceeded to the theater at break of day, wearing a garment entirely of silver and of wonderful texture. And there the silver, illuminated by the reflection of the sun's earliest rays, shone marvelously, gleaming so brightly as to produce a sort of fear and terror in those who gazed upon him.

5. And immediately his flatterers, some from one place, others from another, raised up their voices in a way that was not for his good, calling him a god, and saying, 'Be thou merciful; if up to this time we have feared thee as a man, henceforth we confess that thou art superior to the nature of mortals.'

6. The king did not rebuke them, nor did he reject their impious flattery. But after a little, looking up, he saw an angel sitting above his head. And this he quickly perceived would be the cause of evil as it had once been the cause of good fortune, and he was smitten with a heart-piercing pain.

7. And straightway distress, beginning with the greatest violence, seized his bowels. And looking upon his friends he said, 'I, your god, am now commanded to depart this life; and fate thus I on the spot disproves the lying words you have just uttered concerning me. He who has been called immortal by you is now led away to die; but our destiny must be accepted as God has determined it. For we have passed our life by no means ingloriously, but in that splendor which is pronounced happiness.'

8. And when he had said this he labored with an increase of pain. He was accordingly carried in haste to the palace, while the report spread among all that the king would undoubtedly soon die. But the multitude, with their wives and children, sitting on sackcloth after the custom of their fathers, implored God in behalf of the king, and every place was filled with lamentation and tears. And the king as he lay in a lofty chamber, and saw them below lying prostrate on the ground, could not refrain from weeping himself.

9. And after suffering continually for five days with pain in the bowels, he departed this life, in the fifty-fourth year of his age, and in the seventh year of his reign. Four years he ruled under the Emperor Caius—three of them over the tetrarchy of Philip, to which was added in the fourth year that of Herod—and three years during the reign of the Emperor Claudius."

10. I marvel greatly that Josephus, in these things as well as in others, so fully agrees with the divine Scriptures. But if there should seem to any one to be a disagreement in respect to the name of the

king, the time at least and the events show that the same person is meant, whether the change of name has been caused by the error of a copyist, or is due to the fact that he, like so many, bore two names.

Chapter XI.

THE IMPOSTOR THEUDAS AND HIS FOLLOWERS.

1. Luke, in the Acts, introduces Gamaliel as saying, at the consultation which was held concerning the apostles, that at the time referred to, "rose up Theudas boasting himself to be somebody; who was slain; and all, as many as obeyed him, were scattered." Let us therefore add the account of Josephus concerning this man. He records in the work mentioned just above, the following circumstances:

2. "While Fadus was procurator of Judea a certain impostor called Theudas persuaded a very great multitude to take their possessions and follow him to the river Jordan. For he said that he was a prophet, and that the river should be divided at his command, and afford them an easy passage. And with these words he deceived many.

3. But Fadus did not permit them to enjoy their folly, but sent a troop of horsemen against them, who fell upon them unexpectedly and slew many of them and took many others alive, while they took Theudas himself captive, and cut off his head and carried it to Jerusalem." Besides this he also makes mention of the famine, which took place in the reign of Claudius, in the following words.

Chapter XII.

HELEN, THE QUEEN OF THE OSRHŒNIANS.

1. "And at this time" it came to pass that the great famine a took place in Judea, in which the queen Helen, having purchased grain from Egypt with large sums, distributed it to the needy."

2. You will find this statement also in agreement with the Acts of the Apostles, where it is said that the disciples at Antioch, "each according to his ability, determined to send relief to the brethren that dwelt in Judea; which also they did, and sent it to the elders by the hands of Barnabas and Paul."

3. But splendid monuments of this Helen, Of whom the historian has made mention, are still shown in the suburbs of the city which is now called Ælia, But she is said to have been queen of the Adiabeni.

Chapter XIII.

SIMON MAGUS.

1. But faith in our Saviour and Lord Jesus Christ having now been diffused among all men, the enemy of man's salvation contrived a plan for seizing the imperial city for himself. He conducted thither the above-mentioned Simon, aided him in his deceitful arts, led many of the inhabitants of Rome astray, and thus brought them into his own power.

2. This is stated by Justin, one of our distinguished writers who lived not long after the time of the apostles. Concerning him I shall speak in the proper place. Take and read the work of this man, who in the first Apology which he addressed to Antonine in behalf of our religion writes as follows:

3. "And after the ascension of the Lord into heaven the demons put forward certain men who said they were gods, and who were not only allowed by you to go unpersecuted, but were even deemed worthy of honors. One of them was Simon, a Samaritan of the village of Gitto, who in the reign of Claudius Cæsar performed in your imperial city some mighty acts of magic by the art of demons operating in him, and was considered a god, and as a god was honored by you with a statue, which was erected in the river Tiber, between the two bridges, and bore this inscription in the Latin tongue, *Simoni Deo Sancto*, that is, *To Simon the Holy God.*

4. And nearly all the Samaritans and a few even of other nations confess and worship him as the first God. And there went around with him at that time a certain Helena who had formerly been a prostitute in Tyre of Phœnicia; and her they call the first idea that proceeded from him."

5. Justin relates these things, and Irenæus also agrees with him in the first book of his work, Against Heresies, where he gives an account of the man and of his profane and impure teaching. It would be superfluous to quote his account here, for it is possible for those who wish to know the origin and the lives and the false doctrines of each of the heresiarchs that have followed him, as well as the customs practiced by them all, to find them treated at length in the above-mentioned work of Irenæus.

6. We have understood that Simon was the author of all heresy. From his time down to the present those who have followed his heresy have reigned the sober philosophy of the Christians, which is celebrated among all on account of its purity of life. But they nevertheless have embraced again the superstitions of idols, which they seemed to have renounced; and they fall down before pictures and images of Simon

himself and of the above-mentioned Helena who was with him; and they venture to worship them with incense and sacrifices and libations.

7. But those matters which they keep more secret than these, in regard to which they say that one upon first hearing them would be astonished, and, to use one of the written phrases in vogue among them, would be confounded, are in truth full of amazing things, and of madness and folly, being of such a sort that it is impossible not only to commit them to writing, but also for modest men even to utter them with the lips on account of their excessive baseness and lewdness.

8. For what ever could be conceived of, viler than the vilest thing—all that has been outdone by this most abominable sect, which is composed of those who make a sport of those miserable females that are literally overwhelmed with all kinds of vices.

Chapter XIV.

THE PREACHING OF THE APOSTLE PETER IN ROME.

1. The evil power, who hates all that is good and plots against the salvation of men, constituted Simon at that time the father and author of such wickedness, as if to make him a mighty antagonist of the great, inspired apostles of our Saviour.

2. For that divine and celestial grace which co-operates with its ministers, by their appearance and presence, quickly extinguished the kindled flame of evil, and humbled and cast down through them "every high thing that exalted itself against the knowledge of God."

3. Wherefore neither the conspiracy of Simon nor that of any of the others who arose at that period could accomplish anything in those apostolic times. For everything was conquered and subdued by the splendors of the truth and by the divine word itself which had but lately begun to shine from heaven upon men, and which was then flourishing upon earth, and dwelling in the apostles themselves.

4. Immediately the above-mentioned impostor was smitten in the eyes of his mind by a divine and miraculous flash, and after the evil deeds done by him had been first detected by the apostle Peter in Judea, he fled and made a great journey across the sea from the East to the West, thinking that only thus could he live according to his mind.

5. And coming to the city of Rome, by the mighty co-operation of that power which was lying in wait there, he was in a short time so successful in his undertaking that those who dwelt there honored him as a god by the erection of a statue.

6. But this did not last long. For immediately, during the reign of Claudius, the all-good and gracious Providence, which watches over all things, led Peter, that strongest and greatest of the apostles, and the one who on account of his virtue was the speaker for all the others, to Rome

against this great corrupter of life. He like a noble commander of God, clad in divine armor, carried the costly merchandise of the light of the understanding from the East to those who dwelt in the West, proclaiming the light itself, and the word which brings salvation to souls, and preaching the kingdom of heaven.

Chapter XV.

THE GOSPEL ACCORDING TO MARK.

1. And thus when the divine word had made its home among them, the power of Simon was quenched and immediately destroyed, together with the man himself. And so greatly did the splendor of piety illumine the minds of Peter's hearers that they were not satisfied with hearing once only, and were not content with the unwritten teaching of the divine Gospel, but with all sorts of entreaties they besought Mark, a follower of Peter, and the one whose Gospel is extant, that he would leave them a written monument of the doctrine which had been orally communicated to them. Nor did they cease until they had prevailed with the man, and had thus become the occasion of the written Gospel which bears the name of Mark.

2. And they say that Peter when he had learned, through a revelation of the Spirit, of that which had been done, was pleased with the zeal of the men, and that the work obtained the sanction of his authority for the purpose of being used in the churches. Clement in the eighth book of his Hypotyposes gives this account, and with him agrees the bishop of Hierapolis named Papias. And Peter makes mention of Mark in his first epistle which they say that he wrote in Rome itself, as is indicated by him, when he calls the city, by a figure, Babylon, as he does in the following words: "The church that is at Babylon, elected together with you, saluteth you; and so doth Marcus my son."

Chapter XVI.

MARK FIRST PROCLAIMED CHRISTIANITY TO THE INHABITANTS OF EGYPT.

1. And they say that this Mark was the first that was sent to Egypt, and that he proclaimed the Gospel which he had written, and first established churches in Alexandria.

2. And the multitude of believers, both men and women, that were collected there at the very outset, and lived lives of the most philosophical and excessive asceticism, was so great, that Philo thought it worth while to describe their pursuits, their meetings, their entertainments, and their whole manner of life."

Chapter XVII.

PHILO'S ACCOUNT OF THE ASCETICS OF EGYPT.

1. It is also said that Philo in the reign of Claudius became acquainted at Rome with Peter, who was then preaching there. Nor is this indeed improbable, for the work of which we have spoken, and which was composed by him some years later, clearly contains those rules of the Church which are even to this day observed among us.

2. And since he describes as accurately as possible the life of our ascetics, it is clear that he not only knew, but that he also approved, while he venerated and extolled, the apostolic men of his time, who were as it seems of the Hebrew race, and hence observed, after the manner of the Jews, the most of the customs of the ancients.

3. In the work to which he gave the title, *On a Contemplative Life or on Suppliants*, after affirming in the first place that he will add to those things which he is about to relate nothing contrary to truth or of his own invention, he says that these men were called Therapeutæ and the women that were with them Therapeutrides. He then adds the reasons for such a name, explaining it from the fact that they applied remedies and healed the souls of those who came to them, by relieving them like physicians, of evil passions, or from the fact that they served and worshiped the Deity in purity and sincerity.

4. Whether Philo himself gave them this name, employing an epithet well suited to their mode of life, or whether the first of them really called themselves so in the beginning, since the name of Christians was not yet everywhere known, we need not discuss here.

5. He bears witness, however, that first of all they renounce their property. When they begin the philosophical mode of life, he says, they give up their goods to their relatives, and then, renouncing all the cares of life, they go forth beyond the walls and dwell in lonely fields and gardens, knowing well that intercourse with people of a different character is unprofitable and harmful. They did this at that time, as seems probable, under the influence of a spirited and ardent faith, practicing in emulation the prophets' mode of life.

6. For in the Acts of the Apostles, a work universally acknowledged as authentic, it is recorded that all the companions of the apostles sold their possessions and their property and distributed to all according to the necessity of each one, so that no one among them was in want. "For as many as were possessors of lands or houses," as the account says, "sold them and brought the prices of the things that were sold, and laid them at the apostles' feet, so that distribution was made unto every man according as he had need."

7. Philo bears witness to facts very much like those here described

and then adds the following account: "Everywhere in the world is this race found. For it was fitting that both Greek and Barbarian should share in what is perfectly good. But the race particularly abounds in Egypt, in each of its so-called nomes, and especially about Alexandria.

8. The best men from every quarter emigrate, as if to a colony of the Therapeutæ's fatherland, to a certain very suitable spot which lies above the lake Maria upon a low hill excellently situated on account of its security and the mildness of the atmosphere"

9. And then a little further on, after describing the kind of houses which they had, he speaks as follows concerning their churches, which were scattered about here and there: "In each house there is a sacred apartment which is called a sanctuary and monastery, where, quite alone, they perform the mysteries of the religious life. They bring nothing into it, neither drink nor food, nor any of the other things which contribute to the necessities of the body, but only the laws, and the inspired oracles of the prophets, and hymns and such other things as augment and make perfect their knowledge and piety."

10. And after some other matters he says: "The whole interval, from morning to evening, is for them a time of exercise. For they read the holy Scriptures, and explain the philosophy of their fathers in an allegorical manner, regarding the written words as symbols of hidden truth which is communicated in obscure figures.

11. They have also writings of ancient men, who were the founders of their sect, and who left many monuments of the allegorical method. These they use as models, and imitate their principles."

12. These things seem to have been stated by a man who had heard them expounding their sacred writings. But it is highly probable that the works of the ancients, which he says they had, were the Gospels and the writings of the apostles, and probably some expositions of the ancient prophets, such as are contained in the Epistle to the Hebrews, and in many others of Paul's Epistles.

13. Then again he writes as follows concerning the new psalms which they composed: "So that they not only spend their time in meditation, but they also compose songs and hymns to God in every variety of metre and melody, though they divide them, of course, into measures of more than common solemnity."

14. The same book contains an account of many other things, but it seemed necessary to select those facts which exhibit the characteristics of the ecclesiastical mode of life.

15. But if any one thinks that what has been said is not peculiar to the Gospel polity, but that it can be applied to others besides those mentioned, let him be convinced by the subsequent words of the same author, in which, if he is unprejudiced, he will find undisputed testimony on this subject. Philo's words are as follows:

16. "Having laid down temperance as a sort of foundation in the

soul, they build upon it the other virtues. None of them may take food or drink before sunset, since they regard philosophizing as a work worthy of the light, but attention to the wants of the body as proper only in the darkness, and therefore assign the day to the former, but to the latter a small portion of the night.

17. But some, in whom a great desire for knowledge dwells, forget to take food for three days; and some are so delighted and feast so luxuriously upon wisdom, which furnishes doctrines richly and without stint, that they abstain even twice as long as this, and are accustomed, after six days, scarcely to take necessary food." These statements of Philo we regard as referring clearly and indisputably to those of our communion.

18. But if after these things any one still obstinately persists in denying the reference, let him renounce his incredulity and be convinced by yet more striking examples, which are to be found nowhere else than in the evangelical religion of the Christians.

19. For they say that there were women also with those of whom we are speaking, and that the most of them were aged virgins who had preserved their chastity, not out of necessity, as some of the priestesses among the Greeks, but rather by their own choice, through zeal and a desire for wisdom. And that in their earnest desire to live with it as their companion they paid no attention to the pleasures of the body, seeking not mortal but immortal progeny, which only the pious soul is able to bear of itself.

20. Then after a little he adds still more emphatically: "They expound the Sacred Scriptures figuratively by means of allegories. For the whole law seems to these men to resemble a living organism, of which the spoken words constitute the body, while the hidden sense stored up within the words constitutes the soul. This hidden meaning has first been particularly studied by this sect, which sees, revealed as in a mirror of names, the surpassing beauties of the thoughts."

21. Why is it necessary to add to these things their meetings and the respective occupations of the men and of the women during those meetings, and the practices which are even to the present day habitually observed by us, especially such as we are accustomed to observe at the feast of the Saviour's passion, with fasting and night watching and study of the divine Word.

22. These things the above-mentioned author has related in his own work, indicating a mode of life which has been preserved to the present time by us alone, recording especially the vigils kept in connection with the great festival, and the exercises performed during those vigils, and the hymns customarily recited by us, and describing how, while one sings regularly in time, the others listen in silence, and join in chanting only the close of the hymns; and how, on the days referred to they sleep on the ground on beds of straw, and to use his

own words, "taste no wine at all, nor any flesh, but water is their only drink, and the relish with their bread is salt and hyssop."

23. In addition to this Philo describes the order of dignities which exists among those who carry on the services of the church, mentioning the diaconate, and the office of bishop, which takes the precedence over all the others. But whosoever desires a more accurate knowledge of these matters may get it from the history already cited. But that Philo, when he wrote these things, had in view the first heralds of the Gospel and the customs handed down from the beginning by the apostles, is clear to every one.

Chapter XVIII.

THE WORKS OF PHILO THAT HAVE CAME DOWN TO US.

1. Copious in language, comprehensive in thought, sublime and elevated in his views of divine Scripture, Philo has produced manifold and various expositions of the sacred books. On the one hand, he expounds in order the events recorded in Genesis in the books to which he gives the title *Allegories of the Sacred Laws*; on the other hand, he makes successive divisions-of the chapters in the Scriptures which are the subject of investigation, and gives objections and solutions, in the books which he quite suitably calls *Questions and Answers an Genesis and Exodus*.

2. There are, besides these, treatises expressly worked out by him on certain subjects, such as the two books *On Agriculture*, and the same number *On Drunkenness*; and some others distinguished by different titles corresponding to the contents of each; for instance, *Concerning the things which the Sober Mind desires and execrates*, *On the Confusion of Tongues*, *On Flight and Discovery*, *On Assembly for the sake of Instruction*, *On the question, 'Who is heir to things divine?'* or *On the division of things into equal and unequal*, and still further the work *On the three Virtues which with others have been described by Moses*.

3. In addition to these is the work *On those whose Names have been changed and why they have been changed*, in which he says that he had written also two hooks *On Covenants*.

4. And there is also a work of his *On Emigration*, and one *On the life of a Wise Man made perfect in Righteousness*, or *On unwritten Laws*; and still further the work *On Giants or On the Immutability of God*, and a first, second, third, fourth and fifth book *On the proposition, that Dreams according to Moses are sent by God*. These are the hooks on Genesis that have come down to us.

5. But on Exodus we are acquainted with the first, second, third, fourth and fifth books of *Questions and Answers*; also with that *On the*

Tabernacle, and that *On the ten Commandments*, and the four books *On the laws which refer especially to the principal divisions of the ten Commandments*, and another *On animals intended for sacrifice* and *On the kinds of sacrifice*, and another *On the rewards fixed in the law for the good, and on the punishments and curses fixed for the wicked.*

6. In addition to all these there are extant also some single-volumed works of his; as for instance, the work *On Providence*, and the book composed by him *On the Jews*, and *The Statesman*; and still further, *Alexander*, or *On the possession of reason by the irrational animals*: Besides these there is a work *On the proposition that every wicked man is a slave*, to which is subjoined the work *On the proposition that every good man is free.*

7. After these was composed by him the work *On the contemplative life*, or *On suppliants*, from which we have drawn the facts concerning the life of the apostolic men; and still further, the *Interpretation of the Hebrew names in the law and in the prophets* are said to be the result of his industry.

8. And he is said to have read in the presence of the whole Roman Senate during the reign of Claudius the work which he had written, when he came to Rome under Coins, concerning Coins' hatred of the gods, and to which, with ironical reference to its character, he had given the title *On the Virtues*. And his discourses were so much admired as to be deemed worthy of a place in the libraries.

9. At this time, while Paul was completing his journey "from Jerusalem and round about unto Illyricum," Claudius drove the Jews out of Rome; and Aquila and Priscilla, leaving Rome with the other Jews, came to Asia, and there abode with the apostle Paul, who was confirming the churches of that region whose foundations he had newly laid. The sacred book of the Acts informs us also of these things.

Chapter XIX.

THE CALAMITY WHICH BEFELL THE JEWS IN JERUSALEM
ON THE DAY OF THE PASSOVER.

1. While Claudius was still emperor, it happened that so great a tumult and disturbance took place in Jerusalem at the feast of the Passover, that thirty thousand of those Jews alone who were forcibly crowded together at the gate of the temple perished, being trampled under foot by one another. Thus the festival became a season of mourning for all the nation, and there was weeping in every house. These things are related literally by Josephus.

2. But Claudius appointed Agrippa, son of Agrippa, king of the Jews, having sent Felix as procurator of the whole country of Samaria and Galilee, and of the land called Perea. And after he had reigned

thirteen years and eight months a he died, and left Nero as his successor
in the empire.

Chapter XX.

THE EVENTS WHICH TOOK PLACE IN JERUSALEM
DURING THE REIGN OF NERO.

1. Josephus again, in the twentieth book of his Antiquities, relates
the quarrel which arose among the priests during the reign of Nero,
while Felix was procurator of Judea. His words are as follows:

2. "There arose a quarrel between the high priests on the one hand
and the priests and leaders of the people of Jerusalem on the other. And
each of them collected a body of the boldest and most restless men, and
put himself at their head, and whenever they met they hurled invectives
and stones at each other. And there was no one that would interpose;
but these things were done at will as if in a city destitute of a ruler.

3. And so great was the shamelessness and audacity of the high
priests that they dared to send their servants to the threshing-floors to
seize the tithes due to the priests; and thus those of the priests that were
poor were seen to be perishing of want. In this way did the violence of
the factions prevail over all justice."

4. And the same author again relates that about the same time there
sprang up in Jerusalem a certain kind of robbers, "who by day," as he
says, "and in the middle of the city slew those who met them."

5. For, especially at the feasts, they mingled with the multitude,
and with short swords, which they concealed under their garments, they
stabbed the most distinguished men. And when they fell, the murderers
themselves were among those who expressed their indignation. And
thus on account of the confidence which was reposed in them by all,
they remained undiscovered.

6. The first that was slain by them was Jonathan the high priest;
and after him many were killed every day, until the fear became worse
than the evil itself, each one, as in battle, hourly expecting death.

Chapter XXI.

THE EGYPTIAN, WHO IS MENTIONED ALSO IN
THE ACTS OF THE APOSTLES.

1. After other matters he proceeds as follows: "But the Jews were
afflicted with a greater plague than these by the Egyptian false prophet.
For there appeared in the land an impostor who aroused faith in himself
as a prophet, and collected about thirty thousand of those whom he had
deceived, and led them from the desert to the so-called Mount of Olives

whence he was prepared to enter Jerusalem by force and to overpower the Roman garrison and seize the government of the people, using those who made the attack with him as bodyguards.

2. But Felix anticipated his attack, and went out to meet him with the Roman legionaries, and all the people joined in the defense, so that when the battle was fought the Egyptian fled with a few followers, but the most of them were destroyed or taken captive."

3. Josephus relates these events in the second book of his History. But it is worth while comparing the account of the Egyptian given here with that contained in the Acts of the Apostles. In the time of Felix it was said to Paul by the centurion in Jerusalem, when the multitude of the Jews raised a disturbance against the apostle, "Art not thou he who before these days made an uproar, and led out into the wilderness four thousand men that were murderers?" These are the events which took place in the time of Felix.

Chapter XXII.

PAUL HAVING BEEN SENT BOUND FROM JUDEA TO ROME, MADE HIS DEFENSE, AND WAS ACQUITTED OF EVERY CHARGE.

1. Festus was sent by Nero to be Felix's successor. Under him Paul, having made his defense, was sent bound to Rome Aristarchus was with him, whom he also somewhere in his epistles quite naturally calls his fellow-prisoner. And Luke, who wrote the Acts of the Apostles, brought his history to a close at this point, after stating that Paul spent two whole years at Rome as a prisoner at large, and preached the word of God without restraint.

2. Thus after he had made his defense it is said that the apostle was sent again upon the ministry of preaching, and that upon coming to the same city a second time he suffered martyrdom. In this imprisonment he wrote his second epistle to Timothy, in which he mentions his first defense and his impending death.

3. But hear his testimony on these matters: "At my first answer," he says, "no man stood with me, but all men forsook me: I pray God that it may not be laid to their charge. Notwithstanding the Lord stood with me, and strengthened me; that by me the preaching might be fully known, and that all the Gentiles might hear: and I was delivered out of the mouth of the lion."

4. He plainly indicates in these words that on the former occasion, in order that the preaching might be fulfilled by him, he was rescued from the mouth of the lion, referring, in this expression, to Nero, as is probable on account of the latter's cruelty. He did not therefore afterward add the similar statement, "He will rescue me from the mouth

of the lion"; for he saw in the spirit that his end would not be long delayed.

5. Wherefore he adds to the words, "And he delivered me from the mouth of the lion," this sentence: "The Lord shall deliver me from every evil work, and will preserve me unto his heavenly kingdom," indicating his speedy martyrdom; which he also foretells still more clearly in the same epistle, when he writes, "For I am now ready to be offered, and the time of my departure is at hand."

6. In his second epistle to Timothy, moreover, he indicates that Luke was with him when he wrote, but at his first defense not even he. Whence it is probable that Luke wrote the Acts of the Apostles at that time, continuing his history down to the period when he was with Paul.

7. But these things have been adduced by us to show that Paul's martyrdom did not take place at the time of that Roman sojourn which Luke records.

8. It is probable indeed that as Nero was more disposed to mildness in the beginning, Paul's defense of his doctrine was more easily received; but that when he had advanced to the commission of lawless deeds of daring, he made the apostles as well as others the subjects of his attacks.

Chapter XXIII.

THE MARTYRDOM OF JAMES, WHO WAS CALLED THE BROTHER OF THE LORD.

1. But after Paul, in consequence of his appeal to Cæsar, had been sent to Rome by Festus, the Jews, being frustrated in their hope of entrapping him by the snares which they had laid for him, turned against James, the brother of the Lord, to whom the episcopal seat at Jerusalem bad been entrusted by the apostles. The following daring measures were undertaken by them against him.

2. Leading him into their midst they demanded of him that he should renounce faith in Christ in the presence of all the people. But, contrary to the opinion of all, with a clear voice, and with greater boldness than they had anticipated, he spoke out before the whole multitude and confessed that our Saviour and Lord Jesus is the Son of God. But they were unable to bear longer the testimony of the man who, on account of the excellence of ascetic virtue and of piety which he exhibited in his life, was esteemed by all as the most just of men, and consequently they slew him. Opportunity for this deed of violence was furnished by the prevailing anarchy, which was caused by the fact that Festus had died just at this time in Judea, and that the province was thus without a governor and head.

3. The manner of James' death has been already indicated by the

above-quoted words of Clement, who records that he was thrown from the pinnacle of the temple, and was beaten to death with a club. But Hegesippus, who lived immediately after the apostles, gives the most accurate account in the fifth book of his Memoirs. He writes as follows:

4. "James, the brother of the Lord, succeeded to the government of the Church in conjunction with the apostles. He has been called the Just by all from the time of our Saviour to the present day; for there were many that bore the name of James.

5. He was holy from his mother's womb; and he drank no wine nor strong drink, nor did he eat flesh. No razor came upon his head; he did not anoint himself with oil, and he did not use the bath.

6. He alone was permitted to enter into the holy place; for he wore not woolen but linen garments. And he was in the habit of entering alone into the temple, and was frequently found upon his knees begging forgiveness for the people, so that his knees became hard like those of a camel, in consequence of his constantly bending them in his worship of God, and asking forgiveness for the people.

7. Because of his exceeding great justice he was called the Just, and Oblias, which signifies in Greek, Bulwark of the people' and 'Justice,' in accordance with what the prophets declare concerning him.

8. Now some of the seven sects, which existed among the people and which have been mentioned by me in the Memoirs, asked him, 'What is the gate of Jesus?' and he replied that he was the Saviour.

9. On account of these words some believed that Jesus is the Christ. But the sects mentioned above did not believe either in a resurrection or in one's coming to give to every man according to his works. But as many as believed did so on account of James.

10. Therefore when many even of the rulers believed, there was a commotion among the Jews and Scribes and Pharisees, who said that there was danger that the whole people would be looking for Jesus as the Christ. Coming therefore in a body to James they said, 'We entreat thee, restrain the people; for they are gone astray in regard to Jesus, as if he were the Christy We entreat thee to persuade all that have come to the feast of the Passover concerning Jesus; for we all have confidence in thee. For we bear thee witness, as do all the people, that thou art just, and dost not respect per sons.

11. Do thou therefore persuade the multitude not to be led astray concerning Jesus. For the whole people, and all of us also, have confidence in thee. Stand therefore upon the pinnacle of the temple, that from that high position thou mayest be clearly seen, and that thy words may be readily heard by all the people. For all the tribes, with the Gentiles also, are come together on account of the Passover.'

12. The aforesaid Scribes and Pharisees therefore placed James upon the pinnacle of the temple, and cried out to him and said: Thou just one, in whom we ought all to have: confidence, forasmuch as the

people are led, astray after Jesus, the crucified one, declare to us, what is the gate of Jesus.'

13. And he answered with a loud voice,' Why do ye ask me concerning Jesus, the Son of Man? He himself sitteth in heaven at the right hand of the great Power, and is about to come upon the clouds of heaven.'

14. And when many were fully convinced and gloried in the testimony of James, and said, 'Hosanna to the Son of David,' these same Scribes and Pharisees said again to one another, 'We have done badly in supplying such testimony to Jesus. But let us go up and throw him down, in order that they may be afraid to believe him.'

15. And they cried out, saying, 'Oh! oh! the just man is also in error.' And they fulfilled the Scripture written in Isaiah, 'Let us take away the just man, because he is troublesome to us: therefore they shall eat the fruit of their doings.'

16. So they went up and threw down the just man, and said to each other, 'Let us stone James the Just.' And they began to stone him, for he was not killed by the fall; but he turned and knelt down and said, 'I entreat thee, Lord God our Father, forgive them, for they know not what they do.'

17. And while they were thus stoning him one of the priests of the sons of Rechab, the son of the Rechabites, who are mentioned by Jeremiah the prophet, cried out, saying, 'Cease, what do ye? The just one prayeth for you.'

18. And one of them, who was a fuller, took the club with which he beat out clothes and struck the just man on the head. And thus he suffered martyrdom. And they buried him on the spot, by the temple, and his monument still remains by the temple. He became a true witness, both to Jews and Greeks, that Jesus is the Christ. And immediately Vespasian besieged them."

19. These things are related at length by Hegesippus, who is in agreement with Clement. James was so admirable a man and so celebrated among all for his justice, that the more sensible even of the Jews were of the opinion that this was the cause of the siege of Jerusalem, which happened to them immediately after his martyrdom for no other reason than their daring act against him.

20. Josephus, at least, has not hesitated to testify this in his writings, where he says, "These things happened to the Jews to avenge James the Just, who was a brother of Jesus, that is called the Christ. For the Jews slew him, although he was a most just man."

21. And the same writer records his death also in the twentieth book of his Antiquities in the following words: "But the emperor, when he learned of the death of Festus, sent Albinus to be procurator of Judea. But the younger Ananus, who, as we have already said, had obtained the high priesthood, was of an exceedingly bold and reckless

disposition. He belonged, moreover, to the sect of the Sadducees, who are the most cruel of all the Jews in the execution of judgment, as we have already shown.

22. Ananus, therefore, being of this character, and supposing that he had a favorable opportunity on account of the fact that Festus was dead, and Albinus was still on the way, called together the Sanhedrim, and brought before them the brother of Jesus, the so-called Christ, James by name, together with some others, and accused them of violating the law, and condemned them to be stoned.

23. But those in the city who seemed most moderate and skilled in the law were very angry at this, and sent secretly to the king, requesting him to order Ananus to cease such proceedings. For he had not done right even this first time. And certain of them also went to meet Albinus, who was journeying from Alexandria, and reminded him that it was not lawful for Ananus to summon the Sanhedrim without his knowledge.

24. And Albinus, being persuaded by their representations, wrote in anger to Ananus, threatening him with punishment. And the king, Agrippa, in consequence, deprived him, of the high priesthood, which he had held three months, and appointed Jesus, the son of Damnæus."

25. These things are recorded in regard to James, who is said to be the author of the first of the so-called catholic epistles. But it is to be observed that it is disputed; at least, not many of the ancients have mentioned it, as is the case likewise with the epistle that bears the name of Jude, which is also one of the seven so-called catholic epistles. Nevertheless we know that these also, with the rest, have been read publicly in very many churches.

Chapter XXIV.

ANNIANUS THE FIRST BISHOP OF THE CHURCH OF ALEXANDRIA AFTER MARK.

1. When Nero was in the eighth year of his reign, Annianus succeeded Mark the evangelist in the administration of the parish of Alexandria.

Chapter XXV.

THE PERSECUTION UNDER NERO IN WHICH PAUL
AND PETER WERE HONORED AT ROME WITH
MARTYRDOM IN BEHALF OF RELIGION.

1. When the government of Nero was now firmly established, he began to plunge into unholy pursuits, and armed himself even against the religion of the God of the universe.

2. To describe the greatness of his depravity does not lie within the plan of the present work. As there are many indeed that have recorded his history in most accurate narratives, every one may at his pleasure learn from them the coarseness of the man's extraordinary madness, under the influence of which, after he had accomplished the destruction of so many myriads without any reason, he ran into such blood-guiltiness that he did not spare even his nearest relatives and dearest friends, but destroyed his mother and his brothers and his wife, with very many others of his own family as he would private and public enemies, with various kinds of deaths.

3. But with all these things this particular in the catalogue of his crimes was still wanting, that he was the first of the emperors who showed himself an enemy of the divine religion.

4. The Roman Tertullian is likewise a witness of this. He writes as follows: "Examine your records. There you will find that Nero was the first that persecuted this doctrine, particularly then when after subduing all the east, he exercised his cruelty against all at Rome. We glory in having such a man the leader in our punishment. For whoever knows him can understand that nothing was condemned by Nero unless it was something of great excellence."

5. Thus publicly announcing himself as the first among God's chief enemies, he was led on to the slaughter of the apostles. It is, therefore, recorded that Paul was beheaded in Rome itself, and that Peter likewise was crucified under Nero. This account of Peter and Paul is substantiated by the fact that their names are preserved in the cemeteries of that place even to the present day.

6. It is confirmed likewise by Caius, a member of the Church, who arose under Zephyrinus, bishop of Rome. He, in a published disputation with Proclus, the leader of the Phrygian heresy, speaks as follows concerning the places where the sacred corpses of the aforesaid apostles are laid:

7. "But I can show the trophies of the apostles. For if you will go to the Vatican or to the Ostian way, you will find the trophies of those who laid the foundations of this church."

8. And that they both suffered martyrdom at the same time is stated

by Dionysius, bishop of Corinth, in his epistle to the Romans, in the following words: "You have thus by such an admonition bound together the planting of Peter and of Paul at Rome and Corinth. For both of them planted and likewise taught us in our Corinth. And they taught together in like manner in Italy, and suffered martyrdom at the same time." I have quoted these things in order that the truth of the history might be still more confirmed.

Chapter XXVI.

THE JEWS, AFFLICTED WITH INNUMERABLE EVILS, COMMENCED THE LAST WAR AGAINST THE ROMANS.

1. Josephus again, after relating many things in connection with the calamity which came upon the whole Jewish nation, records, in addition to many other circumstances, that a great many of the most honorable among the Jews were scourged in Jerusalem itself and then crucified by Florus. It happened that he was procurator of Judea when the war began to be kindled, in the twelfth year of Nero.
2. Josephus says that at that time a terrible commotion was stirred up throughout all Syria in consequence of the revolt of the Jews, and that everywhere the latter were destroyed without mercy, like enemies, by the inhabitants of the cities, "so that one could see cities filled with unburied corpses, and the dead bodies of the aged scattered about with the bodies of infants, and women without even a covering for their nakedness, and the whole province full of indescribable calamities, while the dread of those things that were threatened was greater than the sufferings themselves which they anywhere endured." Such is the account of Josephus; and such was the condition of the Jews at that time.

Book III.

Chapter I.

THE PARTS OF THE WORLD IN WHICH THE APOSTLES PREACHED CHRIST.

1. Such was the condition of the Jews. Meanwhile the holy apostles and disciples of our Saviour were dispersed throughout the world. Parthia, according to tradition, was allotted to Thomas as his field of labor, Scythia to Andrew, and Asia to John, who, after he had lived some time there, died at Ephesus.
2. Peter appears to have preached in Pontus, Galatia, Bithynia, Cappadocia, and Asia to the Jews of the dispersion. And at last, having

come to Rome, he was crucified head-downwards; for he had requested that he might suffer in this way. What do we need to say concerning Paul, who preached the Gospel of Christ from Jerusalem to Illyricum, and afterwards suffered martyrdom in Rome under Nero? These facts are related by Origen in the third volume of his Commentary on Genesis.

Chapter II.

THE FIRST RULER OF THE CHURCH OF ROME.

1. After the martyrdom of Paul and of Peter, Linus was the first to obtain the episcopate of the church at Rome. Paul mentions him, when writing to Timothy from Rome, in the salutation at the end of the epistle.

Chapter III.

THE EPISTLES OF THE APOSTLES.

1. One epistle of Peter, that called the first, is acknowledged as genuine. And this the ancient elders used freely in their own writings as an undisputed work. But we have learned that his extant second Epistle does not belong to the canon; yet, as it has appeared profitable to many, it has been used with the other Scriptures.

2. The so-called Acts of Peter, however, and the Gospel which bears his name, and the Preaching and the Apocalypse, as they are called, we know have not been universally accepted, because no ecclesiastical writer, ancient or modern, has made use of testimonies drawn from them.

3. But in the course of my history I shall be careful to show, in addition to the official succession, what ecclesiastical writers have from time to time made use of any of the disputed works, and what they have said in regard to the canonical and accepted writings, as well as in regard to those which are not of this class.

4. Such are the writings that bear the name of Peter, only one of which I know to be genuine and acknowledged by the ancient elders.

5. Paul's fourteen epistles are well known and undisputed. It is not indeed right to overlook the fact that some have rejected the Epistle to the Hebrews, saying that it is disputed by the church of Rome, on the ground that it was not written by Paul. But what has been said concerning this epistle by those who lived before our time I shall quote in the proper place. In regard to the so-called Acts of Paul, I have not found them among the undisputed writings.

6. But as the same apostle, in the salutations at the end of the

Epistle to the Romans, has made mention among others of Hermas, to whom the book called The Shepherd is ascribed, it should be observed that this too has been disputed by some, and on their account cannot be placed among the acknowledged books; while by others it is considered quite indispensable, especially to those who need instruction in the elements of the faith. Hence, as we know, it has been publicly read in churches, and I have found that some of the most ancient writers used it.

7. This will serve to show the divine writings that are undisputed as well as those that are not universally acknowledged.

Chapter IV.

THE FIRST SUCCESSORS OF THE APOSTLES.

1. That Paul preached to the Gentiles and laid the foundations of the churches "from Jerusalem round about even unto Illyricum," is evident both from his own words, and from the account which Luke has given in the Acts.

2. And in how many provinces Peter preached Christ and taught the doctrine of the new covenant to those of the circumcision is clear from his own words in his epistle already mentioned as undisputed, in which he writes to the Hebrews of the dispersion in Pontus, Galatia, Cappadocia, Asia, and Bithynia.

3. But the number and the names of those among them that became true and zealous followers of the apostles, and were judged worthy to tend the churches rounded by them, it is not easy to tell, except those mentioned in the writings of Paul.

4. For he had innumerable fellow-laborers, or "fellow-soldiers," as he called them, and most of them were honored by him with an imperishable memorial, for he gave enduring testimony concerning them in his own epistles.

5. Luke also in the Acts speaks of his friends, and mentions them by name.

6. Timothy, so it is recorded, was the first to receive the episcopate of the parish in Ephesus, Titus of the churches in Crete.

7. But Luke, who was of Antiochian parentage and a physician by profession, and who was especially intimate with Paul and well acquainted with the rest of the apostles, has left us, in two inspired books, proofs of that spiritual healing art which he learned from them. One of these books is the Gospel, which he testifies that he wrote as those who were from the beginning eye witnesses and ministers of the word delivered unto him, all of whom, as he says, he followed accurately from the first. The other book is the Acts of the Apostles which he composed not from the accounts of others, but from what he

had seen himself.

8. And they say that Paul meant to refer to Luke's Gospel wherever, as if speaking of some gospel of his own, he used the words, "according to my Gospel."

9. As to the rest of his followers, Paul testifies that Crescens was sent to Gaul; but Linus, whom he mentions in the Second Epistle to Timothy as his companion at Rome, was Peter's successor in the episcopate of the church there, as has already been shown.

10. Clement also, who was appointed third bishop of the church at Rome, was, as Paul testifies, his co-laborer and fellow-soldier.

11. Besides these, that Areopagite, named Dionysius, who was the first to believe after Paul's address to the Athenians in the Areopagus (as recorded by Luke in the Acts) is mentioned by another Dionysius, an ancient writer and pastor of the parish in Corinth, as the first bishop of the church at Athens.

12. But the events connected with the apostolic succession we shall relate at the proper time. Meanwhile let us continue the course of our history.

Chapter V.

THE LAST SIEGE OF THE JEWS AFTER CHRIST.

1. After Nero had held the power thirteen years, and Galba and Otho had ruled a year and six months, Vespasian, who had become distinguished in the campaigns against the Jews, was proclaimed sovereign in Judea and received the title of Emperor from the armies there. Setting out immediately, therefore, for Rome, he entrusted the conduct of the war against the Jews to his son Titus.

2. For the Jews after the ascension of our Saviour, in addition to their crime against him, had been devising as many plots as they could against his apostles. First Stephen was stoned to death by them, and after him James, the son of Zebedee and the brother of John, was beheaded, and finally James, the first that had obtained the episcopal seat in Jerusalem after the ascension of our Saviour, died in the manner already described. But the rest of the apostles, who had been incessantly plotted against with a view to their destruction, and had been driven out of the land of Judea, went unto all nations to preach the Gospel, relying upon the power of Christ, who had said to them, "Go ye and make disciples of all the nations in my name."

3. But the people of the church in Jerusalem had been commanded by a revelation, vouchsafed to approved men there before the war, to leave the city and to dwell in a certain town of Perea called Pella. And when those that believed in Christ had come thither from Jerusalem, then, as if the royal city of the Jews and the whole land of Judea were

entirely destitute of holy men, the judgment of God at length overtook those who had committed such outrages against Christ and his apostles, and totally destroyed that generation of impious men.

4. But the number of calamities which every where fell upon the nation at that time; the extreme misfortunes to which the inhabitants of Judea were especially subjected, the thousands of men, as well as women and children, that perished by the sword, by famine, and by other forms of death innumerable—all these things, as well as the many great sieges which were carried on against the cities of Judea, and the excessive. sufferings endured by those that fled to Jerusalem itself, as to a city of perfect safety, and finally the general course of the whole war, as well as its particular occurrences in detail, and how at last the abomination of desolation, proclaimed by the prophets, stood in the very temple of God, so celebrated of old, the temple which was now awaiting its total and final destruction by fire—all these things any one that wishes may find accurately described in the history written by Josephus.

5. But it is necessary to state that this writer records that the multitude of those who were assembled from all Judea at the time of the Passover, to the number of three million souls, were shut up in Jerusalem "as in a prison," to use his own words.

6. For it was right that in the very days in which they had inflicted suffering upon the Saviour and the Benefactor of all, the Christ of God, that in those days, shut up "as in a prison," they should meet with destruction at the hands of divine justice.

7. But passing by the particular calamities which they suffered from the attempts made upon them by the sword and by other means, I think it necessary to relate only the misfortunes which the famine caused, that those who read this work may have some means of knowing that God was not long in executing vengeance upon them for their wickedness against the Christ of God.

Chapter VI.

THE FAMINE WHICH OPPRESSED THEM.

1. Taking the fifth book of the History of Josephus again in our hands, let us go through the tragedy of events which then occurred.

2. "For the wealthy," he says, "it was equally dangerous to remain. For under pretense that they were going to desert men were put to death for their wealth. The madness of the seditions increased with the famine and both the miseries were inflamed more and more day by day.

3. Nowhere was food to be seen; but, bursting into the houses men searched them thoroughly, and whenever they found anything to eat they tormented the owners on the ground that they had denied that they

had anything; but if they found nothing, they tortured them on the ground that they had more carefully concealed it.

4. The proof of their having or not having food was found in the bodies of the poor wretches. Those of them who were still in good condition they assumed were well supplied with food, while those who were already wasted away they passed by, for it seemed absurd to slay those who were on the point of perishing for want.

5. Many, indeed, secretly sold their possessions for one measure of wheat, if they belonged to the wealthier class, of barley if they were poorer. Then shutting themselves up in the innermost parts of their houses, some ate the grain uncooked on account of their terrible want, while others baked it according as necessity and fear dictated.

6. Nowhere were tables set, but, snatching the yet uncooked food from the fire, they tore it in pieces. Wretched was the fare, and a lamentable spectacle it was to see the more powerful secure an abundance while the weaker mourned.

7. Of all evils, indeed, famine is the worst, and it destroys nothing so effectively as shame. For that which under other circumstances is worthy of respect, in the midst of famine is despised. Thus women snatched the food from the very mouths of their husbands and children, from their fathers, and what was most pitiable of all, mothers from their babes, And while their dearest ones were wasting away in their arms, they were not ashamed to take away froth them the last drops that supported life.

8. And even while they were eating thus they did not remain undiscovered. But everywhere the rioters appeared, to rob them even of these portions of food. For whenever they saw a house shut up, they regarded it as a sign that those inside were taking food. And immediately bursting open the doors they rushed in and seized what they were eating, almost forcing it out of their very throats.

9. Old men who clung to their food were beaten, and if the women concealed it in their hands, their hair was torn for so doing. There was pity neither for gray hairs nor for infants, but, taking up the babes that clung to their morsels of food, they dashed them to the ground. But to those that anticipated their entrance and swallowed what they were about to seize, they were still more cruel, just as if they had been wronged by them.

10. And they devised the most terrible modes of torture to discover food, stopping up the privy passages of the poor wretches with bitter herbs, and piercing their seats with sharp rods. And men suffered things horrible even to hear of, for the sake of compelling them to confess to the possession of one loaf of bread, or in order that they might be made to disclose a single drachm of barley which they had concealed. But the tormentors themselves did not suffer hunger.

11. Their conduct might indeed have seemed less barbarous if they

had been driven to it by necessity; but they did it for the sake of exercising their madness and of providing sustenance for themselves for days to come.

12. And when any one crept out of the city by night as far as the outposts of the Romans to collect wild herbs and grass, they went to meet him; and when he thought he had already escaped the enemy, they seized what he had brought with him, and even though oftentimes the man would entreat them, and, calling upon the most awful name of God, adjure them to give him a portion of what he had obtained at the risk of his life, they would give him nothing back. Indeed, it was fortunate if the one that was plundered was not also slain." To this account Josephus, after relating other things, adds the following:

13. "The possibility of going out of the city being brought to an end, all hope of safety for the Jews was cut off. And the famine increased and devoured the people by houses and families. And the rooms were filled with dead women and children, the lanes of the city with the corpses of old men.

14. Children and youths, swollen with the famine, wandered about the market-places like shadows, and fell down wherever the death agony overtook them. The sick were not strong enough to bury even their own relatives, and those who had the strength hesitated because of the multitude of the dead and the uncertainty as to their own fate. Many, indeed, died while they were burying others, and many betook themselves to their graves before death came upon them.

15. There was neither weeping nor lamentation under these misfortunes; but the famine stifled the natural affections. Those that were dying a lingering death looked with dry eyes upon those that had gone to their rest before them. Deep silence and death-laden night encircled the city.

16. But the robbers were more terrible than these miseries; for they broke open the houses, which were now mere sepulchres, robbed the dead and stripped the covering from their bodies, and went away with a laugh. They tried the points of their swords in the dead bodies, and some that were lying on the ground still alive they thrust through in order to test their weapons. But those that prayed that they would use their right hand and their sword upon them, they contemptuously left to be destroyed by the famine. Every one of these died with eyes fixed upon the temple; and they left the seditious alive.

17. These at first gave orders that the dead should be buried out of the public treasury, for they could not endure the stench. But afterward, when they were not able to do this, they threw the bodies from the walls into the trenches.

18. And as Titus went around and saw the trenches filled with the dead, and the thick blood oozing out of the putrid bodies, he groaned aloud, and, raising his hands, called God to witness that this was not his

doing."

19. After speaking of some other things, Josephus proceeds as follows: "I cannot hesitate to declare what my feelings compel me to. I suppose, if the Romans had longer delayed in coming against these guilty wretches, the city would have been swallowed up by a chasm, or overwhelmed with a flood, or struck with such thunderbolts as destroyed Sodom. For it had brought forth a generation of men much more godless than were those that suffered such punishment. By their madness indeed was the whole people brought to destruction."

20. And in the sixth book he writes as follows: "Of those that perished by famine in the city the number was countless, and the miseries they underwent unspeakable. For if so much as the shadow of food appeared in any house, there was war, and the dearest friends engaged in hand-to-hand conflict with one another, and snatched from each other the most wretched supports of life.

21. Nor would they believe that even the dying were without food; but the robbers would search them while they were expiring, lest any one should feign death while concealing food in his bosom. With mouths gaping for want of food, they stumbled and staggered along like mad dogs, and beat the doors as if they were drunk, and in their impotence they would rush into the same houses twice or thrice in one hour.

22. Necessity compelled them to eat anything they could find, and they gathered and devoured things that were not fit even for the filthiest of irrational beasts. Finally they did not abstain even from their girdles and shoes, and they stripped the hides off their shields and devoured them. Some used even wisps of old hay for food, and others gathered stubble and sold the smallest weight of it for four Attic drachm'.

23. "But why should I speak of the shamelessness which was displayed during the famine toward inanimate things? For I am going to relate a fact such as is recorded neither by Greeks nor Barbarians; horrible to relate, incredible to hear. And indeed I should gladly have omitted this calamity, that I might not seem to posterity to be a teller of fabulous tales, if I had not innumerable witnesses to it in my own age. And besides, I should render my country poor service if I suppressed the account of the sufferings which she endured.

24. "There was a certain woman named Mary that dwelt beyond Jordan, whose father was Eleazer, of the village of Bathezor (which signifies the *house of hyssop*). She was distinguished for her family and her wealth, and had fled with the rest of the multitude to Jerusalem and was shut up there with them during the siege.

25. The tyrants had robbed her of the rest of the property which she had brought with her into the city from Perea. And the remnants of her possessions and whatever food was to be seen the guards rushed in daily and snatched away from her. This made the woman terribly

angry, and by her frequent reproaches and imprecations she aroused the anger of the rapacious villains against herself.

26. But no one either through anger or pity would slay her; and she grew weary of finding food for others to eat. The search, too, was already become everywhere difficult, and the famine was piercing her bowels and marrow, and resentment was raging more violently than famine. Taking, therefore, anger and necessity as her counsellors, she proceeded to do a most unnatural thing.

27. Seizing her child, a boy which was sucking at her breast, she said, Oh, wretched child, in war, in famine, in sedition, for what do I preserve thee? Slaves among the Romans we shall be even if we are allowed to live by them. But even slavery is anticipated by the famine, and the rioters are more cruel than both. Come, be food for me, a fury for these rioters, and a bye-word to the world, for this is all that is wanting to complete the calamities of the Jews.

28. And when she had said this she slew her son; and having roasted him, she ate one half herself, and covering up the remainder, she kept it. Very soon the rioters appeared on the scene, and, smelling the nefarious odor, they threatened to slay her immediately unless she should show them what she had prepared. She replied that she had saved an excellent portion for them, and with that she uncovered the remains of the child.

29. They were immediately seized with horror and amazement and stood transfixed at the sight. But she said This is my own son, and the deed is mine. Eat for I too have eaten. Be not more merciful than a woman, nor more compassionate than a mother. But if you are too pious and shrink from my sacrifice, I have already eaten of it; let the rest also remain for me.

30. At these words the men went out trembling, in this one case being affrighted; yet with difficulty did they yield that food to the mother. Forthwith the whole city was filled with the awful crime, and as all pictured the terrible deed before their own eyes, they trembled as if they had done it themselves.

31. Those that were suffering from the famine now longed for death; and blessed were they that had died before hearing and seeing miseries like these."

32. Such was the reward which the Jews received for their wickedness and impiety, against the Christ of God.

Chapter VII.

THE PREDICTIONS OF CHRIST.

1. It is fitting to add to these accounts the true prediction of our Saviour in which he foretold these very events.

2. His words are as follows: "Woe unto them that are with child, and to them that give suck in those days! But pray ye that your flight be not in the winter, neither on the Sabbath day; For there shall be great tribulation, such as was not since the beginning of the world to this time, no, nor ever shall be."

3. The historian, reckoning the whole number of the slain, says that eleven hundred thousand persons perished by famine and sword, and that the rest of the rioters and robbers, being betrayed by each other after the taking of the city, were slain. But the tallest of the youths and those that were distinguished for beauty were preserved for the triumph. Of the rest of the multitude, those that were over seventeen years of age were sent as prisoners to labor in the works of Egypt, while still more were scattered through the provinces to meet their death in the theaters by the sword and by beasts. Those under seventeen years of age were carried away to be sold as slaves, and of these alone the number reached ninety thousand.

4. These things took place in this manner in the second year of the reign of Vespasian, in accordance with the prophecies of our Lord and Saviour Jesus Christ, who by divine power saw them beforehand as if they were already present, and wept and mourned according to the statement of the holy evangelists, who give the very words which be uttered, when, as if addressing Jerusalem herself, he said:

5. "If thou hadst known, even thou, in this day, the things which belong unto thy peace! But now they are hid from thine eyes. For the days shall come upon thee, that thine enemies shall cast a rampart about thee, and compass thee round, and keep thee in on every side, and shall lay thee and thy children even with the ground."

6. And then, as if speaking concerning the people, he says, "For there shall be great distress in the land, and wrath upon this people. And they shall fall by the edge of the sword, and shall be led away captive into all nations. And Jerusalem shall be trodden down of the Gentiles, until the times of the Gentiles be fulfilled." And again: "When ye shall see Jerusalem compassed with armies, then know that the desolation thereof is nigh."

7. If any one compares the words of our Saviour with the other accounts of the historian concerning the whole war, how can one fail to wonder, and to admit that the foreknowledge and the prophecy of our Saviour were truly divine and marvellously strange.

8. Concerning those calamities, then, that befell the whole Jewish nation after the Saviour's passion and after the words which the multitude of the Jews uttered, when they begged the release of the robber and murderer, but besought that the Prince of Life should be taken from their midst, it is not necessary to add anything to the account of the historian.

9. But it may be proper to mention also those events which exhibited the graciousness of that all-good Providence which held back their destruction full forty years after their crime against Christ—during which time many of the apostles and disciples, and James himself the first bishop there, the one who is called the brother of the Lord, were still alive, and dwelling in Jerusalem itself, remained the surest bulwark of the place. Divine Providence thus still proved itself long-suffering toward them in order to see whether by repentance for what they had done they might obtain pardon and salvation; and in addition to such long-suffering, Providence also furnished wonderful signs of the things which were about to happen to them if they did not repent.

10. Since these matters have been thought worthy of mention by the historian already cited, we cannot do better than to recount them for the benefit of the readers of this work.

Chapter VIII.

THE SIGNS WHICH PRECEDED THE WAR.

1. Taking, then, the work of this author, read what he records in the sixth book of his History. His words are as follows: "Thus were the miserable people won over at this time by the impostors and false prophets; but they did not heed nor give credit to the visions and signs that foretold the approaching desolation. On the contrary, as if struck by lightning, and as if possessing neither eyes nor understanding, they slighted the proclamations of God.

2. At one time a star, in form like a sword, stood over the city, and a comet, which lasted for a whole year; and again before the revolt and before the disturbances that led to the war, when the people were gathered for the feast of unleavened bread, on the eighth of the month Xanthicus, at the ninth hour of the night, so great a light shone about the altar and the temple that it seemed to be bright day; and this continued for half an hour. This seemed to the unskillful a good sign, but was interpreted by the sacred scribes as portending those events which very soon took place.

3. And at the same feast a cow, led by the high priest to be sacrificed, brought forth a lamb in the midst of the temple.

4. And the eastern gate of the inner temple, which was of bronze and very massive, and which at evening was closed with difficulty by

twenty men, and rested upon iron-bound beams, and had bars sunk deep in the ground, was seen at the sixth hour of the night to open of itself.

5. And not many days after the feast, on the twenty-first of the month Artemisium, a certain marvelous vision was seen which passes belief. The prodigy might seem fabulous were it not related by those who saw it, and were not the calamities which followed deserving of such signs. For before the setting of the sun chariots and armed troops were seen throughout the whole region in mid-air, wheeling through the clouds and encircling the cities.

6. And at the feast which is called Pentecost, when the priests entered the temple at night, as was their custom, to perform the services, they said that at first they perceived a movement and a noise, and afterward a voice as of a great multitude, saying, 'Let us go hence.'

7. But what follows is still more terrible; for a certain Jesus, the son of Ananias, a common countryman, four years before the war, when the city was particularly prosperous and peaceful, came to the feast, at which it was customary for all to make tents at the temple to the honor of God, and suddenly began to cry out: 'A voice from the east, a voice from the west, a voice from the four winds, a voice against Jerusalem and the temple, a voice against bridegrooms and brides, a voice against all the people.' Day and night he went through all the alleys crying thus.

8. But certain of the more distinguished citizens, vexed at the ominous cry, seized the man and beat him with many stripes. But without uttering a word in his own behalf, or saying anything in particular to those that were present, he continued to cry out in the same words as before.

9. And the rulers, thinking, as was true, that the man was moved by a higher power, brought him before the Roman governor. And then, though he was scourged to the bone, he neither made supplication nor shed tears, but, changing his voice to the most lamentable tone possible, he answered each stroke with the words, 'Woe, woe unto Jerusalem.'"

10. The same historian records another fact still more wonderful than this. He says that a certain oracle was found in their sacred writings which declared that at that time a certain person should go forth from their country to rule the world. He himself understood that this was fulfilled in Vespasian.

11. But Vespasian did not rule the whole world, but only that part of it which was subject to the Romans. With better right could it be applied to Christ; to whom it was said by the Father, "Ask of me, and I will give thee the heathen for thine inheritance, and the ends of the earth for thy possession." At that very time, indeed, the voice of his holy apostles "went throughout all the earth, and their words to the end

of the world."

Chapter IX.

JOSEPHUS AND THE WORKS WHICH HE HAS LEFT.

1. After all this it is fitting that we should know something in regard to the origin and family of Josephus, who has contributed so much to the history in hand. He himself gives us information on this point in the following words: "Josephus, the son of Mattathias, a priest of Jerusalem, who himself fought against the Romans in the beginning and was compelled to be present at what happened afterward."

2. He was the most noted of all the Jews of that day, not only among his own people, but also among the Romans, so that he was honored by the erection of a statue in Rome, and his works were deemed worthy of a place in the library.

3. He wrote the whole of the Antiquities of the Jews in twenty books, and a history of the war with the Romans which took place in his time, in seven books? He himself testifies that the latter work was not only written in Greek, but that it was also translated by himself into his native tongue. He is worthy of credit here because of his truthfulness in other matters.

4. There are extant also two other books of his which are worth reading. They treat of the antiquity of the Jews, and in them he replies to Apion the Grammarian, who had at that time written a treatise against the Jews, and also to others who had attempted to vilify the hereditary institutions of the Jewish people.

5. In the first of these books he gives the number of the canonical books of the so-called Old Testament. Apparently drawing his information from ancient tradition, he shows what books were accepted without dispute among the Hebrews. His words are as follows.

Chapter X.

THE MANNER IN WHICH JOSEPHUS MENTIONS THE DIVINE BOOKS.

1. "We have not, therefore, a multitude of books disagreeing and conflicting with one another; but we have only twenty-two, which contain the record of all time and are justly held to be divine.

2. Of these, five are by Moses, and contain the laws and the tradition respecting the origin of man, and continue the history down to his own death. This period embraces nearly three thousand years.

3. From the death of Moses to the death of Artaxerxes, who succeeded Xerxes as king of Persia, the prophets that followed Moses

wrote the history of their own times in thirteen books. The other four books contain hymns to God, and precepts for the regulation of the life of men.

4. From the time of Artaxerxes to our own day all the events have been recorded, but the accounts are not worthy of the same confidence that we repose in those which preceded them, because there has not been during this time an exact succession of prophets.

5. How much we are attached to our own writings is shown plainly by our treatment of them. For although so great a period has already passed by, no one has ventured either to add to or to take from them, but it is inbred in all Jews from their very birth to regard them as the teachings of God, and to abide by them, and, if necessary, cheerfully to die for them." These remarks of the historian I have thought might advantageously be introduced in this connection.

6. Another work of no little merit has been produced by the same writer, On the Supremacy of Reason, which some have called Maccabaicum, because it contains an account of the struggles of those Hebrews who contended manfully for the true religion, as is related in the books called Maccabees.

7. And at the end of the twentieth book of his Antiquities Josephus himself intimates that he had purposed to write a work in four books concerning God and his existence, according to the traditional opinions of the Jews, and also concerning the laws, why it is that they permit some things while prohibiting others. And the same writer also mentions in his own works other books written by himself.

8. In addition to these things it is proper to quote also the words that are found at the close of his Antiquities, in confirmation of the testimony which we have drawn from his accounts. In that place he attacks Justus of Tiberias, who, like himself, had attempted to write a history of contemporary events, on the ground that he had not written truthfully. Having brought many other accusations against the man, he continues in these words:

9. "I indeed was not afraid in respect to my writings as you were, but, on the contrary, I presented my books to the emperors themselves when the events were almost under men's eyes. For I was conscious that I had preserved the truth in my account, and hence was not disappointed in my expectation of obtaining their attestation.

10. And I presented my history also to many others, some of whom were present at the war, as, for instance, King Agrippa and some of his relatives.

11. For the Emperor Titus desired so much that the knowledge of the events should be communicated to men by my history alone, that he indorsed the books with his own hand and commanded that they should be published. And King Agrippa wrote sixty-two epistles testifying to the truthfulness of my account." Of these epistles Josephus subjoins

two.

12. But this will suffice in regard to him. Let us now proceed with our history.

Chapter XI.

SYMEON RULES THE CHURCH OF JERUSALEM AFTER JAMES.

1. After the martyrdom of James and the conquest of Jerusalem which immediately followed, it is said that those of the apostles and disciples of the Lord that were still living came together from all directions with those that were related to the Lord according to the flesh (for the majority of them also were still alive) to take counsel as to who was worthy to succeed James.

2. They all with one consent pronounced Symeon, the son of Clopas, of whom the Gospel also makes mention; to be worthy of the episcopal throne of that parish. He was a cousin, as they say, of the Saviour. For Hegesippus records that Clopas was a brother of Joseph.

Chapter XII.

VESPASIAN COMMANDS THE DESCENDANTS OF DAVID TO BE SOUGHT.

1. He also relates that Vespasian after the conquest of Jerusalem gave orders that all that belonged to the lineage of David should be sought out, in order that none of the royal race might be left among the Jews; and in consequence of this a most terrible persecution again hung over the Jews.

Chapter XIII.

ANENCLETUS, THE SECOND BISHOP OF ROME.

1. After Vespasian had reigned ten years Titus, his son, succeeded him. In the second year of his reign, Linus, who had been bishop of the church of Rome for twelve years, delivered his office to Anencletus. But Titus was succeeded by his brother Domitian after he had reigned two years and the same number of months.

Chapter XIV.

ABILIUS, THE SECOND BISHOP OF ALEXANDRIA.

1. In the fourth year of Domitian, Annianus, the first bishop of the parish of Alexandria, died after holding office twenty-two years, and was succeeded by Abilius, the second bishop.

Chapter XV.

CLEMENT, THE THIRD BISHOP OF ROME.

1. In the twelfth year of the same reign Clement succeeded Anencletus after the latter had been bishop of the church of Rome for twelve years. The apostle in his Epistle to the Philippians informs us that this Clement was his fellow-worker. His words are as follows: "With Clement and the rest of my fellow-laborers whose names are in the book of life."

Chapter XVI.

THE EPISTLE OF CLEMENT.

1. There is extant an epistle of this Clement which is acknowledged to be genuine and is of considerable length and of remarkable merit. He wrote it in the name of the church of Rome to the church of Corinth, when a sedition had arisen in the latter church. We know that this epistle also has been publicly used in a great many churches both in former times and in our own. And of the fact that a sedition did take place in the church of Corinth at the time referred to Hegesippus is a trustworthy witness.

Chapter XVII.

THE PERSECUTION UNDER DOMITIAN.

1. Domitian, having shown great cruelty toward many, and having unjustly put to death no small number of well-born and notable men at Rome, and having without cause exiled and confiscated the property of a great many other illustrious men, finally became a successor of Nero in his. hatred and enmity toward God. He was in fact the second that stirred up a persecution against us, although his father Vespasian had undertaken nothing prejudicial to us.

Chapter XVIII.

THE APOSTLE JOHN AND THE APOCALYPSE.

1. It is said that in this persecution the apostle and evangelist John, who was still alive, was condemned to dwell on the island of Patmos in consequence of his testimony to the divine word.

2. Irenæus, in the fifth book of his work Against Heresies, where he discusses the number of the name of Antichrist which is given in the so-called Apocalypse of John, speaks as follows concerning him:

3. "If it were necessary for his name to be proclaimed openly at the present time, it would have been declared by him who saw the revelation. For it was seen not long ago, but almost in our own generation, at the end of the reign of Domitian."

4. To such a degree, indeed, did the teaching of our faith flourish at that time that even those writers who were far from our religion did not hesitate to mention in their histories the persecution and the martyrdoms which took place during it.

5. And they, indeed, accurately indicated the time. For they recorded that in the fifteenth year of Domitian Flavia Domitilla, daughter of a sister of Flavius Clement, who at that time was one of the consuls of Rome, was exiled with many others to the island of Pontia in consequence of testimony borne to Christ.

Chapter XIX.

DOMITIAN COMMANDS THE DESCENDANTS OF DAVID TO BE SLAIN.

1. But when this same Domitian had commanded that the descendants of David should be slain, an ancient tradition says that some of the heretics brought accusation against the descendants of Jude (said to have been a brother of the Saviour according to flesh), on the ground that they were of the lineage of David and were related to Christ himself. Hegesippus relates these facts in the following words.

Chapter XX.

THE RELATIVES OF OUR SAVIOUR.

1. "Of the family of the Lord there were still living the grandchildren of Jude, who is said to have been the Lord's brother according to the flesh.

2. Information was given that they belonged to the family of

David, and they were brought to the Emperor Domitian by the Evocatus. For Domitian feared the coming of Christ as Herod also had feared it. And he asked them if they were descendants of David, and they confessed that they were.

3. Then he asked them how much property they had, or how much money they owned.

4. And both of them answered that they had only nine thousand denarii, half of which belonged to each of them; and this property did not consist of silver, but of a piece of land which contained only thirty-nine acres, and from which they raised their taxes and supported themselves by their own labor."

5. Then they showed their hands, exhibiting the hardness of their bodies and the callousness produced upon their hands by continuous toil as evidence of their own labor.

6. And when they were asked concerning Christ and his kingdom, of what sort it was and where and when it was to appear, they, answered that it was not a temporal nor an earthly kingdom, but a heavenly and angelic one, which would appear at the end of the world, when he should come in glory to judge the quick and the dead, and to give unto every one according to his works.

7. Upon hearing this, Domitian did not pass judgment against them, but, despising them as of no account, he let them go, and by a decree put a stop to the persecution of the Church.

8. But when they were released they ruled the churches because they were witnesses and were also relatives of the Lord. And peace being established, they lived until the time of Trojan. These things are related by Hegesippus.

9. Tertullian also has mentioned Domitian in the following words: "Domitian also, who possessed a share of Nero's cruelty, attempted once to do the same thing that the latter did. But because he had, I suppose, some intelligence, he very soon ceased, and even recalled those whom he had banished."

10. But after Domitian had reigned fifteen years, and Nerva had succeeded to the empire, the Roman Senate, according to the writers that record the history of those days, voted that Domitian's honors should be cancelled, and that those who had been unjustly banished should return to their homes and have their property restored to them.

11. It was at this time that the apostle John returned from his banishment in the island and took up his abode at Ephesus, according to an ancient Christian tradition.

Chapter XXI.

CERDON BECOMES THE THIRD RULER OF
THE CHURCH OF ALEXANDRIA.

1. After Nerva had reigned a little more than a year he was succeeded by Trojan. It was during the first year of his reign that Abilius, who had ruled the church of Alexandria for thirteen years, was succeeded by Cerdon.

2. He was the third that presided over that church after Annianus, who was the first. At that time Clement still ruled the church of Rome, being also the third that held the episcopate there after Paul and Peter.

3. Linus was the first, and after him came Anencletus,

Chapter XXII.

IGNATIUS, THE SECOND BISHOP OF ANTIOCH.

1. At this time Ignatius was known as the second bishop of Antioch, Evodius having been the first. Symeon likewise was at that time the second ruler of the church of Jerusalem, the brother of our Saviour having been the first.

Chapter XXIII.

NARRATIVE CONCERNING JOHN THE APOSTLE.

1. At that time the apostle and evangelist John, the one whom Jesus loved, was still living in Asia, and governing the churches of that region, having returned after the death of Domitian from his exile on the island.

2. And that he was still alive at that time may be established by the testimony of two witnesses. They should be trustworthy who have maintained the orthodoxy of the Church; and such indeed were Irenæus and Clement of Alexandria.

3. The former in the second book of his work Against Heresies, writes as follows: "And all the elders that associated with John the disciple of the Lord in Asia bear witness that John delivered it to them. For he remained among them until the time of Trajan."

4. And in the third book of the same work he attests the same thing in the following words: "But the church in Ephesus also, which was founded by Paul, and where John remained until the time of Trajan, is a faithful witness of the apostolic tradition."

5. Clement likewise in his book entitled What Rich Man Can be

Saved? indicates the time, and subjoins a narrative which is most attractive to those that enjoy hearing what is beautiful and profitable. Take and read the account which rims as follows:

6. "Listen to a tale, which is not a mere tale, but a narrative concerning John the apostle, which has been handed down and treasured up in memory. For when, after the tyrant's death, he returned from the isle of Patmos to Ephesus, he went away upon their invitation to the neighboring territories of the Gentiles, to appoint bishops in some places, in other places to set in order whole churches, elsewhere to choose to the ministry some one of those that were pointed out by the Spirit.

7. When he had come to one of the cities not far away (the name of which is given by some), and had consoled the brethren in other matters, he finally turned to the bishop that had been appointed, and seeing a youth of powerful physique, of pleasing appearance, and of ardent temperament, he said, 'This one I commit to thee in all earnestness in the presence of the Church and with Christ as witness.' And when the bishop had accepted the Charge and had promised all, he repeated the same injunction with an appeal to the same witnesses, and then departed for Ephesus.

8. But the presbyter, taking home the youth committed to him, reared, kept, cherished, and finally baptized him. After this he relaxed his stricter care and watchfulness, with the idea that in putting upon him the seal of the Lord he had given him a perfect protection.

9. But some youths of his own age, idle and dissolute, and accustomed to evil practices, corrupted him when he was thus prematurely freed from restraint. At first they enticed him by costly entertainments; then, when they went forth at night for robbery, they took him with them, and finally they demanded that he should unite with them in some greater crime.

10. He gradually became accustomed to such practices, and on account of the positiveness of his character, leaving the right path, and taking the bit in his teeth like a hard-mouthed and powerful horse, he rushed the more violently down into the depths.

11. And finally despairing of salvation in God, he no longer meditated what was insignificant, but having committed some great crime, since he was now lost once for all, he expected to suffer a like fate with the rest. Taking them, therefore, and forming a band of robbers, he became a bold bandit-chief, the most violent, most bloody, most cruel of them all.

12. Time passed, and some necessity having arisen, they sent for John. But he, when he had set in order the other matters on account of which he had come, said, 'Come, O bishop, restore us the deposit which both I and Christ committed to thee, the church, over which thou presidest, being witness.'

13. But the bishop was at first confounded, thinking that he was falsely charged in regard to money which he had not received, and he could neither believe the accusation respecting what he had not, nor could he disbelieve John. But when he said, 'I demand the young man and the soul of the brother,' the old man, groaning deeply and at the same time bursting into tears, said, 'He is dead.' 'How and what kind of death?' 'He is dead to God,' he said; 'for he turned wicked and abandoned, and at last a robber. And now, instead of the church, he haunts the mountain with a band like himself.'

14. But the Apostle rent his clothes, and beating his head with great lamentation, he said, 'A fine guard I left for a brother's soul! But let a horse be brought me, and let some one show me the way.' He rode away from the church just as he was, and coming to the place, he was taken prisoner by the robbers' outpost.

15. He, however, neither fled nor made entreaty, but cried out, 'For this did I come; lead me to your captain.'

16. The latter, meanwhile, was waiting, armed as he was. But when he recognized John approaching, he turned in shame to flee.

17. But John, forgetting his age, pursued him with all his might, crying out, 'Why, my son, dost thou flee from me, thine own father, unarmed, aged? Pity me, my son; fear not; thou hast still hope of life. I will give account to Christ for thee. If need be, I will willingly endure thy death as the Lord suffered death for us. For thee will I give up my life. Stand, believe; Christ hath sent me.'

18. And he, when he heard, first stopped and looked down; then he threw away his arms, and then trembled and wept bitterly. And when the old man approached, he embraced him, making confession with lamentations as he! was able, baptizing himself a second time with tears, and concealing only his right hand,

19. But John, pledging himself, and assuring him on oath that he would find forgiveness with the Saviour, besought him, fell upon his knees, kissed his right hand itself as if now purified by repentance, and led him back to the church. And making intercession for him with copious prayers, and struggling together with him in continual fastings, and subduing his mind by various utterances, he did not depart, as they say, until he had restored him to the church, furnishing a great example of true repentance and a great proof of regeneration, a trophy of a visible resurrection."

Chapter XXIV.

THE ORDER OF THE GOSPELS.

1. This extract from Clement I have inserted here for the sake of the history and for the benefit of my readers. Let us now point out the undisputed writings of this apostle.

2. And in the first place his Gospel, which is known to all the churches under heaven, must be acknowledged as genuine. That it has with good reason been put by the ancients in the fourth place, after the other three Gospels, may be made evident in the following way.

3. Those great and truly divine men, I mean the apostles of Christ, were purified in their life, and were adorned with every virtue of the soul, but were uncultivated in speech. They were confident indeed in their trust in the divine and wonder-working power which was granted unto them by the Saviour, but they did not know how, nor did they attempt to proclaim the doctrines of their teacher in studied and artistic language, but employing only the demonstration of the divine Spirit, which worked with them, and the wonder-working power of Christ, which was displayed through them, they published the knowledge of the kingdom of heaven throughout the whole world, paying little attention to the composition of written works.

4. And this they did because they were assisted in their ministry by one greater than man. Paul, for instance, who surpassed them all in vigor of expression and in richness of thought, committed to writing no more than the briefest epistles, although he had innumerable mysterious matters to communicate, for he had attained even unto the sights of the third heaven, had been carried to the very paradise of God, and had been deemed worthy to hear unspeakable utterances there.

5. And the rest of the followers of our Saviour, the twelve apostles, the seventy disciples, and countless others besides, were not ignorant of these things. Nevertheless, of all the disciples of the Lord, only Matthew and John have left us written memorials, and they, tradition says, were led to write only under the pressure of necessity.

6. For Matthew, who had at first preached to the Hebrews, when he was about to go to other peoples, committed his Gospel to writing in his native tongue, and thus compensated those whom he was obliged to leave for the loss of his presence.

7. And when Mark and Luke had already published their Gospels, they say that John, who had employed all his time in proclaiming the Gospel orally, finally proceeded to write for the following reason. The three Gospels already mentioned having come into the hands of all and into his own too, they say that he accepted them and bore witness to their truthfulness; but that there was lacking in them an account of the

deeds done by Christ at the beginning of his ministry.

8. And this indeed is true. For it is evident that the three evangelists recorded only the deeds done by the Saviour for one year after the imprisonment of John the Baptist, and indicated this in the beginning of their account.

9. For Matthew, after the forty days' fast and the temptation which followed it, indicates the chronology of his work when he says: "Now when he heard that John was delivered up he withdrew from Judea into Galilee."

10. Mark likewise says: "Now after that John was delivered up Jesus came into Galilee." And Luke, before commencing his account of the deeds of Jesus, similarly marks the time, when he says that Herod, "adding to all the evil deeds which he had done, shut up John in prison."

11. They say, therefore, that the apostle John, being asked to do it for this reason, gave in his Gospel an account of the period which had been omitted by the earlier evangelists, and of the deeds done by the Saviour during that period; that is, of those which were done before the imprisonment of the Baptist. And this is indicated by him, they say, in the following words: "This beginning of miracles did Jesus"; and again when he refers to the Baptist, in the midst of the deeds of Jesus, as still baptizing in Ænon near Salim; where he states the matter clearly in the words: "For John was not yet cast into prison."

12. John accordingly, in his Gospel, records the deeds of Christ which were performed before the Baptist was cast into prison, but the other three evangelists mention the events which happened after that time.

13. One who understands this can no longer think that the Gospels are at variance with one another, inasmuch as the Gospel according to John contains the first acts of Christ, while the others give an account of the latter part of his life. And the genealogy of our Saviour according to the flesh John quite naturally omitted, because it had been already given by Matthew and Luke, and began with the doctrine of his divinity, which had, as it were, been reserved for him, as their superior, by the divine Spirit.

14. These things may suffice, which we have said concerning the Gospel of John. The cause which led to the composition of the Gospel of Mark has been already stated by us.

15. But as for Luke, in the beginning of his Gospel, he states that since many others had more rashly undertaken to compose a narrative of the events of which he had acquired perfect knowledge, he himself, feeling the necessity of freeing us from their uncertain opinions, delivered in his own Gospel an accurate account of those events in regard to which he had learned the full truth, being aided by his intimacy and his stay with Paul and by his acquaintance with the rest of

the apostles.

16. So much for our own account of these things. But in a more fitting place we shall attempt to show by quotations from the ancients, what others have said concerning them.

17. But of the writings of John, not only his Gospel, but also the former of his epistles, has been accepted without dispute both now and in ancient times. But the other two are disputed.

18. In regard to the Apocalypse, the opinions of most men are still divided. But at the proper time this question likewise shall be decided from the testimony of the ancients.

Chapter XXV.

THE DIVINE SCRIPTURES THAT ARE ACCEPTED AND THOSE THAT ARE NOT.

1. Since we are dealing with this subject it is proper to sum up the writings of the New Testament which have been already mentioned. First then must be put the holy quaternion of the Gospels; following them the Acts of the Apostles.

2. After this must be reckoned the epistles of Paul; next in order the extant former epistle of John, and likewise the epistle of Peter, must be maintained. After them is to be placed, if it really seem proper, the Apocalypse of John, concerning which we shall give the different opinions at the proper time. These then belong among the accepted writings.

3. Among the disputed writings, which are nevertheless recognized by many, are extant the so-called epistle of James and that of Jude, also the second epistle of Peter, and those that are called the second and third of John, whether they belong to the evangelist or to another person of the same name.

4. Among the rejected writings must be reckoned also the Acts of Paul, and the so-called Shepherd, and the Apocalypse of Peter, and in addition to these the extant epistle of Barnabas, and the so-called Teachings of the Apostles; and besides, as I said, the Apocalypse of John, if it seem proper, which some, as I said, reject, but which others class with the accepted books.

5. And among these some have placed also the Gospel according to the Hebrews, with which those of the Hebrews that have accepted Christ are especially delighted. And all these may be reckoned among the disputed books.

6. But we have nevertheless felt compelled to give a catalogue of these also, distinguishing those works which according to ecclesiastical tradition are true and genuine and commonly accepted, from those others which, although not canonical but disputed, are yet at the same

time known to most ecclesiastical writers—we have felt compelled to give this catalogue in order that we might be able to know both these works and those that are cited by the heretics under the name of the apostles, including, for instance, such books as the Gospels of Peter, of Thomas, of Matthias, or of any others besides them, and the Acts of Andrew and John and the other apostles, which no one belonging to the succession of ecclesiastical writers has deemed worthy of mention in his writings.

7. And further, the character of the style is at variance with apostolic usage, and both the thoughts and the purpose of the things that are related in them are so completely out of accord with true orthodoxy that they clearly show themselves to be the fictions of heretics. Wherefore they are not to be placed even among the rejected writings, but are all of them to be cast aside as absurd and impious. Let us now proceed with our history.

Chapter XXVI.

MENANDER THE SORCERER.

1. Menander, who succeeded Simon Magus, showed himself in his conduct another instrument of diabolical power, not inferior to the former. He also was a Samaritan and carried his sorceries to no less an extent than his teacher had done, and at the same time reveled in still more marvelous tales than he.

2. For he said that he was himself the Saviour, who had been sent down from invisible æons for the salvation of men; and he taught that no one could gain the mastery over the world-creating angels themselves unless he had first gone through the magical discipline imparted by him and had received baptism from him. Those who were deemed worthy of this would partake even in the present life of perpetual immortality, and would never die, but would remain here forever, and without growing old become immortal. These facts can be easily learned from the works of Irenæus.

3. And Justin, in the passage in which he mentions Simon, gives an account of this man also, in the following words: "And we know that a certain Menander, who was also a Samaritan, from the village of Capparattea, was a disciple of Simon, and that he also, being driven by the demons, came to Antioch and deceived many by his magical art. And he persuaded his followers that they should not die. And there are still some of them that assert this."

4. And it was indeed an artifice of the devil to endeavor, by means of such sorcerers, who assumed the name of Christians, to defame the great mystery of godliness by magic art, and through them to make ridiculous the doctrines of the Church concerning the immortality of

the soul and the resurrection of the dead. But they that have chosen these men as their saviours have fallen away from the true hope.

Chapter XXVII.

THE HERESY OF THE EBIONITES.

1. The evil demon, however, being unable to tear certain others from their allegiance to the Christ of God, yet found them susceptible in a different direction, and so brought them over to his own purposes. The ancients quite properly called these men Ebionites, because they held poor and mean opinions concerning Christ.

2. For they considered him a plain and common man, who was justified only because of his superior virtue, and who was the fruit of the intercourse of a man with Mary. In their opinion the observance of the ceremonial law was altogether necessary, on the ground that they could not be saved by faith in Christ alone and by a corresponding life.

3. There were others, however, besides them, that were of the same name, but avoided the strange and absurd beliefs of the former, and did not deny that the Lord was born of a virgin and of the Holy Spirit. But nevertheless, inasmuch as they also refused to acknowledge that he pre-existed, being God, Word, and Wisdom, they turned aside into the impiety of the former, especially when they, like them, endeavored to observe strictly the bodily worship of the law.

4. These men, moreover, thought that it was necessary to reject all the epistles of the apostle, whom they called an apostate from the law; and they used only the so-called Gospel according to the Hebrews and made small account of the rest.

5. The Sabbath and the rest of the discipline of the Jews they observed just like them, but at the same time, like us, they celebrated the Lord's days as a memorial of the resurrection of the Saviour.

6. Wherefore, in consequence of such a course they received the name of Ebionites, which signified the poverty of their understanding. For this is the name by which a poor man is called among the Hebrews.

Chapter XXVIII.

CERINTHUS THE HERESIARCH.

1. We have understood that at this time Cerinthus, the author of another heresy, made his appearance. Caius, whose words we quoted above, in the Disputation which is ascribed to him, writes as follows concerning this man:

2. "But Cerinthus also, by means of revelations which he pretends were written by a great apostle, brings before us marvelous things

which he falsely claims were shown him by angels; and he says that after the resurrection the kingdom of Christ will be set up on earth, and that the flesh dwelling in Jerusalem will again be subject to desires and pleasures. And being an enemy of the Scriptures of God, he asserts, with the purpose of deceiving men, that there is to be a period of a thousand years a for marriage festivals."

3. And Dionysius, who was bishop of the parish of Alexandria in our day, in the second book of his work On the Promises, where he says some things concerning the Apocalypse of John which he draws from tradition, mentions this same man in the following words:

4. "But (they say that) Cerinthus, who founded the sect which was called, after him, the Cerinthian, desiring reputable authority for his fiction, prefixed the name. For the doctrine which he taught was this: that the kingdom of Christ will be an earthly one.

5. And as he was himself devoted to the pleasures of the body and altogether sensual in his nature, he dreamed that that kingdom would consist in those things which he desired, namely, in the delights of the belly and of sexual passion, that is to say, in eating and drinking and marrying, and in festivals and sacrifices and the slaying of victims, under the guise of which he thought he could indulge his appetites with a better grace." These are the words of Dionysius.

6. But Irenæus, in the first book of his work Against Heresies, gives some more abominable false doctrines of the same man, and in the third book relates a story which deserves to be recorded. He says, on the authority of Polycarp, that the apostle John once entered a bath to bathe; but, learning that Cerinthus was within, he sprang from the place and rushed out of the door, for he could not bear to remain under the same roof with him. And he advised those that were with him to do the same, saying, "Let us flee, lest the bath fall for Cerinthus, the enemy of the truth, is within."

Chapter XXIX.

NICOLAUS AND THE SECT NAMED AFTER HIM.

1. At this time the so-called sect of the Nicolaitans made its appearance and lasted for a very short time. Mention is made of it in the Apocalypse of John. They boasted that the author of their sect was Nicolaus, one of the deacons who, with Stephen, were appointed by the apostles for the purpose of ministering to the poor. Clement of Alexandria, in the third book of his Stromata, relates the following things concerning him.

2. "They say that he had a beautiful wife, and after the ascension of the Saviour, being accused by the apostles of jealousy, he led her into their midst and gave permission to any one that wished to marry her.

For they say that this was in accord with that saying of his, that one ought to abuse the flesh. And those that have followed his heresy, imitating blindly and foolishly that which was done and said, commit fornication without shame.

3. But I understand that Nicolaus had to do with no other woman than her to whom he was married, and that, so far as his children are concerned, his daughters continued in a state of virginity until old age, and his son remained uncorrupt. If this is so, when he brought his wife, whom he jealously loved, into the midst of the apostles, he was evidently renouncing his passion; and when he used the expression, 'to abuse the flesh,' he was inculcating self-control in the face of those pleasures that are eagerly pursued. For I suppose that, in accordance with the command of the Saviour, he did not wish to serve two masters, pleasure and the Lord.

4. But they say that Matthias also taught in the same manner that we ought to fight against and abuse the flesh, and not give way to it for the sake of pleasure, but strengthen the soul by faith and knowledge." So much concerning those who then attempted to pervert the truth, but in less time than it has taken to tell it became entirely extinct.

Chapter XXX.

THE APOSTLES THAT WERE MARRIED.

1. Clement, indeed, whose words we have just quoted, after the above-mentioned facts gives a statement, on account of those who rejected marriage, of the apostles that had wives. "Or will they," says he, "reject even the apostles? For Peter and Philip begat children; and Philip also gave his daughters in marriage. And Paul does not hesitate, in one of his epistles, to greet his wife, whom he did not take about with him, that he might not be inconvenienced in his ministry."

2. And since we have mentioned this subject it is not improper to subjoin another account which is given by the same author and which is worth reading. In the seventh book of his Stromata he writes as follows: "They say, accordingly, that when the blessed Peter saw his own wife led out to die, he rejoiced because of her summons and her return home, and called to her very encouragingly and comfortingly, addressing her by name, and saying, 'Oh thou, remember the Lord.' Such was the marriage of the blessed, and their perfect disposition toward those dearest to them." This account being in keeping with the subject in hand, I have related here in its proper place.

Chapter XXXI.

THE DEATH OF JOHN AND PHILIP.

1. The time and the manner of the death of Paul and Peter as well as their burial places, have been already shown by us.

2. The time of John's death has also been given in a general way, but his burial place is indicated by an epistle of Polycrates (who was bishop of the parish of Ephesus), addressed to Victor, bishop of Rome. In this epistle he mentions him together with the apostle Philip and his daughters in the following words:

3. "For in Asia also great lights have fallen asleep, which shall rise again on the last day, at the coming of the Lord, when he shall come with glory from heaven and shall seek out all the saints. Among these are Philip, one of the twelve apostles, who sleeps in Hierapolis, and his two aged virgin daughters, and another daughter who lived in the Holy Spirit and now rests at Ephesus; and moreover John, who was both a witness and a teacher, who reclined upon the bosom of the Lord, and being a priest wore the sacerdotal plate. He also sleeps at Ephesus." So much concerning their death.

4. And in the Dialogue of Caius which we mentioned a little above, Proclus, against whom he directed his disputation, in agreement with what has been quoted, speaks thus concerning the death of Philip and his daughters: "After him there were four prophetesses, the daughters of Philip, at Hierapolis in Asia. Their tomb is there and the tomb of their father." Such is his state-merit.

5. But Luke, in the Acts of the Apostles, mentions the daughters of Philip who were at that time at Cæsarea in Judea with their father, and were honored with the gift of prophecy. His words are as follows: "We came unto Cæsarea; and entering into the house of Philip the evangelist, who was one of the seven, we abode with him. Now this man had four daughters, virgins, which did prophesy."

6. We have thus set forth in these pages what has come to our knowledge concerning the apostles themselves and the apostolic age, and concerning the sacred writings which they have left us, as well as concerning those which are disputed, but nevertheless have been publicly used by many in a great number of churches, and moreover, concerning those that are altogether rejected and are out of harmony with apostolic orthodoxy. Having done this, let us now proceed with our history.

Chapter XXXII.

SYMEON, BISHOP OF JERUSALEM, SUFFERS MARTYRDOM.

1. It is reported that after the age of Nero and Domitian, under the emperor whose times we are now recording, a persecution was stirred up against us in certain cities in consequence of a popular uprising. In this persecution we have understood that Symeon, the son of Clopas, who, as we have shown, was the second bishop of the church of Jerusalem, suffered martyrdom.

2. Hegesippus, whose words we have already quoted in various places, is a witness to this fact also. Speaking of certain heretics he adds that Symeon was accused by them at this time; and since it was clear that he was a Christian, he was tortured in various ways for many days, and astonished even the judge himself and his attendants in the highest degree, and finally he suffered a death similar to that of our Lord.

3. But there is nothing like hearing the historian himself, who writes as follows: "Certain of these heretics brought accusation against Symeon, the son of Clopas, on the ground that he was a descendant of David and a Christian; and thus he suffered martyrdom, at the age of one hundred and twenty years, while Trajan was emperor and Atticus governor."

4. And the same writer says that his accusers also, when search was made for the descendants of David, were arrested as belonging to that family. And it might be reasonably assumed that Symeon was one of those that saw and heard the Lord, judging from the length of his life, and from the fact that the Gospel makes mention of Mary, the wife of Clopas, who was the father of Symeon, as has been already shown.

5. The same historian says that there were also others, descended from one of the so-called brothers of the Saviour, whose name was Judas, who, after they had borne testimony before Domitian, as has been already recorded, in behalf of faith in Christ, lived until the same reign.

6. He writes as follows: "They came, therefore, and took the lead of every church as witness and as relatives of the Lord. And profound peace being established in every church, they remained until the reign of the Emperor Trajan, and until the above-mentioned Symeon, son of Clopas, an uncle of the Lord, was informed against by the heretics, and was himself in like manner accused for the same cause before the governor Atticus. And after being tortured for many days he suffered martyrdom, and all, including even the proconsul, marveled that, at the age of one hundred and twenty years, he could endure so much. And orders were given that he should be crucified."

7. In addition to these things the same man, while recounting the events of that period, records that the Church up to that time had remained a pure and uncorrupted virgin, since, if there were any that attempted to corrupt the sound norm of the preaching of salvation, they lay until then concealed in obscure darkness.

8. But when the sacred college of apostles had suffered death in various forms, and the generation of those that had been deemed worthy to hear the inspired wisdom with their own ears had passed away, then the league of godless error took its rise as a result of the folly of heretical teachers, who, because none of the apostles was still living, attempted henceforth, with a bold face, to proclaim, in opposition to the preaching of the truth, the 'knowledge which is falsely so-called.'

Chapter XXXIII.

TRAJAN FORBIDS THE CHRISTIANS TO BE SOUGHT AFTER.

1. So great a persecution was at that time opened against us in many places that Plinius Secundus, one of the most noted of governors, being disturbed by the great number of martyrs, communicated with the emperor concerning the multitude of those that were put to death for their faith. At the same time, he informed him in his communication that he had not heard of their doing anything profane or contrary to the laws—except that they arose at dawn and sang hymns to Christ as a God; but that they renounced adultery and murder and like criminal offenses, and did all things in accordance with the laws.

2. In reply to this Trajan made the following decree: that the race of Christians should not be sought after, but when found should be punished. On account of this the persecution which had threatened to be a most terrible one was to a certain degree checked, but there were still left plenty of pretexts for those who wished to do us harm. Sometimes the people, sometimes the rulers in various places, would lay plots against us, so that, although no great persecutions took place, local persecutions were nevertheless going on in particular provinces, and many of the faithful endured martyrdom in various forms.

3. We have taken our account from the Latin Apology of Tertullian which we mentioned above. The translation runs as follows: "And indeed we have found that search for us has been forbidden. For when Plinius Secundus, the governor of a province, had condemned certain Christians and deprived them of their dignity, he was confounded by the multitude, and was uncertain what further course to pursue. He therefore communicated with Trajan the emperor, informing him that, aside from their unwillingness to sacrifice, he had found no impiety in them.

4. And he reported this also, that the Christians arose early in the morning and sang hymns unto Christ as a God, and for the purpose of preserving their discipline forbade murder, adultery, avarice, robbery, and the like. In reply to this Trajan wrote that the race of Christians should not be sought after, but when found should be punished." Such were the events which took place at that time.

Chapter XXXIV.

EVARESTUS, THE FOURTH BISHOP OF THE CHURCH OF ROME.

1. In the third year of the reign of the emperor mentioned above, Clement committed the episcopal government of the church of Rome to Evarestus, and departed this life after he had superintended the teaching of the divine word nine years in all.

Chapter XXXV.

JUSTUS, THE THIRD BISHOP OF JERUSALEM.

1. But when Symeon also had died in the manner described, a certain Jew by the name of Justus succeeded to the episcopal throne in Jerusalem. He was one of the many thousands of the circumcision who at that time believed in Christ.

Chapter XXXVI.

IGNATIUS AND HIS EPISTLES.

1. At that time Polycarp, a disciple of the apostles, was a man of eminence in Asia, having been entrusted with the episcopate of the church of Smyrna by those who had seen and heard the Lord.

2. And at the same time Papias, bishop of the parish of Hierapolis, became well known, as did also Ignatius, who was chosen bishop of Antioch, second in succession to Peter, and whose fame is still celebrated by a great many.

3. Report says that he was sent from Syria to Rome, and became food for wild beasts on account of his testimony to Christ.

4. And as he made the journey through Asia under the strictest military surveillance, he fortified the parishes in the various cities where he stopped by oral homilies and exhortations, and warned them above all to be especially on their guard against the heresies that were then beginning to prevail, and exhorted them to hold fast to the tradition of the apostles. Moreover, he thought it necessary to attest that

tradition in writing, and to give it a fixed form for the sake of greater security.

5. So when he came to Smyrna, where Polycarp was, he wrote an epistle to the church of Ephesus, in which he mentions Onesimus, its pastor; and another to the church of Magnesia, situated upon the Mæander, in which he makes mention again of a bishop Damas; and finally one to the church of Tralles, whose bishop, he states, was at that time Polybius.

6. In addition to these he wrote also to the church of Rome, entreating them not to secure his release from martyrdom, and thus rob him of his earnest hope. In confirmation of what has been said it is proper to quote briefly from this epistle. He writes as follows:

7. "From Syria even unto Rome I fight with wild beasts, by land and by sea, by night and by day, being bound amidst ten leopards? that is, a company of soldiers who only become worse when they are well treated. In the midst of their wrongdoings, however, I am more fully learning discipleship, but I am not thereby justified.

8. May I have joy of the beasts that are prepared for me; and I pray that I may find them ready; I will even coax them to devour me quickly that they may not treat me as they have some whom they have refused to touch through fear. And if they are unwilling, I will compel them. Forgive me.

9. I know what is expedient for me. Now do I begin to be a disciple. May naught of things visible and things invisible envy me; that I may attain unto Jesus Christ. Let fire and cross and attacks of wild beasts, let wrenching of bones, cutting of limbs, crushing of the whole body, tortures of the devil—let all these come upon me if only I may attain unto Jesus Christ."

10. These things he wrote from the above-mentioned city to the churches referred to. And when he had left Smyrna he wrote again from Troas to the Philadelphians and to the church of Smyrna; and particularly to Polycarp, who presided over the latter church. And since he knew him well as an apostolic man, he commended to him, like a true and good shepherd, the flock at Antioch, and besought him to care diligently for it.

11. And the same man, writing to the Smyrnæans, used the following words concerning Christ, taken I know not whence: "But I know and believe that he was in the flesh after the resurrection. And when he came to Peter and his companions he said to them, Take, handle me, and see that I am not an incorporeal spirit. And immediately they touched him and believed."

12. Irenæus also knew of his martyrdom and mentions his epistles in the following words: "As one of our people said, when he was condemned to the beasts on account of his testimony unto God, I am God's wheat, and by the teeth of wild beasts am I ground, that I may be

found pure bread."

13. Polycarp also mentions these letters in the epistle to the Philippians which is ascribed to him. His words are as follows: "I exhort all of you, therefore, to be obedient and to practice all patience such as ye saw with your own eyes not only in the blessed Ignatius and Rufus and Zosimus, but also in others from among yourselves as well as in Paul himself and the rest of the apostles; being persuaded that all these ran not in vain, but in faith and righteousness, and that they are gone to their rightful place beside the Lord, with whom also they suffered. For they loved not the present world, but him that died for our sakes and was raised by God for us."

14. And afterwards he adds: "You have written to me, both you and Ignatius, that if any one go to Syria he may carry with him the letters from you. And this I will do if I have a suitable opportunity, either I myself or one whom I send to be an ambassador for you also. The epistles of Ignatius which were sent to us by him and the others which we had with us we sent to you as you gave charge. They are appended to this epistle, and from them you will be able to derive great advantage. For they comprise faith and patience, and every kind of edification that pertaineth to our Lord." So much concerning Ignatius. But he was succeeded by Heros in the episcopate of the church of Antioch.

Chapter XXXVII.

THE EVANGELISTS THAT WERE STILL
EMINENT AT THAT TIME.

1. Among those that were celebrated at that time was Quadratus, who, report says, was renowned along with the daughters of Philip for his prophetical gifts. And there were many others besides these who were known in those days, and who occupied the first place among the successors of the apostles. And they also, being illustrious disciples of such great men, built up the foundations of the churches which had been laid by the apostles in every place, and preached the Gospel more and more widely and scattered the saving seeds of the kingdom of heaven far and near throughout the whole world.

2. For indeed most of the disciples of that time, animated by the divine word with a more ardent love for philosophy, had already fulfilled the command of the Saviour, and had distributed their goods to the needy. Then starting out upon long journeys they performed the office of evangelists, being filled with the desire to preach Christ to those who had not yet heard the word of faith, and to deliver to them the divine Gospels.

3. And when they had only laid the foundations of the faith in

foreign places, they appointed others as pastors, and entrusted them with the nurture of those that had recently been brought in, while they themselves went on again to other countries and nations, with the grace and the co-operation of God. For a great many wonderful works were done through them by the power of the divine Spirit, so that at the first hearing whole multitudes of men eagerly embraced the religion of the Creator of the universe.

4. But since it is impossible for us to enumerate the names of all that became shepherds or evangelists in the churches throughout the world in the age immediately succeeding the apostles, we have recorded, as was fitting, the names of those only who have transmitted the apostolic doctrine to us in writings still extant.

Chapter XXXVIII.

THE EPISTLE OF CLEMENT AND THE WRITINGS FALSELY ASCRIBED TO HIM.

1. Thus Ignatius has done in the epistles which we have mentioned, and Clement in his epistle which is accepted by all, and which he wrote in the name of the church of Rome to the church of Corinth. In this epistle he gives many thoughts drawn from the Epistle to the Hebrews, and also quotes verbally some of its expressions, thus showing most plainly that it is not a recent production.

2. Wherefore it has seemed reasonable to reckon it with the other writings of the apostle. For as Paul had written to the Hebrews in his native tongue, some say that the evangelist Luke, others that this Clement himself, translated the epistle.

3. The latter seems more probable, because the epistle of Clement and that to the Hebrews have a similar character in regard to style, and still further because the thoughts contained in the two works are not very different.

4. But it must be observed also that there is said to be a second epistle of Clement. But we do not know that this is recognized like the former, for we do not find that the ancients have made any use of it.

5. And certain men Lengthy writings under his name, containing dialogues of Peter and Apion. But no mention has been made of these by the ancients; for they do not even preserve the pure stamp of apostolic orthodoxy. The acknowledged writing of Clement is well known. We have spoken also of the works of Ignatius and Polycarp.

Chapter XXXIX.

THE WRITINGS OF PAPIAS.

1. There are extant five books of Papias, which bear the title Expositions of Oracles of the Lord. Irenæus makes mention of these as the only works written by him, in the following words: "These things are attested by Papias, an ancient man who was a hearer of John and a companion of Polycarp, in his fourth book. For five books have been written by him." These are the words of Irenæus.

2. But Papias himself in the preface to his discourses by no means declares that he was himself a hearer and eye-witness of the holy apostles, but he shows by the words which he uses that he received the doctrines of the faith from those who were their friends.

3. He says: "But I shall not hesitate also to put down for you along with my interpretations whatsoever things I have at any time learned carefully from the elders and carefully remembered, guaranteeing their truth. For I did not, like the multitude, take pleasure in those that speak much, but in those that teach the truth; not in those that relate strange commandments, but in those that deliver the commandments given by the Lord to faith, and springing from the truth itself.

4. If, then, any one came, who had been a follower of elders, I questioned him in regard to the words of the elders,—what Andrew or what Peter said, or what was said by Philip, or by Thomas, or by James, or by John, or by Matthew, or by any other of the disciples of the Lord, and what things Aristion and the presbyter John, the disciples of the Lord, say. For I did not think that what was to be gotten from the books would profit me as much as what came from the living and abiding voice."

5. It is worth while observing here that the name John is twice enumerated by him. The first one he mentions in connection with Peter and James and Matthew and the rest of the Apostles, clearly meaning the evangelist; but the other John he mentions after an interval, and places him among others outside of the number of the apostles, putting Aristion before him, and he distinctly calls him a presbyter.

6. This shows that the statement of those is true, who say that there were two persons in Asia that bore the same name, and that there were two tombs in Ephesus, each of which, even to the present day, is called John's. It is important to notice this. For it is probable that it was the second, if one is not willing to admit that it was the first that saw the Revelation, which is ascribed by name to John.

7. And Papias, of whom we are now speaking, confesses that he received the words of the apostles from those that followed them, but says that he was himself a hearer of Aristion and the presbyter John. At

least he mentions them frequently by name, and gives their traditions in his writings. These things, we hope, have not been uselessly adduced by us.

8. But it is fitting to subjoin to the words of Papias which have been quoted, other passages from his works in which he relates some other wonderful events which he claims to have received from tradition.

9. That Philip the apostle dwelt in Hierapolis with his daughters has been already stated. But it must be noted here that Papias, their contemporary, says that he heard a wonderful tale from the daughters of Philip. For he relates that in his time one rose from the dead. And he tells another wonderful story of Justus, surnamed Barsabbas: that he drank a deadly poison, and yet, by grace of the Lord, suffered no harm.

10. The Book of Acts records that the holy apostles after the ascension of the Saviour, put forward this Justus, together with Matthias, and prayed that one might be chosen in place of the traitor Judas, to fill up their number. The account is as follows: "And they put forward two, Joseph, called Barsabbas, who was surnamed Justus, and Matthias; and they prayed and said."

11. The same writer gives also other accounts which he says came to him through unwritten tradition, certain strange parables and teachings of the Saviour, and some other mythical things.

12. To these belong his statement that there will be a period of some thousand years after the resurrection of the dead, and that the kingdom of Christ will be set up in material form on this very earth. I suppose he got these ideas through a misunderstanding of the apostolic accounts, not perceiving that the things said by them were spoken mystically in figures.

13. For he appears to have been of very limited understanding, as one can see from his discourses. But it was due to him that so many of the Church Fathers after him adopted a like opinion, urging in their own support the antiquity of the man; as for instance Irenæus and any one else that may have proclaimed similar views.

14. Papias gives also in his own work other accounts of the words of the Lord on the authority of Aristion who was mentioned above, and traditions as handed down by the presbyter John; to which we refer those who are fond of learning. But now we must add to the words of his which we have already quoted the tradition which he gives in regard to Mark, the author of the Gospel.

15. It is in the following words: "This also the presbyter said: Mark, having become the interpreter of Peter, wrote down accurately, though not indeed in order, whatsoever he remembered of the things said or done by Christ. For he neither heard the Lord nor followed him, but afterward, as I said, he followed Peter, who adapted his teachings to the needs of his hearers, but with no intention of giving a connected

account of the Lord's discourses, so that Mark committed no error while he thus wrote some things as he remembered them. For he was careful of one thing, not to omit any of the things which he had heard, and not to state any of them falsely. "These things are related by Papias concerning Mark.

16. But concerning Matthew he writes as follows: "So then Matthew wrote the oracles in the Hebrew language, and every one interpreted them as he was able." And the same writer uses testimonies from the Epistle of John and from that of Peter likewise. And he relates another story of a woman, who was accused of many sins before the Lord, which is contained in the Gospel according to the Hebrews. These things we have thought it necessary to observe in addition to what has been already stated.

Book IV.

Chapter I.

THE BISHOPS OF ROME AND OF ALEXANDRIA DURING THE REIGN OF TRAJAN.

1. About the twelfth year of the reign of Trajan the above-mentioned bishop of the parish of Alexandria died, and Primus, the fourth in succession from the apostles, was chosen to the office.

2. At that time also Alexander, the fifth in the line of succession from Peter and Paul, received the episcopate at Rome, after Evarestus had held the office eight years.

Chapter II.

THE CALAMITIES OF THE JEWS DURING TRAJAN'S REIGN.

1. The teaching and the Church of our Saviour flourished greatly and made progress from day to day; but the calamities of the Jews increased, and they underwent a constant succession of evils. In the eighteenth year of Trajan's reign there was another disturbance of the Jews, through which a great multitude of them perished.'

2. For in Alexandria and in the rest of Egypt, and also in Cyrene, as if incited by some terrible and factious spirit, they rushed into seditious measures against their fellow-inhabitants, the Greeks. The insurrection increased greatly, and in the following year, while Lupus was governor of all Egypt, it developed into a war of no mean magnitude.

3. In the first attack it happened that they were victorious over the Greeks, who fled to Alexandria and imprisoned and slew the Jews that

were in the city. But the Jews of Cyrene, although deprived of their aid, continued to plunder the land of Egypt and to devastate its districts, under the leadership of Lucuas. Against them the emperor sent Marcius Turbo with a foot and naval force and also with a force of cavalry.

4. He carried on the war against them for a long time and fought many battles, and slew many thousands of Jews, not only of those of Cyrene, but also of those who dwelt in Egypt and had come to the assistance of their king Lucuas.

5. But the emperor, fearing that the Jews in Mesopotamia would also make an attack upon the inhabitants of that country, commanded Lucius Quintus to clear the province of them. And he having marched against them slew a great multitude of those that dwelt there; and in consequence of his success he was made governor of Judea by the emperor. These events are recorded also in these very words by the Greek historians that have written accounts of those times.

Chapter III.

THE APOLOGISTS THAT WROTE IN DEFENSE OF THE FAITH DURING THE REIGN OF ADRIAN.

1. After Trajan had reigned for nineteen and a half years Ælius Adrian became his successor in the empire. To him Quadratus addressed a discourse containing an apology for our religion, because certain wicked men had attempted to trouble the Christians. The work is still in the hands of a great many of the brethren, as also in our own, and furnishes clear proofs of the man's understanding and of his apostolic orthodox.

2. He himself reveals the early date at which he lived in the following words: "But the works of our Saviour were always present, for they were genuine:-those that were healed, and those that were raised from the dead, who were seen not only when they were healed and when they were raised, but were also always present; and not merely while the Saviour was on earth, but also after his death, they were alive for quite a while, so that some of them lived even to our day." Such then was Quadratus.

3. Aristides also, a believer earnestly devoted to our religion, left, like Quadratus, an apology for the faith, addressed to Adrian. His work, too, has been preserved even to the present day by a great many persons.

Chapter IV.

THE BISHOPS OF ROME AND OF ALEXANDRIA UNDER THE SAME EMPEROR.

1. In the third year of the same reign, Alexander, bishop of Rome, died after holding office ten years. His successor was Xystus. About the same time Primus, bishop of Alexandria, died in the twelfth year of his episcopate, and was succeeded by Justus.

Chapter V.

THE BISHOPS OF JERUSALEM FROM THE AGE OF OUR SAVIOUR TO THE PERIOD UNDER CONSIDERATION.

1. The chronology of the bishops of Jerusalem I have nowhere found preserved in writing; for tradition says that they were all short lived.

2. But I have learned this much from writings, that until the siege of the Jews, which took place under Adrian, there were fifteen bishops in succession there. all of whom are said to have been of Hebrew descent, and to have received the knowledge of Christ in purity, so that they were approved by those who were able to judge of such matters, and were deemed worthy of the episcopate. For their whole church consisted then of believing Hebrews who continued from the days of the apostles until the siege which took place at this time; in which siege the Jews, having again rebelled against the Romans, were conquered after severe battles.

3. But since the bishops of the circumcision ceased at this time, it is proper to give here a list of their names from the beginning. The first, then, was James, the so-called brother of the Lord; the second, Symeon; the third, Justus; the fourth, Zacchæus; the fifth, Tobias; the sixth, Benjamin; the seventh, John; the eighth, Matthias; the ninth, Philip; the tenth, Seneca; the eleventh, Justus; the twelfth, Levi; the thirteenth, Ephres; the fourteenth, Joseph; and finally, the fifteenth, Judas.

4. These are the bishops of Jerusalem that lived between the age of the apostles and the time referred to, all of them belonging to the circumcision.

5. In the twelfth year of the reign of Adrian, Xystus, having completed the tenth year of his episcopate, was succeeded by Telesphorus, the seventh in succession from the apostles. In the meantime, after the lapse of a year and some months, Eumenes, the sixth in order, succeeded to the leadership of the Alexandrian church, his predecessor having held office eleven years.

Chapter VI.

THE LAST SIEGE OF THE JEWS UNDER ADRIAN.

1. As the rebellion of the Jews at this time grew much more serious, Rufus, governor of Judea, after an auxiliary force had been sent him by the emperor, using their madness as a pretext, proceeded against them without mercy, and destroyed indiscriminately thousands of men and women and children, and in accordance with the laws of war reduced their country to a state of complete subjection.

2. The leader of the Jews at this time was a man by the name of Barcocheba (which signifies a star), who possessed the character of a robber and a murderer, but nevertheless, relying upon his name, boasted to them, as if they were slaves, that he possessed wonderful powers; and he pretended that he was a star that had come down to them out of heaven to bring them light in the midst of their misfortunes.

3. The war raged most fiercely in the eighteenth year of Adrian, at the city of Bithara, which was a very secure fortress, situated not far from Jerusalem. When the siege had lasted a long time, and the rebels had been driven to the last extremity by hunger and thirst, and the instigator of the rebellion had suffered his just punishment, the whole nation was prohibited from this time on by a decree, and by the commands of Adrian, from ever going up to the country about Jerusalem. For the emperor gave orders that they should not even see from a distance the land of their fathers. Such is the account of Aristo of Pella.

4. And thus, when the city had been emptied of the Jewish nation and had suffered the total destruction of its ancient inhabitants, it was colonized by a different race, and the Roman city which subsequently arose changed its name and was called Ælia, in honor of the emperor Ælius Adrian. And as the church there was now composed of Gentiles, the first one to assume the government of it after the bishops of the circumcision was Marcus.

Chapter VII.

THE PERSONS THAT BECAME AT THAT TIME LEADERS OF KNOWLEDGE FALSELY SO-CALLED.

1. As the churches throughout the world were now shining like the most brilliant stars, and faith in our Saviour and Lord Jesus Christ was flourishing among the whole human race, the demon who hates everything that is good, and is always hostile to the truth, and most bitterly opposed to the salvation of man, turned all his arts against the

Church. In the beginning he armed himself against it with, external persecutions.

2. But now, being shut off from the use of such means, he devised all sorts of plans, and employed other methods in his conflict with the Church, using base and deceitful men as instruments for the ruin of souls and as ministers of destruction. Instigated by him, impostors and deceivers, assuming the name of our religion, brought to the depth of ruin such of the believers as they could win over and at the same time, by means of the deeds which they practiced, turned away from the path which leads to the word of salvation those who were ignorant of the faith.

3. Accordingly there proceeded from that Menander, whom we have already mentioned as the successor of Simon, a certain serpent-like power, double-tongued and two-headed, which produced the leaders of two different heresies, Saturninus, an Antiochian by birth, and Basilides, an Alexandrian. The former of these established schools of godless heresy in Syria, the latter in Alexandria.

4. Irenæus states that the false teaching of Saturninus agreed in most respects with that of Menander, but that Basilides, under the pretext of unspeakable mysteries, invented monstrous fables, and carried the fictions of his impious heresy quite beyond bounds.

5. But as there were at that time a great many members of the Church who were fighting for the truth and defending apostolic and ecclesiastical doctrine with uncommon eloquence, so there were some also that furnished posterity through their writings with means of defense against the heresies to which we have referred.

6. Of these there has come down to us a most powerful refutation of Basilides by Agrippa Castor, one of the most renowned writers of that day, which shows the terrible imposture of the man.

7. While exposing his mysteries he says that Basilides wrote twenty-four books upon the Gospel, and that he invented prophets for himself named Barcabbas and Barcoph, and others that had no existence, and that he gave them barbarous names in order to amaze those who marvel at such things; that he taught also that the eating of meat offered to idols and the unguarded renunciation of the faith in times of persecution were matters of indifference; and that he enjoined upon his followers, like Pythagoras, a silence of five years.

8. Other similar things the above-mentioned writer has recorded concerning Basilides, and has ably exposed the error of his heresy.

9. Irenæus also writes that Carpocrates was a contemporary of these men, and that he was the father of another heresy, called the heresy of the Gnostics, who did not wish to transmit any longer the magic arts of Simon, as that one had done, in secret, but openly. For they boasted—as of something great—of love potions that were carefully prepared by them, and of certain demons that sent them

dreams and lent them their protection, and of other similar agencies; and in accordance with these things they taught that it was necessary for those who wished to enter fully into their mysteries, or rather into their abominations, to practice all the worst kinds of wickedness, on the ground that they could escape the cosmic powers, as they called them, in no other way than by discharging their obligations to them all by infamous-conduct.

10. Thus it came to pass that the malignant demon, making use of these ministers, on the one hand enslaved those that were so pitiably led astray by them to their own destruction, while on the other hand he furnished to the unbelieving heathen abundant opportunities for slandering the divine word, inasmuch as the reputation of these men brought infamy upon the whole race of Christians.

11. In this way, therefore, it came to pass that there was spread abroad in regard to us among the unbelievers of that age, the infamous and most absurd suspicion that we practiced unlawful commerce with mothers and sisters, and enjoyed impious feasts.

12. He did not, however, long succeed in these artifices, as the truth established itself and in time shone with great brilliancy.

13. For the machinations of its enemies were refuted by its power and speedily vanished. One new heresy arose after another, and the former ones always passed away, and now at one time, now at another, now in one way, now in other ways, were lost in ideas of various kinds and various forms. But the splendor of the catholic and only true Church, which is always the same, grew in magnitude and power, and reflected its piety and simplicity and freedom, and the modesty and purity of its inspired life and philosophy to every nation both of Greeks and of Barbarians.

14. At the same time the slanderous accusations which had been brought against the whole Church also vanished, and there remained our teaching alone, which has prevailed over all, and which is acknowledged to be superior to all in dignity and temperance, and in divine and philosophical doctrines. So that none of them now ventures to affix a base calumny upon our faith, or any such slander as our ancient enemies formerly delighted to utter.

15. Nevertheless, in those times the truth again called forth many champions who fought in its defense against the godless heresies, refuting them not only with oral, but also with written arguments.

Chapter VIII.

ECCLESIASTICAL WRITERS.

1. Among these Hegesippus was well known. We have already quoted his words a number of times, relating events which happened in the time of the apostles according to his account.

2. He records in five books the true tradition of apostolic doctrine in a most simple style, and he indicates the time in which he flourished when he writes as follows concerning those that first set up idols: "To whom they erected cenotaphs and temples, as is done to the present day. Among whom is also Antinous, a slave of the Emperor Adrian, in whose honor are celebrated also the Antinoian games, which were instituted in our day. For he [i.e. Adrian] also founded a city named after Antinous, and appointed prophets."

3. At the same time also Justin, a genuine lover of the true philosophy, was still continuing to busy himself with Greek literature. He indicates "We do not think it out of place to mention here Antinous also, who lived in our day, and whom all were driven by fear to worship as a god, although they knew who he was and whence he came."

4. The same writer, speaking of the Jewish war which took place at that time, adds the following: "For in the late Jewish war Barcocheba, the leader of the Jewish rebellion, commanded that Christians alone should be visited with terrible punishments unless they would deny and blaspheme Jesus Christ."

5. And in the same work he shows that his conversion from Greek philosophy to Christianity was not without reason, but that it was the result of deliberation on his part. His words are as follows: "For I myself, while I was delighted with the doctrines of Plato, and heard the Christians slandered, and saw that they were afraid neither of death nor of anything else ordinarily looked upon as terrible, concluded that it was impossible that they could be living in wickedness and pleasure. For what pleasure-loving or intemperate man, or what man that counts it good to feast on human flesh, could welcome death that he might be deprived of his enjoyments, and would not rather strive to continue permanently his present life, and to escape the notice of the rulers, instead of giving himself up to be put to death?"

6. The same writer, moreover, relates that Adrian having received from Serennius Granianus, a most distinguished governor, a letter in behalf of the Christians, in which he stated that it was not just to slay the Christians without a regular accusation and trial, merely for the sake of gratifying the outcries of the populace, sent a rescript to Minucius Fundanus, proconsul of Asia, commanding him to condemn

no one without an indictment and a well-grounded accusation.

7. And he gives a copy of the epistle, preserving the original Latin in which it was written, and prefacing it with the following words: "Although from the epistle of the greatest and most illustrious Emperor Adrian, your father, we have good ground to demand that you order judgment to be given as we have desired, yet we have asked this not because it was ordered by Adrian, but rather because we know that what we ask is just. And we have subjoined the copy of Adrian's epistle that you may know that we are speaking the truth in this matter also. And this is the copy."

8. After these words the author referred to gives the rescript in Latin, which we have translated into Greek as accurately as we could. It reads as follows:

Chapter IX.

THE EPISTLE OF ADRIAN, DECREEING THAT WE SHOULD NOT BE PUNISHED WITHOUT A TRIAL.

1. "To Minucius Fundanus. I have received an epistle, written to me by Serennius Granianus, a most illustrious man, whom you have succeeded. It does not seem right to me that the matter should be passed by without examination, lest the men be harassed and opportunity be given to the informers for practicing villainy.

2. If, therefore, the inhabitants of the province can clearly sustain this petition against the Christians so as to give answer in a court of law, let them pursue this course alone, but let them not have resort to men's petitions and outcries. For it is far more proper, if any one wishes to make an accusation, that you should examine into it.

3. If any one therefore accuses them and shows that they are doing anything contrary to the laws, do you pass judgment according to the heinousness of the crime. But, by Hercules! if any one bring an accusation through mere calumny, decide in regard to his criminality, and see to it that you inflict punishment." Such are the contents of Adrian's rescript.

Chapter X.

THE BISHOPS OF ROME AND OF ALEXANDRIA DURING THE REIGN OF ANTONINUS.

1. Adrian having died after a reign of twenty-one years, was succeeded in the government of the Romans by Antoninus, called the Pious. In the first year of his reign Telesphorus died in the eleventh year of his episcopate, and Hyginus became bishop of Rome. Irenæus

records that Telesphorus' death was made glorious by martyrdom, and in the same connection he states that in the time of the above-mentioned Roman bishop Hyginus, Valentinus, the founder of a sect of his own, and Cerdon, the author of Marcion's error, were both well known at Rome. He writes as follows:

Chapter XI.

THE HERESIARCHS OF THAT AGE.

1. "For Valentinus came to Rome under Hyginus, flourished under Plus, and remained until Anicetus. Cerdon also, Marcion's predecessor, entered the Church in the time of Hyginus, the ninth bishop, and made confession, and continued in this way, now teaching in secret, now making confession again, and now denounced for corrupt doctrine and withdrawing from the assembly of the brethren." These words are found in the third book of the work Against Heresies.

2. And again in the first book he speaks as follows concerning Cerdon: "A certain Cerdon, who had taken his system from the followers of Simon, and had come to Rome under Hyginus, the ninth in the episcopal succession from the apostles, taught that the God proclaimed by the law and prophets was not the father of our Lord Jesus Christ. For the former was known, but the latter unknown; and the former was just, but the latter good. Marcion of Pontus succeeded Cerdon and developed his doctrine, uttering shameless blasphemies."

3. The same Irenæus unfolds with the greatest vigor the unfathomable abyss of Valentinus' errors in regard to matter, and reveals his wickedness, secret and hidden like a serpent lurking in its nest.

4. And in addition to these men he says that there was also another that lived in that age, Marcus by name, who was remarkably skilled in magic arts. And he describes also their unholy initiations and their abominable mysteries in the following words:

5. "For some of them prepare a nuptial couch an perform a mystic rite with certain forms of expression addressed to those who are being initiated, and they say that it is a spiritual marriage which is celebrated by them, after the likeness of the marriages above. But others lead them to water, and while they baptize them they repeat the following words: Into the name of the unknown father of the universe, into truth, the mother of all things, into the one that descended upon Jesus. Others repeat Hebrew names in order the better to confound those who are being initiated."

6. But Hyginus having died at the close of the fourth year of his episcopate, Pius succeeded him in the government of the church of Rome. In Alexandria Marcus was appointed pastor, after Eumenes had

filled the office thirteen years in all. And Marcus having died after holding office ten years was succeeded by Celadion in the government of the church of Alexandria.

7. And in Rome Pius died in the fifteenth year of his episcopate, and Anicetus assumed the leadership of the Christians there. Hegesippus records that he himself was in Rome at this time, and that he remained there until the episcopate of Eleutherus.

8. But Justin was especially prominent in those days. In the guise of a philospher he preached the divine word, and contended for the faith in his writings. He wrote also a work against Marcion, in which he states that the latter was alive at the time he wrote.

9. He speaks as follows: "And there is a certain Marcion of Pontus, who is even now still teaching his followers to think that there is some other God greater than the creator. And by the aid of the demons he has persuaded many of every race of men to utter blasphemy, and to deny that the maker of this universe is the father of Christ, and to confess that some other, greater than he, was the creator. And all who followed them are, as we have said, called Christians, just as the name of philosophy is given to philosphers, although they may have no doctrines in common."

10. To this he adds: "And we have also written a work against all the heresies that have existed, which we will give you if you wish to read it."

11. But this same Justin contended most successfully against the Greeks, and addressed discourses containing an apology for our faith to the Emperor Antoninus, called Pius, and to the Roman senate. For he lived at Rome. But who and whence he was he shows in his Apology in the following words.

Chapter XII.

THE APOLOGY OF JUSTIN ADDRESSED TO ANTONINUS.

1. "To the Emperor Titus Ælius Adrian Antoninus Pius Cæsar Augustus, and to Verissimus his son, the philosopher, and to Lucius the philosopher, own son of Cæsar and adopted son of Pius, a lover of learning, and to the sacred senate and to the whole Roman people, I, Justin, son of Priscus and grandson of Bacchius, of Flavia Neapolis in Palestine, Syria, present this address and petition in behalf of those men of every nation who are unjustly hated and persecuted, I myself being one of them." And the same emperor having learned also from other brethren in Asia of the injuries of all kinds which they were suffering from the inhabitants of the province, thought it proper to address the following ordinance to the Common Assembly of Asia.

Chapter XIII.

THE EPISTLE OF ANTONINUS TO THE COMMON ASSEMBLY OF ASIA IN REGARD TO OUR DOCTRINE.

1. The Emperor Cæsar Marcus Aurelius Antoninus Augustus, Armenicus, Pontifex Maximus, for the fifteenth time Tribune, for the third time Consul, to the Common Assembly of Asia, Greeting.

2. I know that the gods also take care that such persons do not escape detection. For they would much rather punish those who will not worship them than you would.

3. But you throw them into confusion, and while you accuse them of atheism you only confirm them in the opinion which they hold. It would indeed be more desirable for them, when accused, to appear to die for their God, than to live. Wherefore also they come off victorious when they give up their lives rather than yield obedience to your commands.

4. And in regard to the earthquakes which have been and are still taking place, it is not improper to admonish you who lose heart whenever they occur, and nevertheless are accustomed to compare your conduct with theirs.

5. They indeed become the more confident in God, while you, during the whole time, neglect, in apparent ignorance, the other gods and the worship of the Immortal, and oppress and persecute even unto death the Christians who worship him.

6. But in regard to these persons, many of the governors of the provinces wrote also to our most divine father, to whom he wrote in reply that they should not trouble these people unless it should appear that they were attempting something affecting the Roman government. And to me also may have sent communications concerning these men, but I have replied to them in the same way that my father did.

7. But if any one still persists in bringing accusations against any of these people as such, the person who is accused shall be acquitted of the charge, even if it appear that he is one of them, but the accuser shall be punished. Published in Ephesus in the Common Assembly of Asia."

8. To these things Melito, bishop of the church of Sardis, and a man well known at that time, is a witness, as is clear from his words in the Apology which he addressed to the Emperor Verus in behalf of our doctrine.

Chapter XIV.

THE CIRCUMSTANCES RELATED OF POLYCARP, A FRIEND OF THE APOSTLES.

1. At this time, while Anicetus was at the head of the church of Rome, Irenæus relates that Polycarp, who was still alive, was at Rome, and that he had a conference with Anicetus on a question concerning the day of the paschal feast.

2. And the same writer gives another account of Polycarp which I feel constrained to add to that which has been already related in regard to him. The account is taken from the third book of Irenæus' work Against Heresies, and is as follows:

3. "But Polycarp also was not only instructed by the apostles, and acquainted with many that had seen Christ, but was also appointed by apostles in Asia bishop of the church of Smyrna.

4. We too saw him in our early youth; for he lived a long time, and died, when a very old man, a glorious and most illustrious martyr's death, having always taught the things which he had learned form the apostles, which the Church also hands down, and which alone are true.

5. To these things all the Asiatic churches testify, as do also those who, down to the present time, have succeeded Polycarp, who was a much more trustworthy and certain witness of the truth than Valentinus and Marcion and the rest of the heretics. He also was in Rome in the time of Anicetus and caused many to turn away from the above-mentioned heretics to the Church of God, proclaiming that he had received from the apostles this one and only system of truth which has been transmitted by the Church.

6. And there are those that heard from him that John, the disciple of the Lord, going to bathe in Ephesus and seeing Cerinthus within, ran out of the bath-house without bathing, crying, 'Let us flee, lest even the bath fall, because Cerinthus, the enemy of the truth, is within.'

7. And Polycarp himself, when Marcion once met him and said, 'Knowest thou us?' replied, 'I know the first born of Satan.' Such caution did the apostles and their disciples exercise that they might not even converse with any of those who perverted the truth; as Paul also said, 'A man that is a heretic, after the first and second admonition, reject; knowing he that is such is subverted, and sinneth, being condemned of himself.'

8. There is also a very powerful epistle of Polycarp written to the Philippians, from which those that wish to do so, and that are concerned for their own salvation, may learn the character of his faith and the preaching of the truth."

9. Such is the account of Irenæus. But Polycarp, in his above-

mentioned epistle to the Philippians, which is still extant, has made use of certain testimonies drawn from the First Epistle of Peter.

10. And when Antoninus, called Pius, had completed the twenty-second year of his reign, Marcus Aurelius Verus, his son, who was also called Antoninus, succeeded him, together with his brother Lucius.

Chapter XV.

UNDER VERUS, POLYCARP WITH OTHERS SUFFERED MARTYRDOM AT SMYRNA.

1. At this time, when the greatest persecutions were exciting Asia, Polycarp ended his life by martyrdom. But I consider it most important that his death, a written account of which is still extant, should be recorded in this history.

2. There is a letter, written in the name of the church over which he himself presided, to the parishes in Pontus, which relates the events that befell him, in the following words:

3. "The church of God which dwelleth in Philomelium, and to all the parishes of the holy catholic Church in every place; mercy and peace and love from God the Father be multiplied. We write unto you, brethren, an account of what happened to those that suffered martyrdom and to the blessed Polycarp, who put an end to the persecution, having, as it were, sealed it by his martyrdom."

4. After these words, before giving the account of Polycarp, they record the events which befell the rest of the martyrs, and describe the great firmness which they exhibited in the midst of their pains. For they say that the bystanders were struck with amazement when they saw them lacerated with scourges even to the innermost veins and arteries, so that the hidden inward parts of the body, both their bowels and their members, were exposed to view; and then laid upon sea-shells and certain pointed spits, and subjected to every species of punishment and of torture, and finally thrown as food to wild beasts.

5. And they record that the most noble Germanicus especially distinguished himself, overcoming by the grace of God the fear of bodily death implanted by nature. When indeed the proconsul wished to persuade him, and urged his youth, and besought him, as he was very young and vigorous, to take compassion on himself, he did not hesitate, but eagerly lured the beast toward himself, all but compelling and irritating him, in order that he might the sooner be freed from their unrighteous and lawless life.

6. After his glorious death the whole multitude marveling at the bravery of the God-beloved martyr and at the fortitude of the whole race of Christians, began to cry out suddenly, "Away with the atheists; let Polycarp be sought."

7. And when a very great tumult arose in consequence of the cries, a certain Phrygian, Quintus by name, who was newly come from Phrygia, seeing the beasts and the additional tortures, was smitten with cowardice and gave up the attainment of salvation.

8. But the above-mentioned epistle shows that he, too hastily and without proper discretion, had rushed forward with others to the tribunal, but when seized had furnished a clear proof to all, that it is not right for such persons rashly and recklessly to expose themselves to danger. Thus did matters turn out in connection with them.

9. But the most admirable Polycarp, when he first heard of these things, continued: undisturbed, preserved a quiet and unshaken mind, and determined to remain in the city. But being persuaded by his friends who en-treated and exhorted him to retire secretly, he went out to a farm not far distant from the city and abode there with a few companions, night and day doing nothing but wrestle with the Lord in prayer, beseeching and imploring, and asking peace for the churches throughout the whole world. For this was always his custom.

10. And three days before his arrest, while he was praying, he saw in a vision at night the pillow under his head suddenly seized by fire and consumed; and upon this awakening he immediately interpreted the vision to those that were present, almost foretelling that which was about to happen, and declaring plainly to those that were with him that it would be necessary for him for Christ's sake to die by fire.

11. Then, as those who were seeking him pushed the search with vigor, they say that he was again constrained by the solicitude and love of the brethren to go to another farm. Thither his pursuers came after no long time, and seized two of the servants there, and tortured one of them for the purpose of learning from him Polycarp's hiding-place.

12. And coming late in the evening, they found him lying in an upper room, whence he might have gone to another house, but he would not, saying, "The will of God be done."

13. And when he learned that they were present, as the account says, he went down and spoke to them with a very cheerful and gentle countenance, so that those who did not already know the man thought that they beheld a miracle when they observed his advanced age and the gravity and firmness of his bearing, and they marveled that so much effort should be made to capture a man like him.

14. But he did not hesitate, but immediately gave orders that a table should be spread for them. Then he invited them to partake of a bounteous meal, and asked of them one hour that he might pray undisturbed. And when they had given permission, he stood up and prayed, being full of the grace of the Lord, so that those who were present and heard him praying were amazed, and many of them now repented that such a venerable and godly old man was about to be put to death.

15. In addition to these things the narrative concerning him contains the following account: "But when at length he had brought his prayer to an end, after remembering all that had ever come into contact with him, small and great, famous and obscure, and the whole catholic Church throughout the world, the hour of departure being come, they put him upon an ass and brought him to the city, it being a great Sabbath. And he was met by Herod, the captain of police, and by his father Nicetes, who took him into their carriage, and sitting beside him endeavored to persuade him, saying, 'For what harm is there in saying, Lord Cæsar, and sacrificing and saving your, life?'

16. He at first did not answer; but when they persisted, he said, 'I am not going to do what you advise me.' And when they failed to persuade him, they uttered dreadful words, and thrust him down with violence, so that as he descended from the carriage he lacerated his shin. But without turning round, he went on his way promptly and rapidly, as if nothing had happened to him, and was taken to the stadium.

17. But there was such a tumult in the stadium that not many heard a voice from heaven, which came to Polycarp as he was entering the place: 'Be strong, Polycarp, and play the man.' And no one saw the speaker, but many of our people heard the voice.

18. And when he was led forward, there was a great tumult, as they heard that Polycarp was taken. Finally, when he came up, the proconsul asked if he were Polycarp. And when he confessed that he was, he endeavored to persuade him to deny, saying, 'Have regard for thine age,' and other like things, which it is their custom to say:

19. 'Swear by the genius of Cæsar; repent and say, Away with the Atheists.' But Polycarp, looking with dignified countenance upon the whole crowd that was gathered in the stadium, waved his hand to them, and groaned, and raising his eyes toward heaven, said, 'Away with the Atheists.'

20. But when the magistrate pressed him, and said, Swear, and I will release thee; revile Christ,' Polycarp said, 'Fourscore and six years have I been serving him, and he hath done me no wrong; how then can I blaspheme my king who saved me?'

21. "But when he again persisted, and said, 'Swear by the genius of Cæsar,' Polycarp replied, 'If thou vainly supposest that I will swear by the genius of Cæsar, as thou sayest, feigning to be ignorant who I am, hear plainly: I am a Christian. But if thou desirest to learn the doctrine of Christianity, assign a day and hear.'

22. The proconsul said, 'Persuade the people.' But Polycarp said, 'As for thee, I thought thee worthy of an explanation; for we have been taught to render to princes and authorities ordained by God the honor that is due, so long as it does not injure us; but as for these, I do not esteem them the proper persons to whom to make my defense.'

23. But the proconsul said, 'I have wild beasts; I will throw thee to them unless thou repent.' But he said, 'Call them; for repentance from better to worse is a change we cannot make. But it is a noble thing to turn from wickedness to righteousness.'

24. But he again said to him, 'If thou despisest the wild beasts, I will cause thee to be consumed by fire, unless thou repent.' But Polycarp said, 'Thou threatenest a fire which burneth for an hour, and after a little is quenched; for thou knowest not the fire of the future judgment and of the eternal punishment which is reserved for the impious. But why dost thou delay? Do what thou wilt.'

25. Saying these and other words besides, he was filled with courage and joy, and his face was suffused with grace, so that not only was he not terrified and dismayed by the words that were spoken to him, but, on the contrary, the proconsul was amazed, and sent his herald to proclaim three times in the midst of the stadium: 'Polycarp hath confessed that he is a Christian.'

26. And when this was proclaimed by the herald, the whole multitude, both of Gentiles and of Jews, who dwelt in Smyrna, cried out with ungovernable wrath and with a great shout, 'This is the teacher of Asia, the father of the Christians, the over-thrower of our gods, who teacheth many not to sacrifice nor to worship.'

27. When they had said this, they cried out and asked the Asiarch Philip to let a lion loose upon Polycarp. But he said that it was not lawful for him, since he had closed the games. Then they thought fit to cry out with one accord that Polycarp should be burned alive.

28. For it was necessary that the vision should be fulfilled which had been shown him concerning his pillow, when he saw it burning while he was praying, and turned and said prophetically to the faithful that were with him, 'I must needs be burned alive.'

29. These things were done with great speed—more quickly than they were said—the crowds immediately collecting from the workshops and baths timber and fagots, the Jews being especially zealous in the work, as is their wont.

30. But when the pile was ready, taking off all his upper garments, and loosing his girdle, he attempted also to remove his shoes, although he had never before done this, because of the effort which each of the faithful always made to touch his skin first; for he had been treated with all honor on account of his virtuous life even before his gray hairs came.

31. Forthwith then the materials prepared for the pile were placed about him; and as they were also about to nail him to the stake, he said, 'Leave me thus; for he who hath given me strength to endure the fire, will also grant me strength to remain in the fire unmoved without being secured by you with nails.'

32. So they did not nail him, but bound him.

33. And he, with his hands behind him, and bound like a noble ram taken from a great flock, an acceptable burnt-offering unto God omnipotent, said, 'Father of thy beloved and blessed Son Jesus Christ, through whom we have received the knowledge of thee, the God of angels and of powers and of the whole creation and of the entire race of the righteous who live in thy presence, I bless thee that thou hast deemed me worthy of this day and hour that I might receive a portion in the number of the martyrs, in the cup of Christ, unto resurrection of eternal life, both of soul and of body, in the immortality of the Holy Spirit.

34. Among these may I be received before thee this day, in a rich and acceptable sacrifice, as thou, the faithful and true God, hast beforehand prepared and revealed, and hast fulfilled.

35. Wherefore I praise thee also for everything; I bless thee, I glorify thee, through the eternal high priest, Jesus Christ, thy beloved Son, through whom, with him, in the Holy Spirit, be glory unto thee, both now and for the ages to come, Amen.'

36. When he had offered up his Amen and had finished his prayer, the firemen lighted the fire and as a great flame blazed out, we, to whom it was given to see, saw a wonder, and we were preserved that we might relate what happened to the others.

37. For the fire presented the appearance of a vault, like the sail of a vessel filled by the wind, and made a wall about the body of the martyr, and it was in the midst not like flesh burning, but like gold and silver refined in a furnace. For we perceived such a fragrant odor, as of the fumes of frankincense or of some other precious spices.

38. So at length the lawless men, when they saw that the body could not be consumed by the fire, commanded an executioner to approach and pierce him with the sword.

39. And when he had done this there came forth a quantity of blood so that it extinguished the fire; and the whole crowd marveled that there should be such a difference between the unbelievers and the elect, of whom this man also was one, the most wonderful teacher in our times, apostolic and prophetic, who was bishop of the catholic Church in Smyrna. For every word which came from his mouth was accomplished and will be accomplished.

40. But the jealous and envious Evil One, the adversary of the race of the righteous, when he saw the greatness of his martyrdom, and his blameless life from the beginning, and when he saw him crowned with the crown of immortality and bearing off an incontestable prize, took care that not even his body should be taken away by us, although many desired to do it and to have communion with his holy flesh.

41. Accordingly certain ones secretly suggested to Nicetes, the father of Herod and brother of Alce, that he should plead with the magistrate not to give up his body, 'lest,' it was said, 'they should

abandon the crucified One and begin to worship this man.' They said these things at the suggestion and impulse of the Jews, who also watched as we were about to take it from the fire, not knowing that we shall never be able either to forsake Christ, who suffered for the salvation of the whole world of those that are saved, or to worship any other.

42. For we worship him who is the Son of God, but the martyrs, as disciples and imitators of the Lord, we love as they deserve on account of their matchless affection for their own king and teacher. May we also be made partakers and fellow-disciples with them.

43. The centurion, therefore, when he saw the contentiousness exhibited by the Jews, placed him in the midst and burned him, as was their custom. And so we afterwards gathered up his bones. which were more valuable than precious stones and more to be esteemed than gold, and laid them in a suitable place.

44. There the Lord will permit us to come together as we are able, in gladness and joy to celebrate the birthday of his martyrdom, for the commemoration of those who have already fought and for the training and preparation of those who shall hereafter do the same.

45. Such are the events that befell the blessed Polycarp, who suffered martyrdom in Smyrna with the eleven from Philadelphia. This one man is remembered more than the others by all, so that even by the heathen he is talked about in every place."

46. Of such an end was the admirable and apostolic Polycarp deemed worthy, as recorded by the brethren of the church of Smyrna in their epistle which we have mentioned. In the same volume concerning him are subjoined also other martyrdoms which took place in the same city, Smyrna, about the same period of time with Polycarp's martyrdom. Among them also Metrodorus, who appears to have been a proselyte of the Marcionitic sect, suffered death by fire.

47. A celebrated martyr of those times was a certain man named Pionius. Those who desire to know his several confessions, and the boldness of his speech, and his apologies in behalf of the faith before the people and the rulers, and his instructive addresses and moreover, his greetings to those who had yielded to temptation in the persecution, and the words of encouragement which he addressed to the brethren who came to visit him in prison, and the tortures which he endured in addition, and besides these the sufferings and the nailings, and his firmness on the pile, and his death after all the extraordinary trials,—those we refer to that epistle which has been given in the Martyrdoms of the Ancients, collected by us, and which contains a very full account of him.

48. And there are also records extant of others that suffered martyrdom in Pergamus, a city of Asia—of Carpus and Papylus, and a woman named Agathonice, who, after many and illustrious testimonies,

gloriously ended their lives.

Chapter XVI.

JUSTIN THE PHILOSOPHER PREACHES THE WORD OF CHRIST IN ROME AND SUFFERS MARTYRDOM.

1. About this time Justin, who was mentioned by us just above, after he had addressed a second work in behalf of our doctrines to the rulers already named, was crowned with divine martyrdom, in consequence of a plot laid against him by Crescens, a philosopher who emulated the life and manners of the Cynics, whose name he bore. After Justin had frequently refuted him in public discussions he won by his martyrdom the prize of victory, dying in behalf of the truth which he preached.

2. And he himself, a man most learned in the truth, in his Apology already referred to clearly predicts how this was about to happen to him, although it had not yet occurred. His words are as follows:

3. "I, too, therefore, expect to be plotted against and put in the stocks by some one of those whom I have named, or perhaps by Crescens, that unphilosophical and vainglorious man. For the man is not worthy to be called a philosopher who publicly bears witness against those concerning whom he knows nothing, declaring, for the sake of captivating and pleasing the multitude, that the Christians are atheistical and impious. Doing this he errs greatly.

4. For if he assails us without having read the teachings of Christ, he is thoroughly depraved, and is much worse than the illiterate, who often guard against discussing and bearing false witness about matters which they do not understand. And if he has read them and does not understand the majesty that is in them, or, understanding it, does these things in order that he may not be suspected of being an adherent, he is far more base and totally depraved, being enslaved to vulgar applause and irrational fear.

5. For I would have you know that when I proposed certain questions of the sort and asked him in regard to them, I learned and proved that he indeed knows nothing. And to show that I speak the truth I am ready, if these disputations have not been reported to you, to discuss the questions again in your presence. And this indeed would be an act worthy of an emperor.

6. But if my questions and his answers have been made known to you, it is obvious to you that he knows nothing about our affairs; or if he knows, but does not dare to speak because of those who hear him, he shows himself to be, as I have already said, not a philosopher, but a vainglorious man, who indeed does not even regard that most admirable saying of Socrates." These are the words of Justin.

7. And that he met his death as he had predicted that he would, in consequence of the machinations of Crescens, is stated by Tatian, a than who early in life lectured upon the sciences of the Greeks and won no little fame in them, and who has left a great many monuments of himself in his writings. He records this fact in his work against the Greeks, where he writes as follows: "And that most admirable Justin declared with truth that the aforesaid persons were like robbers."

8. Then, after making some remarks about the philosophers, he continues as follows: "Crescens, indeed, who made his nest in the great city, surpassed all in his unnatural lust, and was wholly devoted to the love of money.

9. And he who taught that death should be despised, was himself so greatly in fear of it that he endeavored to inflict death, as if it were a great evil, upon Justin, because the latter, when preaching the truth, had proved that the philosophers were gluttons and impostors." And such was the cause of Justin's martyrdom.

Chapter XVII.

THE MARTYRS WHOM JUSTIN MENTIONS IN HIS OWN WORK.

1. The same man, before his conflict, mentions in his first Apology others that suffered martyrdom before him, and most fittingly records the following events. He writes thus:

2. "A certain woman lived with a dissolute husband; she herself, too, having formerly been of the same character. But when she came to the knowledge of the teachings of Christ, she became temperate, and endeavored to persuade her husband likewise to be temperate, repeating the teachings, and declaring the punishment in eternal fire which shall come upon those who do not live temperately and conformably to right reason.

3. But he, continuing in the same excesses, alienated his wife by his conduct. For she finally, thinking it wrong to live as a wife with a man who, contrary to the law of nature and right, sought every possible means of pleasure, desired to be divorced from him.

4. And when she was earnestly entreated by her friends, who counseled her still to remain with him, on the ground that her husband might some time give hope of amendment, she did violence to herself and remained.

5. But when her husband had gone to Alexandria, and was reported to be conducting himself still worse, she in order that she might not, by continuing in wedlock, and by sharing his board and bed, become a partaker in his lawlessness and impiety—gave him what we a call a bill of divorce and left him.

6. But her noble and excellent husband—instead of rejoicing, as he ought to have done, that she had given up those actions which she had formerly recklessly committed with the servants and hirelings, when she delighted in drunkenness and in every vice, and that she desired him likewise to give them up—when she had gone from him contrary to his wish, brought an accusation concerning her, declaring that she was a Christian.

7. And she petitioned you, the emperor, that she might be permitted first to set her affairs in order, and afterwards, after the settlement of her affairs, to make her defense against the accusation. And this you granted.

8. But he who had once been her husband, being no longer able to prosecute her, directed his attacks against a certain Ptolemæus, who had been her teacher in the doctrines of Christianity, and whom Urbicius had punished. Against him he proceeded in the following manner:

9. "He persuaded a centurion who was his friend to cast Ptolemæus into prison, and to take him and ask him this only: whether he were a Christian? And when Ptolemæus, who was a lover of truth, and not of a deceitful and false disposition, confessed that he was a Christian, the centurion bound him and punished him for a long time in the prison.

10. And finally, when the man was brought before Urbicius he was likewise asked this question only: whether he were a Christian? And again, conscious of the benefits which he enjoyed through the teaching of Christ, he confessed his schooling in divine virtue.

11. For whoever denies that he is a Christian, either denies because he despises Christianity, or he avoids confession because he is conscious that he is unworthy and an alien to it; neither of which is the case with the true Christian.

12. And when Urbicius commanded that he be led away to punishment, a certain Lucius, who was also a Christian, seeing judgment so unjustly passed, said to Urbicius, 'Why have you punished this I man who is not an adulterer, nor a fornicator, nor a murderer, nor a thief, nor a robber, nor has been convicted of committing any crime at all, but has confessed that he beam the name of Christian? You do not judge, O Urbicius, in a manner befitting the Emperor Pins, or the philosophical son of Cæsar, or the sacred senate.'

13. And without making any other reply, he said to Lucius, 'Thou also seemest to me to be such an one.' And when Lucius said, 'Certainly,' he again commanded that he too should be led away to punishment. But he professed his thanks, for he was liberated, he added, from such wicked rulers and was going to the good Father and King, God. And still a third having come forward was condemned to be punished."

14. To this, Justin fittingly and consistently adds the words which

we quoted above, saying, "I, too, therefore expect to be plotted against by some one of those whom I have named," etc."

Chapter XVIII.

THE WORKS OF JUSTIN WHICH HAVE COME DOWN TO US.

1. This writer has left us a great many monuments of a mind educated and practiced in divine things, which are replete with profitable matter of every kind. To them we shall refer the studious, noting as we proceed those that have come to our knowledge.

2. There is a certain discourse of his in defense of our doctrine addressed to Antoninus surnamed the Pious, and to his sons, and to the Roman senate. Another work contains his second Apology in behalf of our faith, which he offered to him who was the successor of the emperor mentioned and who bore the same name, Antoninus Verus, the one whose times we are now recording.

3. Also another work against the Greeks, in which he discourses at length upon most of the questions at issue between us and the Greek philosophers, and discusses the nature of demons. It is not necessary for me to add any of these things here.

4. And still another work of his against the Greeks has come down to us, to which he gave the title Refutation. And besides these another, On the Sovereignty of God, which he establishes not only from our Scriptures, but also from the books of the Greeks.

5. Still further, a work entitled Psaltes, and another disputation On the Soul, in which, after propounding various questions concerning the problem under discussion, he gives the opinions of the Greek philosophers, promising to refute it, and to present his own view in another work.

6. He composed also a dialogue against the Jews, which he held in the city of Ephesus with Trypho, a most distinguished man among the Hebrews of that day. In it he shows how the divine grace urged him on to the doctrine of the faith, and with what earnestness he had formerly pursued philosophical studies, and how ardent a search he had made for the truth.

7. And he records of the Jews in the same work, that they were plotting against the teaching of Christ, asserting the same things against Trypho: "Not only did you not repent of the wickedness which you had committed, but you selected at that time chosen men, and you sent them out from Jerusalem through all the land, to announce that the godless heresy of the Christians had made its appearance, and to accuse them of those things which all that are ignorant of us say against us, so that you become the causes not only of your own injustice, but also of all other men's."

8. He writes also that even down to his time prophetic gifts shone in the Church. And he mentions the Apocalypse of John, saying distinctly that it was the apostle's. He also refers to certain prophetic declarations, and accuses Trypho on the ground that the Jews had cut them out of the Scripture. A great many other works of his are still in the hands of many of the brethren.

9. And the discourses of the man were thought so worthy of study even by the ancients, that Irenæus quotes his words: for instance, in the fourth book of his work Against Heresies, where he writes as follows: "And Justin well says in his work against Marcion, that he would not have believed the Lord himself if he had preached another God besides the Creator"; and again in the fifth book of the same work he says: "And Justin well said that before the coming of the Lord Satan never dared to blaspheme God, because he did not yet know his condemnation."

10. These things I have deemed it necessary to say for the sake of stimulating the studious to peruse his works with diligence. So much concerning him.

Chapter XIX.

THE RULERS OF THE CHURCHES OF ROME AND ALEXANDRIA DURING THE REIGN OF VERUS.

1. In the eighth year of the above-mentioned reign Soter succeeded Anicetus as bishop of the church of Rome, after the latter had held office eleven years in all. But when Celadion had presided over the church of Alexandria for fourteen years tie was succeeded by Agrippinus.

Chapter XX.

THE RULERS OF THE CHURCH OF ANTIOCH.

1. At that time also in the church of Antioch, Theophilus was well known as the sixth from the apostles. For Cornelius, who succeeded Hero, was the fourth, and after him Eros, the fifth in order, had held the office of bishop.

Chapter XXI.

THE ECCLESIASTICAL WRITERS THAT
FLOURISHED IN THOSE DAYS.

1. At that time there flourished in the Church Hegesippus, whom we know from what has gone before, and Dionysius, bishop of Corinth, and another bishop, Pinytus of Crete, and besides these, Philip, and Apolinarius, and Melito, and Musanus, and Modestus, and finally, Irenæus. From them has come down to us in writing, the sound and orthodox faith received from apostolic tradition..

Chapter XXII.

HEGESIPPUS AND THE EVENTS WHICH HE MENTIONS.

1. Hegesippus in the five books of Memoirs which have come down to us has left a most complete record of his own views. In them he states that on a journey to Rome he met a great many bishops, and that he received the same doctrine from all. It is fitting to hear what he says after making some remarks about the epistle of Clement to the Corinthians. His words are as follows:

2. "And the church of Corinth continued in the true faith until Primus was bishop in Corinth. I conversed with them on my way to Rome, and abode with the Corinthians many days, during which we were mutually refreshed in the true doctrine.

3. And when I had come to Rome I remained a there until Anicetus, whose deacon was Eleutherus. And Anicetus was succeeded by Soter, and he by Eleutherus. In every succession, and in every city that is held which is preached by the law and the prophets and the Lord."

4. The same author also describes the beginnings of the heresies which arose in his time, in the following words: "And after James the Just had suffered martyrdom, as the Lord had also on the same account, Symeon, the son of the Lord's uncle, Clopas, was appointed the next bishop. All proposed him as second bishop because he was a cousin of the Lord.

5. "Therefore, they called the Church a virgin, for it was not yet corrupted by vain discourses. But Thebuthis, because he was not made bishop, began to corrupt it. He also was sprung from the seven sects among the people, like Simon, from whom came the Simonians, and Cleobius, from whom came the Cleobians, and Dositheus, from whom came the Dositheans, and Gorthæus, from whom came the Goratheni, and Masbotheus, from whom came the Masbothæans. From them

sprang the Menandrianists, and Marcionists, and Carpocratians, and Valentinians, and Basilidians, and Saturnilians. Each introduced privately and separately his own peculiar opinion. From them came false Christs, false prophets, false apostles, who divided the unity of the Church by corrupt doctrines uttered against God and against his Christ."

6. The same writer also records the ancient heresies which arose among the Jews, in the following words: "There were, moreover, various opinions in the circumcision, among the children of Israel. The following were those that were opposed to the tribe of Judah and the Christ: Essenes, Galileans, Hemerobaptists, Masbothæans, Samaritans, Sadducees, Pharisees."

7. And he wrote of many other matters, which we have in part already mentioned, introducing the accounts in their appropriate places. And from the Syriac Gospel according to the Hebrews he quotes some passages in the Hebrew tongue, showing that he was a convert from the Hebrews, and he mentions other matters as taken from the unwritten tradition of the Jews.

8. And not only he, but also Irenæus and the whole company of the ancients, called the Proverbs of Solomon All-virtuous Wisdom. And when speaking of the books called Apocrypha, he records that some of them were composed in his day by certain heretics. But let us now pass on to another.

Chapter XXIII.

DIONYSIUS, BISHOP OF CORINTH, AND THE EPISTLES WHICH HE WROTE.

1. And first we must speak of Dionysius, who was appointed bishop of the church in Corinth, and communicated freely of his inspired labors not only to his own people, but also to those in foreign lands, and rendered the greatest service to all in the catholic epistles which he wrote to the churches.

2. Among these is the one addressed to the Lacedæmonians, containing instruction in the orthodox faith and an admonition to peace and unity; the one also addressed to the Athenians, exciting them to faith and to the life prescribed by the Gospel, which he accuses them of esteeming lightly, as if they had almost apostatized from the faith since the martyrdom of their ruler Publius, which had taken place during the persecutions of those days.

3. He mentions Quadratus also, stating that he was appointed their bishop after the martyrdom of Publius, and testifying that through his zeal they were brought together again and their faith revived. He records, moreover, that Dionysius the Areopagite, who was converted

to the faith by the apostle Paul, according to the statement in the Acts of the Apostles, first obtained the episcopate of the church at Athens.

4. And there is extant another epistle of his addressed to the Nicomedians, in which he attacks the heresy of Marcion, and stands fast by the canon of the truth.

5. Writing also to the church that is in Gortyna, together with the other parishes in Crete, he commends their bishop Philip, because of the many acts of fortitude which are testified to as performed by the church under him, and he warns them to be on their guard against the aberrations of the heretics.

6. And writing to the church that is in Amastris, together with those in Pontus, he refers to Bacchylides and Elpistus, as having urged him to write, and he adds explanations of passages of the divine Scriptures, and mentions their bishop Palmas by name. He gives them much advice also in regard to marriage and chastity, and commands them to receive those who come back again after any fall, whether it be delinquency or heresy.

7. Among these is inserted also another epistle addressed to the Cnosians, in which he exhorts Pinytus, bishop of the parish, not to lay upon the brethren a grievous and compulsory burden in regard to chastity, but to have regard to the weakness of the multitude.

8. Pinytus, replying to this epistle, admires and commends Dionysius, but exhorts him in turn to impart some time more solid food, and to feed the people under him, when he wrote again, with more advanced teaching, that they might not be fed continually on these milky doctrines and imperceptibly grow old under a training calculated for children. In this epistle also Pinytus' orthodoxy in the faith and his care for the welfare of those placed under him, his learning and his comprehension of divine things, are revealed as in a most perfect image.

9. There is extant also another epistle written by Dionysius to the Romans, and addressed to Soter, who was bishop at that time. We cannot do better than to subjoin some passages from this epistle, in which he commends the practice of the Romans which has been retained down to the persecution in our own days. His words are as follows:

10. "For from the beginning it has been your practice to do good to all the brethren in various ways, and to send contributions to many churches in every city. Thus relieving the want of the needy, and making provision for the brethren in the mines by the gifts which you have sent from the beginning, you Romans keep up the hereditary customs of the Romans, which your blessed bishop Soter has not only maintained, but also added to, furnishing an abundance of supplies to the saints, and encouraging the brethren from abroad with blessed words, as a loving father his children."

11. In this same epistle he makes mention also of Clement's epistle to the Corinthians, showing that it had been the custom from the beginning to read it in the church. His words are as follows: "To-day we have passed the Lord's holy day, in which we have read your epistle. From it, whenever we read it, we shall always be able to draw advice, as also from the former epistle, which was written to us through Clement."

12. The same writer also speaks as follows concerning his own epistles, alleging that they had been mutilated: "As the brethren desired me to write epistles, I wrote. And these epistles the apostles of the devil have filled with tares, cutting out some things and adding others. For them a woe is reserved. It is, therefore, not to be wondered at if some have attempted to adulterate the Lord's writings also, since they have formed designs even against writings which are of less accounts." There is extant, in addition to these, another epistle of Dionysius, written to Chrysophora a most faithful sister. In it he writes what is suitable, and imparts to her also the proper spiritual food. So much concerning Dionysius.

Chapter XXIV.

THEOPHILUS BISHOP OF ANTIOCH.

1. Of Theophilus, whom we have mentioned as bishop of the church of Antioch, three elementary works addressed to Autolycus are extant; also another writing entitled Against the Heresy of Hermogenes, in which he makes use of testimonies from the Apocalypse of John, and finally certain other catechetical books.

2. And as the heretics, no less then than at other times, were like tares, destroying the pure harvest of apostolic teaching, the pastors of the churches everywhere hastened to restrain them as wild beasts from the fold of Christ, at one time by admonitions and exhortations to the brethren, at another time by contending more openly against them in oral discussions and refutations, and again by correcting their opinions with most accurate proofs in written works.

3. And that Theophilus also, with the others, contended against them, is manifest from a certain discourse of no common merit written by him against Marcion. This work too, with the others of which we have spoken, has been preserved to the present day. Maximinus, the seventh from the apostles, succeeded him as bishop of the church of Antioch.

Chapter XXV.

PHILIP AND MODESTUS.

1. Philip who, as we learn from the words of Dionysius, was bishop of the parish of Gortyna, likewise wrote a most elaborate work against Marcion, as did also Irenæus and Modestus. The last named has exposed the error of the man more clearly than the rest to the view of all. There are a number of others also whose works are still presented by a great many of the brethren.

Chapter XXVI.

MELITO AND THE CIRCUMSTANCES WHICH HE RECORDS.

1. In those days also Melito, bishop of the parish in Sardis, and Apolinarius, bishop of Hierapolis, enjoyed great distinction. Each of them on his own part addressed apologies in behalf of the faith to the above-mentioned emperor of the Romans who was reigning at that time.

2. The following works of these writers have come to our knowledge. Of Melito, the two books On the Passover, and one On the Conduct of Life and the Prophets, the discourse On the Church, and one On the Lord's Day, still further one On the Faith of Man, and one On his Creation, another also On the Obedience of Faith, and one On the Senses; besides these the work On the Soul and Body, and that On Baptism, and the one On Truth, and On the Creation and Generation of Christ; his discourse also On Prophecy, and that On Hospitality; still further, The Key, and the books On the Devil and the Apocalypse of John, and the work On the Corporeality of God, and finally the book addressed to Antoninus.

3. In the books On the Passover he indicates the time at which he wrote, beginning with these words: "While Servilius Paulus was proconsul of Asia, at the time when Sagaris suffered martyrdom, there arose in Laodicea a great strife concerning the Passover, which fell according to rule in those days; and these were written."

4. And Clement of Alexandria refers to this work in his own discourse On the Passover, which, he says, he wrote on occasion of Melito's work.

5. But in his book addressed to the emperor he records that the following events happened to us under him: "For, what never before happened, the race of the pious is now suffering persecution, being driven about in Asia by new decrees. For the shameless informers and coveters of the property of others, taking occasion from the decrees,

openly carry on robbery night and day, despoiling those who are guilty of no wrong." And a little further on he says: "If these things are done by thy command, well and good. For a just ruler will never take unjust measures; and we indeed gladly accept the honor of such a death.

6. But this request alone we present to thee, that thou wouldst thyself first examine the authors of such strife, and justly judge whether they be worthy of death and punishment, or of safety and quiet. But if, on the other hand, this counsel and this new decree, which is not fit to be executed even against barbarian enemies, be not from thee, much more do we beseech thee not to leave us exposed to such lawless plundering by the populace."

7. Again he adds the following: "For our philosophy formerly flourished among the Barbarians; but having sprung up among the nations under thy rule, during the great reign of thy ancestor Augustus, it became to thine empire especially a blessing of auspicious omen. For from that time the power of the Romans has grown in greatness and splendor. To this power thou hast succeeded, as the desired possessor, and such shalt thou continue with thy son, if thou guardest the philosophy which grew up with the empire and which came into existence with Augustus; that philosophy which thy ancestors also honored along with the other religions.

8. And a most convincing proof that our doctrine flourished for the good of an empire happily begun, is this—that there has no evil happened since Augustus' reign, but that, on the contrary, all things have been splendid and glorious, in accordance with the prayers of all.

9. Nero and Domitian, alone, persuaded by certain calumniators, have wished to slander our doctrine, and from them it has come to pass that the falsehood has been handed down, in consequence of an unreasonable practice which prevails of bringing slanderous accusations against the Christians.

10. But thy pious fathers corrected their ignorance, having frequently rebuked in writing many who dared to attempt new measures against them. Among them thy grandfather Adrian appears to have written to many others, and also to Fundanus, the proconsul and governor of Asia. And thy father, when thou also wast ruling with him, wrote to the cities, forbidding them to take any new measures against us; among the rest to the Larissæans, to the Thessalonians, to the Athenians, and to all the Greeks.

11. And as for thee—since thy opinions respecting the Christians are the same as theirs, and indeed much more benevolent and philosophic—we are the more persuaded that thou wilt do all that we ask of thee." These words are found in the above-mentioned work.

12. But in the Extracts made by him the same writer gives at the beginning of the introduction a catalogue of the acknowledged books of the Old Testament, which it is necessary to quote at this point. He

writes as follows:

13. "Melito to his brother Onesimus, greeting: Since thou hast often, in thy zeal for the word, expressed a wish to have extracts made from the Law and the Prophets concerning the Saviour and concerning our entire faith, and hast also desired to have an accurate statement of the ancient book, as regards their number and their order, I have endeavored to perform the task, knowing thy zeal for the faith, and thy desire to gain information in regard to the word, and knowing that thou, in thy yearning after God, esteemest these things above all else, struggling to attain eternal salvation.

14. Accordingly when I went East and came to the place where these things were preached and done, I learned accurately the books of the Old Testament, and send them to thee as written below. Their names are as follows: Of Moses, five books: Genesis, Exodus, Numbers, Leviticus, Deuteronomy; Jesus Nave, Judges, Ruth; of Kings, four books; of Chronicles, two; the Psalms of David, the Proverbs of Solomon, Wisdom also, Ecclesiastes, Song off Songs, Job; of Prophets, Isaiah, Jeremiah; of the twelve prophets, one book; Daniel, Ezekiel, Esdras. From which also I have made the extracts, dividing them into six books." Such are the words of Melito.

Chapter XXVII.

APOLINARIUS, BISHOP OF THE CHURCH OF HIERAPOLIS.

1. A number of works of Apolinarius have been preserved by many, and the following have reached us: the Discourse addressed to the above-mentioned emperor, five books Against the Greeks, On Truth, a first and second book, and those which he subsequently wrote against the heresy of the Phrygians, which not long afterwards came out with its innovations, but at that time was, as it were, in its incipiency, since Montanus, with his false prophetesses, was then laying the foundations of his error.

Chapter XXVIII.

MUSANUS AND HIS WRITINGS.

1. And as for Musanus, whom we have mentioned among the foregoing writers, a certain very elegant discourse is extant, which was written by him against some brethren that had gone over to the heresy of the so-called Encratites, which had recently sprung up, and which introduced a strange and pernicious error. It is said that Tatian was the author of this false doctrine.

Chapter XXIX.

THE HERESY OF TATIAN.

1. He is the one whose words we quoted a little above in regard to that admirable man, Justin, and whom we stated to have been a disciple of the martyr. Irenæus declares this in the first book of his work Against Heresies, where he writes as follows concerning both him and his heresy:

2. "Those who are called Encratites, and who sprung from Saturninus and Marcion, preached celibacy, setting aside the original arrangement of God and tacitly censuring him who made male and female for the propagation of the human race. They introduced also abstinence from the things called by them animate, thus showing ingratitude to the God who made all things. And they deny the salvation of the first man?

3. But this has been only recently discovered by them, a certain Tatian being the first to introduce this blasphemy. He was a hearer of Jus-tin, and expressed no such opinion while he was with him, but after the martyrdom of the latter he left the Church, and becoming exalted with the thought of being a teacher, and puffed up with the idea that he was superior to others, he established a peculiar type of doctrine of his own, inventing certain invisible æons like the followers of Valentinus, while, like Marcion and Saturninus, he pronounced marriage to be corruption and fornication. His argument against the salvation of Adam, however, he devised for himself." Irenæus at that time wrote thus.

4. But a little later a certain man named Severus put new strength into the aforesaid heresy, and thus brought it about that those who took their origin from it were called, after him, Severians.

5. They, indeed, use the Law and Prophets and Gospels, but interpret in their own way the utterances of the Sacred Scriptures. And they abuse Paul the apostle and reject his epistles, and do not accept even the Acts of the Apostles.

6. But their original founder, Tatian, formed a certain combination and collection of the Gospels, I know not how, to which he gave the title *Diatessaron*, and which is still in the hands of some. But they say that he ventured to paraphrase certain words of the apostle, in order to improve their style.

7. He has left a great many writings. Of these the one most in use among many persons is his celebrated Address to the Greeks, which also appears to be the best and most useful of all his works. In it he deals with the most ancient times, and shows that Moses and the Hebrew prophets were older than all the celebrated men among the

Greeks. So much in regard to these men.

Chapter XXX.

BARDESANES THE SYRIAN AND HIS EXTANT WORKS.

1. In the same reign, as heresies were abounding in the region between the rivers, a certain Bardesanes, a most able man and a most skillful disputant in the Syriac tongue, having composed dialogues against Marcion's followers and against certain others who were authors of various opinions, committed them to writing in his own language, together with many other works. His pupils, of whom he had very many (for he was a powerful defender of the faith), translated these productions from the Syriac into Greek.

2. Among them there is also his most able dialogue On Fate, addressed to Antoninus, and other works which they say he wrote on occasion of the persecution which arose at that time.

3. He indeed was at first a follower of Valentinus, but afterward, having rejected his teaching and having refuted most of his fictions, he fancied that he had come over to the more correct opinion. Nevertheless he did not entirely wash off the filth of the old heresy. About this time also Soter, bishop of the church of Rome, departed this life.

Book V.

Introduction.

1. Soter, bishop of the church of Rome, died after an episcopate of eight years, and was succeeded by Eleutherus, the twelfth from the apostles. In the seventeenth year of the Emperor Antoninus Verus, the persecution of our people was rekindled more fiercely in certain districts on account of an insurrection of the masses in the cities; and judging by the number in a single nation, myriads suffered martyrdom throughout the world. A record of this was written for posterity, and in truth it is worthy of perpetual remembrance.

2. A full account, containing the most reliable information on the subject, is given in our Collection of Martyrdoms, which constitutes a narrative instructive as well as historical. I will repeat here such portions of this account as may be needful for the present purpose.

3. Other writers of history record the victories of war and trophies won from enemies, the skill of generals, and the manly bravery of soldiers, defiled with blood and with innumerable slaughters for the sake of children and country and other possessions.

4. But our narrative of the government of God will record in ineffaceable letters the most peaceful wars waged in behalf of the peace

of the soul, and will tell of men doing brave deeds for truth rather than country, and for piety rather than dearest friends. It will hand down to imperishable remembrance the discipline and the much-tried fortitude of the athletes of religion, the trophies won from demons, the victories over invisible enemies, and the crowns placed upon all their heads.

Chapter I.

THE NUMBER OF THOSE WHO FOUGHT FOR RELIGION IN GAUL UNDER VERUS AND THE NATURE OF THEIR CONFLICTS.

1. The country in which the arena was prepared for them was Gaul, of which Lyons and Vienne are the principal and most celebrated cities. The Rhone passes through both of them, flowing in a broad stream through the entire region.

2. The most celebrated churches in that country sent an account of the witnesses to the churches in Asia and Phrygia, relating in the following manner what was done among them. I will give their own words.

3. "The servants of Christ residing at Vienne and Lyons, in Gaul, to the brethren through out Asia and Phrygia, who hold the same faith and hope of redemption, peace and grace and glory from God the Father and Christ Jesus our Lord."

4. Then, having related some other matters they begin their account in this manner: "The greatness of the tribulation in this region, and the fury of the heathen against the saints, and the sufferings of the blessed witnesses we cannot recount accurately, nor indeed could they possibly be recorded.

5. For with all his might the adversary fell upon us, giving us a foretaste of his unbridled activity at his future coming. He endeavored in every manner to practice and exercise his servants against the servants of God, not only shutting us out from houses and baths and markets, but forbidding any of us to be seen in any place whatever.

6. But the grace of God led the conflict against him, and delivered the weak, and set them as firm pillars, able through patience to endure all the wrath of the Evil One. And they joined battle with him, undergoing all kinds of shame and injury; and regarding their great sufferings as little, they hastened to Christ, manifesting truly that 'the sufferings of this present time are not worthy to be compared with the glory which shall be revealed to us-ward.'

7. First of all, they endured nobly the injuries heaped upon them by the populace; clamors and blows and draggings and robberies and stonings and imprisonments, and all things which an infuriated mob delight in inflicting on enemies and adversaries.

8. Then, being taken to the forum by the chiliarch and the authorities of the city, they were examined in the presence of the whole multitude, and having confessed, they were imprisoned until the arrival of the governor.

9. When, afterwards, they were brought before him, and he treated us with the utmost cruelty, Vettius Epagathus, one of the brethren, and a man filled with love for God and his neighbor, interfered. His life was so consistent that, although young, he had attained a reputation equal to that of the elder Zacharias: for he 'walked in all the commandments and ordinances of the Lord blameless,' and was untiring in every good work for his neighbor, zealous for God and fervent in spirit. Such being his character, he could not endure the unreasonable judgment against us, but was filled with indignation, and asked to be permitted to testify in behalf of his brethren, that there is among us nothing ungodly or impious.

10. But those about the judgment seat cried out against him, for he was a man of distinction; and the governor refused to grant his just request, and merely asked if he also were a Christian. And he, confessing this with a loud voice, was himself taken into the order of the witnesses, being called the Advocate of the Christians, but having the Advocate in himself, the Spirit more abundantly than Zacharias. He showed this by the fullness of his love, being well pleased even to lay down his life in defense of the brethren. For he was and is a true disciple of Christ, 'following the Lamb whithersoever he goeth.'

11. "Then the others were divided, and the proto-witnesses were manifestly ready, and finished their confession with all eagerness. But some appeared unprepared and untrained, weak as yet, and unable to endure so great a conflict. About ten of these proved abortions, causing us great grief and sorrow beyond measure, and impairing the zeal of the others who had not yet been seized, but who, though suffering all kinds of affliction, continued constantly with the witnesses and did not forsake them.

12. Then all of us feared greatly on account of uncertainty as to their confession not because we dreaded the sufferings to be endured, but because we looked to the end, and were afraid that some of them might fall away.

13. But those who were worthy were seized day by day, filling up their number, so that all the zealous persons, and those through whom especially our affairs had been established, were collected together out of the two churches.

14. And some of our heathen servants also were seized, as the governor had commanded that all of us should be examined publicly. These, being ensnared by Satan, and fearing for themselves the tortures which they beheld the saints endure, and being also urged on by the soldiers, accused us falsely of Thyestean banquets and Edipodean

intercourse, and of deeds which are not only unlawful for us to speak of or to think, but which we cannot believe were ever done by men.

15. When these accusations were reported, all the people raged like wild beasts against us, so that even if any had before been moderate on account of friendship, they were now exceedingly furious and gnashed their teeth against us. And that which was spoken by our Lord was fulfilled: 'The time will come when whosoever killeth you will think that he doeth God service.'

16. Then finally the holy witnesses endured sufferings beyond description, Satan striving earnestly that some of the slanders might be uttered by them also?

17. "But the whole wrath of the populace, and governor, and soldiers was aroused exceedingly against Sanctus, the deacon from Vienne, and Maturus, a late convert, yet a noble combatant, and against Attalus, a native of Pergamos where he had always been a pillar and foundation, and Blandina, through whom Christ showed that things which appear mean and obscure and despicable to men are with God of great glory, through love toward him manifested in power, and not boasting in appearance.

18. For while we all trembled, and her earthly mistress, who was herself also one of the witnesses, feared that on account of the weakness of her body, she would be unable to make bold confession, Blandina was filled with such power as to be delivered and raised above those who were torturing her by turns from morning till evening in every manner, so that they acknowledged that they were conquered, and could do nothing more to her. And they were astonished at her endurance, as her entire body was mangled and broken; and they testified that one of these forms of torture was sufficient to destroy life, not to speak of so many and so great sufferings.

19. But the blessed woman, like a noble athlete, renewed her strength in her confession; and her comfort and recreation and relief from the pain of her sufferings was in exclaiming, 'I am a Christian, and there is nothing vile done by us.'

20. "But Sanctus also endured marvelously and superhumanly all the outrages which he suffered. While the wicked men hoped, by the continuance and severity of his tortures to wring something from him which he ought not to say, he girded himself against them with such firmness that he would not even tell his name, or the nation or city to which he belonged, or whether he was bond or free, but answered in the Roman tongue to all their questions, 'I am a Christian.' He confessed this instead of name and city and race and everything besides, and the people heard from him no other word.

21. There arose therefore on the part of the governor and his tormentors a great desire to conquer him but having nothing more that they could do to him, they finally fastened red-hot brazen plates to the

most tender parts of his body.

22. And these indeed were burned, but he continued unbending and unyielding, firm in his confession, and refreshed and strengthened by the heavenly fountain of the water of life, flowing from the bowels of Christ.

23. And his body was a witness of his sufferings, being one complete wound and bruise, drawn: out of shape, and altogether unlike a human form. Christ, suffering in him, manifested his glory, delivering him from his adversary, and making him an example for the others, showing that nothing is fearful where the love of the Father is, and nothing painful where there is the glory of Christ.

24. For when the wicked men tortured him a second time after some days, supposing that with his body swollen and inflamed to such a degree that he could not bear the touch of a hand, if they should again apply the same instruments, they would overcome him, or at least by his death under his sufferings others would be made afraid, not only did not this occur, but, contrary to all human expectation, his body arose and stood erect in the midst of the subsequent torments, and resumed its original appearance and the use of its limbs so that, through the grace of Christ, these second sufferings became to him, not torture, but healing.

25. "But the devil, thinking that he had already consumed Biblias, who was one of those who had denied Christ, desiring to increase her condemnation through the utterance of blasphemy, brought her again to the torture, to compel her, as already feeble and weak, to report impious things concerning us.

26. But she recovered herself under the suffering, and as if awaking from a deep sleep, and reminded by the present anguish of the eternal punishment in hell, she contradicted the blasphemers. 'How,' she said, 'could those eat children who do not think it lawful to taste the blood even of irrational animals?' And thenceforward she confessed herself a Christian, and was given a place in the order of the witnesses.

27. "But as the tyrannical tortures were made by Christ of none effect through the patience of the blessed, the devil invented other contrivances,—confinement in the dark and most loathsome parts of the prison, stretching of the feet to the fifth hole in the stocks, and the other outrages which his servants are accustomed to inflict upon the prisoners when furious and filled with the devil. A great many were suffocated in prison, being chosen by the Lord for this manner of death, that he might manifest in them his glory.

28. For some, though they had been tortured so cruelly that it seemed impossible that they could live, even with the most careful nursing, yet, destitute of human attention, remained in the prison, being strengthened by the Lord, and invigorated both in body and soul; and they exhorted and encouraged the rest. But such as were young, and

arrested recently, so that their bodies had not become accustomed to torture, were unable to endure the severity of their confinement, and died in prison.

29. "The blessed Pothinus, who had been entrusted with the bishopric of Lyons, was dragged to the judgment seat. He was more than ninety years of age, and very infirm, scarcely indeed able to breathe because of physical weakness; but he was strengthened by spiritual zeal through his earnest desire for martyrdom. Though his body was worn out by old age and disease, his life was preserved that Christ might triumph in it.

30. When he was brought by the soldiers to the tribunal, accompanied by the civil magistrates and a multitude who shouted against him in every manner as if he were Christ himself, he bore noble witness.

31. Being asked by the governor, Who was the God of the Christians, he replied, 'If thou art worthy, thou shalt know.' Then he was dragged away harshly, and received blows of every kind. Those near him struck him with their hands and feet, regardless of his age; and those at a distance hurled, at him whatever they could seize; all of them thinking that they would be guilty of great wickedness and impiety if any possible abuse were omitted. For thus they thought to avenge their own deities. Scarcely able to breathe, he was cast into prison and died after two days.

32. "Then a certain great dispensation of God occurred, and the compassion of Jesus appeared beyond measure, in a manner rarely seen among the brotherhood, but not beyond the power of Christ.

33. For those who had recanted at their first arrest were imprisoned with the others, and endured terrible sufferings, so that their denial was of no profit to them even for the present. But those who confessed what they were imprisoned as Christians, no other accusation being brought against them. But the first were treated afterwards as murderers and defiled, and were punished twice as severely as the others.

34. For the joy of martyrdom, and the hope of the promises, and love for Christ, and the Spirit of the Father supported the latter; but their consciences so greatly distressed the former that they were easily distinguishable from all the rest by their very countenances when they were led forth.

35. For the first went out rejoicing, glory and grace being blended in their faces, so that even their bonds seemed like beautiful ornaments, as those of a bride adorned with variegated golden fringes; and they were perfumed with the sweet savor of Christ, so that some supposed they had been anointed with earthly ointment. But the others were downcast and humble and dejected and filled with every kind of disgrace, and they were reproached by the heathen as ignoble and weak, bearing the accusation of murderers, and having lost the one

honorable and glorious and life-giving Name. The rest, beholding this, were strengthened, and when apprehended, they confessed without hesitation, paying no attention to the persuasions of the devil."

36. After certain other words they continue: "After these things, finally, their martyrdoms For plaiting a crown of various colors and of all kinds of flowers, they presented it to the Father. It was proper therefore that the noble athletes, having endured a manifold strife, and conquered grandly, should receive the crown, great and incorruptible.

37. "Maturus, therefore, and Sanctus and Blandina and Attalus were led to the amphitheater to be exposed to the wild beasts, and to give to the heathen public a spectacle of cruelty, a day for fighting with wild beasts being specially appointed on account of our people.

38. Both Maturus and Sanctus passed again through every torment in the amphitheater, as if they had suffered nothing before, or rather, as if, having already conquered their antagonist in many contests, they were now striving for the crown itself. They endured again the customary running of the gauntlet and the violence of the wild beasts, and everything which the furious people called for or desired, and at last, the iron chair in which their bodies being roasted, tormented them with the fumes.

39. And not with this did the persecutors cease, but were yet more mad against them, determined to overcome their patience. But even thus they did not hear a word from Sanctus except the confession which he had uttered from the beginning.

40. These, then, after their life had continued for a long time through the great conflict, were at last sacrificed, having been made throughout that day a spectacle to the world, in place of the usual variety of combats.

41. "But Blandina was suspended on a stake, and exposed to be devoured by the wild beasts who should attack her. And because she appeared as if hanging on a cross, and because of her earnest prayers, she inspired the combatants with great zeal. For they looked on her in her conflict, and beheld with their outward eyes, in the form of their sister, him who was crucified for them, that he might persuade those who believe on him, that every one who suffers for the glory of Christ has fellowship always with the living God.

42. As none of the wild beasts at that time touched her, she was taken down from the stake, and cast again into prison. She was preserved thus for another contest, that, being victorious in more conflicts, she might make the punishment of the crooked serpent irrevocable; and, though small and weak and despised, yet clothed with Christ the mighty and conquering Athlete, she might arouse the zeal of the brethren, and, having overcome the adversary many times might receive, through her conflict, the crown incorruptible.

43. "But Attalus was called for loudly by! the people, because he

was a person of distinction. He entered the contest readily on account of a good conscience and his genuine practice in Christian discipline, and as he had always been a witness for the truth among us.

44. He was led around the amphitheater, a tablet being carried before him on which was written in the Roman language 'This is Attalus the Christian,' and the people were filled with indignation against him. But when the governor learned that he was a Roman, he commanded him to be taken back with the rest of those who were in prison concerning whom he had written to Cæsar, and whose answer he was awaiting.

45. "But the intervening time was not wasted nor fruitless to them; for by their patience the measureless compassion of Christ was manifested. For through their continued life the dead were made alive, and the witnesses showed favor to those who had failed to witness. And the virgin mother had much joy in receiving alive those whom she had brought forth as dead.

46. For through their influence many who had denied were restored, and re-be-gotten, and rekindled with life, and learned to confess. And being made alive and strengthened, they went to the judgment seat to be again interrogated by the governor; God, who desires not the death of the sinner, but mercifully invites to repentance, treating them with kindness.

47. For Cæsar commanded that they should be put to death, but that any who might deny should be set free. Therefore, at the beginning of the public festival which took place there, and which was attended by crowds of men from all nations, the governor brought the blessed ones to the judgment seat, to make of them a show and spectacle for the multitude. Wherefore also he examined them again, and beheaded those who appeared to possess Roman citizenship, but he sent the others to the wild beasts.

48. "And Christ was glorified greatly in those who had formerly denied him, for, contrary to the expectation of the heathen, they confessed. For they, were examined by themselves, as about to be set free; but confessing, they were added to the order of the witnesses. But some continued without, who had never possessed a trace of faith, nor any apprehension of the wedding garment, nor an understanding of the fear of God; but, as sons of perdition, they blasphemed the Way through their apostasy.

49. But all the others were added to the Church. While these were being examined, a certain Alexander, a Phrygian by birth, and physician by profession, who had resided in Gaul for many years, and was well known to all on account of his love to God and boldness of speech (for he was not without a share of apostolic grace), standing before the judgment seat, and by signs encouraging them to confess, appeared to those standing by as if in travail.

50. But the people being enraged because those who formerly denied now confessed, cried out against Alexander as if he were the cause of this. Then the governor summoned him and inquired who he was. And when he answered that he was a Christian, being very angry he condemned him to the wild beasts. And on the next day he entered along with Attalus. For to please the people, the governor had ordered Attalus again to the wild beasts.

51. And they were tortured in the amphitheater with all the instruments contrived for that purpose, and having endured a very great conflict, were at last sacrificed. Alexander neither groaned nor murmured in any manner, but communed in his heart with God.

52. But when Attalus was placed in the iron seat, and the fumes arose from his burning body, he said to the people in the Roman language: 'Lo! this which ye do is devouring men; but we do not devour men; nor do any other wicked thing.' And being asked, what name God has, he replied, 'God has not a name as man has.'

53. "After all these, on the last day of the contests, Blandina was again brought in, with Ponticus, a boy about fifteen years old. They had been brought every day to witness the sufferings of the others, and had been pressed to swear by the idols. But because they remained steadfast and despised them, the multitude became furious, so that they had no compassion for the youth of the boy nor respect for the sex of the woman.

54. Therefore they exposed them to all the terrible sufferings and took them through the entire round of torture, repeatedly urging them to swear, but being unable to effect this; for Ponticus, encouraged by his sister so that even the heathen could see that she was confirming and strengthening him, having nobly endured every torture, gave up the ghost.

55. But the blessed Blandina, last of all, having, as a noble mother, encouraged her children and sent them before her victorious to the King, endured herself all their conflicts and hastened after them, glad and rejoicing in her departure as if called to a marriage supper, rather than east to wild beasts.

56. And, after the scourging, after the wild beasts, after the roasting seat, she was finally enclosed in a net, and thrown before a bull. And having been tossed about by the animal, but feeling none of the things which were happening to her, on account of her hope and firm hold upon what had been entrusted to her, and her communion with Christ, she also was sacrificed. And the heathen themselves confessed that never among them had a woman endured so many and such terrible tortures.

57. "But not even thus was their madness and cruelty toward the saints satisfied. For incited by the Wild Beast, wild and barbarous tribes were not easily appeased, and their violence found another peculiar

opportunity in the dead bodies.

58. For, through their lack of manly reason, the fact that they had been conquered did not put them to shame, but rather the more enkindled their wrath as that of a wild beast, and aroused alike the hatred of governor and people to treat us unjustly; that the Scripture might be fulfilled: 'He that is lawless, let him be lawless still, and he that is righteous, let him be righteous still.'

59. For they cast to the dogs those who had died of suffocation in the prison, carefully guarding them by night and day, lest any one should be buried by us. And they exposed the remains left by the wild beasts and by fire, mangled and charred, and placed the heads of the others by their bodies, and guarded them in like manner from burial by a watch of soldiers for many days.

60. And some raged and gnashed their teeth against them, desiring to execute more severe vengeance upon them; but others laughed and mocked at them, magnifying their own idols, and imputed to them the punishment of the Christians. Even the more reasonable, and those who had seemed to sympathize somewhat, reproached them often, saying, 'Where is their God, and what has their religion, which they have chosen rather than life, profited them?'

61. So various was their conduct toward us; but we were in deep affliction because we could not bury the bodies. For neither did night avail us for this purpose, nor did money persuade, nor entreaty move to compassion; but they kept watch in every way, as if the prevention of the burial would be of some great advantage to them." In addition, they say after other things:

62. "The bodies of the martyrs, having thus in every manner been exhibited and exposed for six days, were afterward burned and reduced to ashes, and swept into the Rhone by the wicked men, so that no trace of them might appear on the earth.

63. And this they did, as if able to conquer God, and prevent their new birth; 'that,' as they said, 'they may have no hope of a resurrection, through trust in which they bring to us this foreign and new religion, and despise terrible things, and are ready even to go to death with joy. Now let us see if they will rise again, and if their God is able to help them, and to deliver them out of our hands.'"

Chapter II.

THE MARTYRS, BELOVED OF GOD, KINDLY MINISTERED UNTO THOSE WHO FELL IN THE PERSECUTION.

1. Such things happened to the churches of Christ under the above-mentioned emperor, from which we may reasonably conjecture the occurrences in the other provinces. It is proper to add other selections

from the same letter, in which the moderation and compassion of these witnesses is recorded in the following words:

2. "They were also so zealous in their imitation of Christ—'who, being in the form of God, counted it not a prize to be on an equality with God,'—that, though they had attained such honor, and had borne witness, not once or twice, but many times, having been brought back to prison from the wild beasts, covered with burns and scars and wounds—yet they did not proclaim themselves witnesses, nor did they suffer us to address them by this name. If any one of us, in letter or conversation, spoke of them as witnesses, they rebuked him sharply.

3. For they conceded cheerfully the appellation of Witness to Christ 'the faithful and true Witness,' and 'firstborn of the dead,' and prince of the life of God; and they reminded us of the witnesses who had already departed, and said, 'They are already witnesses whom Christ has deemed worthy to be taken up in their confession, having sealed their testimony by their departure; but we are lowly and humble confessors.' And they besought the brethren with tears that earnest prayers should be offered that they might be made perfect.

4. They showed in their deeds the power of 'testimony,' manifesting great boldness toward all the brethren, and they made plain their nobility through patience and fearlessness and courage, but they refused the title of Witnesses as distinguishing them from their brethren, being filled with the fear of God."

5. A little further on they say: "They humbled themselves under the mighty hand, by which they are now greatly exalted. They defended all, but accused none. They absolved all, but bound none. And they prayed for those who had inflicted cruelties upon them, even as Stephen, the perfect witness, 'Lord, lay not this sin to their charge.' But if he prayed for those who stoned him, how much more for the brethren!"

6. And again after mentioning other matters, they say: "For, through the genuineness of their love, their greatest contest with him was that the Beast, being choked, might cast out alive those whom he supposed he had swallowed. For they did not boast over the fallen, but helped them in their need with those things in which they themselves abounded, having the compassion of a mother, and shedding many tears on their account before the Father.

7. They asked for life, and he gave it to them, and they shared it with their neighbors. Victorious; over everything, they departed to God. Having always loved peace, and having commended peace to us they went in peace to God, leaving no sorrow to their mother, nor division or strife to the brethren, but joy and peace and concord and love."

8. This record of the affection of those blessed ones toward the brethren that had fallen may be profitably added on account of the inhuman and unmerciful disposition of those who, after these events,

acted unsparingly toward the members of Christ.

Chapter III.

THE VISION WHICH APPEARED IN A DREAM TO THE WITNESS ATTALUS.

1. The same letter of the abovementioned witnesses contains another account worthy of remembrance. No one will object to our bringing it to the knowledge of our readers. It runs as follows:

2. "For a certain Alcibiades, who was one of them, led a very austere life, partaking of nothing whatever but bread and water. When he endeavored to continue this same sort of life in prison, it was revealed to Attalus after his first conflict in the amphitheater that Alcibiades was not doing well in refusing the creatures of God and placing a stumbling-block before others.

3. And Alcibiades obeyed; and partook of all things without restraint, giving thanks to God. For they were not deprived of the grace of God, but the Holy Ghost was their counselor." Let this suffice for these matters.

4. The followers of Montanus, Alcibiades and Theodotus in Phrygia were now first giving wide circulation to their assumption in regard to prophecy—for the many other miracles that, through the gift of God, were still wrought in the different churches caused their prophesying to be readily credited by many—and as dissension arose concerning them, the brethren in Gaul set forth their own prudent and most orthodox judgment in the matter, and published also several epistles from the witnesses that had been put to death among them. These they sent, while they were still in prison, to the brethren throughout Asia and Phrygia, and also to Eleutherus, who was then bishop of Rome, negotiating for the peace of the churches.

Chapter IV.

IRENÆUS COMMENDED BY THE WITNESSES IN A LETTER.

1. The same witnesses also recommended Irenæus, who was already at that time a presbyter of the parish of Lyons, to the above-mentioned bishop of Rome, saying many favorable things in regard to him, as the following extract shows:

2. "We pray, father Eleutherus, that you may rejoice in God in all things and always. We have requested our brother and comrade Irenæus to carry this letter to you, and we ask you to hold him in esteem, as zealous for the covenant of Christ. For if we thought that office could confer righteousness upon any one, we should commend him among

the first as a presbyter of the church, which is his position."

3. Why should we transcribe the catalogue of the witnesses given in the letter already mentioned, of whom some were beheaded, others cast to the wild beasts, and others fell asleep in prison, or give the number of confessors still surviving at that time? For whoever desires can readily find the full account by consulting the letter itself, which, as I have said, is recorded in our Collection of Martyrdoms. Such were the events which happened under Antoninus.

Chapter V.

GOD SENT RAIN FROM HEAVEN FOR MARCUS AURELIUS CÆSAR IN ANSWER TO THE PRAYERS OF OUR PEOPLE.

1. It is reported that Marcus Aurelius Cæsar, brother of Antoninus, being about to engage in battle with the Germans and Sarmatians, was in great trouble on account of his army suffering from thirst. But the soldiers of the so-called Melitene legion, through the faith which has given strength from that time to the present, when they were drawn up before the enemy, kneeled on the ground, as is our custom in prayer, and engaged in supplications to God.

2. This was indeed a strange sight to the enemy, but it is reported that a stranger thing immediately followed. The lightning drove the enemy to flight and destruction, but a shower refreshed the army of those who had called on God, all of whom had been on the point of perishing with thirst.

3. This story is related by non-Christian writers who have been pleased to treat the times referred to, and it has also been recorded by our own people. By those historians who were strangers to the faith, the marvel is mentioned, but it is not acknowledged as an answer to our prayers. But by our own people, as friends of the truth, the occurrence is related in a simple and artless manner.

4. Among these is Apolinarius, who says that from that time the legion through whose prayers the wonder took place received from the emperor a title appropriate to the event, being called in the language of the Romans the Thundering Legion.

5. Tertullian is a trustworthy witness of these things. In the Apology for the Faith, which he addressed to the Roman Senate, and which work we have already mentioned, he confirms the history with greater and stronger proofs.

6. He writes that there are still extant letters of the most intelligent Emperor Marcus in which he testifies that his army, being on the point of perishing with thirst in Germany, was saved by the prayers of the Christians. And he says also that this emperor threatened death to those who brought accusation against us.

7. He adds further: "What kind of laws are those which impious, unjust, and cruel persons use against us alone? which Vespasian, though he had conquered the Jews, did not regard; which Trajan partially annulled, forbidding Christians to be sought after; which neither Adrian, though inquisitive in all matters, nor he who was called Plus sanctioned." But let any one treat these things as he chooses; we must pass on to what followed.

8. Pothinus having died with the other martyrs in Gaul at ninety years of age, Irenæus succeeded him in the episcopate of the church at Lyons. We have learned that, in his youth, he was a hearer of Polycarp.

9. In the third book of his work Against Heresies he has inserted a list of the bishops of Rome, bringing it down as far as Eleutherus (whose times we are now considering), under whom he composed his work. He writes as follows:

Chapter VI.

CATALOGUE OF THE BISHOPS OF ROME.

1. "The blessed apostles having founded and established the church, entrusted the office of the episcopate to Linus. Paul speaks of this Linus in his Epistles to Timothy.

2. Anencletus succeeded him, and after Anencletus, in the third place from the apostles, Clement received the episcopate. He had seen and conversed with the blessed apostles, and their preaching was still sounding in his ears, and their tradition was still before his eyes. Nor was he alone in this, for many who had been taught by the apostles yet survived.

3. In the times of Clement, a serious dissension having arisen among the brethren in Corinth, the church of Rome sent a most suitable letter to the Corinthians, reconciling them in peace, renewing their faith, and proclaiming the doctrine lately received from the apostles."

4. A little farther on he says: "Evarestus succeeded Clement, and Alexander, Evarestus. Then Xystus, the sixth from the apostles, was appointed. After him Telesphorus, who suffered martyrdom gloriously; then Hyginus; then Pius; and after him Anicetus; Sorer succeeded Anicetus; and now, in the twelfth place from the apostles,

5. Eleutherus holds the office of bishop. In the same order and succession the tradition in the Church and the preaching of the truth has descended from the apostles unto us."

Chapter VII.

EVEN DOWN TO THOSE TIMES MIRACLES WERE PERFORMED BY THE FAITHFUL.

1. These things Irenæus, in agreement with the accounts already given by us, records in the work which comprises five books, and to which he gave the title Refutation and Overthrow of the Knowledge Falsely So-called. In the second book of the same treatise he shows that manifestations of divine and miraculous power continued to his time in some of the churches.

2. He says: "But so far do they come short of raising the dead, as the Lord raised them, and the apostles through prayer. And oftentimes in the brotherhood, when, on account of some necessity, our entire Church has besought with fasting and much supplication, the spirit of the dead has returned, and the man has been restored through the prayers of the saints."

3. And again, after other remarks, he says: "If they will say that even the Lord did these things in mere appearance, we will refer them to the prophetic writings, and show from them that all things were beforehand spoken of him in this manner, and were strictly fulfilled; and that he alone is the Son of God. Wherefore his true disciples, receiving grace from him, perform such works in his Name for the benefit of other men, as each has received the gift from him.

4. For some of them drive out demons effectually and truly, so that those who have been cleansed from evil spirits frequently believe and unite with the Church. Others have a foreknowledge of future events, and visions, and prophetic revelations. Still others heal the sick by the laying on of hands, and restore them to health. And, as we have said, even dead persons have been raised, and remained with us many years.

5. But why should we say more? It is not possible to recount the number of gifts which the Church, throughout all the world, has received from God in the name of Jesus Christ, who was crucified under Pontius Pilate, and exercises every day for the benefit of the heathen, never deceiving any nor doing it for money. For as she has received freely from God, freely also does she minister."

6. And in another place the same author writes: "As also we hear that many brethren in the Church possess prophetic gifts, and speak, through the Spirit, with all kinds of tongues, and bring to light the secret things of men for their good, and declare the mysteries of God." So much in regard to the fact that various gifts remained among those who were worthy even until that time.

Chapter VIII.

THE STATEMENTS OF IRENÆUS IN REGARD TO THE DIVINE SCRIPTURES.

1. Since, in the beginning of this work, we promised to give, when needful, the words of the ancient presbyters and writers of the Church, in which they have declared those traditions which came down to them concerning the canonical books, and since Irenæus was one of them, we will now give his words and, first, what he says of the sacred Gospels:

2. "Matthew published his Gospel among the Hebrews in their own language, while Peter and Paul were preaching and founding the church in Rome.

3. After their departure Mark, the disciple and interpreter of Peter, also transmitted to us in writing those things which Peter had preached; and Luke, the attendant of Paul, recorded in a book the Gospel which Paul had declared.

4. Afterwards John, the disciple of the Lord, who also reclined on his bosom, published his Gospel, while staying at Ephesus in Asia."

5. He states these things in the third book of his above-mentioned work. In the fifth book he speaks as follows concerning the Apocalypse of John, and the number of the name of Antichrist: "As these things are so, and this number is found in all the approved and ancient copies, and those who saw John face to face confirm it, and reason teaches us that the number of the name of the beast, according to the mode of calculation among the Greeks, appears in its letters...."

6. And farther on he says concerning the same: "We are not bold enough to speak confidently of the name of Antichrist. For if it were necessary that his name should be declared clearly at the present time, it would have been announced by him who saw the revelation. For it was seen, not long ago, but almost in our generation, toward the end of the reign of Domitian."

7. He states these things concerning the Apocalypse in the work referred to. He also mentions the first Epistle of John, taking many proofs from it, and likewise the first Epistle of Peter. And he not only knows, but also receives, The Shepherd, writing as follows: "Well did the Scripture speak, saying, 'First of all believe that God is one, who has created and completed all things,'" etc.

8. And he uses almost the precise words of the Wisdom of Solomon, saying: "The vision of God produces immortality, but immortality renders us near to God." He men-lions also the memoirs of a certain apostolic presbyter, whose name he passes by in silence, and gives his expositions of the sacred Scriptures.

9. And he refers to Justin the Martyr, and to Ignatius, using

testimonies also from their writings. Moreover, he promises to refute Marcion from his own writings, in a special work.

10. Concerning the translation of the inspired Scriptures by the Seventy, hear the very words which he writes: "God in truth became man, and the Lord himself saved us, giving the sign of the virgin but not as some say, who now venture to translate the Scripture, 'Behold, a young woman shall conceive and bring forth a son,' as Theodotion of Ephesus and Aquila of Pontus, both of them Jewish proselytes, interpreted; following whom, the Ebionites say that he was begotten by Joseph."

11. Shortly after he adds: "For before the Romans had established their empire, while the Macedonians were still holding Asia, Ptolemy, the son of Lagus, being desirous of adorning the library which he had rounded in Alexandria with the meritorious writings of all men, requested the people of Jerusalem to have their Scriptures translated into the Greek language.

12. But, as they were then subject to the Macedonians, they sent to Ptolemy seventy elders, who were the most skilled among them in the Scriptures and in both languages. Thus God accomplished his purpose.

13. But wishing to try them individually, as he feared lest, by taking counsel together, they might conceal the truth of the Scriptures by their interpretation, he separated them from one another, and commanded all of them to write the same translation. He did this for all the books.

14. But when they came together in the presence of Ptolemy, and compared their several translations, God was glorified, and the Scriptures were recognized as truly divine. For all of them had rendered the same things in the same words and with the same names from beginning to end, so that the heathen perceived that the Scriptures had been translated by the inspiration of God.

15. And this was nothing wonderful for God to do, who, in the captivity of the people trader Nebuchadnezzar, when the Scriptures had been destroyed, and the Jews had returned to their own country after seventy years, afterwards, in the time of Artaxerxes, king of the Persians, inspired Ezra the priest, of the tribe of Levi, to relate all the words of the former prophets, and to restore to the people the legislation of Moses." Such are the words of Irenæus.

Chapter IX.

THE BISHOPS UNDER COMMODUS.

1. After Antoninus had been emperor for nineteen years, Commodus received the government. In his first year Julian became bishop of the Alexandrian churches, after Agrippinus had held the office for twelve years.

Chapter X.

PANTÆNUS THE PHILOSOPHER.

1. About that time, Pantænus, a man highly distinguished for his learning, had charge of the school of the faithful in Alexandria. A school of sacred learning, which continues to our day, was established there in ancient times, and as we have been informed, was managed by men of great ability and zeal for divine things. Among these it is reported that Pantænus was at that time especially conspicuous, as he had been educated in the philosophical system of those called Stoics.

2. They say that he displayed such zeal for the divine Word, that he was appointed as a herald of the Gospel of Christ to the nations in the East, and was sent as far as India. For indeed there were still many evangelists of the Word who sought earnestly to use their inspired zeal, after the examples of the apostles, for the increase and building up of the Divine Word.

3. Pantænus was one of these, and is said to have gone to India. It is reported that among persons there who knew of Christ, he found the Gospel according to Matthew, which had anticipated his own arrival. For Bartholomew, one of the apostles, had preached to them, and left with them the writing of Matthew in the Hebrew language, which they had preserved till that time.

4. After many good deeds, Pantænus finally became the head of the school at Alexandria, and expounded the treasures of divine doctrine both orally and in writing.

Chapter XI.

CLEMENT OF ALEXANDRIA.

1. At this time Clement, being trained with him in the divine Scriptures at Alexandria, became well known. He had the same name as the one who anciently was at the head of the Roman church, and who was a disciple of the apostles.

2. In his Hypotyposes he speaks of Pantænus by name as his teacher. It seems to me that he alludes to the same person also in the first book of his Stromata, when, referring to the more conspicuous of the successors of the apostles whom he had met, he says:

3. "This work is not a writing artfully constructed for display; but my notes are stored up for old age, as a remedy against forgetfulness; an image without art, and a rough sketch of those powerful and animated words which it was my privilege to hear, as well as of blessed and truly remarkable men.

4. Of these the one—the Ionian—was in Greece, the other in Magna Græcia; the one of them was from Cœle-Syria, the other from Egypt. There were others in the East, one of them an Assyrian, the other a Hebrew in Palestine? But when I met with the last,—in ability truly he was first—having hunted him out in his concealment in Egypt, I found rest.

5. These men, preserving the true tradition of the blessed doctrine, directly from the holy apostles, Peter and James and John and Paul, the son receiving it from the father (but few were like fathers), have come by God's will even to us to deposit those ancestral and apostolic seeds."

Chapter XII.

THE BISHOPS IN JERUSALEM.

1. At this time Narcissus was the bishop of the church at Jerusalem, and he is celebrated by many to this day. He was the fifteenth in succession from the siege of the Jews under Adrian. We have shown that from that time first the church in Jerusalem was composed of Gentiles, after those of the circumcision, and that Marcus was the first Gentile bishop that presided over them.

2. After him the succession in the episcopate was: first Cassianus; after him Publius; then Maximus; following them Julian; then Gaius; after him Symmachus and another Gaius, and again another Julian; after these Capito and Valens and Dolichianus; and after all of them Narcissus, the thirtieth in regular succession from the apostles.

Chapter XIII.

RHODO AND HIS ACCOUNT OF THE
DISSENSION OF MARCION.

1. At this time Rhodo, a native of Asia, who had been instructed, as he himself states, by Tatian, with whom we have already become acquainted, having written several books, published among the rest one against the heresy of Marcion. He says that this heresy was divided in

his time into various opinions; and while describing those who occasioned the division, he refutes accurately the falsehoods devised by each of them.

2. But hear what he writes: "Therefore also they disagree among themselves, maintaining an inconsistent opinion. For Apelles, one of the herd, priding himself on his manner of life and his age, acknowledges one principle, but says that the prophecies are from an opposing spirit, being led to this view by the responses of a maiden by name Philumene, who was possessed by a demon.

3. But others, among whom are Potitus and Basilicus, hold to two principles, as does the mariner Marcion himself.

4. These following the wolf of Pontus, and, like him, unable to fathom the division of things, became reckless, and without giving any proof asserted two principles. Others, again, drifting into a worse error, consider that there are not only two, but three natures. Of these, Syneros is the leader and chief, as those who defend his teaching say."

5. The same author writes that he engaged in conversation with Apelles. He speaks as follows: "For the old man Apelles, when conversing with us, was refuted in many things which he spoke falsely; whence also he said that it was not at all necessary to examine one's doctrine, but that each one should continue to hold what he believed. For he asserted that those who trusted in the Crucified would be saved, if only they were found doing good works. But as we have said before, his opinion concerning God was the most obscure of all. For he spoke of one principle, as also our doctrine does."

6. Then, after stating fully his own opinion, he adds: "When I said to him, Tell me how you know this or how can you assert that there is one principle, he replied that the prophecies refuted themselves, because they have said nothing true; for they are inconsistent, and false, and self-contradictory. But how there is one principle he said that he did not know, but that he was thus persuaded.

7. As I then adjured him to speak the truth, he swore that he did so when he said that he did not know how there is one unbegotten God, but that he believed it. Thereupon I laughed and reproved him because, though calling himself a teacher, he knew not how to confirm what he taught."

8. In the same work, addressing Callistio, the same writer acknowledges that he had been instructed at Rome by Tatian. And he says that a book of Problems had been prepared by Tatian, in which he promised to explain the obscure and hidden parts of the divine Scriptures. Rhodo himself promises to give in a work of his: own solutions of Tatian's problems. There is also extant a Commentary of his on the Hexæmeron.

9. But this Apelles wrote many things, an impious manner, of the law of Moses, blaspheming the divine words in many of his works,

being, as it seemed, very zealous for their refutation and overthrow. So much concerning these.

Chapter XIV.

THE FALSE PROPHETS OF THE PHRYGIANS.

1. The enemy of God's Church, who is emphatically a hater of good and a lover of evil, and leaves untried no manner of craft against men, was again active in causing strange heresies to spring up against the Church. For some persons, like venomous reptiles, crawled over Asia and Phrygia, boasting that Montanus was the Paraclete, and that the women that followed him, Priscilla and Maximilla, were prophetesses of Montanus.

Chapter XV.

THE SCHISM OF BLASTUS AT ROME.

1. Others, of whom Florinus was chief, flourished at Rome. He fell from the presbyterate of the Church, and Blastus was involved in a similar fall. They also drew away many oft the Church to their opinion, each striving to introduce his own innovations in respect to the truth

Chapter XVI.

THE CIRCUMSTANCES RELATED OF MONTANUS AND HIS FALSE PROPHETS.

1. Against the so-called Phrygian heresy, the power which always contends for the truth raised up a strong and invincible weapon, Apolinarius of Hierapolis, whom we have mentioned before, and with him many other men of ability, by whom abundant material for our history has been left.

2. A certain one of these, in the beginning of his work against them, first intimates that he had contended with them in oral controversies.

3. He commences his work in this manner: "Having for a very long and sufficient time, O beloved Avircius Marcellus, been urged by you to write a treatise against the heresy of those who are called after Miltiades, I have hesitated till the present time, not through lack of ability to refute the falsehood or bear testimony for the truth, but from fear and apprehension that I might seem to some to be making additions to the doctrines or precepts of the Gospel of the New Testament, which it is impossible for one who has chosen to live

according to the Gospel, either to increase or to diminish.

4. But being recently in Ancyra in Galatia, I found the church there greatly agitated by this novelty, not prophecy, as they call it, but rather false prophecy, as will be shown. Therefore, to the best of our ability, with the Lord's help, we disputed in the church many days concerning these and other matters separately brought forward by them, so that the church rejoiced and was strengthened in the truth, and those of the opposite side were for the time confounded, and the adversaries were grieved.

5. The presbyters in the place, our fellow-presbyter Zoticus of Otrous also being present, requested us to leave a record of what had been said against the opposers of the truth. We did not do this, but we promised to write it out as soon as the Lord permitted us, and to send it to them speedily."

6. Having said this with other things, in the beginning of his work, he proceeds to state the cause of the above-mentioned heresy as follows: "Their opposition and their recent heresy which has separated them from the Church arose on the following account.

7. There is said to be a certain village called Ardabau in that part of Mysia, which borders upon Phrygia. There first, they say, when Gratus was proconsul of Asia, a recent convert, Montanus by name, through his unquenchable desire for leadership, gave the adversary opportunity against him. And he became beside himself, and being suddenly in a sort of frenzy and ecstasy, he raved, and began to babble and utter strange things, prophesying in a manner contrary to the constant custom of the Church handed down by tradition from the beginning.

8. Some of those who heard his spurious utterances at that time were indignant, and they rebuked him as one that was possessed, and that was under the control of a demon, and was led by a deceitful spirit, and was distracting the multitude; and they forbade him to talk, remembering the distinction drawn by the Lord and his warning to guard watchfully against the coming of false prophets? But others imagining themselves possessed of the Holy Spirit and of a prophetic gift, were elated and not a little puffed up; and forgetting the distinction of the Lord, they challenged the mad and insidious and seducing spirit, and were cheated and deceived by him. In consequence of this, he could no longer be held in check, so as to keep silence.

9. Thus by artifice, or rather by such a system of wicked craft, the devil, devising destruction for the disobedient, and being unworthily honored by them, secretly excited and inflamed their understandings which had already become estranged from the true faith. And he stirred up besides two women, and filled them with the false spirit, so that they talked wildly and unreasonably and strangely, like the person already mentioned. And the spirit pronounced them blessed as they rejoiced and gloried in him, and puffed them up by the magnitude of his

promises. But sometimes he rebuked them openly in a wise and faithful manner, that he might seem to be a reprover. But those of the Phrygians that were deceived were few in number. "And the arrogant spirit taught them to revile the entire universal Church under heaven, because the spirit of false prophecy received neither honor from it nor entrance into it.

10. For the faithful in Asia met often in many places throughout Asia to consider this matter, and examined the novel utterances and pronounced them profane, and rejected the heresy, and thus these persons were expelled from the Church and debarred from communion."

11. Having related these things at the outset, and continued the refutation of their delusion through his entire work, in the second book he speaks as follows of their end:

12. "Since, therefore, they called us slayers of the prophets because we did not receive their loquacious prophets, who, they say, are those that the Lord promised to send to the people, let them answer as in God's presence: Who is there, O friends, of these who began to talk, from Montanus and the women down, that was persecuted by the Jews, or slain by lawless men? None. Or has any of them been seized and crucified for the Name? Truly not. Or has one of these women ever been scourged in the synagogues of the Jews, or stoned? No; never anywhere.

13. But by another kind of death Montanus and Maximilla are said to have died. For the report is that, incited by the spirit of frenzy, they both hung themselves; not at the same time, but at the time which common report gives for the death of each. And thus they died, and ended their lives like the traitor Judas.

14. So also, as general report says, that remarkable person, the first steward, as it were, of their so-called prophecy, one Theodotus—who, as if at sometime taken up and received into heaven, fell into trances, and entrusted himself to the deceitful spirit—was pitched like a quoit, and died miserably?

15. They say that these things happened in this manner. But as we did not see them, O friend, we do not pretend to know. Perhaps in such a manner, perhaps not, Montanus and Theodotus and the above-mentioned woman died."

16. He says again in the same book that the holy bishops of that time attempted to refute the spirit in Maximilla, but were prevented by others who plainly co-operated with the spirit.

17. He writes as follows: "And let not the spirit, in the same work of Asterius Urbanus, say through Maximilla, 'I am driven away from the sheep like a wolf. I am not a wolf. I am word and spirit and power.' But let him show clearly and prove the power in the spirit. And by the spirit let him compel those to confess him who were then present for

the purpose of proving and reasoning with the talkative spirit, those eminent men and bishops, Zoticus, from the village Comana and Julian, from Apamea, whose mouths the followers of Themiso muzzled, refusing to per-knit the false and seductive spirit to be refuted by them."

18. Again in the same work, after saying other things in refutation of the false prophecies of Maximilla, he indicates the time when he wrote these accounts, and mentions her predictions in which she prophesied wars and anarchy. Their falsehood he censures in the following manner:

19. "And has not this been shown clearly to be false? For it is to-day more than thirteen years since the woman died, and there has been neither a partial nor general war in the world; but rather, through the mercy of God, continued peace even to the Christians." These things are taken from the second book.

20. I will add also short extracts from the third book, in which he speaks thus against their boasts that many of them had suffered, martyrdom: "When therefore they are at a loss, being refuted in all that they say, they try to take refuge in their martyrs, alleging that they have many martyrs, and that this is sure evidence of the, power of the so-called prophetic spirit that is with them. But this, as it appears, is entirely fallacious.

21. For some of the heresies have a great many martyrs; but surely we shall not on that account agree with them or confess that they hold the truth. And first, indeed, those called Marcionites, from the heresy of Marcion, say that they have a multitude of martyrs for Christ; yet they do not confess Christ himself in truth."

22. A little farther on he continues: "When those called to martyrdom from the Church for the truth of the faith have met with any of the so-called martyrs of the Phrygian heresy, they have separated from them, and died without any fellowship with them, because they did not wish to give their assent to the spirit of Montanus and the women. And that this is true and took place in our own time in Apamea on the Mæander, among those who suffered martyrdom with Gaius and Alexander of Eumenia, is well known."

Chapter XVII.

MILTIADES AND HIS WORKS.

1. In this work he mentions a writer, Miltiades, stating that he also wrote a certain book against the above-mentioned heresy. After quoting some of their words, he adds: "Having found these things in a certain work of theirs in opposition to the work of the brother Alcibiades, in which he shows that a prophet ought not to speak in ecstasy, I made an

abridgment."

2. A little further on in the same work he gives a list of those who prophesied under the new covenant, among whom he enumerates a certain Ammia and Quadratus, saying "But the false prophet falls into an ecstasy, in which he is without shame or fear. Beginning with purposed ignorance, he passes on, as has been stated, involuntary madness of soul.

3. They cannot show that one of the old or one of the new prophets was thus carried away in spirit. Neither can they boast of Agabus, or Judas, or Silas, or the daughters of Philip, or Ammia in Philadelphia, or Quadratus, or any others not belonging to them."

4. And again after a little he says: "For if after Quadratus and Ammia in Philadelphia, as they assert, the women with Montanus received the prophetic gift, let them show who among them received it from Montanus and the women. For the apostle thought it necessary that the prophetic gift should continue in all the Church until the final coming. But they cannot show it, though this is the fourteenth year since the death of Maximilla."

5. He writes thus. But the Miltiades to whom he refers has left other monuments of his own zeal for the Divine Scriptures, in the discourses which he composed against the Greeks and against the Jews, answering each of them separately in two books. And in addition he addresses an apology to the earthly rulers, in behalf of the philosophy which he embraced.

Chapter XVIII.

THE MANNER IN WHICH APOLLONIUS REFUTED THE PHRYGIANS, AND THE PERSONS WHOM HE MENTIONS.

1. As the so-called Phrygian heresy was still flourishing in Phrygia in his time, Apollonius also, an ecclesiastical writer, undertook its refutation, and wrote a special work against it, correcting in detail the false prophecies current among them and reproving the life of the founders of the heresy. But hear his own words respecting Montanus:

2. "His actions and his teaching show who this new teacher is. This is he who taught the dissolution of marriage; who made laws for fasting; who named Pepuza and Tymion, small towns in Phrygia, Jerusalem, wishing to gather people to them from all directions; who appointed collectors of money; who contrived the receiving of gifts under the name of offerings; who provided salaries for those who preached his doctrine, that its teaching might prevail through gluttony."

3. He writes thus concerning Montanus; and a little farther on he writes as follows concerning his prophetesses: "We show that these first prophetesses themselves, as soon as they were filled with the

Spirit, abandoned their husbands. How falsely therefore they speak who call Prisca a virgin."

4. Afterwards he says: "Does not all Scripture seem to you to forbid a prophet to receive gifts and money? When therefore I see the prophetess receiving gold and silver and costly garments, how can I avoid reproving her?"

5. And again a little farther on he speaks thus concerning one of their confessors: "So also Themiso, who was clothed with plausible covetousness, could not endure the sign of confession, but threw aside bonds for an abundance of possessions. Yet, though he should have been humble on this account, he dared to boast as a martyr, and in imitation of the apostle, he wrote a certain catholic epistle, to instruct those whose faith was better than his own, contending for words of empty sound, and blaspheming against the Lord and the apostles and the holy Church."

6. And again concerning others of those honored among them as martyrs, he writes as follows: "Not to speak of many, let the prophetess herself tell us of Alexander, who called himself a martyr, with whom she is in the habit of banqueting, and who is worshiped by many. We need not mention his robberies and other daring deeds for which he was punished, but the archives contain them.

7. Which of these forgives the sins of the other? Does the prophet the robberies of the martyr, or the: martyr the covetousness of the prophet? For although the Lord said,' Provide neither gold, nor silver, neither two coats,' these men, in complete opposition, transgress in respect to the possession of the forbidden things. For we will show that those whom they call prophets and martyrs gather their gain not only from rich men, but also from the poor, and orphans, and widows.

8. But if they are confident, let them stand up and discuss these matters, that if convicted they may hereafter cease transgressing. For the fruits of the prophet must be tried; 'for the tree is known by its fruit.'

9. But that those who wish may know concerning Alexander, he was tried by Æmilius Frontinus, proconsul at Ephesus; not on account of the Name, but for the robberies which he had committed, being already an apostate. Afterwards, having falsely declared for the name of the Lord, he was released, having deceived the faithful that were there. And his own parish, from which he came, did not receive him, because he was a robber. Those who wish to learn about him have the public records of Asia. And yet the prophet with whom he spent many years knows nothing about him!

10. Exposing him, through him we expose also the pretense of the prophet. We could show the same thing of many others. But if they are confident, let them endure the test."

11. Again, in another part of his work he speaks as follows of the

prophets of whom they boast: "If they deny that their prophets have received gifts, let them acknowledge this: that if they are convicted of receiving them, they are not prophets. And we will bring a multitude of proofs of this. But it is necessary that all the fruits of a prophet should be examined. Tell me, does a prophet dye his hair? Does a prophet stain his eyelids? Does a prophet delight in adornment? Does a prophet play with tables and dice? Does a prophet lend on usury? Let them confess whether these things are lawful or not; but I will show that they have been done by them."

12. This same Apollonius states in the same work that, at the time of his writing, it was the fortieth year since Montanus had begun his pretended prophecy.

13. And he says also that Zoticus, who was mentioned by the former writer, when Maximilla was pretending to prophesy in Pepuza, resisted her and endeavored to refute the spirit that was working in her; but was prevented by those who agreed with her. He mentions also a certain Thraseas among the martyrs of that time. He speaks, moreover, of a tradition that the Saviour commanded his apostles not to depart from Jerusalem for twelve years. He uses testimonies also from the Revelation of John, and he relates that a dead man had, through the Divine power, been raised by John himself in Ephesus. He also adds other things by which he fully and abundantly exposes the error of the heresy of which we have been speaking. These are the matters recorded by Apollonius.

Chapter XIX.

SERAPION ON THE HERESY OF THE PHRYGIANS.

1. Serapion, who, as report says, succeeded Maximinus at that time as bishop of the church of Antioch, mentions the works of Apolinarius against the above-mentioned heresy. And he alludes to him in a private letter to Caricus and Pontius, in which he himself exposes the same heresy, and adds the following words:

2. "That you may see that the doings of this lying band of the new prophecy, so called, are an abomination to all the brotherhood throughout the world, I have sent you writings of the most blessed Claudius Apolinarius, bishop of Hierapolis in Asia."

3. In the same letter of Serapion the signatures of several bishops are found, one of whom subscribes himself as follows: "I, Aurelius Cyrenius, a witness, pray for your health." And another in this manner: "Ælius Publius Julius, bishop of Debeltum, a colony of Thrace. As God liveth in the heavens, the blessed Sotas in Anchialus desired to cast the demon out of Priscilla, but the hypocrites did not permit him."

4. And the autograph signatures of many other bishops who agreed

with them are contained in the same letter. So much for these persons.

Chapter XX.

THE WRITINGS OF IRENÆUS AGAINST THE SCHISMATICS AT ROME.

1. Irenæus wrote several letters against those who were disturbing the sound ordinance of the Church at Rome. One of them was to Blastus On Schism; another to Florinus On Monarchy, or That God is not the Author of Evil. For Florinus seemed to be defending this opinion. And because he was being drawn away by the error of Valentinus, Irenæus wrote his work On the Ogdoad, in which he shows that he himself had been acquainted with the first successors of the apostles.

2. At the close of the treatise we have found a most beautiful note which we are constrained to insert in this work. It runs as follows: "I adjure thee who mayest copy this book, by our Lord Jesus Christ, and by his glorious advent when he comes to judge the living and the dead, to compare what thou shalt write, and correct it carefully by this manuscript, and also to write this adjuration, and place it in the copy."

3. These things may be profitably read in his work, and related by us, that we may have those ancient and truly holy men as the best example of painstaking carefulness.

4. In the letter to Florinus, of which we have spoken, Irenæus mentions again his intimacy with Polycarp, saying: "These doctrines, O Florinus, to speak mildly, are not of sound judgment. These doctrines disagree with the Church, and drive into the greatest impiety those who accept them. These doctrines, not even the heretics outside of the Church, have ever dared to publish. These doctrines, the presbyters who were before us, and who were companions of the apostles, did not deliver to thee.

5. For when I was a boy, I saw thee in lower Asia with Polycarp, moving in splendor in the royal court, and endeavoring to gain his approbation.

6. I remember the events of that time more clearly than those of recent years. For what boys learn, growing with their mind, becomes joined with it; so that I am able to describe the very place in which the blessed Polycarp sat as he discoursed, and his goings out and his comings in, and the manner of his life, and his physical appearance, and his discourses to the people, and the accounts which he gave of his intercourse with John and with the others who had seen the Lord. And as he remembered their words, and what he heard from them concerning the Lord, and concerning his miracles and his teaching, having received them from eyewitnesses of the 'Word of life,' Polycarp

related all things in harmony with the Scriptures.

7. These things being told me by the mercy of God, I listened to them attentively, noting them down, not on paper, but in my heart. And continually, through God's grace, I recall them faithfully. And I am able to bear witness before God that if that blessed and apostolic presbyter had heard any such thing, he would have cried out, and stopped his ears, and as was his custom, would have exclaimed, O good God, unto what times hast thou spared me that I should endure these things? And he would have fled from the place where, sitting or standing, he had heard such words.

8. And this can be shown plainly from the letters which he sent, either to the neighboring churches for their confirmation, or to some of the brethren, admonishing and exhorting them." Thus far Irenæus.

Chapter XXI.

HOW APOLLONIUS SUFFERED MARTYRDOM AT ROME.

1. About the same time, in the reign of Commodus, our condition became more favorable, and through the grace of God the churches throughout the entire world enjoyed peace, and the word of salvation was leading every soul, from every race of man to the devout worship of the God of the universe. So that now at Rome many who were highly distinguished for wealth and family turned with all their household and relatives unto their salvation.

2. But the demon who hates what is good, being malignant in his nature, could not endure this, but prepared himself again for conflict, contriving many devices against us. And he brought to the judgment seat Apollonius, of the city of Rome, a man renowned among the faithful for learning and philosophy, having stirred up one of his servants, who was well fitted for such a purpose, to accuse him.

3. But this wretched man made the charge unseasonably, because by a royal decree it was unlawful that informers of such things should live. And his legs were broken immediately, Perennius the judge having pronounced this sentence upon him.

4. But the martyr, highly beloved of God, being earnestly entreated and requested by the judge to give an account of himself before the Senate, made in the presence of all an eloquent defense of the faith for which he was witnessing. And as if by decree of the Senate he was put to death by decapitation; an ancient law requiring that those who were brought to the judgment seat and refused to recant should not be liberated.

5. Whoever desires to know his arguments before the judge and his answers to the questions of Perennius, and his entire defense before the Senate will find them in the records of the ancient martyrdoms which

we have collected.

Chapter XXII.

THE BISHOPS THAT WERE WELL KNOWN AT THIS TIME.

1. In the tenth year of the reign of Commodus, Victor succeeded Eleutherus, the latter having held the episcopate for thirteen years. In the same year, after Julian a had completed his tenth year, Demetrius received the charge of the parishes at Alexandria. At this time the above-mentioned Serapion, the eighth from the apostles, was still well known as bishop of the church at Antioch. Theophilus presided at Cæsarea in Palestine; and Narcissus, whom we have mentioned before, still had charge of the church at Jerusalem. Bacchylus at the same time was bishop of Corinth in Greece, and Polycrates of the parish of Ephesus. And besides these a multitude of others, as is likely, were then prominent. But we have given the names of those alone, the soundness of whose faith has come down to us in writing.

Chapter XXIII.

THE QUESTION THEN AGITATED CONCERNING THE PASSOVER.

1. A Question of no small importance arose at that time. For the parishes of all Asia, as from an older tradition, held that the fourteenth day of the moon, on which day the Jews were commanded to sacrifice the lamb, should be observed as the feast of the Saviour's passover. It was therefore necessary to end their fast on that day, whatever day of the week it should happen to be. But it was not the custom of the churches in the rest of the world to end it at this time, as they observed the practice which, from apostolic tradition, has prevailed to the present time, of terminating the fast on no other day than on that of the resurrection of our Saviour.

2. Synods and assemblies of bishops were held on this account, and all, with one consent, through mutual correspondence drew up an ecclesiastical decree, that the mystery of the resurrection of the Lord should be celebrated on no other but the Lord's day, and that we should observe the close of the paschal fast on this day only. There is still extant a writing of those who were then assembled in Palestine, over whom Theophilus, bishop of Cæsarea, and Narcissus, bishop of Jerusalem, presided.

3. And there is also another writing extant of those who were assembled at Rome to consider the same question, which bears the name of Bishop Victor; also of the bishops in Pontus over whom

Palmas, as the oldest, presided; and of the parishes in Gaul of which Irenæus was bishop, and of those in Osrhoene and the cities there; and a personal letter of Bacchylus, bishop of the church at Corinth, and of a great many others, who uttered the same opinion and judgment, and cast the same vote. And that which has been given above was their unanimous decision.

Chapter XXIV.

THE DISAGREEMENT IN ASIA.

1. But the bishops of Asia, led by Polycrates, decided to hold to the old custom handed down to them. He himself, in a letter which he addressed to Victor and the church of Rome, set forth in the following words the tradition which had come down to him:

2. "We observe the exact day; neither adding, nor taking away. For in Asia also great lights have fallen asleep, which shall rise again on the day of the Lord's coming, when he shall come with glory from heaven, and shall seek out all the saints.

3. Among these are Philip, one of the twelve apostles, who fell asleep in Hierapolis; and his two aged virgin daughters, and another daughter, who lived in the Holy Spirit and now rests at Ephesus; and, moreover, John, who was both a witness and a teacher, who reclined upon the bosom of the Lord, and, being a priest, wore the sacerdotal plate. He fell asleep at Ephesus.

4. And Polycarp in Smyrna, who was a bishop and martyr; and Thraseas, bishop and martyr from Eumenia, who fell asleep in Smyrna.

5. Why need I mention the bishop and martyr Sagaris who fell asleep in Laodicea, or the blessed Papirius, or Melito, the Eunuch who lived altogether in the Holy Spirit, and who lies in Sardis, awaiting the episcopate from heaven, when he shall rise from the dead?

6. All these observed the fourteenth day of the passover according to the Gospel, deviating in no respect, but following the rule of faith. And I also, Polycrates, the least of you all, do according to the tradition of my relatives, some of whom I have closely followed. For seven of my relatives were bishops; and I am the eighth. And my relatives always observed the day when the people put away the leaven.

7. I, therefore, brethren, who have lived sixty-five years in the Lord, and have met with the brethren throughout the world, and have gone through every Holy Scripture, am not affrighted by terrifying words. For those greater than I have said 'We ought to obey God rather than man.'"

8. He then writes of all the bishops who were present with him and thought as he did. His words are as follows: "I could mention the bishops who were present, whom I summoned at your desire; whose

names, should I write them, would constitute a great multitude. And they, beholding my littleness, gave their consent to the letter, knowing that I did not bear my gray hairs in vain, but had always governed my life by the Lord Jesus."

9. Thereupon Victor, who presided over the church at Rome, immediately attempted to cut off from the common unity the parishes of all Asia, with the churches that agreed with them, as heterodox; and he wrote letters and declared all the brethren there wholly excommunicate.

10. But this did not please all the bishops. And they besought him to consider the things of peace, and of neighborly unity and love. Words of theirs are extant, sharply rebuking Victor.

11. Among them was Irenæus, who, sending letters in the name of the brethren in Gaul over whom he presided, maintained that the mystery of the resurrection of the Lord should be observed only on the Lord's day. He fittingly admonishes Victor that he should not cut off whole churches of God which observed the tradition of an ancient custom and after many other words he proceeds as follows:

12. "For the controversy is not only concerning the day, but also concerning the very manner of the fast. For some think that they should fast one day, others two, yet others more; some, moreover, count their day as consisting of forty hours day and night.

13. And this variety in its observance has not originated in our time; but long before in that of our ancestors. It is likely that they did not hold to strict accuracy, and thus formed a custom for their posterity according to their own simplicity and peculiar mode. Yet all of these lived none the less in peace, and we also live in peace with one another; and the disagreement in regard to the fast confirms the agreement in the faith."

14. He adds to this the following account, which I may properly insert: "Among these were the presbyters before Soter, who presided over the church which thou now rulest. We mean Anicetus, and Pius, and Hyginus, and Telesphorus, and Xystus. They neither observed it themselves, nor did they permit those after them to do so. And yet though not observing it, they were none the less at peace with those who came to them from the parishes in which it was observed; although this observance was more opposed to those who did not observe it.

15. But none were ever cast out on account of this form; but the presbyters before thee who did not observe it, sent the eucharist to those of other parishes who observed it.

16. And when the blessed Polycarp was at Rome in the time of Anicetus, and they disagreed a little about certain other things, they immediately made peace with one another, not caring to quarrel over this matter. For neither could Anicetus persuade Polycarp not to observe what he had always observed with John the disciple of our

Lord, and the other apostles with whom he had associated; neither could Polycarp persuade Anicetus to observe it as he said that he ought to follow the customs of the presbyters that had preceded him.

17. But though matters were in this shape, they communed together, and Anicetus conceded the administration of the eucharist in the church to Polycarp, manifestly as a mark of respect. And they parted from each other in peace, both those who observed, and those who did not, maintaining the peace of the whole church."

18. Thus Irenæus, who truly was well named, became a peacemaker in this matter, exhorting and negotiating in this way in behalf of the peace of the churches. And he conferred by letter about this mooted question, not only with Victor, but also with most of the other rulers of the churches.

Chapter XXV.

HOW ALL CAME TO AN AGREEMENT RESPECTING THE PASSOVER.

1. Those in Palestine whom we have recently mentioned, Narcissus and Theophilus, and with them Cassius, bishop of the church of Tyre, and Clarus of the church of Ptolemais, and those who met with them, having stated many things respecting the tradition concerning the passover which had come to them in succession from the apostles, at the close of their writing add these words:

2. "Endeavor to send copies of our letter to every church, that we may not furnish occasion to those who easily deceive their souls. We show you indeed that also in Alexandria they keep it on the same day that we do. For letters are carried from us to them and from them to us, so that in the same manner and at the same time we keep the sacred day."

Chapter XXVI.

THE ELEGANT WORKS OF IRENÆUS WHICH HAVE COME DOWN TO US.

1. Besides the works and letters of Irenæus which we have mentioned, a certain book of his On Knowledge, written against the Greeks, very concise and remarkably forcible, is extant; and another, which he dedicated to a brother Martian, In Demonstration of the Apostolic Preaching; and a volume containing various Dissertations, in which he mentions the Epistle to the Hebrews and the so-called Wisdom of Solomon, making quotations from them. These are the works of Irenæus which have come to our knowledge. Commodus

having ended his reign after thirteen years, Severus became emperor in less than six months after his death, Pertinax having reigned during the intervening time.

Chapter XXVII.

THE WORKS OF OTHERS THAT FLOURISHED AT THAT TIME.

1. Numerous memorials of the faithful zeal of the ancient ecclesiastical men of that time are still preserved by many. Of these we would note particularly the writings of Heraclitus On the Apostle, and those of Maximus on the question so much discussed among heretics, the Origin of Evil, and on the Creation of Matter. Also those of Candidus on the Hexæmeron, and of Apion on the same subject; likewise of Sextus on the Resurrection, and another treatise of Arabianus, and writings of a multitude of others, in regard to whom, because we have no data, it is impossible to state in our work when they lived, or to give any account of their history. And works of many others have come down to us whose names we are unable to give, orthodox and ecclesiastical, as their interpretations of the Divine Scriptures show, but unknown to us, because their names are not stated in their writings.

Chapter XXVIII.

THOSE WHO FIRST ADVANCED THE HERESY OF ARTEMON; THEIR MANNER OF LIFE, AND HOW THEY DARED TO CORRUPT THE SACRED SCRIPTURES.

1. In a laborious work by one of these writers against the heresy of Artemon, which Paul of Samosata attempted to revive again in our day, there is an account appropriate to the history which we are now examining.

2. For he criticises, as a late innovation, the above-mentioned heresy which teaches that the Saviour was a mere man, because they were attempting to magnify it as ancient? Having given in his work many other arguments in refutation of their blasphemous falsehood, he adds the following words:

3. "For they say that all the early teachers and the apostles received and taught what they now declare, and that the truth of the Gospel was preserved until the times of Victor, who was the thirteenth bishop of Rome from Peter, but that from his successor, Zephyrinus, the truth had been corrupted.

4. And what they say might be plausible, if first of all the Divine Scriptures did not contradict them. And there are writings of certain

brethren older than the times of Victor, which they wrote in behalf of the truth against the heathen, and against the heresies which existed in their day. I refer to Justin and Miltiades and Tatian and Clement and many others, in all of whose works Christ is spoken of as God.

5. For who does not know the works of Irenæus and of Melito and of others which teach that Christ is God and man? And how many psalms and hymns, written by the faithful brethren from the beginning, celebrate Christ the Word of God, speaking of him as Divine.

6. How then since the opinion held by the Church has been preached for so many years, can its preaching have been delayed as they affirm, until the times of Victor? And how is it that they are not ashamed to speak thus falsely of Victor, knowing well that he cut off from communion Theodotus, the cobbler, the leader and father of this God-denying apostasy, and the first to declare that Christ is mere man? For if Victor agreed with their opinions, as their slander affirms, how came he to cast out Theodotus, the inventor of this heresy?"

7. So much in regard to Victor. His bishopric lasted ten years, and Zephyrinus was appointed his successor about the ninth year of the reign of Severus. The author of the above-mentioned book, concerning the founder of this heresy, narrates another event which occurred in the time of Zephyrinus, using these words:

8. "I will remind many of the brethren of a fact which took place in our time, which, had it happened in Sodom, might, I think, have proved a warning to them. There was a certain confessor, Natalius, not long ago, but in our own day.

9. This man was deceived at one time by Asclepiodotus and another Theodotus, a money-changer. Both of them were disciples of Theodotus, the cobbler, who, as I have said, was the first person excommunicated by Victor, bishop at that time, on account of this sentiment, or rather senselessness.

10. Natalius was persuaded by them to allow himself to be chosen bishop of this heresy with a salary, to be paid by them, of one hundred and fifty denarii a month.

11. When he had thus connected himself with them, he was warned oftentimes by the Lord through visions. For the compassionate God and our Lord Jesus Christ was not willing that a witness of his own sufferings, being cast out of the Church, should perish.

12. But as he paid little regard to the visions, because he was ensnared by the first position among them and by that shameful covetousness which destroys a great many, he was scourged by holy angels, and punished severely through the entire night. Thereupon having risen in the morning, he put on sackcloth and covered himself with ashes, and with great haste and tears he fell down before Zephyrinus, the bishop, rolling at the feet not only of the clergy, but also of the laity; and he moved with his tears the compassionate Church

of the merciful Christ. And though he used much supplication, and showed the welts of the stripes which he had received, yet scarcely was he taken back into communion."

13. We will add from the same writer some other extracts concerning them, which run as follows: "They have treated the Divine Scriptures recklessly and without fear. They have set aside the rule of ancient faith; and Christ they have not known. They do not endeavor to learn what the Divine Scriptures declare, but strive laboriously after any form of syllogism which may be devised to sustain their impiety. And if any one brings before them a passage of Divine Scripture, they see whether a conjunctive or disjunctive form of syllogism can be made from it.

14. And as being of the earth and speaking of the earth, and as ignorant of him who cometh from above, they forsake the holy writings of God to devote themselves to geometry. Euclid is laboriously measured by some of them; and Aristotle and Theophrastus are admired; and Galen, perhaps, by some is even worshiped.

15. But that those who use the arts of unbelievers for their heretical opinions and adulterate the simple faith of the Divine Scriptures by the craft of the godless, are far from the faith, what need is there to say? Therefore they have laid their hands boldly upon the Divine Scriptures, alleging that they have corrected them.

16. That I am not speaking falsely of them in this matter, whoever wishes may learn. For if any one will collect their respective copies, and compare them one with another, he will find that they differ greatly.

17. Those of Asclepiades, for example, do not agree with those of Theodotus. And many of these can be obtained, because their disciples have assiduously written the corrections, as they call them, that is the corruptions, of each of them. Again, those of Hermophilus do not agree with these, and those of Apollonides are not consistent with themselves. For you can compare those prepared by them at an earlier date with those which they corrupted later, and you will find them widely different.

18. But how daring this offense is, it is not likely that they themselves are ignorant. For either they do not believe that the Divine Scriptures were spoken by the Holy Spirit, and thus are unbelievers, or else they think themselves wiser than the Holy Spirit, and in that case what else are they than demoniacs? For they cannot deny the commission of the crime, since the copies have been written by their own hands. For they did not receive such Scriptures from their instructors, nor can they produce any copies from which they were transcribed.

19. But some of them have not thought it worth while to corrupt them, but simply deny the law and the prophets, and thus through their

lawless and impious teaching under pretense of grace, have sunk to the lowest depths of perdition." Let this suffice for these things.

Book VI.

Chapter I.

THE PERSECUTION UNDER SEVERUS.

1. When Severus began to persecute the churches, glorious testimonies were given everywhere by the athletes of religion. This was especially the case in Alexandria, to which city, as to a most prominent theater, athletes of God were brought from Egypt and all Thebais according to their merit, and won crowns from God through their great patience under many tortures and every mode of death. Among these was Leonides, who was called the father of Origen, and who was beheaded while his son was still young. How remarkable the predilection of this son was for the Divine Word, in consequence of his father's instruction, it will not be amiss to state briefly, as his fame has been very greatly celebrated by many.

Chapter II.

THE TRAINING OF ORIGEN FROM CHILDHOOD.

1. Many things might be said in attempting to describe the life of the man while in school; but this subject alone would require a separate treatise. Nevertheless, for the present, abridging most things, we shall state a few facts concerning him as briefly as possible, gathering them from certain letters, and from the statement of persons still living who were acquainted with him.

2. What they report of Origen seems to me worthy of mention, even, so to speak, from his swathing-bands. It was the tenth year of the reign of Severus, while Lætus was governor of Alexandria and the rest of Egypt, and Demetrius had lately received the episcopate of the parishes there, as successor of Julian.

3. As the flame of persecution had been kindled greatly, and multitudes had gained the crown of martyrdom, such desire for martyrdom seized the soul of Origen, although yet a boy, that he went close to danger, springing forward and rushing to the conflict in his eagerness.

4. And truly the termination of his life had been very near had not the divine and heavenly Providence, for the benefit of many, prevented his desire through the agency of his mother.

5. For, at first, entreating him, she begged him to have compassion

on her motherly feelings toward him; but finding, that when he had learned that his father had been seized and imprisoned, he was set the more resolutely, and completely carried away with his zeal for martyrdom, she hid all his clothing, and thus compelled him to remain at home.

6. But, as there was nothing else that he could do, and his zeal beyond his age would not suffer him to be quiet, he sent to his father an encouraging letter on martyrdom, in which he exhorted him, saying, "Take heed not to change your mind on our account." This may be recorded as the first evidence of Origen's youthful wisdom and of his genuine love for piety.

7. For even then he had stored up no small resources in the words of the faith, having been trained in the Divine Scriptures from childhood. And he had not studied them with indifference, for his father, besides giving him the usual liberal education, had made them a matter of no secondary importance.

8. First of all, before inducting him into the Greek sciences, he drilled him in sacred studies, requiring him to learn and recite every day.

9. Nor was this irksome to the boy, but he was eager and diligent in these studies. And he was not satisfied with learning what was simple and obvious in the sacred words, but sought for something more, and even at that age busied himself with deeper speculations. So that he puzzled his father with inquiries for the true meaning of the inspired Scriptures.

10. And his father rebuked him seemingly to his face, telling him not to search beyond his age, or further than the manifest meaning. But by himself he rejoiced greatly and thanked God, the author of all good, that he had deemed him worthy to be the father of such a child.

11. And they say that often, standing by the boy when asleep, he uncovered his breast as if the Divine Spirit were enshrined within it, and kisses it reverently; considering himself blessed in his goodly offspring. These and other things like them are related to Origen when a boy.

12. But when his father ended his life in martyrdom, he was left with his mother and six younger brothers when he was not quite seventeen years old.

13. And the poverty of his father being confiscated to the royal treasury, he and his family were in want of the necessaries of life. But he was deemed worthy of Divine care. And he found welcome and rest with a woman of great wealth, and distinguished in her manner of life and in other respects. She was treating with great honor a famous heretic then in Alexandria; who, however, was born in Antioch. He was with her as an adopted son, and she treated him with the greatest kindness.

14. But although Origen was under the necessity of associating with him, he nevertheless gave from this time on strong evidences of his orthodoxy in the faith. For when on account of the apparent skill in argument of Paul—for this was the man's name—a great multitude came to him, not only of heretics but also of our people, Origen could never be induced to join with him in prayer; for he held, although a boy, the rule of the Church, and abominated, as he somewhere expresses it, heretical teachings. Having been instructed in the sciences of the Greeks by his father, he devoted him after his death more assiduously and exclusively to the study of literature, so that he obtained considerable preparation in philology ad was able not long after the death of his father, by devoting himself to that subject, to earn a compensation amply sufficient for his needs at his age.

Chapter III.

WHILE STILL VERY YOUNG, HE TAUGHT DILIGENTLY THE WORD OF CHRIST.

1. But while he was lecturing in the school, as he tells us himself, and there was no one at Alexandria to give instruction in the faith, as all were driven away by the threat of persecution, some of the heathen came to him to hear the word of God.

2. The first of them, he says, was Plutarch, who after living well, was honored with divine martyrdom. The second was Heraclas, a brother of Plutarch; who after he too had given with him abundant evidence of a philosophic ad ascetic life, was esteemed worthy to succeed Demetrius in the bishopric of Alexandria.

3. He was in his eighteenth year when he took charge of the catechetical school. He was prominent also at this time, during the persecution under Aquila, the governor of Alexandria, when his name became celebrated among the leaders in the faith, through the kindness and goodwill which he manifested toward all the holy martyrs, whether known to him or strangers.

4. For not only was he with them while in bonds, and until their final condemnation, but when the holy martyrs were led to death, he was very bold and went with them into danger. So that as he acted bravely, and with great boldness saluted the martyrs with a kiss, oftentimes the heathen multitude round about them became infuriated, and were on the point of rushing upon him.

5. But through the helping hand of God, he escaped absolutely and marvelously. And this same divine and heavenly power, again and again, it is impossible to say how often, on account of his great zeal and boldness for the words of Christ, guarded him when thus endangered. So great was the enmity of the unbelievers toward him, on account of

the multitude that were instructed by him in the sacred faith, that they placed bands of soldiers around the house where he abode.

6. Thus day by day the persecution burned against him, so that the whole city could no longer contain him; but he removed from house to house and was driven in every direction because of the multitude who attended upon the divine instruction which he gave. For his life also exhibited right and admirable conduct according to the practice of genuine philosophy.

7. For they say that his manner of life was as his doctrine, and his doctrine as his life. Therefore, by the divine Power working with him he aroused a great many to his own zeal.

8. But when he saw yet more coming to him for instruction, and the catechetical school had been entrusted to him alone by Demetrius, who presided over the church, he considered the teaching of grammatical science inconsistent with training in divine subjects, and forthwith he gave up his grammatical school as unprofitable and a hindrance to sacred learning.

9. Then, with becoming consideration, that he might not need aid from others, he disposed of whatever valuable books of ancient literature he possessed, being satisfied with receiving from the purchaser four oboli a day. For many years he lived philosophically in this manner, putting away all the incentives of youthful desires. Through the entire day he endured no small amount of discipline; and for the greater part of the night he gave himself to the study of the Divine Scriptures. He restrained himself as much as possible by a most philosophic life; sometimes by the discipline of fasting, again by limited time for sleep. And in his zeal he never lay upon a bed, but upon the ground.

10. Most of all, he thought that the words of the Saviour in the Gospel should be observed, in which he exhorts not to have two coats nor to use shoes, nor to occupy oneself with cares for the future.

11. With a zeal beyond his age he continued in cold and nakedness; and, going to the very extreme of poverty, he greatly astonished those about him. And indeed he grieved may of his friends who desired to share their possessions with him, on account of the wearisome toil which they saw him enduring in the teaching of divine things.

12. But he did not relax his perseverance. He is said to have walked for a number of years never wearing a shoe, and, for a great many years, to have abstained from the use of wine, and of all other things beyond his necessary food; so that he was in danger of breaking down and destroying his constitution.

13. By giving such evidences of a philosophic life to those who saw him,, he aroused may of his pupils to similar zeal; so that prominent men even of the unbelieving heathen and men that followed

learning and philosophy were led to his instruction. Some of them having received from hi into the depth of their souls faith in the Divine Word, became prominent in the persecution then prevailing; and some of them were seized and suffered martyrdom.

Chapter IV.

THE PUPILS OF ORIGEN THAT BECAME MARTYRS.

1. The first of these was Plutarch, who was mentioned just above. As he was led to death the man of whom we are speaking being with him at the end of hiss life, came near being slain by his fellow-citizens, as if he were the cause of his death. But the providence of God preserved him at this time also.

2. After Plutarch, the second martyr among the pupils of Origen was Serenus, who gave through fire a proof of the faith which he had received.

3. The third martyr from the same school was Heraclides, and after him the fourth was Hero. The former of these was as yet a catechumen, and the latter had but recently been baptized. Both of them were beheaded. After them, the fifth from the same school proclaimed as an athlete of piety was another Serenus, who, it is reported, was beheaded, after a long endurance of tortures. And of women, Herais died while yet a catechumen, receiving baptism by fire, as Origen himself somewhere says.

Chapter V.

POTAMIÆNA.

1. Basilides may be counted the seventh of these. He led to martyrdom the celebrated Potamiæna, who is still famous among the people of the country for the many things which she endured for the preservation of her chastity and virginity. For she was blooming in the perfection of her mind and her physical graces. Having suffered much for the faith of Christ, finally after tortures dreadful and terrible to speak of, she with her mother, Marcella, was put to death by fire.

2. They say that the judge, Aquila by name, having inflicted severe tortures upon her entire body, at last threatened to hand her over to the gladiators for bodily abuse. After a little consideration, being asked for her decision, she made a reply which was regarded as impious.

3. Thereupon she received sentence immediately, and Basilides, one of the officers of the army, led her to death. But as the people attempted to annoy and insult her with abusive words, he drove back her insulters, showing her much pity and kindness. And perceiving the

man's sympathy for her, she exhorted him to be of good courage, for she would supplicate her Lord for him after her departure, and he would soon received a reward for the kindness he had shown her.

4. Having said this, she nobly sustained the issue, burning pitch being poured little by little, over various parts of her body, from the sole of her feet to the crown of her head. Such was the conflict endured by this famous maiden.

5. Not long after this Basilides, being asked by his fellow-soldiers to swear for a certain reason, declared that it was not lawful for him to swear at all, for he was a Christian, and he confessed this openly. At first they thought that he was jesting, but when he continued to affirm it, he was led to the judge, and, acknowledging his conviction before him, he was imprisoned.

6. But the brethren in God coming to him and inquiring the reason of this sudden and remarkable resolution, he is reported to have said that Potamiæna, for three days after her martyrdom, stood beside him by night and placed a crown on his head and said that she had besought the Lord for him and had obtained what she asked, and that soon she would take him with her. Thereupon the brethren gave him the seal of the Lord; and on the next day, after giving glorious testimony for the Lord, he was beheaded.

7. And many others in Alexandria are recorded to have accepted speedily the word of Christ in those times. For Potamiæna appeared to them in their dreams and exhorted them. But let this suffice in regard to this matter.

Chapter VI.

CLEMENT OF ALEXANDRIA.

1. Clement having succeeded Pantænus, had charge at that time of the catechetical instruction in Alexandria, so that Origen also, while still a boy, was one of his pupils. In the first book of the work called Stromata, which Clement wrote, he gives a chronological table, bringing events down to the death of Commodus. So it is evident that that work was written during the reign of Severus, whose times we are now recording.

Chapter VII.

THE WRITER, JUDAS.

1. At this time another writer, Judas, discoursing about the seventy weeks in Daniel, brings down the chronology to the tenth year of the reign of Severus. He thought that the coming of Antichrist, which was

much talked about, was then near. So greatly did the agitation caused by the persecution of our people at this time disturb the minds of many.

Chapter VIII.

ORIGEN'S DARING DEED.

1. At this time while Origen was conducting catechetical instruction at Alexandria, a deed was done by him which evidenced an immature and youthful mind, but at the same time gave the highest proof of faith and continence.

2. For he took the words, "There are eunuchs who have made themselves eunuchs for the kingdom of heaven's sake," in too literal ad extreme a sense. And in order to fulfill the Saviour's word, and at the same time to take away from the unbelievers all opportunity for scandal—for, although young, he met for the study of divine things with women as well as men—he carried out in action the word of the Saviour. He thought that this would not be known by many of his acquaintances. But it was impossible for him, though desiring to do so, to keep such an action secret.

3. When Demetrius, who presided over that parish, at last learned of this, he admired greatly the daring nature of the act, and as he perceived his zeal and the genuineness of his faith, he immediately exhorted him to courage, and urged him the more to continue his work of catechetical instruction.

4. Such was he at that time. But soon afterward, seeing that he was prospering, and becoming great and distinguished among all men, the same Demetrius, overcome by human weakness, wrote of his deed as most foolish to the bishops throughout the world. But the bishops of Cesarea and Jerusalem, who were especially notable and distinguished among the bishops of Palestine, considering Origen worthy in the highest degree of the honor, ordained him a presbyter.

5. Thereupon his fame increased greatly, and his name became renowned everywhere, and he obtained no small reputation for virtue and wisdom. But Demetrius, having nothing else that he could say against him, save this deed of his boyhood, accused him bitterly, and dared to include with him in these accusations those who had raised him to the presbyterate.

6. These things, however, took place a little later. But at this time Origen continued fearlessly the instruction in divine things at Alexandria by day and night to all who came to him; devoting his entire leisure without cessation to divine studies and to his pupils.

7. Severus, having held the government for eighteen years, was succeeded by his son, Antoninus. Among those who had endured courageously the persecution of that time, and had been preserved by

the Providence of God through the conflicts of confession, was Alexander, of whom we have spoken already as bishop of the church in Jerusalem. On account of his pre-eminence in the confession of Christ he was thought worthy of that bishopric, while Narcissus, his predecessor, was still living.

Chapter IX.

THE MIRACLES OF NARCISSUS.

1. The citizens of that parish mention many other miracles of Narcissus, on the tradition of the brethren who succeeded him; among which they relate the following wonder as performed by him.

2. They say that the oil once failed while the deacons were watching through the night at the great paschal vigil. Thereupon the whole multitude being dismayed, Narcissus directed those who attended to the lights, to draw water and bring it to him.

3. This being immediately done he prayed over the water, and with firm faith in the Lord, commanded them to pour it into the lamps. And when they had done so, contrary to all expectation by a wonderful and divine power, the nature of the water was changed into that of oil. A small portion of it has been preserved even to our day by many of the brethren there as a memento of the wonder.

4. They tell many other things worthy to be noted of the life of this man, among which is this. Certain base men being unable to endure the strength and firmness of his life, and fearing punishment for the many evil deeds of which they were conscious, sought by plotting to anticipate him, and circulated a terrible slander against him.

5. And to persuade those who heard of it, they confirmed their accusations with oaths: one invoked upon himself destruction by fire; another the wasting of his body by a foul disease; the third the loss of his eyes. But though they swore in this manner, they could not affect the mind of the believers; because the continence and virtuous life of Narcissus were well known to all.

6. But he could not in any wise endure the wickedness of these men; and as he had followed a philosophic life for a long time, he fled from the whole body of the Church, and hid himself in desert and secret places, and remained there many years.

7. But the great eye of judgment was not unmoved by these things, but soon looked down upon these impious men, and brought on them the curses with which they had bound themselves. The residence of the first, from nothing but a little spark failing upon it, was entirely consumed by night, and he perished with all his family. The second was speedily covered with the disease which he had imprecated upon himself, from the sole of his feet to his head.

8. But the third, perceiving what had happened to the others, and fearing the inevitable judgment of God, the ruler of all, confessed publicly what they had plotted together. And in his repentance he became so wasted by his great lamentations, and continued weeping to such an extent, that both his eyes were destroyed. Such were the punishments which these men received for their falsehood.

Chapter X.

THE BISHOPS OF JERUSALEM.

1. Narcissus having departed, and no one knowing where he was, those presiding over the neighboring churches thought it best to ordain another bishop. His name was Dius. He presided but a short time, and Germanio succeeded him. He was followed by Gordius, in whose time Narcissus appeared again, as if raised from the dead. And immediately the brethren besought him to take the episcopate, as all admired him the more on account of his retirement and philosophy, and especially because of the punishment with which God had avenged him.

Chapter XI.

ALEXANDER.

1. But as on account of his great age Narcissus was no longer able to perform his official duties, the Providence of God called to the office with him, by a revelation given him in a night vision, the above-mentioned Alexander, who was then bishop of another parish.

2. Thereupon, as by Divine direction, he journeyed from the land of Cappadocia, where he first held the episcopate, to Jerusalem, in consequence of a vow and for the sake of information in regard to its places. They received, him there with great cordiality, and would not permit him to return, because of another revelation seen by them at night, which uttered the clearest message to the most zealous among them. For it made known that if they would go outside the gates, they would receive the bishop foreordained for them by God. And having done this, with the unanimous consent of the bishops of the neighboring churches, they constrained him to remain.

3. Alexander, himself, in private letters to the Antinoites, which are still preserved among us, mentions the joint episcopate of Narcissus and himself, writing in these words at the end of the epistle:

4. "Narcissus salutes you, who held the episcopate here before me, and is now associated with me in prayers, being one hundred and sixteen years of age; and he exhorts you, as I do, to be of one mind." These things took place in this manner. But, on the death of Serapion,

Asclepiades, who had been himself distinguished among the confessors during the persecution, succeeded to the episcopate of the church at Antioch. Alexander alludes to his appointment, writing thus to the church at Antioch:

5. "Alexander, a servant and prisoner of Jesus Christ, to the blessed church of Antioch, greeting in the Lord. The Lord hath made my bonds during the time of my imprisonment light and easy, since I learned that, by the Divine Providence, Asclepiades, who in regard to the true faith is eminently qualified, has undertaken the bishopric of your holy church at Antioch."

6. He indicates that he sent this epistle by Clement, writing toward its close as follows: "My honored brethren, have sent this letter to you by Clement, the blessed presbyter, a man virtuous and approved, whom ye yourselves also know and will recognize. Being here, in the providence and oversight of the Master, he has strengthened and built up the Church of the Lord."

Chapter XII.

SERAPION AND HIS EXTANT WORKS.

1. It is probable that others have preserved other memorials of Serapion's literary industry, but there have reached us only those addressed to a certain Domninus, who, in the time of persecution, fell away from faith in Christ to the Jewish will-worship; and those addressed to Pontius and Caricus, ecclesiastical men, and other letters to different persons, and still another work composed by him on the so-called Gospel of Peter.

2. He wrote this last to refute the falsehoods which that Gospel contained, on account of some in the parish of Rhossus who had been led astray by it into heterodox notions. It may be well to give some brief extracts from his work, showing his opinion of the book. He writes as follows:

3. "For we, brethren, receive both Peter and the other apostles as Christ; but we reject intelligently the writings falsely ascribed to them, knowing that such were not handed down to us.

4. When I visited you I supposed that all of you held the true faith, and as I had not read the Gospel which they put forward under the name of Peter, I said, 'If this is the only thing which occasions dispute among you, let it be read.' But now having learned, from what has been told me, that their mind was involved in some heresy, I will hasten to come to you again. Therefore, brethren, expect me shortly.

5. But you will learn, brethren, from what has been written to you, that we perceived the nature of the heresy of Marcianus, and that, not understanding', what he was saying, he contradicted himself.

6. For having obtained this Gospel from others who had studied it diligently, namely, from the successors of those who first used it, whom we call Docetæ (for most of their opinions are connected with the teaching of that school) we have been able to read it through, and we find many things in accordance with the true doctrine of the Saviour, but some things added to that doctrine, which we have pointed out for you farther on." So much in regard to Serapion.

Chapter XIII.

THE WRITINGS OF CLEMENT.

1. All the eight Stromata of Clement are preserved among us, and have been given by him the following title: "Titus Flavius Clement's Stromata of Gnostic Notes on the True Philosophy."

2. The books entitled Hypotyposes are of the same number. In them he mentions Pantænus by name as his teacher, and gives his opinions and traditions.

3. Besides these there is his Hortatory Discourse addressed to the Greeks; three books of a work entitled the Instructor; another with the title What Rich Man is Saved? the work on the Passover; discussions on Fasting and on Evil Speaking; the Hortatory Discourse on Patience, or To Those Recently Baptized; and the one bearing the title Ecclesiastical Canon, or Against the Judaizers, which he dedicated to Alexander, the bishop mentioned above.

4. In the Stromata, he has not only treated extensively of the Divine Scripture, but he also quotes from the Greek writers whenever anything that they have said seems to him profitable. He elucidates the opinions of many, both Greeks and barbarians.

5. He also refutes the false doctrines of the heresiarchs, and besides this, reviews a large portion of history, giving us specimens of very various learning; with all the rest he mingles the views of philosophers. It is likely that on this account he gave his work the appropriate title of Stromata.

6. He makes use also in these works of testimonies from the disputed Scriptures, the so-called Wisdom of Solomon, and of Jesus, the son of Sirach, and the Epistle to the Hebrews, and those of Barnabas, and Clement and Jude.

7. He mentions also Tatian's Discourse to the Greeks, and speaks of Cassianus as the author of a chronological work. He refers to the Jewish authors Philo, Aristobulus, Josephus, Demetrius, and Eupolemus, as showing, all of them, in their works, that Moses and the Jewish race existed before the earliest origin of the Greeks.

8. These books abound also in much other learning. In the first of them the author speaks of himself as next after the successors of the

apostles. In them he promises also to write a commentary on Genesis.

9. In his book on the Passover he acknowledges that he had been urged by his friends to commit to writing, for posterity, the traditions which he had heard from the ancient presbyters; and in the same work he mentions Melito and Irenæus, and certain others, and gives extracts from their writings.

Chapter XIV.

THE SCRIPTURES MENTIONED BY HIM.

1. To sum up briefly, he has given in the Hypotyposes abridged accounts of all canonical Scripture, not omitting the disputed books,—I refer to Jude and the other Catholic epistles, and Barnabas and the so-called Apocalypse of Peter.

2. He says that the Epistle to the Hebrews is the work of Paul, and that it was written to the Hebrews in the Hebrew language; but that Luke translated it carefully and published it for the Greeks, and hence the same style of expression is found in this epistle and in the Acts.

3. But he says that the words, Paul the Apostle, were probably not prefixed, because, in sending it to the Hebrews, who were prejudiced and suspicious of him, he wisely did not wish to repel them at the very beginning by giving his name.

4. Farther on he says: "But now, as the blessed presbyter said, since the Lord being the apostle of the Almighty, was sent to the Hebrews, Paul, as sent to the Gentiles, on account of his modesty did not subscribe himself an apostle of the Hebrews, through respect for the Lord, and because being a herald and apostle of the Gentiles he wrote to the Hebrews out of his superabundance."

5. Again, in the same books, Clement gives the tradition of the earliest presbyters, as to the order of the Gospels, in the following manner: The Gospels containing the genealogies, he says, were written first.

6. The Gospel according to Marks had this occasion. As Peter had preached the Word publicly at Rome, and declared the Gospel by the Spirit, many who were present requested that Mark, who had followed him for a long time and remembered his sayings, should write them out. And having composed the Gospel he gave it to those who had requested it.

7. When Peter learned of this, he neither directly forbade nor encouraged it. But, last of all, John, perceiving that the external facts had been made plain in the Gospel, being urged by his friends, and inspired by the Spirit, composed a spiritual Gospel. This is the account of Clement.

8. Again the above-mentioned Alexander, in a certain letter to

Origen, refers to Clement, and at the same time to Pantænus, as being among his familiar acquaintances. He writes as follows: "For this, as thou knowest, was the will of God, that the ancestral friendship existing between us should remain unshaken; nay, rather should be warmer and stronger.

9. For we know well those blessed fathers who have trodden the way before us, with whom we shall soon be; Pantænus, the truly blessed man and master, and the holy Clement, my master and benefactor, and if there is any other like them, through whom I became acquainted with thee, the best in everything, my master and brother."

10. So much for these matters. But Adamantius,—for this also was a name of Origen,—when Zephyrinus was bishop of Rome, visited Rome, "desiring," as he himself somewhere says, "to see the most ancient church of Rome." After a short stay there he returned to Alexandria.

11. And he performed the duties of catechetical instruction there with great zeal; Demetrius, who was bishop there at that time, urging and even entreating him to work diligently for the benefit of the brethren.

Chapter XV.

HERACLAS.

1. But when he saw that he had not time for the deeper study of divine things, and for the investigation and interpretation of the Sacred Scriptures, and also for the instruction of those who came to him—for coming, one after another, from morning till evening to be taught by him, they scarcely gave him time to breathe—he divided the multitude. And from those whom he knew well, he selected Heraclas, who was a zealous student of divine things, and in other respects a very learned man, not ignorant of philosophy, and made him his associate in the work of instruction. He entrusted to him the elementary training of beginners, but reserved for himself the teaching of those who were farther advanced.

Chapter XVI.

ORIGEN'S EARNEST STUDY OF THE DIVINE SCRIPTURES.

1. So earnest and assiduous was Origen's research into the divine words that he learned the Hebrew language, and procured as his own the original Hebrew Scriptures which were in the hands of the Jews. He investigated also the works of other translators of the Sacred Scriptures besides the Seventy. And in addition to the well-known translations of

Aquila, Symmachus, and Theodotion, he discovered certain others which had been concealed from remote times—in what out-of-the-way corners I know not—and by his search he brought them to light.

2. Since he did not know the authors, he simply stated that he had found this one in Nicopolis near Actium and that one in some other place.

3. In the Hexapla of the Psalms, after the four prominent translations, he adds not only a fifth, but also a sixth and seventh. He states of one of these that he found it in a jar in Jericho in the time of Antoninus, the son of Severus.

4. Having collected all of these, he divided them into sections, and placed them opposite each other, with the Hebrew text itself. He thus left us the copies of the so-called Hexapla. He arranged also separately an edition of Aquila and Symmachus and Theodotion with the Septuagint, in the Tetrapla.

Chapter XVII.

THE TRANSLATOR SYMMACHUS.

1. As to these translators it should be stated that Symmachus was an Ebionite. But the heresy of the Ebionites, as it is called, asserts that Christ was the son of Joseph and Mary, considering him a mere man, and insists strongly on keeping the law in a Jewish manner, as we have seen already in this history. Commentaries of Symmachus are still extant in which he appears to support this heresy by attacking the Gospel of Matthew. Origen states that he obtained these and other commentaries of Symmachus on the Scriptures from a certain Juliana, who, he says, received the books by inheritance from Symmachus himself.

Chapter XVIII.

AMBROSE.

1. About this time Ambrose, who held the heresy of Valentinus, was convinced by Origen's presentation of the truth, and, as if his mind were illumined by light, he accepted the orthodox doctrine of the Church.

2. Many others also, drawn by the fame of Origen's learning, which resounded everywhere, came to him to make trial of his skill in sacred literature. And a great many heretics, and not a few of the most distinguished philosophers, studied under him diligently, receiving instruction from him not only in divine things, but also in secular philosophy.

3. For when he perceived that any persons had superior intelligence he instructed them also in philosophic branches—in geometry, arithmetic, and other preparatory studies—and then advanced to the systems of the philosophers and explained their writings. And he made observations and comments upon each of them, so that he became celebrated as a great philosopher even among the Greeks themselves.

4. And he instructed many of the less learned in the common school branches, saying that these would be no small help to them in the study and understanding of the Divine Scriptures. On this account he considered it especially necessary for himself to be skilled in secular and philosophic learning.

Chapter XIX.

CIRCUMSTANCES RELATED OF ORIGEN.

1. The Greek philosophers of his age are witnesses to his proficiency in these subjects. We find frequent mention of him in their writings. Sometimes they dedicated their own works to him; again, they submitted their labors to him as a teacher for his judgment.

2. Why need we say these things when even Porphyry, who lived in Sicily in our own times and wrote books against us, attempting to traduce the Divine Scriptures by them, mentions those who have interpreted them; and being unable in any way to find a base accusation against the doctrines, for lack of arguments turns to reviling and calumniating their interpreters, attempting especially to slander Origen, whom he says he knew in his youth.

3. But truly, without knowing it, he commends the man; telling the truth about him in some cases where he could not do otherwise; but uttering falsehoods where he thinks he will not be detected. Sometimes he accuses him as a Christian; again he describes his proficiency in philosophic learning. But hear his own words:

4. "Some persons, desiring to find a solution of the baseness of the Jewish Scriptures rather than abandon them, have had recourse to explanations inconsistent and incongruous with the words written, which explanations, instead of supplying a defense of the foreigners, contain rather approval and praise of themselves. For they boast that the plain words of Moses are enigmas, and regard them as oracles full of hidden mysteries; and having bewildered the mental judgment by folly, they make their explanations." Farther on he says:

5. "As an example of this absurdity take a man whom I met when I was young, and who was then greatly celebrated and still is, on account of the writings which he has left. I refer to Origen, who is highly honored by the teachers of these doctrines.

6. For this man, having been a hearer of Ammonius, who had attained the greatest proficiency in philosophy of any in our day, derived much benefit from his teacher in the knowledge of the sciences; but as to the correct choice of life, he pursued a course opposite to his.

7. For Ammonius, being a Christian, and brought up by Christian parents, when he gave himself to study and to philosophy straightway conformed to the life required by the laws. But Origen, having been educated as a Greek in Greek literature, went over to the barbarian recklessness. And carrying over the learning which he had obtained, he hawked it about, in his life conducting himself as a Christian and contrary to the laws, but in his opinions of material things and of the Deity being like a Greek, and mingling Grecian teachings with foreign fables.

8. For he was continually studying Plato, and he busied himself with the writings of Numenius and Cronius, Apollophanes, Longinus, Moderatus, and Nicomachus, and those famous among the Pythagoreans. And he used the books of Chæremon the Stoic, and of Cornutus. Becoming acquainted through them with the figurative interpretation of the Grecian mysteries, he applied it to the Jewish Scriptures."

9. These things are said by Porphyry in the third book of his work against the Christians. He speaks truly of the industry and learning of the man, but plainly utters a falsehood (for what will not an opposer of Christians do?) when he says that he went over from the Greeks, and that Ammonius fell from a life of piety into heathen customs.

10. For the doctrine of Christ was taught to Origen by his parents, as we have shown above. And Ammonius held the divine philosophy unshaken and unadulterated to the end of his life. His works yet extant show this, as he is celebrated among many for the writings which he has left. For example, the work entitled The Harmony of Moses and Jesus, and such others as are in the possession of the learned.

11. These things are sufficient to evince the slander of the false accuser, and also the proficiency of Origen in Grecian learning. He defends his diligence in this direction against some who blamed him for it, in a certain epistle, where he writes as follows:

12. "When I devoted myself to the word, and the fame of my proficiency went abroad, and when heretics and persons conversant with Grecian learning, and particularly with philosophy, came to me, it seemed necessary that I should examine the doctrines of the heretics, and what the philosophers say concerning the truth.

13. And in this we have followed Pantænus, who benefited many before our time by his thorough preparation in such things, and also Heraclas, who is now a member of the presbytery of Alexandria. I found him with the teacher of philosophic learning, with whom he had already continued five years before I began to hear lectures on those

subjects.

14. And though he had formerly worn the common dress, he laid it aside and assumed and still wears the philosopher's garment; and he continues the earnest investigation of Greek works." He says these things in defending himself for his study of Grecian literature.

15. About this time, while he was still at Alexandria, a soldier came and delivered a letter from the governor of Arabia to Demetrius, bishop of the parish, and to the prefect of Egypt who was in office at that time, requesting that they would with all speed send Origen to him for an interview. Being sent by them, he went to Arabia. And having in a short time accomplished the object of his visit, he returned to Alexandria.

16. But sometime after a considerable war broke out in the city, and he departed from Alexandria. And thinking that it would be unsafe for him to remain in Egypt, he went to Palestine and abode in Cæsarea. While there the bishops of the church in that country requested him to preach and expound the Scriptures publicly, although he had not yet been ordained as presbyter.

17. This is evident from what Alexander, bishop of Jerusalem and Theoctistus of Cæsarea, wrote to Demetrius in regard to the matter, defending themselves thus: "He has stated in his letter that such a thing was never heard of before, neither has hitherto taken place, that laymen should preach in the presence of bishops. I know not how he comes to say what is plainly untrue.

18. For whenever persons able to instruct the brethren are found, they are exhorted by the holy bishops to preach to the people. Thus in Laranda, Euelpis by Neon; and in Iconium, Paulinus by Celsus; and in Synada, Theodorus by Atticus, our blessed brethren. And probably this has been done in other places unknown to us." He was honored in this manner while yet a young man, not only by his countrymen, but also by foreign bishops.

19. But Demetrius sent for him by letter, and urged him through members and deacons of the church to return to Alexandria. So he returned and resumed his accustomed duties.

Chapter XX.

THE EXTANT WORKS OF THE WRITERS OF THAT AGE.

1. There flourished many learned men in the Church at that time, whose letters to each other have been preserved and are easily accessible. They have been kept until our time in the library at Ælia, which was established by Alexander, who at that time presided over that church. We have been able to gather from that library material for our present work.

2. Among these Beryllus has left us, besides letters and treatises, various elegant works. He was bishop of Bostra in Arabia. Likewise also Hippolytus, who presided over another church, has left writings.

3. There has reached us also a dialogue of Caius, a very learned man, which was held at Rome under Zephyrinus, with Proclus, who contended for the Phrygian heresy. In this he curbs the rashness and boldness of his opponents in setting forth new Scriptures. He mentions only thirteen epistles of the holy apostle, not counting that to the Hebrews with the others. And unto our day there are some among the Romans who do not consider this a work of the apostle.

Chapter XXI.

THE BISHOPS THAT WERE WELL KNOWN AT THAT TIME.

1. After Antoninus had reigned seven years and six months, Macrinus succeeded him. He held the government but a year, and was succeeded by another Antoninus. During his first year the Roman bishop, Zephyrinus, having held his office for eighteen years, died, and Callistus received the episcopate.

2. He continued for five years, and was succeeded by Urbanus. After this, Alexander became Roman emperor, Antoninus having reigned but four years. At this time Philetus also succeeded Asclepiades in the church of Antioch.

3. The mother of the emperor, Mammæa by name, was a most pious woman, if there ever was one, and of religious life. When the fame of Origen had extended everywhere and had come even to her ears, she desired greatly to see the man, and above all things to make trial of his celebrated understanding of divine things.

4. Staying for a time in Antioch, she sent for him with a military escort. Having remained with her a while and shown her many things which were for the glory of the Lord and of the excellence of the divine teaching, he hastened back to his accustomed work.

Chapter XXII.

THE WORKS OF HIPPOLYTUS WHICH HAVE REACHED US.

1. At that time Hippolytus, besides many other treatises, wrote a work on the passover. He gives in this a chronological table, and presents a certain paschal canon of sixteen years, bringing the time down to the first year of the Emperor Alexander.

2. Of his other writings the following have reached us: On the Hexæmeron, On the Works after the Hexæmeron, Against Marcion, On the Song of Songs, On Portions of Ezekiel, On the Passover, Against

All the Heresies; and you can find many other works preserved by many.

Chapter XXIII.

ORIGEN'S ZEAL AND HIS ELEVATION TO THE PRESBYTERATE.

1. At that time Origen began his commentaries on the Divine Scriptures, being urged thereto by Ambrose, who employed innumerable incentives, not only exhorting him by word, but also furnishing abundant means.

2. For he dictated to more than seven amanuenses, who relieved each other at appointed times. And he employed no fewer copyists, besides girls who were skilled in elegant writing. For all these Ambrose furnished the necessary expense in abundance, manifesting himself an inexpressible earnestness in diligence and zeal for the divine oracles, by which he especially pressed him on to the preparation of his commentaries.

3. While these things were in progress, Urbanus, who had been for eight years bishop of the Roman church, was succeeded by Pontianus, and Zebinus succeeded Philetus in Antioch.

4. At this time Origen was sent to Greece on account of a pressing necessity in connection with ecclesiastical affairs, and went through Palestine, and was ordained as presbyter in Cæsarea by the bishops of that country. The matters that were agitated concerning him on this account, and the decisions on these matters by those who presided over the churches, besides the other works concerning the divine word which he published while in his prime, demand a separate treatise. We have written of them to some extent in the second book of the Defense which we have composed in his behalf.

Chapter XXIV.

THE COMMENTARIES WHICH HE PREPARED AT ALEXANDRIA.

1. It may be well to add that in the sixth book of his exposition of the Gospel of John he states that he prepared the first five while in Alexandria. Of his work on the entire Gospel only twenty-two volumes have come down to us.

2. In the ninth of those on Genesis, of which there are twelve in all, he states that not only the preceding eight had been composed at Alexandria, but also those on the first twenty-five Psalms and on Lamentations. Of these last five volumes have reached us. In them he

mentions also his books On the Resurrection, of which there are two.

3. He wrote also the books De Principiis before leaving Alexandria; and the discourses entitled Stromata, ten in number, he composed in the same city during the reign of Alexander, as the notes by his own hand preceding the volumes indicate.

Chapter XXV.

HIS REVIEW OF THE CANONICAL SCRIPTURES.

1. When expounding the first Psalm, he I gives a catalogue of the sacred Scriptures of the Old Testament as follows: "It should be stated that the canonical books, as the Hebrews have handed them down, are twenty-two; corresponding with the number of their letters." Farther on he says:

2. "The twenty-two books of the Hebrews are the following: That which is called by us Genesis, but by the Hebrews, from the beginning of the book, Bresith, which means, 'In the beginning'; Exodus, Welesmoth, that is, 'These are the names'; Leviticus, Wikra, 'And he called'; Numbers, Ammesphekodeim; Deuteronomy, Eleaddebareim, 'These are the words'; Jesus, the son of Nave, Josoue ben Noun; Judges and Ruth, among them in one book, Saphateim; the First and Second of Kings, among them one, Samouel, that is, 'The called of God'; the Third and Fourth of Kings in one, Wammelch David, that is, 'The kingdom of David'; of the Chronicles, the First and Second in one, Dabreiamein, that is, 'Records of days'; Esdras, First and Second in one, Ezra, that is, 'An assistant'; the book of Psalms, Spharthelleim; the Proverbs of Solomon, Meloth; Ecclesiastes, Koelth; the Song of Songs (not, as some suppose, Songs of Songs), Sir Hassirim; Isaiah, Jessia; Jeremiah, with Lamentations and the epistle in one, Jeremia; Daniel, Daniel; Ezekiel, Jezekiel; Job, Job; Esther, Esther. And besides these there are the Maccabees, which are entitled Sarbeth Sabanaiel. He gives these in the above-mentioned work.

3. In his first book on Matthew's Gospel, maintaining the Canon of the Church, he testifies that he knows only four Gospels, writing as follows:

4. "Among the four Gospels, which are the only indisputable ones in the Church of God under heaven, I have learned by tradition that the first was written by Matthew, who was once a publican, but afterwards an apostle of Jesus Christ, and it was prepared for the converts from Judaism, and published in the Hebrew language.

5. The second is by Mark, who composed it according to the instructions of Peter, who in his Catholic epistle acknowledges him as a son, saying, 'The church that is at Babylon elected together with you, saluteth you, and so doth Marcus, my son.'

6. And the third by Luke, the Gospel commended by Paul, and composed for Gentile converts. Last of all that by John."

7. In the fifth book of his Expositions of John's Gospel, he speaks thus concerning the epistles of the apostles: "But he who was 'made sufficient to be a minister of the New Testament, not of the letter, but of the Spirit,' that is, Paul, who 'fully preached the Gospel from Jerusalem and round about even unto Illyricum,' did not write to all the churches which he had instructed and to those to which he wrote he sent but few lines.

8. And Peter, on whom the Church of Christ is built, 'against which the gates of hell shall not prevail,' has left one acknowledged epistle; perhaps also a second, but this is doubtful.

9. Why need we speak of him who reclined upon the bosom of Jesus, John, who has left us one Gospel, though he confessed that he might write so many that the world could not contain them? And he wrote also the Apocalypse, but was commanded to keep silence and not to write the words of the seven thunders.

10. He has left also an epistle of very few lines; perhaps also a second and third; but not all consider them genuine, and together they do not contain hundred lines."

11. In addition he makes the following statements in regard to the Epistle to the Hebrews in his Homilies upon it: "That the verbal style of the epistle entitled 'To the Hebrews,' is not rude like the language of the apostle, who acknowledged himself 'rude in speech,' that is, in expression; but that its diction is purer Greek, any one who has the power to discern differences of phraseology will acknowledge.

12. Moreover, that the thoughts of the epistle are admirable, and not inferior to the acknowledged apostolic writings, any one who carefully examines the apostolic text will admit."

13. Farther on he adds: "If I gave my opinion, I should say that the thoughts are those of the apostle, but the diction and phraseology are those of some one who remembered the apostolic teachings, and wrote down at his leisure what had been said by his teacher. Therefore if any church holds that this epistle is by Paul, let it be commended for this. For not without reason have the ancients handed it down as Paul's.

14. But who wrote the epistle, in truth, God knows. The statement of some who have gone before us is that Clement, bishop of the Romans, wrote the epistle, and of others that Luke, the author of the Gospel and the Acts, wrote it." But let this suffice on these matters.

Chapter XXVI.

HERACLAS BECOMES BISHOP OF ALEXANDRIA.

1. It was in the tenth year of the above-mentioned reign that Origen removed from Alexandria to Cæsarea, leaving the charge of the catechetical school in that city to Heraclas. Not long afterward Demetrius, bishop of the church of Alexandria, died, having held the office for forty-three full years, and Heraclas succeeded him. At this time Firmilianus, bishop of Cæsarea in Cappadocia, was conspicuous.

Chapter XXVII.

HOW THE BISHOPS REGARDED ORIGEN.

1. He was so earnestly affected toward Origen, that he urged him to come to that country for the benefit of the churches, and moreover he visited him in Judea, remaining with him for some time, for the sake of improvement in divine things. And Alexander, bishop of Jerusalem, and Theoctistus, bishop of Cæsarea, attended on him constantly, as their only teacher, and allowed him to expound the Divine Scriptures, and to perform the other duties pertaining to ecclesiastical discourse.

Chapter XXVIII.

THE PERSECUTION UNDER MAXIMINUS.

1. The Roman emperor, Alexander, having finished his reign in thirteen years, was succeeded by Maximinus Cæsar. On account of his hatred toward the household of Alexander, which contained many believers, he began a persecution, commanding that only the rulers of the churches should be put to death, as responsible for the Gospel teaching. Thereupon Origen composed his work On Martyrdom, and dedicated it to Ambrose and Protoctetus, a presbyter of the parish of Cæsarea, because in the persecution there had come upon them both unusual hardships, in which it is reported that they were eminent in confession during the reign of Maximinus, which lasted but three years. Origen has noted this as the time of the persecution in the twenty-second book of his Commentaries on John, and in several epistles.

Chapter XXIX.

FABIANUS, WHO WAS WONDERFULLY
DESIGNATED BISHOP OF ROME BY GOD.

1. Gordianus succeeded Maximinus as Roman emperor; and Pontianus, who had been bishop of the church at Rome for six years, was succeeded by Anteros. After he had held the office for a month, Fabianus succeeded him.

2. They say that Fabianus having come, after the death of Anteros, with others from the country, was staying at Rome, and that while there he was chosen to the office through a most wonderful manifestation of divine and heavenly grace.

3. For when all the brethren had assembled to select by vote him who should succeed to the episcopate of the church, several renowned and honorable men were in the minds of many, but Fabianus, although present, was in the mind of none. But they relate that suddenly a dove flying down lighted on his head, resembling the descent of the Holy Spirit on the Saviour in the form of a dove.

4. Thereupon all the people, as if moved by one Divine Spirit, with all eagerness and unanimity cried out that he was worthy, and without delay they took him and placed him upon the episcopal seat.

5. About that time Zebinus, bishop of Antioch died, and Babylas succeeded him. And in Alexandria Heraclas, having received the episcopal office after Demetrius, was succeeded in the charge of the catechetical school by Dionysius, who had also been one of Origen's pupils.

Chapter XXX.

THE PUPILS OF ORIGEN.

1. While Origen was carrying on his customary duties in Cæsarea, many pupils came to him not only from the vicinity, but also from other countries. Among these Theodorus, the same that was distinguished among the bishops of our day under the name of Gregory, and his brother Athenodorus, we know to have been especially celebrated. Finding them deeply interested in Greek and Roman learning, he infused into them a love of philosophy, and led them to exchange their old zeal for the study of divinity. Remaining with him five years, they made such progress in divine things, that although they were still young, both of them were honored with a bishopric in the churches of Pontus.

Chapter XXXI.

AFRICANUS.

1. At this time also Africanus, the writer of the books entitled Cesti, was well known. There is extant an epistle of his to Origen, expressing doubts of the story of Susannah in Daniel, as being spurious and fictitious. Origen answered this very fully.

2. Other works of the same Africanus which have reached us are his five books on Chronology, a work accurately and laboriously prepared. He says in this that he went to Alexandria on account of the great fame of Heraclas, who excelled especially in philosophic studies and other Greek learning, and whose appointment to the bishopric of the church there we have already mentioned.

3. There is extant also another epistle from the same Africanus to Aristides on the supposed discrepancy between Matthew and Luke in the Genealogies of Christ. In this he shows clearly the agreement of the evangelists, from an account which had come down to him, which we have already given in its proper place in the first book of this work.

Chapter XXXII.

THE COMMENTARIES WHICH ORIGEN COMPOSED IN CÆSAREA IN PALESTINE.

1. About this time Origen prepared his Commentaries on Isaiah and on Ezekiel. Of the former there have come down to us thirty books, as far as the third part of Isaiah, to the vision of the beasts in the desert; on Ezekiel twenty-five books, which are all that he wrote on the whole prophet.

2. Being at that time in Athens, he finished his work on Ezekiel and commenced his Commentaries on the Song of Songs, which he carried forward to the fifth book. After his return to Cæsarea, he completed these also, ten books in number.

3. But why should we give in this history an accurate catalogue of the man's works, which would require a separate treatise? we have furnished this also in our narrative of the life of Pamphilus, a holy martyr of our own time. After showing how great the diligence of Pamphilus was in divine things, we give in that a catalogue of the library which he collected of the works of Origen and of other ecclesiastical writers, Whoever desires may learn readily from this which of Origen's works have reached us. But we must proceed now with our history.

Chapter XXXIII.

THE ERROR OF BERYLLUS.

1. Beryllus, whom we mentioned recently as bishop of Bostra in Arabia, turned aside from the ecclesiastical standard and attempted to introduce ideas foreign to the faith. He dared to assert that our Saviour and Lord did not pre-exist in a distinct form of being of his own before his abode among men, and that he does not possess a divinity of his own, but only that of the Father dwelling in him.

2. Many bishops carried on investigations and discussions with him on this matter, and Origen having been invited with the others, went down at first for a conference with him to ascertain his real opinion. But when he understood his views, and perceived that they were erroneous, having persuaded him by argument, and convinced him by demonstration, he brought him back to the true doctrine, and restored him to his former sound opinion.

3. There are still extant writings of Beryllus and of the synod held on his account, which contain the questions put to him by Origen, and the discussions which were carried on in his parish, as well as all the things done at that time.

4. The elder brethren among us have handed down many other facts respecting Origen which I think proper to omit, as not pertaining to this work. But whatever it has seemed necessary to record about him can be found in the Apology in his behalf written by us and Pamphilus, the holy martyr of our day. We prepared this carefully and did the work jointly on account of faultfinders.

Chapter XXXIV.

PHILIP CÆSAR.

1. Gordianus had been Roman emperor for six years when Philip, with his son Philip, succeeded him. It is reported that he, being a Christian desired, on the day of the last paschal vigil, to share with the multitude in the prayers of the Church, but that he was not permitted to enter, by him who then presided, until he had made confession and had numbered himself among those who were reckoned as transgressors and who occupied the place of penance. For if he had not done this, he would never have been received by him, on account of the many crimes which he had committed. It is said that he obeyed readily, manifesting in his conduct a genuine and pious fear of God.

Chapter XXXV.

DIONYSIUS SUCCEEDS HERACLAS IN THE EPISCOPATE.

1. In the third year of this emperor, Heraclas died, having held his office for sixteen years, and Dionysius received the episcopate of the churches of Alexandria.

Chapter XXXVI.

OTHER WORKS OF ORIGEN.

1. At this time, as the faith extended and our doctrine was proclaimed boldly before all, Origen, being, as they say, over sixty years old, and having gained great facility by his long practice, very properly permitted his public discourses to be taken down by stenographers, a thing which he had never before allowed.

2. He also at this time composed a work of eight books in answer to that entitled True Discourse, which had been written against us by Celsus the Epicurean, and the twenty-five books on the Gospel of Matthew, besides those on the Twelve Prophets, of which we have found only twenty-five.

3. There is extant also an epistle of his to the Emperor Philip, and another to Severa his wife, with several others to different persons. We have arranged in distinct books to the number of one hundred, so that they might be no longer scattered, as many of these as we have been able to collect, which have been preserved here and there by different persons.

4. He wrote also to Fabianus, bishop of Rome, and to many other rulers of the churches concerning his orthodoxy. You have examples of these in the eighth book of the Apology which we have written in his behalf.

Chapter XXXVII.

THE DISSENSION OF THE ARABIANS.

1. About the same time others arose in Arabia, putting forward a doctrine foreign to the truth. They said that during the present time the human soul dies and perishes with the body, but that at the time of the resurrection they will be renewed together. And at that time also a synod of considerable size assembled, and Origen, being again invited thither, spoke publicly on the question with such effect that the opinions of those who had formerly fallen were changed.

Chapter XXXVIII.

THE HERESY OF THE ELKESITES.

1. Another error also arose at this time, called the heresy of the Elkesites, which was extinguished in the very beginning. Origen speaks of it in this manner in a public homily on the eighty-second Psalm: "A certain man came just now, puffed up greatly with his own ability, proclaiming that godless and impious opinion which has appeared lately in the churches, styled 'of the Elkesites.' I will show you what evil things that opinion teaches, that you may not be carried away by it. It rejects certain parts of every scripture. Again it uses portions of the Old Testament and the Gospel, but rejects the apostle altogether. It says that to deny Christ is an indifferent matter, and that he who understands will, under necessity, deny with his mouth, but not in his heart. They produce a certain book which they say fell from heaven. They hold that whoever hears and believes this shall receive remission of sins, another remission than that which Jesus Christ has given." Such is the account of these persons.

Chapter XXXIX.

THE PERSECUTION UNDER DECIUS, AND THE SUFFERINGS OF ORIGEN.

1. After a reign of seven years Philip was succeeded by Decius. On account of his hatred of Philip, he commenced a persecution of the churches, in which Fabianus suffered martyrdom at Rome, and Cornelius succeeded him in the episcopate.

2. In Palestine, Alexander, bishop of the church of Jerusalem, was brought again on Christ's account before the governor's judgment seat in Cæsarea, and having acquitted himself nobly in a second confession was cast into prison, crowned with the hoary locks of venerable age.

3. And after his honorable and illustrious confession at the tribunal of the governor, he fell asleep in prison, and Mazabanes became his successor in the bishopric of Jerusalem.

4. Babylas in Antioch, having like Alexander passed away in prison after hi confession, was succeeded by Fabius in the episcopate of that church.

5. But how many and how great things came upon Origen in the persecution, and what was their final result—as the demon of evil marshaled all his forces, and fought against the man with his utmost craft and power, assaulting him beyond all others against whom he contended at that time—and what and how many things he endured for

the word of Christ, bonds and bodily tortures and torments under the iron collar and in the dungeon; and how for many days with his feet stretched four spaces in the stocks he bore patiently the threats of fire and whatever other things were inflicted by his enemies; and how his sufferings terminated, as his judge strove eagerly with all his might not to end his life; and what words he left after these things, full of comfort to those needing aid, a great many of his epistles show with truth and accuracy.

Chapter XL.

THE EVENTS WHICH HAPPENED TO DIONYSIUS.

1. I shall quote from the epistle of Dionysius to Germanus an account of what befell the former. Speaking of himself, he writes as follows: "I speak before God, and he knows that I do not lie. I did not flee on my own impulse nor without divine direction.

2. But even before this, at the very hour when the Decian persecution was commanded, Sabinus sent a frumentarius to search for me, and I remained at home four days awaiting his arrival. But he went about examining all places—roads, rivers, and fields—where he thought I might be concealed or on the way. But he was smitten with blindness, and did not find the house, for he did not suppose, that being pursued, I would remain at home.

3. And after the fourth day God commanded me to depart, and made a way for me in a wonderful manner; and I and my attendants and many of the brethren went away together. And that this occurred through the providence of God was made manifest by what followed, in which perhaps we were useful to some."

4. Farther on he relates in this manner what happened to him after his flight: "For about sunset, having been seized with those that were with me, I was taken by the soldiers to Taposiris, but in the providence of God, Timothy was not present and was not captured. But coming later, he found the house deserted and guarded by soldiers, and ourselves reduced to slavery."

5. After a little he says: "And what was the manner of his admirable management? for the truth shall be told. One of the country people met Timothy fleeing and disturbed, and inquired the cause of his haste. And he told him the truth.

6. And when the man heard it (he was on his way to a marriage feast, for it was customary to spend the entire night in such gatherings), he entered and announced it to those at the table. And they, as if on a preconcerted signal, arose with one impulse, and rushed out quickly and came and burst in upon us with a shout. Immediately the soldiers who were guarding us fled, and they came to us lying as we were upon

the bare couches.

7. But I, God knows, thought at first that they were robbers who had come for spoil and plunder. So I remained upon the bed on which I was, clothed only in a linen garment, and offered them the rest of my clothing which was lying beside me. But they directed me to rise and come away quickly.

8. Then I understood why they were come, and I cried out, beseeching and entreating them to depart and leave us alone. And I requested them, if they desired to benefit me in any way, to anticipate those who were carrying me off, and cut off my head themselves. And when I had cried out in this manner, as my companions and partners in everything know, they raised me by force. But I threw myself on my back on the ground; and they seized me by the hands and feet and dragged me away.

9. And the witnesses of all these occurrences followed: Gaius, Faustus, Peter, and Paul. But they who had seized me carried me out of the village hastily, and placing me on an ass without a saddle, bore me away." Dionysius relates these things respecting himself.

Chapter XLI.

THE MARTYRS IN ALEXANDRIA.

1. The same writer, in an epistle to Fabius, bishop of Antioch, relates as follows the sufferings of the martyrs in Alexandria under Decius: "The persecution among us did not begin with the royal decree, but preceded it an entire year. The prophet and author of evils to this city, whoever he was, previously moved and aroused against us the masses of the heathen, rekindling among them the superstition of their country.

2. And being thus excited by him and finding full opportunity for any wickedness, they considered this the only pious service of their demons, that they should slay us.

3. "They seized first an old man named Metras, and commanded him to utter impious words. But as he would not obey, they beat him with clubs, and tore his face and eyes with sharp sticks, and dragged him out of the city and stoned him.

4. Then they carried to their idol temple a faithful woman, named Quinta, that they might force her to worship. And as she turned away in detestation, they bound her feet and dragged her through the entire city over the stone-paved streets, and dashed her against the millstones, and at the same time scourged her; then, taking her to the same place, they stoned her to death.

5. Then all with one impulse rushed to the homes of the pious, and they dragged forth whomsoever any one knew as a neighbor, and

despoiled and plundered them. They took for themselves the more valuable property; but the poorer articles and those made of wood they scattered about and burned in the streets, so that the city appeared as if taken by an enemy.

6. But the brethren withdrew and went away, and 'took joyfully the spoiling of their goods,' like those to whom Paul bore witness. I know of no one unless possibly some one who fell into their hands, who, up to this time, denied the Lord.

7. Then they seized also that most admirable virgin, Apollonia, an old woman, and, smiting her on the jaws, broke out all her teeth. And they made a fire outside the city and threatened to burn her alive if she would not join with them in their impious cries. And she, supplicating a little, was released, when she leaped eagerly into the fire and was consumed.

8. Then they seized Serapion in his own house, and tortured him with harsh cruelties, and having broken all his limbs, they threw him headlong from an upper story. And there was no street, nor public road, nor lane open to us, by night or day; for always and everywhere, all of them cried out that if any one would not repeat their impious words, he should immediately be dragged away and burned.

9. And matters continued thus for a considerable time. But a sedition and civil war came upon the wretched people and turned their cruelty toward us against one another. So we breathed for a little while as they ceased from their rage against us. But presently the change from that milder reign was announced to us, and great fear of what was threatened seized us.

10. For the decree arrived, almost like unto that most terrible time foretold by our Lord, which if it were possible would offend even the elect.

11. All truly were affrighted. And many of the more eminent in their fear came forward immediately; others who were in the public service were drawn on by their official duties; others were urged on by their acquaintances. And as their names were called they approached the impure and impious sacrifices. Some of them were pale and trembled as if they were not about to sacrifice, but to be themselves sacrifices and offerings to the idols; so that they were jeered at by the multitude who stood around, as it was plain to every one that they were afraid either to die or to sacrifice.

12. But some advanced to the altars more readily, declaring boldly that they had never been Christians. Of these the prediction of our Lord is most true that they shall 'hardly' be saved. Of the rest some followed the one, others the other of these classes, some fled and some were seized.

13. And of the latter some continued faithful until bonds and imprisonment, and some who had even been imprisoned for many days

yet abjured the faith before they were brought to trial. Others having for a time endured great tortures finally retracted.

14. But the firm and blessed pillars of the Lord being strengthened by him, and having received vigor and might suitable and appropriate to the strong faith which they possessed, became admirable witnesses of his kingdom.

15. The first of these was Julian, a man who suffered so much with the gout that he was unable to stand or walk. They brought him forward with two others who carried him. One of these immediately denied. But the other, whose name was Cronion, and whose surname was Eunus, and the old man Julian himself, both of them having confessed the Lord, were carried on camels through the entire city, which, as you know, is a very large one, and in this elevated position were beaten and finally burned in a fierce fire, surrounded by all the populace.

16. But a soldier, named Besas, who stood by them as they were led away rebuked those who insulted them. And they cried out against him, and this most manly warrior of God was arraigned, and having done nobly in the great contest for piety, was beheaded.

17. A certain other one, a Libyan by birth, but in name and blessedness a true Macar, was strongly urged by the judge to recant; but as he would not yield he was burned alive. After them Epimachus and Alexander, having remained in bonds for a long time, and endured countless agonies from scrapers and scourges, were also consumed in a fierce fire.

18. And with them there were four women. Ammonarium, a holy virgin, the judge tortured relentlessly and excessively, because she declared from the first that she would utter none of those things which he commanded; and having kept her promise truly, she was dragged away. The others were Mercuria, a very remarkable old woman, and Dionysia, the mother of many children, who did not love her own children above the Lord. As the governor was ashamed of torturing thus ineffectually, and being always defeated by women, they were put to death by the sword, without the trial of tortures. For the champion, Ammonarium, endured these in behalf of all.

19. The Egyptians, Heron and Ater and Isidorus, and with them Dioscorus, a boy about fifteen years old, were delivered up. At first the judge attempted to deceive the lad by fair words, as if he could be brought over easily, and then to force him by tortures, as one who would readily yield. But Dioscorus was neither persuaded nor constrained.

20. As the others remained firm, he scourged them cruelly and then delivered them to the fire. But admiring the manner in which Dioscorus had distinguished himself publicly, and his wise answers to his persuasions, he dismissed him, saying that on account of his youth he would give him time for repentance. And this most godly Dioscorus is

among us now, awaiting a longer conflict and more severe contest.

21. But a certain Nemesion, who also was an Egyptian, was accused as an associate of robbers; but when he had cleared himself before the centurion of this charge most foreign to the truth, he was informed against as a Christian, and taken in bonds before the governor. And the most unrighteous magistrate inflicted on him tortures and scourgings double those which he executed on the robbers, and then burned him between the robbers, thus honoring the blessed man by the likeness to Christ.

22. A band of soldiers, Ammon and Zeno and Ptolemy and Ingenes, and with them an old man, Theophilus, were standing close together before the tribunal. And as a certain person who was being tried as a Christian, seemed inclined to deny, they standing by gnashed their teeth, and made signs with their faces and stretched out their hands, and gestured with their bodies.

23. And when the attention of all was turned to them, before any one else could seize them, they rushed up to the tribunal saying that they were Christians, so that the governor and his council were affrighted. And those who were on trial appeared most courageous in prospect of their sufferings, while their judges trembled. And they went exultingly from the tribunal rejoicing in their testimony; God himself having caused them to triumph gloriously."

Chapter XLII.

OTHERS OF WHOM DIONYSIUS GIVES AN ACCOUNT.

1. "Many others, in cities and villages, were torn asunder by the heathen, of whom I will mention one as an illustration. Ischyrion was employed as a steward by one of the rulers. His employer commanded him to sacrifice, and on his refusal insulted him, and as he remained firm, abused him. And as he still held out he seized a long staff and thrust it through his bowels and slew him.

2. "Why need I speak of the multitude that wandered in the deserts and mountains, and perished by hunger, and thirst, and cold, and sickness, and robbers, and wild beasts? Those of them who survived are witnesses of their election and victory.

3. But I will relate one occurrence as an example. Chæremon, who was very old, was bishop of the city called Nilus. He fled with his wife to the Arabian mountain and did not return. And though the brethren searched diligently they could not find either them or their bodies.

4. And many who fled to the same Arabian mountain were carried into slavery by the barbarian Saracens. Some of them were ransomed with difficulty and at a large price others have not been to the present time. I have related these things, my brother, not without an object, but

that you may understand how many and great distresses came upon us. Those indeed will understand them the best who have had the largest experience of them."

5. A little further on he adds: "These divine martyrs among us, who now are seated with Christ, and are sharers in his kingdom, partakers of his judgment and judges with him, received some of the brethren who had fallen away and become chargeable with the guilt of sacrificing. When they perceived that their conversion and repentance were sufficient to be acceptable with him who by no means desires the death of the sinner, but his repentance, having proved them they received them back and brought them together, and met with them and had fellowship with them in prayers and feasts.

6. What counsel then, brethren, do you give us concerning such persons? What should we do? Shall we have the same judgment and rule as theirs, and observe their decision and charity, and show mercy to those whom they pitied? Or, shall we declare their decision unrighteous, and set ourselves as judges of their opinion, and grieve mercy and overturn order?" These words Dionysius very properly added when making mention of those who had been weak in the time of persecution.

Chapter XLIII.

NOVATUS, HIS MANNER OF LIFE AND HIS HERESY.

1. After this, Novatus, a presbyter of the church at Rome, being lifted up with arrogance against these persons, as if there was no longer for them a hope of salvation, not even if they should do all things pertaining to a genuine and pure conversion, became leader of the heresy of those who, in the pride of their imagination, call themselves Cathari.

2. Thereupon a very large synod assembled at Rome, of bishops in number sixty, and a great many more presbyters and deacons; while the pastors of the remaining provinces deliberated in their places privately concerning what ought to be done. A decree was confirmed by all, that Novatus and those who joined with him, and those who adopted his brother-hating and inhuman opinion, should be considered by the church as strangers; but that they should heal such of the brethren as had fallen into misfortune, and should minister to them with the medicines of repentance.

3. There have reached us epistles of Cornelius, bishop of Rome, to Fabius, of the church at Antioch, which show what was done at the synod at Rome, and what seemed best to all those in Italy and Africa and the regions thereabout. Also other epistles, written in the Latin language, of Cyprian and those with him in Africa, which show that

they agreed as to the necessity of succoring those who had been tempted, and of cutting off from the Catholic Church the leader of the heresy and all that joined with him.

4. Another epistle of Cornelius, concerning the resolutions of the synod, is attached to these; and yet others, on the conduct of Novatus, from which it is proper for us to make selections, that any one who sees this work may know about him.

5. Cornelius informs Fabius what sort of a man Novatus was, in the following words: "But that you may know that a long time ago this remarkable man desired the episcopate, but kept this ambitious desire to himself and concealed it—using as a cloak for his rebellion those confessors who had adhered to him from the beginning—I desire to speak.

6. Maximus, one of our presbyters, and Urbanus, who twice gained the highest honor by confession, with Sidonius, and Celerinus, a man who by the grace of God most heroically endured all kinds of torture, and by the strength of his faith overcame the weakness of the flesh, and mightily conquered the adversary—these men found him out and detected his craft and duplicity, his perjuries and falsehoods, his unsociability and cruel friendship. And they returned to the holy church and proclaimed in the presence of many, both bishops and presbyters and a large number of the laity, all his craft and wickedness, which for a long time he had concealed. And this they did with lamentations land repentance, because through the persuasions of the crafty and malicious beast they had left the church for the time." A little farther on he says:

7. "How remarkable, beloved brother, the change and transformation which we have seen take place in him in a short time. For this most illustrious man, who bound himself with terrible oaths in nowise to seek the bishopric, suddenly appears a bishop as if thrown among us by some machine.

8. For this dogmatist, this defender of the doctrine of the Church, attempting to grasp and seize the episcopate, which had not been given him from above, chose two of his companions who had given up their own salvation. And he sent them to a small and insignificant corner of Italy, that there by some counterfeit argument he might deceive three bishops, who were rustic and very simple men. And they asserted positively and strongly that it was necessary that they should come quickly to Rome, in order that all the dissension which had arisen there might be appeased through their mediation, jointly with other bishops.

9. When they had come, being, as we have stated, very simple in the craft and artifice of the wicked, they were shut up with certain selected men like himself. And by the tenth hour, when they had become drunk and sick, he compelled them by force to confer on him the episcopate through a counterfeit and vain imposition of hands. Because it had not come to him, he avenged himself by craft and

treachery.

10. One of these bishops shortly after came back to the church, lamenting and confessing his transgression. And we communed with him as with a layman, all the people present interceding for him. And we ordained successors of the other bishops, and sent them to the places where they were.

11. This avenger of the Gospel then did not know that there should be one bishop in a catholic church; yet he was not ignorant (for how could he be?) that in it there were forty-six presbyters, seven deacons, seven sub-deacons, forty-two acolyths, fifty-two exorcists, readers, and janitors, and over fifteen hundred widows and persons in distress, all of whom the grace and kindness of the Master nourish.

12. But not even this great multitude, so necessary in the church, nor those who, through God's providence, were rich and full, together with the very many, even innumerable people, could turn him from such desperation and presumption and recall him to the Church."

13. Again, farther on, he adds these words: "Permit us to say further: On account of what works or conduct had he the assurance to contend for the episcopate? Was it that he had been brought up in the Church from the beginning, and had endured many conflicts in her behalf, and had passed through many and great dangers for religion? Truly this is not the fact.

14. But Satan, who entered and dwelt in him for a long time, became the occasion of his believing. Being delivered by the exorcists, he fell into a severe sickness; and as he seemed about to die, he received baptism by affusion, on the bed where he lay; if indeed we can say that such a one did receive it.

15. And when he was healed of his sickness he did not receive the other things which it is necessary to have according to the canon of the Church, even the being sealed by the bishop. And as he did not receive this, how could he receive the Holy Spirit?"

16. Shortly after he says again: "In the time of persecution, through cowardice and love of life, he denied that he was a presbyter. For when he was requested and en-treated by the deacons to come out of the chamber in which he had imprisoned himself and give aid to the brethren as far as was lawful and possible for a presbyter to assist those of the brethren who were in danger and needed help, he paid so little respect to the entreaties of the deacons that he went away and departed in anger. For he said that he no longer desired to be a presbyter, as he was an admirer of another philosophy."

17. Passing by a few things, he adds the following: "For this illustrious man forsook the Church of God, in which, when he believed, he was judged worthy of the presbyterate through the favor of the bishop who ordained him to the presbyterial office. This had been resisted by all the clergy and many of the laity; because it was unlawful

that one who had been affused on his bed on account of sickness as he had been should enter into any clerical office; but the bishop requested that he might be permitted to ordain this one only."

18. He adds to these yet another, the worst of all the man's offenses, as follows: "For when he has made the offerings, and distributed a part to each man, as he gives it he compels the wretched man to swear in place of the blessing. Holding his hands in both of his own, he will not release him until he has sworn in this manner (for I will give his own words): 'Swear to me by the body and blood of our Lord Jesus Christ that you will never forsake me and turn to Cornelius.'

19. And the unhappy man does not taste until he has called down imprecations on himself; and instead of saying Amen, as he takes the bread, he says, I will never return to Cornelius."

20. Farther on he says again: "But know that he has now been made bare and desolate; as the brethren leave him every day and return to the church. Moses also, the blessed martyr, who lately suffered among us a glorious and admirable martyrdom, while he was yet alive, beholding his boldness and folly, refused to commune with him and with the five presbyters who with him had separated themselves from the church."

21. At the close of his letter he gives a list of the bishops who had come to Rome and condemned the silliness of Novatus, with their names and the parish over which each of them presided.

22. He mentions also those who did not come to Rome, but who expressed by letters their agreement with the vote of these bishops, giving their names and the cities from which they severally sent them. Cornelius wrote these things to Fabius, bishop of Antioch.

Chapter XLIV.

DIONYSIUS' ACCOUNT OF SERAPION.

1. To this same Fabius, who seemed to lean somewhat toward this schism, Dionysius of Alexandria also wrote an epistle. He writes in this many other things concerning repentance, and relates the conflicts of those who had lately suffered martyrdom at Alexandria. After the other account he mentions a certain wonderful fact, which deserves a place in this work. It is as follows:

2. "I will give thee this one example which occurred among us. There was with us a certain Serapion, an aged believer who had lived for a long time blamelessly, but had fallen in the trial. He besought often, but no one gave heed to him, because he had sacrificed. But he became sick, and for three successive days continued speechless and senseless.

3. Having recovered somewhat on the fourth day he sent for his

daughter's son, and said, 'How long do you detain me, my child? I beseech you, make haste, and absolve me speedily. Call one of the presbyters to me.' And when he had said this, he became again speechless. And the boy ran to the presbyter. But it was night and he was sick, and therefore unable to come.

4. But as I had commanded that persons at the point of death, if they requested it, and especially if they had asked for it previously, should receive remission, that they might depart with a good hope, he gave the boy a small portion of the eucharist, telling him to soak it and let the drops fall into the old man's mouth.

5. The boy returned with it, and as he drew near, before he entered, Serapion again arousing, said, 'Thou art come, my child, and the presbyter could not come; but do quickly what he directed, and let me depart.' Then the boy soaked it and dropped it into his mouth. And when he had swallowed a little, immediately he gave up the ghost.

6. Is it not evident that he was preserved and his life continued till he was absolved, and, his sin having been blotted out, he could be acknowledged for the many good deeds which he had done?" Dionysius relates these things.

Chapter XLV.

AN EPISTLE OF DIONYSIUS TO NOVATUS.

1. But let us see how the same man addressed Novatus when he was disturbing the Roman brotherhood. As he pretended that some of the brethren were the occasion of his apostasy and schism, as if he had been forced by them to proceed as he had, observe the manner in which he writes to him: "Dionysius to his brother Novatus, greeting. If, as thou sayest, thou hast been led on unwillingly, thou wilt prove this if thou retirest willingly. For it were better to suffer everything, rather than divide the Church of God. Even martyrdom for the sake of preventing division would not be less glorious than for refusing to worship idols. Nay, to me it seems greater. For in the one case a man suffers martyrdom for the sake of his own soul; in the other case in behalf of the entire Church. And now if thou canst persuade or induce the brethren to come to unanimity, thy righteousness will be greater than thine error, and this will not be counted, but that will be praised. But if thou canst not prevail with the disobedient, at least save thine own soul. I pray that thou mayst fare well, maintaining peace in the Lord." This he wrote to Novatus.

Chapter XLVI.

OTHER EPISTLES OF DIONYSIUS.

1. He wrote also an epistle to the brethren in Egypt on Repentance. In this he sets forth what seemed proper to him in regard to those who had fallen, and he describes the classes of transgressions.

2. There is extant also a private letter on Repentance, which he wrote to Conon, bishop of the parish of Hermopolis, and another of an admonitory character, to his flock at Alexandria. Among them also is the one written to Origen on Martyrdom and to the brethren at Laodicea, of whom Thelymidres was bishop. He likewise sent one on Repentance to the brethren in Armenia, of whom Merozanes was bishop.

3. Besides all these, he wrote to Cornelius of Rome, when he had received from him an epistle against Novatus. He states in this that he had been invited by Helenus, bishop of Tarsus, in Cilicia, and the others who were with him, Firmilianus, bishop in Cappadocia, and Theoctistus, of Palestine, to meet them at the synod in Antioch, where some persons were endeavoring to establish the schism of Novatus.

4. Besides this he writes that he had been informed that Fabius had fallen asleep, and that Demetrianus had been appointed his successor in the episcopate of Antioch. He writes also in these words concerning the bishop of Jerusalem: "For the blessed Alexander having been confined in prison, passed away happily."

5. In addition to this there is extant also a certain other diaconal epistle of Dionysius, sent to those in Rome through Hippolytus. And he wrote another to them on Peace, and likewise on Repentance; and yet another to the confessors there who still held to the opinion of Novatus. He sent two more to the same persons after they had returned to the Church. And he communicated with many others by letters, which he has left behind him as a benefit in various ways to those who now diligently study his writings.

Book VII.

Introduction.

1. In this seventh book of the Church History, the great bishop of Alexandria, Dionysius, shall again assist us by his own words; relating the several affairs of his time in the epistles which he has left. I will begin with them.

Chapter I.

THE WICKEDNESS OF DECIUS AND GALLUS.

1. When Decius had reigned not quite two years, he was slain with his children, and Gallus succeeded him. At this time Origen died, being sixty-nine years of age. Dionysius, writing to Hermammon, speaks as follows of Gallus: "Gallus neither recognized the wickedness of Decius, nor considered what had destroyed him; but stumbled on the same stone, though it lay before his eyes. For when his reign was prosperous and affairs were proceeding according to his mind, he attacked the holy men who were interceding with God for his peace and welfare. Therefore with them he persecuted also their prayers in his behalf." So much concerning him.

Chapter II.

THE BISHOPS OF ROME IN THOSE TIMES.

1. Cornelius, having held the episcopate in the city of Rome about three years, was succeeded by Lucius. He died in less than eight months, and transmitted his office to Stephen. Dionysius wrote to him the first of his letters on baptism, as no small controversy had arisen as to whether those who had turned from any heresy should be purified by baptism. For the ancient custom prevailed in regard to such, that they should receive only the laying on of hands with prayers.

Chapter III.

CYPRIAN, AND THE BISHOPS WITH HIM, FIRST TAUGHT THAT IT WAS NECESSARY TO PURIFY BY BAPTISM THOSE CONVERTED FROM HERESY.

1. First of all, Cyprian, pastor of the parish of Carthage, maintained that they should not be received except they had been purified from their error by baptism. But Stephen considering it unnecessary to add any innovation contrary to the tradition which had been held from the beginning, was very indignant at this.

Chapter IV.

THE EPISTLES WHICH DIONYSIUS WROTE ON THIS SUBJECT.

1. Dionysius, therefore, having communicated with him extensively on this question by letter, finally showed him that since the persecution had abated, the churches everywhere had rejected the novelty of Novatus, and were at peace among themselves. He writes as follows:

Chapter V.

THE PEACE FOLLOWING THE PERSECUTION.

1. "But know now, my brethren, that all the churches throughout the East and beyond, which formerly were divided, have become united. And all the bishops everywhere are of one mind, and rejoice greatly in the peace which has come beyond expectation. Thus Demetrianus in Antioch, Theoctistus in Cæsarea, Mazabanes in Ælia, Marinus in Tyre (Alexander having fallen asleep), Heliodorus in Laodicea (Thelymidres being dead), Helenus in Tarsus, and all the churches of Cilicia, Firmilianus, and all Cappadocia. I have named only the more illustrious bishops, that I may not make my epistle too long and my words too burdensome.

2. And all Syria, and Arabia to which you send help when needed, and whither you have just written, Mesopotamia, Pontus, Bithynia, and in short all everywhere are rejoicing and glorifying God for the unanimity and brotherly love." Thus far Dionysius.

3. But Stephen, having filled his office two years, was succeeded by Xystus. Dionysius wrote him a second epistle on baptism, in which he shows him at the same time the opinion and judgment of Stephen and the other bishops, and speaks in this manner of Stephen:

4. "He therefore had written previously concerning Helenus and Firmilianus, and all those in Cilicia and Cappadocia and Galatia and the neighboring nations, saying that he would not commune with them for this same cause; namely, that they re-baptized heretics. But consider the importance of the matter.

5. For truly in the largest synods of the bishops, as I learn, decrees have been passed on this subject, that those coming over from heresies should be instructed, and then should be washed and cleansed from the filth of the old and impure leaven. And I wrote entreating him concerning all these things." Further on he says:

6. "I wrote also, at first in few words, recently in many, to our beloved fellow-presbyters, Dionysius and Philemon, who formerly had

held the same opinion as Stephen, and had written to me on the same matters." So much in regard to the above-mentioned controversy.

Chapter VI.

THE HERESY OF SABELLIUS.

1. He refers also in the same letter to the heretical teachings of Sabellius, which were in his time becoming prominent, and says: "For concerning the doctrine now agitated in Ptolemais of Pentapolis— which is impious and marked by great blasphemy against the Almighty God, the Father, and our Lord Jesus Christ, and contains much unbelief respecting his Only Begotten Son and the first-born of every creature, the Word which became man, and a want of perception of the Holy Spirit—as there came to me communications from both sides and brethren discussing the matter, I wrote certain letters treating the subject as instructively as, by the help. of God, I was able. Of these I send thee copies."

Chapter VII.

THE ABOMINABLE ERROR OF THE HERETICS; THE DIVINE VISION OF DIONYSIUS; AND THE ECCLESIASTICAL CANON WHICH HE RECEIVED.

1. In the third epistle on baptism which this same Dionysius wrote to Philemon, the Roman presbyter, he relates the following: "But I examined the works and traditions of the heretics, defiling my mind for a little time with their abominable opinions, but receiving this benefit from them, that I refuted them by myself, and detested them all the more.

2. And when a certain brother among the presbyters restrained me, fearing that I should be carried away with the filth of their wickedness (for it would defile my soul),—in which also, as I perceived, he spoke the truth,—a vision sent from God came and strengthened me.

3. And the word which came to me commanded me, saying distinctly, 'Read everything which thou canst take in hand, for thou art able to correct and prove all; and this has been to thee from the beginning the cause of thy faith.' I received the vision as agreeing with the apostolic word, which says to them that are stronger, 'Be skillful money-changers.'"

4. Then after saying some things concerning all the heresies he adds: "I received this rule and ordinance from our blessed father, Heraclas. For those who came over from heresies, although they had apostatized from the Church—or rather had not apostatized, but seemed

to meet with them, yet were charged with resorting to some false teacher—when he, had expelled them from the Church he did not receive them back, though they entreated for it, until they had publicly reported all things which they had heard from their adversaries; but then he received them without requiring of them another baptism. For they had formerly received the Holy Spirit from him."

5. Again, after treating the question thoroughly, he adds: "I have learned also that this is not a novel practice introduced in Africa alone, but that even long ago in the times of the bishops before us this opinion has been adopted in the most populous churches, and in synods of the brethren in Iconium and Synnada, and by many others. To overturn their counsels and throw them into strife and contention, I cannot endure. For it is said? 'Thou shalt not remove thy neighbor's landmark, which thy fathers have set.'"

6. His fourth epistle on baptism was written to Dionysius of Rome, who was then a presbyter, but not long after received the episcopate of that church. It is evident from what is stated of him by Dionysius of Alexandria, that he also was a learned and admirable man. Among other things he writes to him as follows concerning Novatus:

Chapter VIII.

THE HETERODOXY OF NOVATUS.

1. "For with good reason do we feel hatred toward Novatian, who has sundered the Church and drawn some of the brethren into impiety and blasphemy, and has introduced impious teaching concerning God, and has calumniated our most compassionate Lord Jesus Christ as unmerciful. And besides all this he rejects the holy baptism, and overturns the faith and confession which precede it, and entirely banishes from them the Holy Ghost, if indeed there was any hope that he would remain or return to them."

Chapter IX.

THE UNGODLY BAPTISM OF THE HERETICS.

1. His fifth epistle was written to Xystus, bishop of Rome. In this, after saying much against the heretics, he relates a certain occurrence of his time as follows: "For truly, brother, I am in need of counsel, and I ask thy judgment concerning a certain matter which has come to me, fearing that I may be in error.

2. For one of the brethren that assemble, who has long been considered a believer, and who, before my ordination, and I think before the appointment of the blessed Heraclas, was a member of the

congregation, was present with those who were recently baptized. And when he heard the questions and answers, he came to me weeping, and bewailing himself; and falling at my feet he acknowledged and protested that the baptism with which he had been baptized among the heretics was not of this character, nor in any respect like this, because it was full of impiety and blasphemy.

3. And he said that his soul was now pierced with sorrow, and that he had not confidence to lift his eyes to God, because he had set out from those impious words and deeds. And on this account he besought that he might receive this most perfect purification, and reception and grace.

4. But I did not dare to do this; and said that his long communion was sufficient for this. For I should not dare to renew from the beginning one who had heard the giving of thanks and joined in repeating the Amen; who had stood by the table and had stretched forth his hands to receive the blessed food; and who had received it, and partaken for a long while of the body and blood of our Lord Jesus Christ. But I exhorted him to be of good courage, and to approach the partaking of the saints with firm faith and good hope.

5. But he does not cease lamenting, and he shudders to approach the table, and scarcely, though entreated, does he dare to be present at the prayers."

6. Besides these there is also extant another epistle of the same man on baptism, addressed by him and his parish to Xystus and the church at Rome. In this he considers the question then agitated with extended argument. And there is extant yet another after these, addressed to Dionysius of Rome, concerning Lucian. So much with reference to these.

Chapter X.

VALERIAN AND THE PERSECUTION UNDER HIM.

1. Gallus and the other rulers, having held the government less than two years, were overthrown, and Valerian, with his son Gallienus, received the empire.

2. The circumstances which Dionysius relates of him we may learn from his epistle to Hermammon, in which he gives the following account: "And in like manner it is revealed to John; 'For there was given to him,' he says, 'a mouth speaking great things and blasphemy; and there was given unto him authority and forty and two months.'

3. It is wonderful that both of these things occurred under Valerian; and it is the more remarkable in this case when we consider his previous conduct, for he had been mild and friendly toward the men of God, for none of the emperors before him had treated them so kindly

and favorably; and not even those who were said openly to be Christians received them with such manifest hospitality and friendliness as he did at the beginning of his reign. For his entire house was filled with pious persons and was a church of God.

4. But the teacher and ruler of the synagogue of the Magi from Egypt persuaded him to change his course, urging him to slay and persecute pure and holy men because they opposed and hindered the corrupt and abominable incantations. For there are and there were men who, being present and being seen, though they only breathed and spoke, were able to scatter the counsels of the sinful demons. And he induced him to practice initiations and abominable sorceries and to offer unacceptable sacrifices; to slay innumerable children and to sacrifice the offspring of unhappy fathers; to divide the bowels of new-born babes and to mutilate and cut to pieces the creatures of God, as if by suck practices they could attain happiness."

5. He adds to this the following: "Splendid indeed were the thank-offerings which Macrianus brought them for the empire which was the object of his hopes. He is said to have been formerly the emperor's general finance minister; yet he did nothing praiseworthy or of general benefit, but fell under the prophetic saying, 'Woe unto those who prophesy from their own heart and do not consider the general good.'

6. For he did not perceive the general Providence, nor did he look for the judgment of Him who is before all, and through all, and over all. Wherefore he became an enemy of his Catholic Church, and alienated and estranged himself from the compassion of God, and fled as far as possible from his salvation. In this he showed the truth of his own name."

7. And again, farther on he says: "For Valerian, being instigated to such acts by this man, was given over to insults and reproaches, according to what was said by Isaiah: 'They have chosen their own ways and their abominations in which their soul delighted; I also will choose their delusions and will render unto them their sins.'

8. But this man madly desired the kingdom though unworthy of it, and being unable to put the royal garment on his crippled body, set forward his two sons to bear their father's sins. For concerning them the declaration which God spoke was plain, 'Visiting the iniquities of the fathers upon the children unto the third and fourth generation of them that hate me.'

9. For heaping on the heads of his sons his own evil desires, in which he had met with success, he wiped off upon them his own wickedness and hatred toward God." Dionysius relates these things concerning Valerian.

Chapter XI.

THE EVENTS WHICH HAPPENED AT THIS TIME
TO DIONYSIUS AND THOSE IN EGYPT.

1. But as regards the persecution which prevailed so fiercely in his reign, and the sufferings which Dionysius with others endured on account of piety toward the God of the universe, his own words shall show, which he wrote in answer to Germanus, a contemporary bishop who was endeavoring to slander him. His statement is as follows:

2. "Truly I am in danger of falling into great folly and stupidity through being forced to relate the wonderful providence of God toward us. But since it is said that 'it is good to keep close the secret of a king, but it is honorable to reveal the works of God,' I will join issue with the violence of Germanus.

3. I went not alone to Æmilianus; but my fellow-presbyter, Maximus, and the deacons Faustus, Eusebius, and Chæremon, and a brother who was present from Rome, went with me.

4. But Æmilianus did not at first say to me: 'Hold no assemblies;' for this was superfluous to him, and the last thing to one who was seeking to accomplish the first. For he was not concerned about our assembling, but that we ourselves should not be Christians. And he commanded me to give this up; supposing if I turned from it, the others also would follow me.

5. But I answered him, neither unsuitably nor in many words: 'We must obey God rather than men.' And I testified openly that I worshiped the one only God, and no other; and that I would not turn from this nor would I ever cease to be a Christian. Thereupon he commanded us to go to a village near the desert, called Cephro.

6. But listen to the very words which were spoken on both sides, as they were recorded: "Dionysius, Faustus, Maximus, Marcellus, and Chæremon being arraigned, Æmilianus the prefect said:

7. 'I have reasoned verbally with you concerning the clemency which our rulers have shown to you; for they have given you the opportunity to save yourselves, if you will turn to that which is according to nature, and worship the gods that preserve their empire, and forget those that are contrary to nature. What then do you say to this? For I do not think that you will be ungrateful for their kindness, since they would turn you to a better course.'

8. Dionysius replied: 'Not all people worship all gods; but each one those whom he approves. We therefore reverence and worship the one God, the Maker of all; who hath given the empire to the divinely favored and august Valerian and Gallienus; and we pray to him continually for their empire, that it may remain unshaken.'

9. Æmilianus, the prefect, said to them: 'But who forbids you to worship him, if he is a god, together with those who are gods by nature. For ye have been commanded to reverence the gods, and the gods whom all know.' Dionysius answered: 'We worship no other.'

10. Æmilianus, the prefect, said to them: 'I see that you are at once ungrateful, and insensible to the kindness of our sovereigns. Wherefore ye shall not remain in this city. But ye shall be sent into the regions of Libya, to a place called Cephro. For I have chosen this place at the command of our sovereigns, and it shall by no means be permitted you or any others, either to hold assemblies, or to enter into the so-called cemeteries.

11. But if any one shall be seen without the place which I have commanded, or be found in any assembly, he will bring peril on himself. For suitable punishment shall not fail. Go, therefore where ye have been ordered.' "And he hastened me away, though I was sick, not granting even a day's respite. What opportunity then did I have, either to hold assemblies, or not to hold them?"

12. Farther on he says: "But through the help of the Lord we did not give up the open assembly. But I called together the more diligently those who were in the city, as if I were with them; being, so to speak, 'absent in body but present in spirit.' But in Cephro a large church gathered with us of the brethren that followed us from the city, and those that joined us from Egypt; and there 'God opened unto us a door for the Word.'

13. At first we were persecuted and stoned; but afterwards not a few of the heathen forsook the idols and turned to God. For until this time they had not heard the Word, since it was then first sown by us.

14. And as if God had brought us to them for this purpose, when we had performed this ministry he transferred us to another place. For Æmilianus, as it appeared, desired to transport us to rougher and more Libyan-like places; so he commanded them to assemble from all quarters in Mareotis, and assigned to them different villages throughout the country. But he ordered us to be placed nearer the highway that we might be seized first. For evidently he arranged and prepared matters so that whenever he wished to seize us he could take all of us without difficulty.

15. When I was first ordered to go to Cephro I did not know where the place was, and had scarcely ever heard the name; yet I went readily and cheerfully. But when I was told that I was to remove to the district of Colluthion, those who were present know how I was affected.

16. For here I will accuse myself. At first I was grieved and greatly disturbed; for though these places were better known and more familiar to us, yet the country was said to be destitute of brethren and of men of character, and to be exposed to the annoyances of travelers and incursions of robbers.

17. But I was comforted when the brethren reminded me that it was nearer the city, and that while Cephro afforded us much intercourse with the brethren from Egypt, so that we were able to extend the Church more widely, as this place was nearer the city we should enjoy more frequently the sight of those who were truly beloved and most closely related and dearest to us. For they would come and remain, and special meetings could be held, as in the more remote suburbs. And thus it turned out." After other matters he writes again as follows of the things which happened to him:

18. "Germanus indeed boasts of many confessions. He can speak forsooth of many adversities which he himself has endured. But is he able to reckon up as many as we can, of sentences, confiscations, proscriptions, plundering of goods, loss of dignities, contempt of worldly glory, disregard for the flatteries of governors and of councilors, and patient endurance of the threats of opponents, of outcries, of perils and persecutions, and wandering and distress, and all kinds of tribulation, such as came upon me under Decius and Sabinus, and such as continue even now under Æmilianus? But where has Germanus been seen? And what account is there of him?

19. But I turn from this great folly into which I am falling on account of Germanus. And for the same reason I desist from giving to the brethren who know it an account of everything which took place."

20. The same writer also in the epistle to! Domitius and Didymus mentions some particulars of the persecution as follows: "As our people are many and unknown to you, it would be superfluous to give their names; but understand that men and women, young and old, maidens and matrons, soldiers and civilians, of every race and age, some by scourging and fire, others by the sword, have conquered in the strife and received their crowns.

21. But in the case of some a very long time was not sufficient to make them appear acceptable to the Lord; as, indeed, it seems also in my own case, that sufficient time has not yet elapsed. Wherefore he has retained me for the time which he knows to be fitting, saying, 'In an acceptable time have I heard thee, and in a day of salvation have I helped thee.'

22. For as you have inquired of our affairs and desire us to tell you how we are situated, you have heard fully that when we—that is, myself and Gaius and Faustus and Peter and Paul—were led away as prisoners by a centurion and magistrates, with their soldiers and servants, certain persons from Mareotis came and dragged us away by force, as we were unwilling to follow them.

23. But now I and Gaius and Peter are alone, deprived of the other brethren, and shut up in a desert and dry place in Libya, three days' journey from Parætonium."

24. He says farther on: "The presbyters, Maximus, Dioscorus,

Demetrius, and Lucius concealed themselves in the city, and visited the brethren secretly; for Faustinus and Aquila, who are more prominent in the world, are wandering in Egypt. But the deacons, Faustus, Eusebius, and Chæremon, have survived those who died in the pestilence. Eusebius is one whom God has strengthened. and endowed from the first to fulfill energetically the ministrations for the imprisoned confessors, and to attend to the dangerous task of preparing for burial the bodies of the perfected and blessed martyrs.

25. For as I have said before, unto the present time the governor continues to put to death in a cruel manner those who are brought to trial. And he destroys some with tortures, and wastes others away with imprisonment and bonds; and he suffers no one to go near them, and investigates whether any one does so. Nevertheless God gives relief to the afflicted through the zeal and persistence of the brethren."

26. Thus far Dionysius. But it should be known that Eusebius, whom he calls a deacon, shortly afterward became bishop of the church of Laodicea in Syria; and Maximus, of whom he speaks as being then a presbyter, succeeded Dionysius himself as bishop of Alexandria. But the Faustus who was with him, and who at that time was distinguished for his confession, was preserved until the persecution in our day, when being very old and full of days, he closed his life by martyrdom, being beheaded. But such are the things which happened at that time to Dionysius.

Chapter XII.

THE MARTYRS IN CÆSAREA IN PALESTINE.

1. During the above-mentioned persecution under Valerian, three men in Cæsarea in Palestine, being conspicuous in their confession of Christ, were adorned with divine martyrdom, becoming food for wild beasts. One of them was called Priscus, another Malchus, and the name of the third was Alexander. They say that these men, who lived in the country, acted at first in a cowardly manner, as if they were careless and thoughtless. For when the opportunity was given to those who longed for the prize with heavenly desire, they treated it lightly, lest they should seize the Crown of martyrdom prematurely. But having deliberated on the matter, they hastened to Cæsarea, and went before the judge and met the end we have mentioned. They relate that besides these, in the same persecution and the same city, a certain woman endured a similar conflict. But it is reported that she belonged to the sect of Marcion.

Chapter XIII.

THE PEACE UNDER GALLIENUS.

1. Shortly after this Valerian was reduced to slavery by the barbarians, and his son having become sole ruler, conducted the government more prudently. He immediately restrained the persecution against us by public proclamations, and directed the bishops to perform in freedom their customary duties, in a rescript which ran as follows:

2. "The Emperor Cæsar Publius Licinius Gallienus, Pius, Felix, Augustus, to Dionysius, Pinnas, Demetrius, and the other bishops. I have ordered the bounty of my gift to be declared through all the world, that they may depart from the places of religious worship. And for this purpose you may use this copy of my rescript, that no one may molest you. And this which you are now enabled lawfully to do, has already for a long time been conceded by me. Therefore Aurelius Cyrenius, who is the chief administrator of affairs, will observe this ordinance which I have given."

3. I have given this in a translation from the Latin, that it may be more readily understood. Another decree of his is extant addressed to other bishops, permitting them to take possession again of the so-called cemeteries.

Chapter XIV.

THE BISHOPS THAT FLOURISHED AT THAT TIME.

1. At that time Xystus was still presiding over the church of Rome, and Demetrianus, successor of Fabius, over the church of Antioch, and Firmilianus over that of Cæsarea in Cappadocia; and besides these, Gregory and his brother Athenodorus, friends of Origen, were presiding over the churches in Pontus; and Theoctistus of Cæsarea in Palestine having died, Domnus received the episcopate there. He held it but a short time, and Theotecnus, our contemporary, succeeded him. He also was a member of Origen's school. But in Jerusalem, after the death of Mazabanes, Hymenæus, who has been celebrated among us for a great many years, succeeded to his seat.

Chapter XV.

THE MARTYRDOM OF MARINUS AT CÆSAREA.

1. At this time, when the peace of the churches had been everywhere restored, Marinus in Cæsarea in Palestine, who was honored for his military deeds, and illustrious by virtue of family and wealth, was beheaded for his testimony to Christ, on the following account.

2. The vine-branch is a certain mark of honor among the Romans, and those who obtain it become, they say, centurions. A place being vacated, the order of succession called Marinus to this position. But when he was about to receive the honor, another person came before the tribunal and claimed that it was not legal, according to the ancient laws, for him to receive the Roman dignity, as he was a Christian and did not sacrifice to the emperors; but that the office belonged rather to him.

3. Thereupon the judge, whose name was Achæus, being disturbed, first asked what opinion Marinus held. And when he perceived that he continually confessed himself a Christian, he gave him three hours for reflection.

4. When he came out from the tribunal, Theotecnus, the bishop there, took him aside and conversed with him, and taking his hand led him into the church. And standing with him within, in the sanctuary, he raised his cloak a little, and pointed to the sword that hung by his side; and at the same time he placed before him the Scripture of the divine Gospels, and told him to choose which of the two he wished. And without hesitation he reached forth his right hand, and took the divine Scripture. "Hold fast then," says Theotecnus to him, "hold fast to God, and strengthened by him mayest thou obtain what thou hast chosen, and go in peace."

5. Immediately on his return the herald cried out calling him to the tribunal, for the appointed time was already completed. And standing before the tribunal, and manifesting greater zeal for the faith, immediately, as he was, he was led away and finished his course by death.

Chapter XVI.

STORY IN REGARD TO ASTYRIUS.

1. Astyrius also is commemorated on account of his pious boldness in connection with this affair. He was a Roman of senatorial rank, and in favor with the emperors, and well known to all on account of his noble birth and wealth. Being present at the martyr's death, he took his body away on his shoulder, and arraying him in a splendid and costly garment, prepared him for the grave in a magnificent manner, and gave him fitting burial. The friends of this man, that remain to our day, relate many other facts, concerning him.

Chapter XVII.

THE SIGNS AT PANEAS OF THE GREAT MIGHT OF OUR SAVIOUR.

1. Among these is also the following wonder. At Cæsarea Philippi, which the Phœnicia ns call Paneas, springs are shown at the foot of the Mountain Panius, out of which the Jordan flows. They say that on a certain feast day, a victim was thrown in, and that through the power of the demon it marvelously disappeared and that which happened was a famous wonder to those who were present. Astyrius was once there when these things were done, and seeing the multitude astonished at the affair, he pitied their delusion; and looking up to heaven he supplicated the God over all through Christ, that he would rebuke the demon who deceived the people, and bring the men's delusion to an end. And they say that when he had prayed thus, immediately the sacrifice floated on the surface of the fountain. And thus the miracle departed; and no wonder was ever afterward performed at the place.

Chapter XVIII.

THE STATUE WHICH THE WOMAN WITH AN ISSUE OF BLOOD ERECTED.

1. Since I have mentioned this city I do not think it proper to omit an account which is worthy of record for posterity. For they say that the woman with an issue of blood, who, as we learn from the sacred Gospel, received from our Saviour deliverance from her affliction, came from this place, and that her house is shown in the city, and that remarkable memorials of the kindness of the Saviour to her remain there.

2. For there stands upon an elevated stone, by the gates of her house, a brazen image of a woman kneeling, with her hands stretched out, as if she were praying. Opposite this is another upright image of a man, made of the same material, clothed decently in a double cloak, and extending his hand toward the woman. At his feet, beside the statue itself, is a certain strange plant, which climbs up to the hem of the brazen cloak, and is a remedy for all kinds of diseases.

3. They say that this statue is an image of Jesus. It has remained to our day, so that we ourselves also saw it when we were staying in the city.

4. Nor is it strange that those of the Gentiles who, of old, were benefited by our Saviour, should have done such things, since we have learned also that the likenesses of his apostles Paul and Peter, and of Christ himself, are preserved in paintings, the ancients being accustomed, as it is likely, according to a habit of the Gentiles, to pay this kind of honor indiscriminately to those regarded by them as deliverers.

Chapter XIX.

THE EPISCOPAL CHAIR OF JAMES.

1. The chair of James, who first received the episcopate of the church at Jerusalem from the Saviour himself and the apostles, and who, as the divine records show, was called a brother of Christ, has been preserved until now, the brethren who have followed him in succession there exhibiting clearly to all the reverence which both those of old times and those of our own day maintained and do maintain for holy men on account of their piety. So much as to this matter.

Chapter XX.

THE FESTAL EPISTLES OF DIONYSIUS, IN WHICH HE ALSO GIVES A PASCHAL CANON.

1. Dionysius, besides his epistles already mentioned, wrote at that time also his extant Festal Epistles, in which he uses words of panegyric respecting the passover feast. He addressed one of these to Flavius, and another to Domitius and Didymus, in which he sets forth a canon of eight years, maintaining that it is not proper to observe the paschal feast until after the vernal equinox. Besides these he sent another epistle to his fellow-presbyters in Alexandria, as well as various others to different persons while the persecution was still prevailing.

Chapter XXI.

THE OCCURRENCES AT ALEXANDRIA.

1. Peace had but just been restored when he returned to Alexandria; but as sedition and war broke out again, rendering it impossible if or him to oversee all the brethren, separated in different places by the insurrection, at the feast of the passover, as if he were still an exile from Alexandria, he addressed them again by letter.

2. And in another festal epistle written later to Hierax, a bishop in Egypt, he mentions the sedition then prevailing in Alexandria, as follows: "What wonder is it that it is difficult for me to communicate by letters with those who live far away, when it is beyond my power even to reason with myself, or to take counsel for my own life?

3. Truly I need to send letters to those who are as my own bowels, dwelling in one home, and brethren of one soul, and citizens of the same church; but how to send them I cannot tell. For it would be easier for one to go, not only beyond the limits of the province, but even from the East to the West, than from Alexandria to Alexandria itself.

4. For the very heart of the city is more intricate and impassable than that great and trackless desert which Israel traversed for two generations. And our smooth and waveless harbors have become like the sea, divided and walled up, through which Israel drove and in whose highway the Egyptians were overwhelmed. For often from the slaughters there committed they appear like the Red Sea.

5. And the river which flows by the city has sometimes seemed drier than the waterless desert, and more parched than that in which Israel, as they passed through it, so suffered for thirst, that they cried out against Moses, and the water flowed for them from the steep rock, through him who alone doeth wonders.

6. Again it has overflowed so greatly as to flood all the surrounding country, and the roads and the fields; threatening to bring back the deluge of water that occurred in the days of Noah. And it flows along, polluted always with blood and slaughter and drownings, as it became for Pharaoh through the agency of Moses, when he changed it into blood, and it stank.

7. And what other water could purify the water which purifies everything? How could the ocean, so great and impassable for men, if poured into it, cleanse this bitter sea? Or how could the great river which flowed out of Eden, if it poured the four heads into which it is divided into the one of Geon, wash away this pollution?

8. Or when can the air poisoned by these noxious exhalations become pure? For such vapors arise from the earth, and winds from the sea, and breezes from the river, and mists from the harbors, that the

dews are, as it were, discharges from dead bodies putrefying in all the elements around us.

9. Yet men wonder and cannot understand whence these continuous pestilences; whence these severe sicknesses; whence these deadly diseases of all kinds; whence this various and vast human destruction; why this great city no longer contains as many inhabitants, from tender infants to those most advanced in life, as it formerly contained of those whom it called hearty old men. But the men from forty to seventy years of age were then so much more numerous that their number cannot now be filled out, even when those from fourteen to eighty years are enrolled and registered for the public allowance of food.

10. And the youngest in appearance have become, as it were, of equal age with those who formerly were the oldest. But though they see the race of men thus constantly diminishing and wasting away, and though their complete destruction is increasing and advancing, they do not tremble."

Chapter XXII.

THE PESTILENCE WHICH CAME UPON THEM.

1. After these events a pestilential disease followed the war, and at the approach of the feast he wrote again to the brethren, describing the sufferings consequent upon this calamity.

2. "To other men the present might not seem to be a suitable time for a festival. Nor indeed is this or any other time suitable for them; neither sorrowful times, nor even such as might be thought especially cheerful. Now, indeed, everything is tears and every one is mourning, and wailings resound daily through the city because of the multitude of the dead and dying.

3. For as it was written of the firstborn of the Egyptians, so now 'there has arisen a great cry, for there is not a house where there is not one dead.' And would that this were all!

4. For many terrible things have happened already. First, they drove us out; and when alone, and persecuted, and put to death by all, even then we kept the feast. And every place of affliction was to us a place of festival: field, desert, ship, inn, prison; but the perfected martyrs kept the most joyous festival of all, feasting in heaven.

5. After these things war and famine followed, which we endured in common with the heathen. But we bore alone those things with which they afflicted us, and at the same time we experienced also the effects of what they inflicted upon and suffered from one another; and again, we rejoiced in the peace of Christ, which he gave to us alone.

6. "But after both we and they had enjoyed a very brief season of

rest this pestilence assailed us; to them more dreadful than any dread, and more intolerable than any other calamity; and, as one of their own writers has said, the only thing which prevails over all hope. But to us this was not so, but no less than the other things was it an exercise and probation. For it did not keep aloof even from us, but the heathen it assailed more severely."

7. Farther on he adds: "The most of our brethren were unsparing in their exceeding love and brotherly kindness. They held fast to each other and visited the sick fearlessly, and ministered to them continually, serving them in Christ. And they died with them most joyfully, taking the affliction of others, and drawing the sickness from their neighbors to themselves and willingly receiving their pains. And many who cared for the sick and gave strength to others died themselves having transferred to themselves their death. And the popular saying which always seems a mere expression of courtesy, they then made real in action, taking their departure as the others' 'offscouring.'

8. "Truly the best of our brethren departed from life in this manner, including some presbyters and deacons and those of the people who had the highest reputation; so that this form of death, through the great piety and strong faith it exhibited, seemed to lack nothing of martyrdom.

9. And they took the bodies of the saints in their open hands and in their bosoms, and closed their eyes and their mouths; and they bore them away on their shoulders and laid them out; and they clung to them and embraced them; and they prepared them suitably with washings and garments. And after a little they received like treatment themselves, for the survivors were continually following those who had gone before them.

10. "But with the heathen everything was quite otherwise. They deserted those who began to be sick, and fled from their dearest friends. And they cast them out into the streets when they were half dead, and left the dead like refuse, unburied. They shunned any participation or fellowship with death; which yet, with all their precautions, it was not easy for them to escape."

11. After this epistle, when peace had been restored to the city, he wrote another festal letter to the brethren in Egypt, and again several others besides this. And there is also a certain one extant On the Sabbath, and another On Exercise.

12. Moreover, he wrote again an epistle to Hermammon and the brethren in Egypt, describing at length the wickedness of Decius and his successors, and mentioning the peace under Gallienus.

Chapter XXIII.

THE REIGN OF GALLIENUS.

1. But there is nothing like hearing his own words, which are as follows: "Then he, having betrayed one of the emperors that preceded him, and made war on the other, perished with his whole family speedily and utterly. But Gallienus was proclaimed and universally acknowledged at once an old emperor and a new, being before them and continuing after them.

2. For according to the word spoken by the prophet Isaiah, 'Behold the things from the beginning have come to pass, and new things shall now arise.' For as a cloud passing over the sun's rays and obscuring them for a little time hides it and appears in its place; but when the cloud has passed by or is dissipated, the sun which had risen before appears again; so Macrianus who put himself forward and approached the existing empire of Gallienus, is not, since he never was. But the other is just as he was.

3. And his kingdom, as if it had cast aside old age, and had been purified from the former wickedness, now blossoms out more vigorously, and is seen and heard farther, and extends in all directions."

4. He then indicates the time at which he wrote this in the following words: "It occurs to me again to review the days of the imperial years. For I perceive that those most impious men, though they have been famous, yet in a short time have become nameless. But the holier and more godly prince, having passed the seventh year, is now completing the ninth, in which we shall keep the feast."

Chapter XXIV.

NEPOS AND HIS SCHISM.

1. Besides all these the two books on the Promises were prepared by him. The occasion of these was Nepos, a bishop in Egypt, who taught that the promises to the holy men in the Divine Scriptures should be understood in a more Jewish manner, and that there would be a certain millennium of bodily luxury upon this earth.

2. As he thought that he could establish his private opinion by the Revelation of John, he wrote a book on this subject, entitled Refutation of Allegorists.

3. Dionysius opposes this in his books on the Promises. In the first he gives his own opinion of the dogma; and in the second he treats of the Revelation of John, and mentioning Nepos at the beginning, writes of him in this manner:

4. "But since they bring forward a certain work of Nepos, on which they rely confidently, as if it proved beyond dispute that there will be a reign of Christ upon earth, I confess that in many other respects I approve and love Nepos, for his faith and industry and diligence in the Scriptures, and for his extensive psalmody, with which many of the brethren are still delighted; and I hold him in the more reverence because he has gone to rest before us. But the truth should be loved and honored most of all. And while we should praise and approve ungrudgingly what is said aright, we ought to examine and correct what does not seem to have been written soundly.

5. Were he present to state his opinion orally, mere unwritten discussion, persuading and reconciling those who are opposed by question and answer, would be sufficient. But as some think his work very plausible, and as certain teachers regard the law and prophets as of no consequence, and do not follow the Gospels, and treat lightly the apostolic epistles, while they make promises as to the teaching of this work as if it were some great hidden mystery, and do not permit our simpler brethren to have any sublime and lofty thoughts concerning the glorious and truly divine appearing of our Lord, and our resurrection from the dead, and our being gathered together unto him, and made like him, but on the contrary lead them to hope for small and mortal things in the kingdom of God, and for things such as exist now—since this is the case, it is necessary that we should dispute with our brother Nepos as if he were present." Farther on he says:

6. "When I was in the district of Arsinoe, where, as you know, this doctrine has prevailed for a long time, so that schisms and apostasies of entire churches have resulted, I called together the presbyters and teachers of the brethren in the villages—such brethren as wished being also present—and I exhorted them to make a public examination of this question.

7. Accordingly when they brought me this book, as if it were a weapon and fortress impregnable, sitting with them from morning till evening for three successive days, I endeavored to correct what was written in it.

8. And I rejoiced over the constancy, sincerity, docility, and intelligence of the brethren, as we considered in order and with moderation the questions and the difficulties and the points of agreement. And we abstained from defending in every manner and contentiously the opinions which we had once held, unless they appeared to be correct. Nor did we evade objections, but we endeavored as far as possible to hold to and confirm the things which lay before us, and if the reason given satisfied us, we were not ashamed to change our opinions and agree with others; but on the contrary, conscientiously and sincerely, and with hearts laid open before God, we accepted whatever was established by the proofs and teachings of the

Holy Scriptures.

9. And finally the author and mover of this teaching, who was called Coracion, in the hearing of all the brethren that were present, acknowledged and testified to us that he would no longer hold this opinion, nor discuss it, nor mention nor teach it, as he was fully convinced by the arguments against it. And some of the other brethren expressed their gratification at the conference, and at the spirit of conciliation and harmony which all had manifested."

Chapter XXV.

THE APOCALYPSE OF JOHN.

1. Afterward he speaks in this manner of the Apocalypse of John. "Some before us have set aside and rejected the book altogether, criticising it chapter by chapter, and pronouncing it without sense or argument, and maintaining that the title is fraudulent.

2. For they say that it is not the work of John, nor is it a revelation, because it is covered thickly and densely by a vail of obscurity. And they affirm that none of the apostles, rend none of the saints, nor any one in the Church is its author, but that Cerinthus, who founded the sect which was called after him the Cerinthian, desiring reputable authority for his fiction, prefixed the name.

3. For the doctrine which he taught was this: that the kingdom of Christ will be an earthly one. And as he was himself devoted to the pleasures of the body and altogether sensual in his nature, he dreamed that that kingdom would consist in those things which he desired, namely, in the delights of the belly and of sexual passion; that is to say, in eating and drinking and marrying, and in festivals and sacrifices and the slaying of victims, under the guise of which he thought he could indulge his appetites with a better grace.

4. "But I could not venture to reject the book, as many brethren hold it in high esteem. But I suppose that it is beyond my comprehension, and that there is a certain concealed and more wonderful meaning in every part. For if I do not understand I suspect that a deeper sense lies beneath the words.

5. I do not measure and judge them by my own reason, but leaving the more to faith I regard them as too high for me to grasp. And I do not reject what I cannot comprehend, but rather wonder because I do not understand it."

6. After this he examines the entire Book of Revelation, and having proved that it is impossible to understand it according to the literal sense, proceeds as follows: "Having finished all the prophecy, so to speak, the prophet pronounces those blessed who shall observe it, and also himself. For he says, 'Blessed is he that keepeth the words of

the prophecy of this book, and I, John, who saw and heard these things.'

7. Therefore that he was called John, and that this book is the work of one John, I do not deny. And I agree also that it is the work of a holy and inspired man. But I cannot readily admit that he was the apostle, the son of Zebedee, the brother of James, by whom the Gospel of John and the Catholic Epistle were written.

8. For I judge from the character of both, and the forms of expression, and the entire execution of the book, that it is not his. For the evangelist nowhere gives his name, or proclaims himself, either in the Gospel or Epistle."

9. Farther on he adds: "But John never speaks as if referring to himself, or as if referring to another person. But the author of the Apocalypse introduces himself at the very beginning: 'The Revelation of Jesus Christ, which he gave him to show unto his servants quickly; and he sent and signified it by his angel unto his servant John, who bare witness of the word of God and of his testimony, even of all things that he saw.'

10. Then he writes also an epistle: 'John to the seven churches which are in Asia, grace be with you, and peace.' But the evangelist did not prefix his name even to the Catholic Epistle; but without introduction he begins with the mystery of the divine revelation itself: 'That which was from the beginning, which we have heard, which we have seen with our eyes.' For because of such a revelation the Lord also blessed Peter, saying, 'Blessed art thou, Simon Bar-Jonah, for flesh and blood hath not revealed it unto thee, but my heavenly Father.'

11. But neither in the reputed second or third epistle of John, though they are very short, does the name John appear; but there is written the anonymous phrase, 'the eider.' But this author did not consider it sufficient to give his name once and to proceed with his work; but he takes it up again: 'I, John, who also am your brother and companion in tribulation, and in the kingdom and in the patience of Jesus Christ, was in the isle that is called Patmos for the Word of God and the testimony of Jesus.' And toward the close he speaks thus: 'Blessed is he that keepeth the words of the prophecy of this book, and I, John, who saw and heard these things.'

12. "But that he who wrote these things was called John must be believed, as he says it; but who he was does not appear. For he did not say, as often in the Gospel, that he was the beloved disciple of the Lord, or the one who lay on his breast, or the brother of James, or the eyewitness and hearer of the Lord.

13. For he would have spoken of these things if he had wished to show himself plainly. But he says none of them; but speaks of himself as our brother and companion, and a witness of Jesus, and blessed because he had seen and heard the revelations.

14. But I am of the opinion that there were many with the same name as the apostle John, who, on account of their love for him, and because they admired and emulated him, and desired to be loved by the Lord as he was, took to themselves the same surname, as many of the children of the faithful are called Paul or Peter.

15. For example, there is also another John, surnamed Mark, mentioned in the Acts of the Apostles, whom Barnabas and Paul took with them; of whom also it is said, 'And they had also John as their attendant.' But that it is he who wrote this, I would not say. For it not written that he went with them into Asia, but, 'Now when Paul and his company set sail from Paphos, they came to Perga in Pamphylia and John departing from them returned to Jerusalem.'

16. But I think that he was some other one of those in Asia; as they say that there are two monuments in Ephesus, each bearing the name of John.

17. "And from the ideas, and from the words and their arrangement, it may be reasonably conjectured that this one is different from that one.

18. For the Gospel and Epistle agree with each other and begin in the same manner. The one says, 'In the beginning was the Word'; the other, 'That which was from the beginning.' The one: 'And the Word was made flesh and dwelt among us, and we beheld his glory, the glory as of the only begotten of the Father'; the other says the same things slightly altered: 'Which we have heard, which we have seen with our eyes; which we have looked upon and our hands have handled of the Word of life—and the life was manifested.'

19. For he introduces these things at the beginning, maintaining them, as is evident from what follows, in opposition to those who said that the Lord had not come in the flesh. Wherefore also he carefully adds, 'And we have seen and bear witness, and declare unto you the eternal life which was with the Father and was manifested unto us. That which we have seen and heard declare we unto you also.'

20. He holds to this and does not digress from his subject, but discusses everything under the same heads and names some of which we will briefly mention.

21. Any one who examines carefully will find the phrases, 'the life,' 'the light,' 'turning from darkness,' frequently occurring in both; also continually, 'truth,' 'grace,' 'joy,' 'the flesh and blood of the Lord,' 'the judgment,' 'the forgiveness of sins,' 'the love of God toward us,' the 'commandment that we love one another,' that we should' keep all the commandments'; the 'conviction of the world, of the Devil, of Anti-Christ,' the 'promise of the Holy Spirit,' the 'adoption of God,' the 'faith continually required of us,' 'the Father and the Son,' occur everywhere. In fact, it is plainly to be seen that one and the same character marks the Gospel and the Epistle throughout.

22. But the Apocalypse is different from these writings and foreign to them; not touching, nor in the least bordering upon them; almost, so to speak, without even a syllable in common with them.

23. Nay more, the Epistle—for I pass by the Gospel—does not mention nor does it contain any intimation of the Apocalypse, nor does the Apocalypse of the Epistle. But Paul, in his epistles, gives some indication of his revelations, though he has not written them out by themselves.

24. "Moreover, it can also be shown that the, diction of the Gospel and Epistle differs from that of the Apocalypse.

25. For they were written not only without error as regards the Greek language, but also with elegance in their expression, in their reasonings, and in their entire structure. They are far indeed from betraying any barbarism or solecism, or any vulgarism whatever. For the writer had, as it seems, both the requisites of discourse,—that is, the gift of knowledge and the gift of expression—as the Lord had bestowed them both upon him.

26. I do not deny that the other writer saw a revelation and received knowledge and prophecy. I perceive, however, that his dialect and language are not accurate Greek, but that he uses barbarous idioms, and, in some places, solecisms.

27. It is unnecessary to point these out here, for I would not have any one think that I have said these things in a spirit of ridicule, for I have said what I have only with the purpose of showing dearly the difference between the writings."

Chapter XXVI.

THE EPISTLES OF DIONYSIUS.

1. Besides these, many other epistles of Dionysius are extant, as those against Sabellius, addressed to Ammon, bishop of the church of Bernice, and one to Telesphorus, and one to Euphranor, and again another to Ammon and Euporus. He wrote also four other books on the same subject, which he addressed to his namesake Dionysius, in Rome.

2. Besides these many of his epistles are with us, and large books written in epistolary form, as those on Nature, addressed to the young man Timothy, and one on Temptations, which he also dedicated to Euphranor.

3. Moreover, in a letter to Basilides, bishop of the parishes in Pentapolis, he says that he had written an exposition of the beginning of Ecclesiastes. And he has left us also various letters addressed to this same person. Thus much Dionysius. But our account of these matters being now completed, permit us to show to posterity the character of our own age.

Chapter XXVII.

PAUL OF SAMOSATA, AND THE HERESY INTRODUCED BY HIM AT ANTIOCH.

1. After Xystus had presided over the church of Rome for eleven years, Dionysius, namesake of him of Alexandria, succeeded him. About the same time Demetrianus died in Antioch, and Paul of Samosata received that episcopate.

2. As he held, contrary to the teaching of the Church, low and degraded views of Christ, namely, that in his nature he was a common man, Dionysius of Alexandria was entreated to come to the synod. But being unable to come on account of age and physical weakness, he gave his opinion on the subject under consideration by letter. But all the other pastors of the churches from all directions, made haste to assemble at Antioch, as against a de-spoiler of the flock of Christ.

Chapter XXVIII.

THE ILLUSTRIOUS BISHOPS OF THAT TIME.

1. Of these, the most eminent were Firmilianus, bishop of Cæsarea in Cappadocia; the brothers Gregory and Athenodorus, pastors of the churches in Pontus; Helenus of the parish of Tarsus, and Nicomas of Iconium moreover, Hymenæus, of the church of Jerusalem, and Theotecnus of the neighboring church of Cæsarea; and besides these Maximus, who presided in a distinguished manner over the brethren in Bostra. If any should count them up he could not fail to note a great many others, besides presbyters and deacons, who were at that time assembled for the same cause in the above-mentioned city. But these were the most illustrious.

2. When all of these assembled at different times and frequently to consider these matters, the arguments and questions were discussed at every meeting; the adherents of the Samosatian endeavoring to cover and conceal his heterodoxy, and the others striving zealously to lay bare and make manifest his heresy and blasphemy against Christ.

3. Meanwhile, Dionysius died in the twelfth year of the reign of Gallienus, having held the episcopate of Alexandria for seventeen years, and Maximus succeeded him.

4. Gallienus after a reign of fifteen years was succeeded by Claudius, who in two years delivered the government to Aurelian.

Chapter XXIX.

PAUL, HAVING BEEN REFUTED BY MALCHION, A PRESBYTER FROM THE SOPHISTS, WAS EXCOMMUNICATED.

1. During his reign a final synod composed of a great many bishops was held, and the leader of heresy in Antioch was detected, and his false doctrine clearly shown before all, and he was excommunicated from the Catholic Church under heaven.

2. Malchion especially drew him out of his hiding-place and refuted him. He was a man learned in other respects, and principal of the sophist school of Grecian learning in Antioch; yet on account of the superior nobility of his faith in Christ he had been made a presbyter of that parish. This man, having conducted a discussion with him, which was taken down by stenographers and which we know is still extant, was alone able to detect the man who dissembled and deceived the others.

Chapter XXX.

THE EPISTLE OF THE BISHOPS AGAINST PAUL.

1. The pastors who had assembled about this matter, prepared by common consent an epistle addressed to Dionysius, bishop of Rome, and Maximus of Alexandria, and sent it to all the provinces. In this they make manifest to all their own zeal and the perverse error of Paul, and the arguments and discussions which they had with him, and show the entire life and conduct of the man. It may be well to put on record at the present time the following extracts from their writing:

2. "To Dionysius and Maximus, and to all our fellow-ministers throughout the world, bishops, presbyters, and deacons, and to the whole Catholic Church under heaven, Helenus, Hymenæus, Theophilus, Theotecnus, Maximus, Proclus, Nicomas, Ælianus, Paul, Bolanus, Protogenes, Hierax, Eutychius, Theodorus, Malchion, and Lucius, and all the others who dwell with us in the neighboring cities and nations, bishops, presbyters, and deacons, and the churches of God, greeting to the beloved brethren in the Lord."

3. A little farther on they proceed thus: "We sent for and called many of the bishops from a distance to relieve us from this deadly doctrine; as Dionysius of Alexandria and Firmilianus of Cappadocia, those blessed men. The first of these not considering the author of this delusion worthy to be addressed, sent a letter to Antioch, not written to him, but to the entire parish, of which we give a copy below.

4. But Firmilianus came twice and condemned his innovations, as

we who were present know and testify, and many others understand. But as he promised to change his opinions, he believed him and hoped that without any reproach to the Word what was necessary would be done. So he delayed the matter, being deceived by him who denied even his own God and Lord, and had not kept the faith which he formerly held.

5. And now Firmilianus was again on his way to Antioch, and had come as far as Tarsus because he had learned by experience his God-denying wickedness. But while we, having come together, were calling for him and awaiting his arrival, he died."

6. After other things they describe as follows the manner of life which he led: "Whereas he has departed from the rule of faith, and has turned aside after base and spurious teachings, it is not necessary—since he is without—that we should pass judgment upon his practices:

7. as for instance in that although formerly destitute and poor, and having received no wealth from his fathers, nor made anything by trade or business, he now possesses abundant wealth through his iniquities and sacrilegious acts, and through those things which he extorts from the brethren, depriving the injured of their rights and promising to assist them for reward, yet deceiving them, and plundering those who in their trouble are ready to give that they may obtain reconciliation with their oppressors,

8. 'supposing that gain is godliness';—or in that he is haughty, and is puffed up, and assumes worldly dignities, preferring to be called ducenarius rather than bishop; and struts in the market-places, reading letters and reciting them as he walks in public, attended by a body-guard, with a multitude preceding and following him, so that the faith is envied and hated on account of his pride and haughtiness of heart;—

9. or in that he practices chicanery in ecclesiastical assemblies, contrives to glorify himself, and deceive with appearances, and astonish the minds of the simple, preparing for himself a tribunal and lofty throne,—not like a disciple of Christ—and possessing a 'secretum,'—like the rulers of the world—and so calling it, and striking his thigh with his hand, and stamping on the tribunal with his feet—or in that he rebukes and insults those who do not applaud, and shake their handkerchiefs as in the theaters, and shout and leap about like the men and women that are stationed around him, and hear him in this unbecoming manner, but who listen reverently and orderly as in the house of God—or in that he violently and coarsely assails in public the expounders of the Word that have departed this life, and magnifies himself, not as a bishop, but as a sophist and juggler,

10. and stops the psalms to our Lord Jesus Christ, as being the modern productions of modern men, and trains women to sing psalms to himself in the midst of the church on the great day of the passover, which any one might shudder to hear, and persuades the bishops and

presbyters of the neighboring districts and cities who fawn upon him, to advance the same ideas in their discourses to the people.

11. For to anticipate something of what we shall presently write, he is unwilling to acknowledge that the Son of God has come down from heaven. And this is not a mere assertion, but it is abundantly proved from the records which we have sent you; and not least where he says 'Jesus Christ is from below.' But those singing to him and extolling him among the people say that their impious teacher has come down an angel from heaven, And he does not forbid such things; but the arrogant man is even present when they are uttered.

12. And there are the women, the 'subintroductæ,' as the people of Antioch call them, belonging to him and to the presbyters and deacons that are with him. Although he knows and has convicted these men, yet he connives at this and their other incurable sins, in order that they may be bound to him, and through fear for themselves may not dare to accuse him for his wicked words and deeds. But he has also made them rich; on which account he is loved and admired by those who covet such things.

13. We know, beloved, that the bishop and all the clergy should be an example to the people of all good works. And we are not ignorant how many have fallen or incurred suspicion, through the women whom they have thus brought in. So that even if we should allow that he commits no sinful act, yet he ought to avoid the suspicion which arises from such a thing, lest he scandalize some one, or lead others to imitate him.

14. For how can he reprove or admonish another not to be too familiar with women—lest he fall, as it is written,—when he has himself sent one away already, and now has two with him, blooming and beautiful, and takes them with him wherever he goes, and at the same time lives in luxury and surfeiting?

15. Because of these things all mourn and lament by themselves; but they so fear his tyranny and power, that they dare not accuse him.

16. But as we have said, while one might call the man to account for this conduct, if he held the Catholic doctrine and was numbered with us, since he has scorned the mystery and struts about in the abominable heresy of Artemas (for why should we not mention his father?), we think it unnecessary to demand of him an explanation of these things."

17. Afterwards, at the close of the epistle, they add these words: "Therefore we have been compelled to excommunicate him, since he sets himself against God, and refuses to obey; and to appoint in his place another bishop for the Catholic Church. By divine direction, as we believe, we have appointed Domnus, who is adorned with all the qualities becoming in a bishop, and who is a son of the blessed Demetrianus, who formerly presided in a distinguished manner over the

same parish. We have informed you of this that you may write to him, and may receive letters of communion from him. But let this man write to Artemas; and let those who think as Artemas does, communicate with him."

18. As Paul had fallen from the episcopate, as well as from the orthodox faith, Domnus, as has been said, became bishop of the church at Antioch.

19. But as Paul refused to surrender the church building, the Emperor Aurelian was petitioned; and he decided the matter most equitably, ordering the building to be given to those to whom the bishops of Italy and of the city of Rome should adjudge it. Thus this man was driven out of the church, with extreme disgrace, by the worldly power.

20. Such was Aurelian's treatment of us at that time; but in the course of his reign he changed his mind in regard to us, and was moved by certain advisers to institute a persecution against us. And there was great talk about this on every side.

21. But as he was about to do it, and was, so to speak, in the very act of signing the decrees against us, the divine judgment came upon him and restrained him at the very verge of his undertaking, showing in a manner that all could see clearly, that the rulers of this world can never find an opportunity against the churches of Christ, except the hand, that defends them permits it, in divine and heavenly judgment, for the sake of discipline and correction, at such times as it sees best.

22. After a reign of six years, Aurelian was succeeded by Probus. He reigned for the same number of years, and Carus, with his sons, Carinus and Numerianus, succeeded him. After they had reigned less than three years the government devolved on Diocletian, and those associated with him. Under them took place the persecution of our time, and the destruction of the churches connected with it. Shortly before this, Dionysius, bishop of Rome, after holding office for nine years, died, and was succeeded by Felix.

Chapter XXXI.

THE PERVERSIVE HERESY OF THE MANICHEANS
WHICH BEGAN AT THIS TIME.

1. At this time, the madman, named from his demoniacal heresy, armed himself in the perversion of his reason, as the devil, Satan, who himself fights against God, put him forward to the destruction of many. He was a barbarian in life, both in word and deed; and in his nature demoniacal and insane. In consequence of this he sought to pose as Christ, and being puffed up in his madness, he proclaimed himself the Paraclete and the very Holy Spirit; and afterwards, like Christ, he chose

twelve disciples as partners of his new doctrine.

2. And he patched together false and godless doctrines collected from a multitude of long-extinct impieties, and swept them, like a deadly poison, from Persia to our part of the world. From him the impious name of the Manicheans is still prevalent among many. Such was the foundation of this "knowledge falsely so-called," which sprang up in those times.

Chapter XXXII.

THE DISTINGUISHED ECCLESIASTICS OF OUR DAY,
AND WHICH OF THEM SURVIVED UNTIL THE
DESTRUCTION OF THE CHURCHES.

1. At this time, Felix, having presided over the church of Rome for five years, was succeeded by Eutychianus, but he in less than ten months left the position to Caius, who lived in our day. He held it about fifteen years, and was in turn succeeded by Marcellinus, who was overtaken by the persecution.

2. About the same time Timæus received the episcopate of Antioch after Domnus, and Cyril, who lived in our day, succeeded him. In his time we became acquainted with Dorotheus, a man of learning among those of his day, who was honored with the office of presbyter in Antioch. He was a lover of the beautiful in divine things, and devoted himself to the Hebrew language, so that he read the Hebrew Scriptures with facility.

3. He belonged to those who were especially liberal, and was not unacquainted with Grecian propædeutics. Besides this he was a eunuch, having been so from his very birth. On this account, as if it were a miracle, the emperor took him into his family, and honored him by placing him over the purple dye-works at Tyre. We have heard him expound the Scriptures wisely in the Church.

4. After Cyril, Tyrannus received the episcopate of the parish of Antioch. In his time occurred the destruction of the churches.

5. Eusebius, who had come from the city of Alexandria, ruled the parishes of Laodicea after Socrates. The occasion of his removal thither was the affair of Paul. He went on this account to Syria, and was restrained from returning home by those there who were zealous in divine things. Among our contemporaries he was a beautiful example of religion, as is readily seen from the words of Dionysius which we have quoted.

6. Anatolius was appointed his successor; one good man, as they say, following another. He also was an Alexandrian by birth. In learning and skill in Greek philosophy, such as arithmetic and geometry, astronomy, and dialectics in general, as well as in the theory

of physics, he stood first among the ablest men of our time, and he was also at the head in rhetorical science. It is reported that for this reason he was requested by the citizens of Alexandria to establish there a school of Aristotelian philosophy.

7. They relate of him many other eminent deeds during the siege of the Pyrucheium in Alexandria, on account of which he was especially honored by all those in high office; but I will give the following only as an example.

8. They say that bread had failed the besieged, so that it was more difficult to withstand the famine than the enemy outside; but he being present provided for them in this manner. As the other part of the city was allied with the Roman army, and therefore was not under siege, Anatolius sent for Eusebius—for he was still there before his transfer to Syria, and was among those who were not besieged, and possessed, moreover, a great reputation and a renowned name which had reached even the Roman general—and he informed him of those who were perishing in the siege from famine.

9. When he learned this he requested the Roman commander as the greatest possible favor, to grant safety to deserters from the enemy. Having obtained his request, he communicated it to Anatolius. As soon as he received the message he convened the senate of Alexandria, and at first proposed that all should come to a reconciliation with the Romans. But when he perceived that they were angered by this advice, he said, "But I do not think you will oppose me, if I counsel you to send the supernumeraries and those who are in nowise useful to us, as old women and children and old men, outside the gates, to go wherever they may please. For why should we retain for no purpose these who must at any rate soon die? and why should we destroy with hunger those who are crippled and maimed in body, when we ought to provide only for men and youth, and to distribute the necessary bread among those who are needed for the garrison of the city?"

10. With such arguments he persuaded the assembly, and rising first he gave his vote that the entire multitude, whether of men or women, who were not needful for the army, should depart from the city, because if they remained and unnecessarily continued in the city, there would be for them no hope of safety, but they would perish with famine.

11. As all the others in the senate agreed to this, he saved almost all the besieged. He provided that first, those belonging to the church, and afterwards, of the others in the city, those of every age should escape, not only the classes included in the decree, but, under cover of these, a multitude of others, secretly clothed in women's garments; and through his management they went out of the gates by night and escaped to the Roman camp. There Eusebius, like a father and physician, received all of them, wasted away through the long siege,

and restored them by every kind of prudence and care.

12. The church of Laodicea was honored by two such pastors in succession, who, in the providence of God, came after the aforesaid war from Alexandria to that city.

13. Anatolius did not write very many works; but in such as have come down to us we can discern his eloquence and erudition. In these he states particularly his opinions on the passover. It seems important to give here the following extracts from them.

14. *From the Paschal Canons of Anatolius.* "There is then in the first year the new moon of the first month, which is the beginning of every cycle of nineteen years, on the twenty-sixth day of the Egyptian Phamenoth; but according to the months of the Macedonians, the twenty-second day of Dystrus, or, as the Romans would say, the eleventh before the Kalends of April.

15. On the said twenty-sixth of Phamenoth, the sun is found not only entered on the first segment, but already passing through the fourth day in it. They are accustomed to call this segment the first dodecatomorion, and the equinox, and the beginning of months, and the head of the cycle, and the starting-point of the planetary circuit. But they call the one preceding this the last of months, and the twelfth segment, and the final dodecatomorion, and the end of the planetary circuit. Wherefore we maintain that those who place the first month in it, and determine by it the fourteenth of the passover, commit no slight or common blunder.

16. And this is not an opinion of our own; but it was known to the Jews of old, even before Christ, and was carefully observed by them. This may be learned from what is said by Philo, Josephus, and Musæus; and not only by them, but also by those yet more ancient, the two Agathobuli, surnamed 'Masters,' and the famous Aristobulus, who was chosen among the seventy interpreters of the sacred and divine Hebrew Scriptures by Ptolemy Philadelphus and his father, and who also dedicated his exegetical books on the law of Moses to the same kings.

17. These writers, explaining questions in regard to the Exodus, say that all alike should sacrifice the passover offerings after the vernal equinox, in the middle of the first month. But this occurs while the sun is passing through the first segment of the solar, or as some of them have styled it, the zodiacal circle. Aristobulus adds that it is necessary for the feast of the passover, that not only the sun should pass through the equinoctial segment, but the moon also.

18. For as there are two equinoctial segments, the vernal and the autumnal, directly opposite each other, and as the day of the passover was appointed on the fourteenth of the month, beginning with the evening, the moon will hold a position diametrically opposite the sun, as may be seen in full moons; and the sun will be in the segment of the

vernal equinox, and of necessity the moon in that of the autumnal.

19. I know that many other things have been said by them, some of them probable, and some approaching absolute demonstration, by which they endeavor to prove that it is altogether necessary to keep the passover and the feast of unleavened bread after the equinox. But I refrain from demanding this sort of demonstration for matters from which the veil of the Mosaic law has been removed, so that now at length with uncovered face we continually behold as in a glass Christ and the teachings and sufferings of Christ. But that with the Hebrews the first month was near the equinox, the teachings also of the Book of Enoch show."

20. The same writer has also left the Institutes of Arithmetic, in ten books, and other evidences of his experience and proficiency in divine things.

21. Theotecnus, bishop of Cæsarea in Palestine, first ordained him as bishop, designing to make him his successor in his own parish after his death. And for a short time both of them presided over the same church. But the synod which was held to consider Paul's case called him to Antioch, and as he passed through the city of Laodicea, Eusebius being dead, he was detained by the brethren there.

22. And after Anatolius had departed this life, the last bishop of that parish before the persecution was Stephen, who was admired by many for his knowledge of philosophy and other Greek learning. But he was not equally devoted to the divine faith, as the progress of the persecution manifested; for it showed that he was a cowardly and unmanly dissembler rather than a true philosopher.

23. But this did not seriously injure the church, for Theodotus restored their affairs, being straightway made bishop of that parish by God himself, the Saviour of all. He justified by his deeds both his lordly name and his office of bishop. For he excelled in the medical art for bodies, and in the healing art for souls. Nor did any other man equal him in kindness, sincerity, sympathy, and zeal in helping such as needed his aid. He was also greatly devoted to divine learning. Such an one was he.

24. In Cæsarea in Palestine, Agapius succeeded Theotecnus, who had most zealously performed the duties of his episcopate. Him too we know to have labored diligently, and to have manifested most genuine providence in his oversight of the people, particularly caring for all the poor with liberal hand.

25. In his time we became acquainted with Pamphilus, that most eloquent man, of truly philosophical life, who was esteemed worthy of the office of presbyter in that parish. It would be no small matter to show what sort of a man he was and whence he came. But we have described, in our special work concerning him, all the particulars of his life, and of the school which he established, and the trials which he

endured in many confessions during the persecution, and the crown of martyrdom with which he was finally honored. But of all that were there he was indeed the most admirable.

26. Among those nearest our times, we have known Pierius, of the presbyters in Alexandria, and Meletius, bishop of the churches in Pontus—rarest of men.

27. The first was distinguished for his life of extreme poverty and his philosophic learning, and was exceedingly diligent in the contemplation and exposition of divine things, and in public discourses in the church. Meletius, whom the learned called the "honey of Attica," was a man whom every one would describe as most accomplished in all kinds of learning; and it would be impossible to admire sufficiently his rhetorical skill. It might be said that he possessed this by nature; but who could surpass the excellence of his great experience and erudition in other respects?

28. For in all branches of knowledge had you undertaken to try him even once, you would have said that he was the most skillful and learned. Moreover, the virtues of his life were not less remarkable. We observed him well in the time of the persecution, when for seven full years he was escaping from its fury in the regions of Palestine.

29. Zambdas received the episcopate of the church of Jerusalem after the bishop Hymenæus, whom we mentioned a little above. He died in a short time, and Hermon, the last before the persecution in our day, succeeded to the apostolic chair, which has been preserved there until the present time.

30. In Alexandria, Maximus, who, after the death of Dionysius, had been bishop for eighteen years, was succeeded by Theonas. In his time Achillas, who had been appointed a presbyter in Alexandria at the same time with Pierius, became celebrated. He was placed over the school of the sacred faith, and exhibited fruits of philosophy most rare and inferior to none, and conduct genuinely evangelical.

31. After Theonas had held the office for nineteen years, Peter received the episcopate in Alexandria, and was very eminent among them for twelve entire years. Of these he governed the church less than three years before the persecution, and for the remainder of his life he subjected himself to a more rigid discipline and cared in no secret manner for the general interest of the churches. On this account he was beheaded in the ninth year of the persecution, and was adorned with the crown of martyrdom.

32. Having written out in these books the account of the successions from the birth of our Saviour to the destruction of the places of worship—a period of three hundred and five years, permit me to pass on to the contests of those who, in our day, have heroically fought for religion, and to leave in writing, for the information of posterity, the extent and the magnitude of those conflicts.

Book VIII.

Introduction.

1. As we have described in seven books the events from the time of the apostles, we think it proper in this eighth book to record for the information of posterity a few of the most important occurrences of our own times, which are worthy of permanent record. Our account will begin at this point.

Chapter I.

THE EVENTS WHICH PRECEDED THE PERSECUTION IN OUR TIMES.

1. It is beyond our ability to describe in a suitable manner the extent and nature of the glory and freedom with which the word of piety toward the God of the universe, proclaimed to the world through Christ, was honored among all men, both Greeks and barbarians, before the persecution in our day.

2. The favor shown our people by the rulers might be adduced as evidence; as they committed to them the government of provinces, and on account of the great friendship which they entertained toward their doctrine, released them from anxiety in regard to sacrificing.

3. Why need I speak of those in the royal palaces, and of the rulers over all, who allowed the members of their households, wives and children and servants, to speak openly before them for the Divine word and life, and suffered them almost to boast of the freedom of their faith? Indeed they esteemed them highly, and preferred them to their fellow-servants.

4. Such an one was that Dorotheus, the most devoted and faithful to them of all, and on this account especially honored by them among those who held the most honorable offices and governments. With him was the celebrated Gorgonius, and as many as had been esteemed worthy of the same distinction on account of the word of God.

5. And one could see the rulers in every church accorded the greatest favor by all officers and governors. But how can any one describe those vast assemblies, and the multitude that crowded together in every city, and the famous gatherings in the houses of prayer; on whose account not being satisfied with the ancient buildings they erected from the foundation large churches in all the cities?

6. No envy hindered the progress of these affairs which advanced gradually, and grew and increased day by day. Nor could any evil demon slander them or hinder them through human counsels, so long as

the divine and heavenly hand watched over and guarded his own people as worthy.

7. But when on account of the abundant freedom, we fell into laxity and sloth, and envied and reviled each other, and were almost, as it were, taking up arms against one another, rulers assailing rulers with words like spears, and people forming parties against people, and monstrous hypocrisy and dissimulation rising to the greatest height of wickedness, the divine judgment with forbearance, as is its pleasure, while the multitudes yet continued to assemble, gently and moderately harassed the episcopacy.

8. This persecution began with the brethren in the army. But as if without sensibility, we were not eager to make the Deity favorable and propitious; and some, like atheists, thought that our affairs were unheeded and ungoverned; and thus we added one wickedness to another. And those esteemed our shepherds, casting aside the bond of piety, were excited to conflicts with one another, and did nothing else than heap up strifes and threats and jealousy and enmity and hatred toward each other, like tyrants eagerly endeavoring to assert their power. Then, truly, according to the word of Jeremiah, "The Lord in his wrath darkened the daughter of Zion, and cast down the glory of Israel from heaven to earth, and remembered not his footstool in the day of his anger. The Lord also overwhelmed all the beautiful things of Israel, and threw down all his strongholds."

9. And according to what was foretold in the Psalms: "He has made void the covenant of his servant, and profaned his sanctuary to the earth—in the destruction of the churches—and has thrown down all his strongholds, and has made his fortresses cowardice. All that pass by have plundered the multitude of the people; and he has become besides a reproach to his neighbors. For he has exalted the right hand of his enemies, and has turned back the help of his sword, and has not taken his part in the war. But he has deprived him of purification, and has cast his throne to the ground. He has shortened the days of his time, and besides all, has poured out shame upon him."

Chapter II.

THE DESTRUCTION OF THE CHURCHES.

1. All these things were fulfilled in us, when we saw with our own eyes the houses of prayer thrown down to the very foundations, and the Divine and Sacred Scriptures committed to the flames in the midst of the market-places, and the shepherds of the churches basely hidden here and there, and some of them captured ignominiously, and mocked by their enemies. When also, according to another prophetic word, "Contempt was poured out upon rulers, and he caused them to wander

in an untrodden and pathless way."

2. But it is not our place to describe the sad misfortunes which finally came upon them, as we do not think it proper, moreover, to record their divisions and unnatural conduct to each other before the persecution. Wherefore we have decided to relate nothing concerning them except the things in which we can vindicate the Divine judgment.

3. Hence we shall not mention those who were shaken by the persecution, nor those who in everything pertaining to salvation were shipwrecked, and by their own will were sunk in the depths of the flood. But we shall introduce into this history in general only those events which may be use-fill first to ourselves and afterwards to posterity. Let us therefore proceed to describe briefly the sacred conflicts of the witnesses of the Divine Word.

4. It was in the nineteenth year of the reign of Diocletian, in the month Dystrus, called March by the Romans, when the feast of the Saviour's passion was near at hand, that royal edicts were published everywhere, commanding that the churches be leveled to the ground and the Scriptures be destroyed by fire, and ordering that those who held places of honor be degraded, and that the household servants, if they persisted in the profession of Christianity, be deprived of freedom.

5. Such was the first edict against us. But not long after, other decrees were issued, commanding that all the rulers of the churches in every place be first thrown into prison, and afterwards by every artifice be compelled to sacrifices.

Chapter III.

THE NATURE OF THE CONFLICTS ENDURED IN THE PERSECUTION.

1. Then truly a great many rulers of the churches eagerly endured terrible sufferings, and furnished examples of noble conflicts. But a multitude of others, benumbed in spirit by fear, were easily weakened at the first onset. Of the rest each one endured different forms of torture. The body of one was scourged with rods. Another was punished with insupportable rackings and scrapings, in which some suffered a miserable death.

2. Others passed through different conflicts. Thus one, while those around pressed him on by force and dragged him to the abominable and impure sacrifices, was dismissed as if he had sacrificed, though he had not. Another, though he had not approached at all, nor touched any polluted thing, when others said that he had sacrificed, went away, bearing the accusation in silence.

3. Another being taken up half dead, was cast aside as if already dead, and again a certain one lying upon the ground was dragged a long

distance by his feet and counted among those who had sacrificed. One cried out and with a loud voice testified his rejection of the sacrifice; another shouted that he was a Christian, being resplendent in the confession of the saving Name. Another protested that he had not sacrificed and never would.

4. But they were struck in the mouth and silenced by a large band of soldiers who were drawn up for this purpose; and they were smitten on the face and cheeks and driven away by force; so important did the enemies of piety regard it, by any means, to seem to have accomplished their purpose. But these things did no+ avail them against the holy martyrs; for an accurate description of whom, what word of ours could suffice?

Chapter IV.

THE FAMOUS MARTYRS OF GOD, WHO FILLED EVERY PLACE WITH THEIR MEMORY AND WON VARIOUS CROWNS IN BEHALF OF RELIGION.

1. For we might tell of many who showed admirable zeal for the religion of the God of the universe, not only from the beginning of the general persecution, but long before that time, while yet peace prevailed.

2. For though he who had received power was seemingly aroused now as from a deep sleep, yet from the time after Decius and Valerian, he had been plotting secretly and without notice against the churches. He did not wage war against all of us at once, but made trial at first only of those in the army. For he supposed that the others could be taken easily if he should first attack and subdue these. Thereupon many of the soldiers were seen most cheerfully embracing private life, so that they might not deny their piety toward the Creator of the universe.

3. For when the commander, whoever he was, began to persecute the soldiers, separating onto tribes an purging those who were enrolled in the army, giving them the choice either by obeying to receive the honor which belonged to them, or on the other hand to be deprived of it if they disobeyed the command, a great many soldiers of Christ's kingdom, without hesitation, instantly preferred the confession of him to the seeming glory and prosperity which they were enjoying.

4. And one and another of them occasionally received in exchange, for their pious constancy, not only the loss of position, but death. But as yet the instigator of this plot proceeded with moderation, and ventured so far as blood only in some instances; for the multitude of believers, as it is likely, made him afraid, and deterred him from waging war at once against all.

5. But when he made the attack more boldly, it is impossible to

relate how many and what sort of martyrs of God could be seen, among the inhabitants of all the cities and countries.

Chapter V.

THOSE IN NICOMEDIA.

1. Immediately on the publication of the decree against the churches in Nicomedia, a certain man, not obscure but very highly honored with distinguished temporal dignities, moved with zeal toward God, and incited with ardent faith, seized the edict as it was posted openly and publicly, and tore it to pieces as a profane and impious thing; and this was done while two of the sovereigns were in the same city—the oldest of all, and the one who held the fourth place in the government after him.

2. But this man, first in that place, after distinguishing himself in such a manner suffered those things which were likely to follow such daring, and kept his spirit cheerful and undisturbed till death.

Chapter VI.

THOSE IN THE PALACE.

1. This period produced divine and illustrious martyrs, above all whose praises have ever been sung and who have been celebrated for courage, whether among Greeks or barbarians, in the person of Dorotheus and the servants that were with him in the palace. Although they received the highest honors from their masters, and were treated by them as their own children, they esteemed reproaches and trials for religion, and the many forms of death that were invented against them, as, in truth, greater riches than the glory and luxury of this life. We will describe the manner in which one of them ended his life, and leave our readers to infer from his case the sufferings of the others.

2. A certain man was brought forward in the above-mentioned city, before the rulers of whom we have spoken. He was then commanded to sacrifice, but as he refused, he was ordered to be stripped and raised on high and beaten with rods over his entire body, until, being conquered, he should, even against his will, do what was commanded.

3. But as he was unmoved by these sufferings, and his bones were already appearing, they mixed vinegar with salt and poured it upon the mangled parts of his body. As he scorned these agonies, a gridiron and fire were brought forward. And the remnants of his body, like flesh intended for eating, were placed on the fire, not at once, lest he should expire instantly, but a little at a time. And those who placed him on the pyre were not permitted to desist until, after such sufferings, he should

assent to the things commanded.

4. But he held his purpose firmly, and victoriously gave up his life while the tortures were still going on. Such was the martyrdom of one of the servants of the palace, who was indeed well worthy of his name, for he was called Peter.

5. The martyrdoms of the rest, though they were not inferior to his, we will pass by for the sake of brevity, recording only that Dorotheus and Gorgonius, with many others of the royal household, after varied sufferings, ended their lives by strangling, and bore away the trophies of God-given victory.

6. At this time Anthimus, who then presided over the church in Nicomedia, was beheaded for his testimony to Christ. A great multitude of martyrs were added to him, a conflagration having broken out in those very days in the palace at Nicomedia, I know not how, which through a false suspicion was laid to our people. Entire families of the pious in that place were put to death in masses at the royal command, some by the sword, and others by fire. It is reported that with a certain divine and indescribable eagerness men and women rushed into the fire. And the executioners bound a large number of others and put them on boats and threw them into the depths of the sea.

7. And those who had been esteemed their masters considered it necessary to dig up the bodies of the imperial servants, who had been committed to the earth with suitable burial and cast them into the sea, lest any, as they thought, regarding them as gods, might worship them lying in their sepulchers. Such things occurred in Nicomedia at the beginning of the persecution.

8. But not long after, as persons in the country called Melitene, and others throughout Syria, attempted to usurp the government, a royal edict directed that the rulers of the churches everywhere should lye thrown into prison and bonds.

9. What was to be seen after this exceeds all description. A vast multitude were imprisoned in every place; and the prisons everywhere, which had long before been prepared for murderers and robbers of graves, were filled with bishops, presbyters and deacons, readers and exorcists, so that room was no longer left in them for those condemned for crimes.

10. And as other decrees followed the first, directing that those in prison if they would sacrifice should be permitted to depart in freedom, but that those who refused should be harassed with many tortures, how could any one, again, number the multitude of martyrs in every province, and especially of those in Africa, and Mauritania, and Thebais, and Egypt? From this last country many went into other cities and provinces, and became illustrious through martyrdom.

Chapter VII.

THE EGYPTIANS IN PHŒNICIA.

1. Those of them that were conspicuous in Palestine we know, as also those that were at Tyre in Phœnicia. Who that saw them was not astonished at the numberless stripes, and at the firmness which these truly wonderful athletes of religion exhibited under them? and at their contest, immediately after the scourging, with bloodthirsty wild beasts, as they were cast before leopards and different kinds of bears and wild boars and bulls goaded with fire and red-hot iron? and at the marvelous endurance of these noble men in the face of all sorts of wild beasts?

2. We were present ourselves when these things occurred, and have put on record the divine power of our martyred Saviour Jesus Christ, which was present and manifested itself mightily in the martyrs. For a long time the man-devouring beasts did not dare to touch or draw near the bodies of those dear to God, but rushed upon the others who from the outside irritated and urged them on. And they would not in the least touch the holy athletes, as they stood alone and naked and shook their hands at them to draw them toward themselves—for they were commanded to do this. But whenever they rushed at them, they were restrained as if by some diviner power and retreated again.

3. This continued for a long time, and occasioned no little wonder to the spectators. And as the first wild beast did nothing, a second and a third were let loose against one and the same martyr.

4. One could not but be astonished at the invincible firmness of these holy men, and the enduring and immovable constancy of those whose bodies were young. You could have seen a youth not twenty years of age standing unbound and stretching out his hands in the form of a cross, with unterrified and untrembling mind, engaged earnestly in prayer to God, and not in the least going back or retreating from the place where he stood, while bears and leopards, breathing rage and death, almost touched his flesh. And yet their mouths were restrained, I know not how, by a divine and incomprehensible power, and they ran back again to their place. Such an one was he.

5. Again you might have seen others, for they were five in all, cast before a wild bull, who tossed into the air with his horns those who approached from the outside, and mangled them, leaving them to be token up half dead; but when he rushed with rage and threatening upon the holy martyrs, who were standing alone, he was unable to come near them; but though he stamped with his feet, and pushed in all directions with his horns, and breathed rage and threatening on account of the irritation of the burning irons, he was, nevertheless, held back by the sacred Providence. And as he in nowise harmed them, they let loose

other wild beasts upon them.

6. Finally, after these terrible and various attacks upon them, they were all slain with the sword; and instead of being buried in the earth they were committed to the waves of the sea.

Chapter VIII.

THOSE IN EGYPT.

1. Such was the conflict of those Egyptians who contended nobly for religion in Tyre. But we must admire those also who suffered martyrdom in their native land; where thousands of men, women, and children, despising the present life for the sake of the teaching of our Saviour, endured various deaths.

2. Some of them, after scrapings and rackings and severest scourgings, and numberless other kinds of tortures, terrible even to hear of, were committed to the flames; some were drowned in the sea; some offered their heads bravely to those who cut them off; some died under their tortures, and others perished with hunger. And yet others were crucified; some according to the method commonly employed for malefactors; others yet more cruelly, being nailed to the cross with their heads downward, and being kept alive until they perished on the cross with hunger.

Chapter IX.

THOSE IN THEBAIS.

1. It would be impossible to describe the outrages and tortures which the martyrs in Thebais endured. They were scraped over the entire body with shells instead of hooks until they died. Women were bound by one foot and raised aloft in the air by machines, and with their bodies altogether bare and uncovered, presented to all beholders this most shameful, cruel, and inhuman spectacle.

2. Others being bound to the branches and trunks of trees perished. For they drew the stoutest branches together with machines, and bound the limbs of the martyrs to them; and then, allowing the branches to assume their natural position, they tore asunder instantly the limbs of those for whom they contrived this.

3. All these things were done, not for a few days or a short time, but for a long series of years. Sometimes more than ten, at other times above twenty were put to death. Again not less than thirty, then about sixty, and yet again a hundred men with young children and women, were slain in one day, being condemned to various and diverse torments.

4. We, also being on the spot ourselves, have observed large crowds in one day; some suffering decapitation, others torture by fire; so that the murderous sword was blunted, and becoming weak, was broken, and the very executioners grew weary and relieved each other.

5. And we beheld the most wonderful ardor, and the truly divine energy and zeal of those who believed in the Christ of God. For as soon as sentence was pronounced against the first, one after another rushed to the judgment seat, and confessed themselves Christians. And regarding with indifference the terrible things and the multiform tortures, they declared themselves boldly and undauntedly for the religion of the God of the universe. And they received the final sentence of death with joy and laughter and cheerfulness; so that they sang and offered up hymns and thanksgivings to the God of the universe till their very last breath.

6. These indeed were wonderful; but yet more wonderful were those who, being distinguished for wealth, noble birth, and honor, and for learning and philosophy, held everything secondary to the true religion and to faith in our Saviour and Lord Jesus Christ.

7. Such an one was Philoromus, who held a high office under the imperial government at Alexandria, and who administered justice every day, attended by a military guard corresponding to his rank and Roman dignity. Such also was Phileas, bishop of the church of Thmuis, a man eminent on account of his patriotism and the services rendered by him to his country, and also on account of his philosophical learning.

8. These persons, although a multitude of relatives and other friends besought them, and many in high position, and even the judge himself entreated them, that they would have compassion on themselves and show mercy to their children and wives, yet were not in the least induced by these things to choose the love of life, and to despise the ordinances of our Saviour concerning confession and denial. But with manly and philosophic minds, or rather with pious and God-loving souls, they persevered against all the threats and insults of the judge; and both of them were beheaded.

Chapter X.

THE WRITINGS OF PHILEAS THE MARTYR DESCRIBING THE OCCURRENCES AT ALEXANDRIA.

1. Since we have mentioned Phileas as having a high reputation for secular learning, let him be his own witness in the following extract, in which he shows us who he was, and at the same time describes more accurately than we can the martyrdoms which occurred in his time at Alexandria:

2. "Having before them all these examples and models and noble

tokens which are given us in the Divine and Sacred Scriptures, the blessed martyrs who were with us did not hesitate, but directing the eye of the soul in sincerity toward the God over all, and having their mind set upon death for religion, they adhered firmly to their calling. For they understood that our Lord Jesus Christ had become man on our account, that he might cut off all sin and furnish us with the means of entrance into eternal life. For 'he counted it not a prize to be on an equality with God, but emptied himself taking the form of a servant; and being found in fashion as a man, he humbled himself unto death, even the death of the cross.'

3. Wherefore also being zealous for the greater gifts, the Christ-bearing martyrs endured all trials and all kinds of contrivances for torture; not once only, but some also a second time. And although the guards vied with each other in threatening them in all sorts of ways, not in words only, but in actions, they did not give up their resolution; because 'perfect love casteth out fear.'

4. "What words could describe their courage and manliness under every torture? For as liberty to abuse them was given to all that wished, some beat them with clubs, others with rods, others with scourges, yet others with thongs, and others with ropes.

5. And the spectacle of the outrages was varied and exhibited great malignity. For some, with their hands bound behind them, were suspended on the stocks, and every member stretched by certain machines. Then the torturers, as commanded, lacerated with instruments their entire bodies; not only their sides, as in the case of murderers, but also their stomachs and knees and cheeks. Others were raised aloft, suspended from the porch by one hand, and endured the most terrible suffering of all, through the distension of their joints and limbs. Others were bound face to face to pillars, not resting on their feet, but with the weight of their bodies bearing on their bonds and drawing them tightly.

6. And they endured this, not merely as long as the governor talked with them or was at leisure, but through almost the entire day. For when he passed on to others, he left officers under his authority to watch the first, and observe if any of them, overcome by the tortures, appeared to yield. And he commanded to cast them into chains without mercy, and afterwards when they were at the last gasp to throw them to the ground and drag them away.

7. For he said that they were not to have the least concern for us, but were to think and act as if we no longer existed, our enemies having invented this second mode of torture in addition to the stripes.

8. "Some, also, after these outrages, were placed on the stocks, and had both their feet stretched over the four holes, so that they were compelled to lie on their backs on the stocks, being unable to keep themselves up on account of the fresh wounds with which their entire

bodies were covered as a result of the scourging. Others were thrown on the ground and lay there under the accumulated infliction of tortures, exhibiting to the spectators a more terrible manifestation of severity, as they bore on their bodies the marks of the various and diverse punishments which had been invented.

9. As this went on, some died under the tortures, shaming the adversary by their constancy. Others half dead were shut up in prison, and suffering with their agonies, they died in a few days; but the rest, recovering under the care which they received, gained confidence by time and their long detention in prison.

10. When therefore they were ordered to choose whether they would be released from molestation by touching the polluted sacrifice, and would receive from them the accursed freedom, or refusing to sacrifice, should be condemned to death, they did not hesitate, but went to death cheerfully. For they knew what had been declared before by the Sacred Scriptures. For it is said, 'He that sacrificeth to other gods shall be utterly destroyed,' and, 'Thou shalt have no other gods before me.'"

11. Such are the words of the truly philosophical and God-loving martyr, which, before the final sentence, while yet in prison, he addressed to the brethren in his parish, showing them his own circumstances, and at the same time exhorting them to hold fast, even after his approaching death, to the religion of Christ.

12. But why need we dwell upon these things, and continue to add fresh instances of the conflicts of the divine martyrs throughout the world, especially since they were dealt with no longer by common law, but attacked like enemies of war?

Chapter XI.

THOSE IN PHRYGIA.

1. A small town of Phrygia, inhabited solely by Christians, was completely surrounded by soldiers while the men were in it. Throwing fire into it, they consumed them with the women and children while they were calling upon Christ. This they did because all the inhabitants of the city, and the curator himself, and the governor, with all who held office, and the entire populace, confessed themselves Christians, and would not in the least obey those who commanded them to worship idols.

2. There was another man of Roman dignity named Adauctus, of a noble Italian family, who had advanced through every honor under the emperors, so that he had blamelessly filled even the general offices of magistrate, as they call it, and of finance minister. Besides all this he excelled in deeds of piety and in the confession of the Christ of God,

and was adorned with the diadem of martyrdom. He endured the conflict for religion while still holding the office of finance minister.

Chapter XII.

MANY OTHERS, BOTH MEN AND WOMEN, WHO SUFFERED IN VARIOUS WAYS.

1. Why need we mention the rest by name, or number the multitude of the men, or picture the various sufferings of the admirable martyrs of Christ? Some of them were slain with the axe, as in Arabia. The limbs of some were broken, as in Cappadocia. Some, raised on high by the feet, with their heads down, while a gentle fire burned beneath them, were suffocated by the smoke which arose from the burning wood, as was done in Mesopotamia. Others were mutilated by cutting off their noses and ears and hands, and cutting to pieces the other members and parts of their bodies, as in Alexandria.

2. Why need we revive the recollection of those in Antioch who were roasted on grates, not so as to kill them, but so as to subject them to a lingering punishment? Or of others who preferred to thrust their right hand into the fire rather than touch the impious sacrifice? Some, shrinking from the trial, rather than be taken and fall into the hands of their enemies, threw themselves from lofty houses, considering death preferable to the cruelty of the impious.

3. A certain holy person—in soul admirable for virtue, in body a woman—who was illustrious beyond all in Antioch for wealth and family and reputation, had brought up in the principles of religion her two daughters, who were now in the freshness and bloom of life. Since great envy was excited on their account, every means was used to find them in their concealment; and when it was ascertained that they were away, they were summoned deceitfully to Antioch. Thus they were caught in the nets of the soldiers. When the woman saw herself and her daughters thus helpless, and knew the things terrible to speak of that men would do to them—and the most unbearable of all terrible things, the threatened violation of their chastity,—she exhorted herself and the maidens that they ought not to submit even to hear of this. For, she said, that to surrender their souls to the slavery of demons was worse than all deaths and destruction; and she set before them the only deliverance from all these things—escape to Christ.

4. They then listened to her advice. And after arranging their garments suitably, they went aside from the middle of the road, having requested of the guards a little time for retirement, and cast themselves into a river which was flowing by.

5. Thus they destroyed themselves. But there were two other virgins in the same city of Antioch who served God in all things, and

were true sisters, illustrious in family and distinguished in life, young and blooming, serious in mind, pious in deportment, and admirable for zeal. As if the earth could not bear such excellence, the worshipers of demons commanded to cast them into the sea. And this was done to them.

6. In Pontus, others endured sufferings horrible to hear. Their fingers were pierced with sharp reeds under their nails. Melted lead, bubbling and boiling with the heat, was poured down the backs of others, and they were roasted in the most sensitive parts of the body.

7. Others endured on their bowels and privy members shameful and inhuman and unmentionable torments, which the noble and law-observing judges, to show their severity, devised, as more honorable manifestations of wisdom. And new tortures were continually invented, as if they were endeavoring, by surpassing one another, to gain! prizes in a contest.

8. But at the close of these calamities, when finally they could contrive no greater cruelties, and were weary of putting to death, and were filled and satiated with the shedding of blood, they turned to what they considered merciful and humane treatment, so that they seemed to be no longer devising terrible things against us.

9. For they said that it was not fitting that the cities should be polluted with the blood of their own people, or that the government of their rulers, which was kind and mild toward all, should be defamed through excessive cruelty; but that rather the beneficence of the humane and royal authority should be extended to all, and we should no longer be put to death. For the infliction of this punishment upon us should be stopped in consequence of the humanity of the rulers.

10. Therefore it was commanded that our eyes should be put out, and that we should be maimed in one of our limbs. For such things were humane in their sight, and the lightest of punishments for us. So that now on account of this kindly treatment accorded us by the impious, it was impossible to tell the incalculable number of those whose right eyes had first been cut out with the sword, and then had been cauterized with fire; or who had been disabled in the left foot by burning the joints, and afterward condemned to the provincial copper mines, not so much for service as for distress and hardship. Besides all these, others encountered other trials, which it is impossible to recount; for their manly endurance surpasses all description.

11. In these conflicts the noble martyrs of Christ shone illustrious over the entire world, and everywhere astonished those who beheld their manliness; and the evidences of the truly divine and unspeakable power of our Saviour were made manifest through them. To mention each by name would be a long task, if not indeed impossible.

Chapter XIII.

THE BISHOPS OF THE CHURCH THAT EVINCED BY THEIR BLOOD THE GENUINENESS OF THE RELIGION WHICH THEY PREACHED.

1. As for the rulers of the Church that suffered martyrdom in the principal cities, the first martyr of the kingdom of Christ whom we shall mention among the monuments of the pious is Anthimus, bishop of the city of Nicomedia, who was beheaded.

2. Among the martyrs at Antioch was Lucian, a presbyter of that parish, whose entire life was most excellent. At Nicomedia, in the presence of the emperor, he proclaimed the heavenly kingdom of Christ, first in an oral defense, and afterwards by deeds as well.

3. Of the martyrs in Phœnicia the most distinguished were those devoted pastors of the spiritual flocks of Christ: Tyrannion, bishop of the church of Tyre; Zenobius, a presbyter of the church at Sidon; and Silvanus, bishop of the churches about Emesa.

4. The last of these, with others, was made food for wild beasts at Emesa, and was thus received into the ranks of martyrs. The other two glorified the word of God at Antioch through patience unto death. The bishop was thrown into the depths of the sea. But Zenobius, who was a very skillful physician, died through severe tortures which were applied to his sides.

5. Of the martyrs in Palestine, Silvanus, bishop of the churches about Gaza, was beheaded with thirty-nine others at the copper mines of Phæno. There also the Egyptian bishops, Peleus and Nilus, with others, suffered death by fire.

6. Among these we must mention Pamphilus, a presbyter, who was the great glory of the parish of Cæsarea, and among the men of our time most admirable. The virtue of his manly deeds we have recorded in the proper place.

7. Of those who suffered death illustriously at Alexandria and throughout Egypt and Thebais, Peter, bishop of Alexandria, one of the most excellent teachers of the religion of Christ, should first be mentioned; and of the presbyters with him Faustus, Dius and Ammonius, perfect martyrs of Christ; also Phileas, Hesychius, Pachymius and Theodorus, bishops of Egyptian churches, and besides them many other distinguished persons who are commemorated by the parishes of their country and region. It is not for us to describe the conflicts of those who suffered for the divine religion throughout the entire world, and to relate accurately what happened to each of them. This would be the proper work of those who were eyewitnesses of the events. I will describe for posterity in another work those which I

myself witnessed.

8. But in the present book I will add to what I have given the revocation issued by our persecutors, and those events that occurred at the beginning of the persecution, which will be most profitable to such as shall read them.

9. What words could sufficiently describe the greatness and abundance of the prosperity of the Roman government before the war against us, while the rulers were friendly and peaceable toward us? Then those who were highest in the government, and had held the position ten or twenty years, passed their time in tranquil peace, in festivals and public games and most joyful pleasures and cheer.

10. While thus their authority was growing uninterruptedly, and increasing day by day, suddenly they changed their peaceful attitude toward us, and began an implacable war. But the second year of this movement was not yet past, when a revolution took place in the entire government and overturned all things.

11. For a severe sickness came upon the chief of those of whom we have spoken, by which his understanding was distracted; and with him who was honored with the second rank, he retired into private life. Scarcely had he done this when the entire empire was divided; a thing which is not recorded as having ever occurred before.

12. Not long after, the Emperor Constantius, who through his entire life was most kindly and favorably disposed toward his subjects, and most friendly to the Divine Word, ended his life in the common course of nature, and left his own son, Constantine, as emperor and Augustus in his stead. He was the first that was ranked by them among the gods, and received after death every honor which one could pay to an emperor.

13. He was the kindest and mildest of emperors, and the only one of those of our day that passed all the time of his government in a manner worthy of his office. Moreover, he conducted himself toward all most favorably and beneficently. He took not the smallest part in the war against us, but preserved the pious that were under him unharmed and unabused. He neither threw down the church buildings, nor did he devise anything else against us. The end of his life was honorable and thrice blessed. He alone at death left his empire happily and gloriously to his own son as his successor—one who was in all respects most prudent and pious.

14. His son Constantine entered on the government at once, being proclaimed supreme emperor and Augustus by the soldiers, And long before by God himself, the King of all. He showed himself an emulator of his father's piety toward our doctrine. Such an one was he. But after this, Licinius was declared emperor and Augustus by a common vote of the rulers.

15. These things grieved Maximinus greatly, for until that time he

had been entitled by all only Cæsar. He therefore, being exceedingly imperious, seized the dignity for himself, and became Augustus, being made such by himself. In the mean time he whom we have mentioned as having resumed his dignity after his abdication, being detected in conspiring against the life of Constantine, perished by a most shameful death. He was the first whose decrees and statues and public monuments were destroyed because of his wickedness and impiety.

Chapter XIV.

THE CHARACTER OF THE ENEMIES OF RELIGION.

1. Maxentius his son, who obtained the government at Rome, at first feigned our faith, in complaisance and flattery toward the Roman people. On this account he commanded his subjects to cease persecuting the Christians, pretending to religion that he might appear merciful and mild beyond his predecessors.

2. But he did not prove in his deeds to be such a person as was hoped, but ran into all wickedness and abstained from no impurity or licentiousness, committing adulteries and indulging in all kinds of corruption. For having separated wives from their lawful consorts, he abused them and sent them back most dishonor-ably to their husbands. And he not only practiced this against the obscure and unknown, but he insulted especially the most prominent and distinguished members of the Roman senate.

3. All his subjects, people and rulers, honored and obscure, were worn out by grievous oppression. Neither, although they kept quiet, and bore the bitter servitude, was there any relief from the murderous cruelty of the tyrant. Once, on a small pretense, he gave the people to be slaughtered by his guards; and a great multitude of the Roman populace were slain in the midst of the city, with the spears and arms, not of Scythians and barbarians, but of their own fellow-citizens.

4. It would be impossible to recount the number of senators who were put to death for the sake of their wealth; multitudes being slain on various pretenses.

5. To crown all his wickedness, the tyrant resorted to magic. And in his divinations he cut open pregnant women, and again inspected the bowels of newborn infants. He slaughtered lions, and performed various execrable acts to invoke demons and avert war. For his only hope was that, by these means, victory would be secured to him.

6. It is impossible to tell the ways in which this tyrant at Rome oppressed his subjects, so that they were reduced to such an extreme dearth of the necessities of life as has never been known, according to our contemporaries, either at Rome or elsewhere.

7. But Maximinus, the tyrant in the East, having secretly formed a

friendly alliance with the Roman tyrant as with a brother in wickedness, sought to conceal it for a long time. But being at last detected, he suffered merited punishment.

8. It was wonderful how akin he was in wickedness to the tyrant at Rome, or rather how far he surpassed him in it. For the chief of sorcerers and magi-clans were honored by him with the highest rank. Becoming exceedingly timid and superstitious, he valued greatly the error of idols and demons. Indeed, without soothsayers and oracles he did not venture to move even a finger, so to speak.

9. Therefore he persecuted us more violently and incessantly than his predecessors. He ordered temples to be erected in every city, and the sacred groves which had been destroyed through lapse of time to be speedily restored. He appointed idol priests in every place and city; and he set over them in every province, as high priest, some political official who had especially distinguished himself in every kind of service, giving him a band of soldiers and a body-guard. And to all jugglers, as if they were pious and beloved of the gods, he granted governments and the greatest privileges.

10. From this time on he distressed and harassed, not one city or country, but all the provinces under his authority, by extreme exactions of gold and silver and goods, and most grievous prosecutions and various fines. He took away from the wealthy the property which they had inherited from their ancestors, and bestowed vast riches and large sums of money on the flatterers about him.

11. And he went to such an excess of folly. and drunkenness that his mind was deranged and crazed in his carousals; and he gave commands when intoxicated of which he repented afterward when sober. He suffered no one to surpass him in debauchery and profligacy, but made himself an instructor in wickedness to those about him, both rulers and subjects. He urged on the army to live wantonly in every kind of revelry and intemperance, and encouraged the governors and generals to abuse their subjects with rapacity and covetousness, almost as if they were rulers with him.

12. Why need we relate the licentious, shameless deeds of the man, or enumerate the multitude with whom he committed adultery? For he could not pass through a city without continually corrupting women and ravishing virgins.

13. And in this he succeeded with all except the Christians. For as they despised death, they cared nothing for his power. For the men endured fire and sword and crucifixion and wild beasts and the depths of the sea, and cutting off of limbs, anti burnings, and pricking and digging out of eyes, and mutilations of the entire body, and besides these, hunger and mines and bonds. In all they showed patience in behalf of religion rather than transfer to idols the reverence due to God.

14. And the women were not less manly than the men in behalf of

the teaching of the Divine Word, as they endured conflicts with the men, and bore away equal prizes of virtue. And when they were dragged away for corrupt purposes, they surrendered their lives to death rather than their bodies to impurity.

15. One only of those who were seized for adulterous purposes by the tyrant, a most distinguished and illustrious Christian woman in Alexandria, conquered the passionate and intemperate soul of Maximinus by most heroic firmness. Honorable on account of wealth and family and education, she esteemed all of these inferior to chastity. He urged her many times, but although she was ready to die, he could not put her to death, for his desire was stronger than his anger.

16. He therefore punished her with exile, and took away all her property. Many others, unable even to listen to the threats of violation from the heathen rulers, endured every form of tortures, and rackings, and deadly punishment. These indeed should be admired. But far the most admirable was that woman at Rome, who was truly the most noble and modest of all, whom the tyrant Maxentius, fully resembling Maximinus in his actions, endeavored to abuse.

17. For when she learned that those who served the tyrant in such matters were at the house (she also was a Christian), and that her husband, although a prefect of Rome, would suffer them to take and lead her away, having requested a little time for adorning her body, she entered her chamber, and being alone, stabbed herself with a sword. Dying immediately, she left her corpse to those who had come for her. And by her deeds, more powerfully than by any words, she has shown to all men now and hereafter that the virtue which prevails among Christians is the only invincible and indestructible possession?

18. Such was the career of wickedness which was carried forward at one and the same time by the two tyrants who held the East and the West. Who is there that would hesitate, after careful examination, to pronounce the persecution against us the cause of such evil? Especially since this extreme confusion of affairs did not cease until the Christians had obtained liberty.

Chapter XV.

THE EVENTS WHICH HAPPENED TO THE HEATHEN.

1. During the entire ten years of the persecution, they were constantly plotting and warring against one another. For the sea could not be navigated, nor could men sail from any port without being exposed to all kinds of outrages; being stretched on the rack and lacerated in their sides, that it might be ascertained through various tortures, whether they came from the enemy; and finally being subjected to punishment by the cross or by fire.

2. And besides these things shields and breastplates were preparing, and darts and spears and other warlike accoutrements were making ready, and galleys and naval armor were collecting in every place. And no one expected anything else than to be attacked by enemies any day. In addition to this, famine and pestilence came upon them, in regard to which we shall relate what is necessary in the proper place.

Chapter XVI.

THE CHANGE OF AFFAIRS FOR THE BETTER.

1. Such was the state of affairs during the entire persecution. But in the tenth year, through the grace of God, it ceased altogether, having begun to decrease after the eighth year. For when the divine and heavenly grace showed us favorable and propitious oversight, then truly our rulers, and the very persons by whom the war against us had been earnestly prosecuted, most remarkably changed their minds, and issued a revocation, and quenched the great fire of persecution which had been kindled, by merciful proclamations and ordinances concerning us.

2. But this was not due to any human agency; nor was it the result, as one might say, of the compassion or philanthropy of our rulers—far from it, for daily from the beginning until that time they were devising more and more severe measures against us, and continually inventing outrages by a greater variety of instruments—but it was manifestly due to the oversight of Divine Providence, on the one I hand becoming reconciled to his people, and on the other, attacking him a who instigated these evils, and showing anger toward him as the author of the cruelties of the entire persecution.

3. For though it was necessary that these things should take place, according to the divine judgment, yet the Word saith, "Woe to him through whom the offense cometh." Therefore punishment from God came upon him, beginning with his flesh, and proceeding to his soul.

4. For an abscess suddenly appeared in the midst of the secret parts of his body, and from it a deeply perforated sore, which spread irresistibly into his inmost bowels. An indescribable multitude of worms sprang from them, and a deathly odor arose, as the entire bulk of his body had, through his gluttony, been changed, before his sickness, into an excessive mass of soft fat, which became putrid, and thus presented an awful and intolerable sight to those who came near.

5. Some of the physicians, being wholly unable to endure the exceeding offensiveness of the odor, were slain; others, as the entire mass had swollen and passed beyond hope of restoration, and they were unable to render any help, were put to death without mercy.

Chapter XVII.

THE REVOCATION OF THE RULERS.

1. Wrestling with so many evils, he thought of the cruelties which he had committed against the pious. Turning, therefore, his thoughts toward himself, he first openly confessed to the God of the universe, and then summoning his attendants, he commanded that without delay they should stop the persecution of the Christians, and should by law and royal decree, urge them forward to build their churches and to perform their customary worship, offering prayers in behalf of the emperor. Immediately the deed followed the word.

2. The imperial decrees were published in the cities, containing the revocation of the acts against us in the following form:

3. "The Emperor Cæsar Galerius Valerius Maximinus, Invictus, Augustus, Pontifex Maximus, conqueror of the Germans, conqueror of the Egyptians, conqueror of the Thebans, five times conqueror of the Sarmatians, conqueror of the Persians, twice conqueror of the Carpathians, six times conqueror of the Armenians, conqueror of the Medes, conqueror of the Adiabeni, Tribune of the people the twentieth time, Emperor the nineteenth time, Consul the eighth time, Father of his country, Proconsul;

4. and the Emperor Cæsar Flavius Valerius Constantinus, Pins, Felix, Invictus, Augustus, Pontifex Maximus, Tribune of the people, Emperor the fifth time, Consul, Father of his country, Proconsul;

5. and the Emperor Cæsar Valerius Licinius, Pins, Felix, Invictus, Augustus, Pontifex Maximus, Tribune of the people the fourth time, Emperor the third time, Consul, Father of his country, Proconsul; to the people of their provinces, greeting:

6. "Among the other things which we have ordained for the public advantage and profit, we formerly wished to restore everything to conformity with the ancient laws and public discipline of the Romans, and to provide that the Christians also, who have forsaken the religion of their ancestors, should return to a good disposition.

7. For in some way such arrogance had seized them and such stupidity had overtaken them, that they did not follow the ancient institutions which possibly their own ancestors had formerly established, but made for themselves laws according to their own purpose, as each one desired, and observed them, and thus assembled as separate congregations in various places.

8. When we had issued this decree that they should return to the institutions established by the ancients, a great many submitted under danger, but a great many being harassed endured all kinds of death.

9. And since many continue in the same folly, and we perceive that

they neither offer to the heavenly gods the worship which is due, nor pay regard to the God of the Christians, in consideration of our philanthropy and our invariable custom, by which we are wont to extend pardon to all, we have determined that we ought most cheerfully to extend our indulgence in this matter also; that they may again be Christians, and may rebuild the conventicles in which they were accustomed to assemble, on condition that nothing be done by them contrary to discipline. In another letter we shall indicate to the magistrates what they have to observe.

10. Wherefore, on account of this indulgence of ours, they ought to supplicate their God for our safety, and that of the people, and their own, that the public welfare may be preserved in every place, and that they may live securely in their several homes." Such is the tenor of this edict, translated, as well as possible, from the Roman tongue into the Greek? It is time to consider what took place after these events.

Appendix.

THAT WHICH FOLLOWS IS FOUND IN SOME COPIES IN THE EIGHTH BOOK.

1. The author of the edict very shortly after this confession was released from his pains and died. He is reported to have been the original author of the misery of the persecution, having endeavored, long before the movement of the other emperors, to turn from the faith the Christians in the army, and first of all those in his own house, degrading some from the military rank, and abusing others most shamefully, and threatening still others with death, and finally inciting his partners in the empire to the general persecution. It is not proper to pass over the death of these emperors in silence.

2. As four of them held the supreme authority, those who were advanced in age and honor, after the persecution had continued not quite two years, abdicated the government, as we have already stated, and passed the remainder of their lives in a common and private station.

3. The end of their lives was as follows. He who was first in honor and age perished through a long and most grievous physical infirmity. He who held the second place ended his life by strangling, suffering thus according to a certain demoniacal prediction, on account of his many daring crimes.

4. Of those after them, the last, of whom we have spoken as the originator of the entire persecution, suffered such things as we have related. But he who preceded him, the most merciful and kindly emperor Constantius, passed all the time of his government in a manner worthy of his office. Moreover, he conducted himself towards all most favorably and beneficently. He took not the smallest part in the war

against us, and preserved the pious that were under him unharmed and unabused. Neither did he throw down the church buildings, nor devise anything else against us. The end of his life was happy and thrice blessed. He alone at death left his empire happily and gloriously to his own son as his successor, one who was in all respects most prudent and pious. He entered on the government at once, being proclaimed supreme emperor and Augustus by the soldiers; and he showed himself an emulator of his father's piety toward our doctrine.

5. Such were the deaths of the four of whom we have written, which took place at different times.

6. Of these, moreover, only the one referred to a little above by us, with those who afterward shared in the government, finally published openly to all the above-mentioned confession, in the written edict which he issued.

Supplement to Book VIII.

THE MARTYRS OF PALESTINE.

The Following also we found in a Certain Copy in the Eighth Book.

Introduction.

1. It was in the nineteenth year of the reign of Diocletian, in the month Xanthicus, which is called April by the Romans, about the time of the feast of our Saviour's passion, while Flavianus was governor of the province of Palestine, that letters were published everywhere, commanding that the churches be leveled to the ground and the Scriptures be destroyed by fire, and ordering that those who held places of honor be degraded, and that the household servants, if they persisted in the profession of Christianity, be deprived of freedom.

2. Such was the force of the first edict against us. But not long after other letters were issued, commanding that all the bishops of the churches everywhere be first thrown into prison, and afterward, by every artifice, be compelled to sacrifice.

Chapter I.

1. The first of the martyrs of Palestine was Procopius, who, before he had received the trial of imprisonment, immediately on his first appearance before the governor's tribunal, having been ordered to sacrifice to the so-called gods, declared that he knew only one to whom it was proper to sacrifice, as he himself wills. But when he was commanded to offer libations to the four emperors, having quoted a sentence which displeased them, he was immediately beheaded. The

quotation was from the poet: "The rule of many is not good; let there be one ruler and one king."

2. It was the seventh day of the month Desius, the seventh before the ides of June, as the Romans reckon, and the fourth day of the week, when this first example was given at Caesura in Palestine.

3. Afterwards, in the same city, many rulers of the country churches readily endured terrible sufferings, and furnished to the beholders an example of noble conflicts. But others, benumbed in spirit by terror, were easily weakened at the first onset. Of the rest, each one endured different forms of torture, as scourgings without number, and rackings, and tearings of their sides, and insupportable fetters, by which the hands of some were dislocated.

4. Yet they endured what came upon them, as in accordance with the inscrutable purposes of God. For the hands of one were seized, and he was led to the altar, while they thrust into his right hand the polluted and abominable offering, and he was dismissed as if he had sacrificed. Another had not even touched it, yet when others said that he had sacrificed, he went away in silence. Another, being taken up half dead, was cast aside as if already dead, and released from his bonds, and counted among the sacrificers. When another cried out, and testified that he would not obey, he was struck in the mouth, and silenced by a large band of those who were drawn up for this purpose, and driven away by force, even though he had not sacrificed. Of such consequence did they consider it, to seem by any means to have accomplished their purpose.

5. Therefore, of all this number, the only ones who were honored with the crown of the holy martyrs were Alphæus and Zacchæus. After stripes and scrapings and severe bonds and additional tortures and various other trials, and after having their feet stretched for a night and day over four holes in the stocks, on the seventeenth day of the month Dius,—that is, according to the Romans, the fifteenth before the Kalends of December—having confessed one only God and Christ Jesus as king, as if they had uttered some blasphemy, they were beheaded like the former martyr.

Chapter II.

1. What occurred to Romanus on the same day at Antioch, is also worthy of record. For he was a native of Palestine, a deacon and exorcist in the parish of Cæsarea; and being present at the destruction of the churches, he beheld many men, with women and children, going up in crowds to the idols and sacrificing. But, through his great zeal for religion, he could not endure the sight, and rebuked them with a loud voice.

2. Being arrested for his boldness, he proved a most noble witness

of the truth, if there ever was one. For when the judge informed him that he was to die by fire, he received the sentence with cheerful countenance and most ready mind, and was led away. When he was bound to the stake, and the wood piled up around him, as they were awaiting the arrival of the emperor before lighting the fire, he cried, "Where is the fire for me?"

3. Having said this, he was summoned again before the emperor, and subjected to the unusual torture of having his tongue cut out. But he endured this with fortitude and showed to all by his deeds that the Divine Power is present with those who endure any hardship whatever for the sake of religion, lightening their sufferings and strengthening their zeal. When he learned of this strange mode of punishment, the noble man was not terrified, but put out his tongue readily, and offered it with the greatest alacrity to those who cut it off.

4. After this punishment he was thrown into prison, and suffered there for a very long time. At last the twentieth anniversary of the emperor being near, when, according to an established gracious custom, liberty was proclaimed everywhere to all who were in bonds, he alone had both his feet stretched over five holes in the stocks, and while he lay there was strangled, and was thus honored with martyrdom, as he desired.

5. Although he was outside of his country, yet, as he was a native of Palestine, it is proper to count him among the Palestinian martyrs. These things occurred in this manner during the first year, when the persecution was directed only against the rulers of the Church.

Chapter III.

1. In the course of the second year, the persecution against us increased greatly. And at that time Urbanus being governor of the province, imperial edicts were first issued to him, commanding by a general decree that all the people should sacrifice at once in the different cities, and offer libations to the idols. In Gaza, a city of Palestine, Timotheus endured countless tortures, and afterwards was subjected to a slow and moderate fire. Having given, by his patience in all his sufferings, most genuine evidence of sincerest piety toward the Deity, he bore away the crown of the victorious athletes of religion. At the same time Agapius and our contemporary, Thecla, having exhibited most noble constancy, were condemned as food for the wild beasts.

2. But who that beheld these things would not have admired, or if they heard of them by report, would not have been astonished? For when the heathen everywhere were holding a festival and the customary shows, it was noised abroad that besides the other entertainments, the public combat of those who had lately been condemned to wild beasts would also take place.

3. As this report increased and spread in all directions, six young men, namely, Timolaus, a native of Pontus, Dionysius from Tripolis in Phœnicia, Romulus, a sub-deacon of the parish of Diospolis, Pæsis and Alexander, both Egyptians, and another Alexander from Gaza, having first bound their own hands, went in haste to Urbanus, who was about to open the exhibition, evidencing great zeal for martyrdom. They confessed that they were Christians, and by their ambition for all terrible things, showed that those who glory in the religion of the God of the universe do not cower before the attacks of wild beasts.

4. Immediately, after creating no ordinary astonishment in the governor and those who were with him, they were cast into prison. After a few days two others were added to them. One of them, named Agapius, had in former confessions endured dreadful torments of various kinds. The other, who had supplied them with the necessaries of life, was called Dionysius. All of these eight were beheaded on one day at Cæsarea, on the twenty-fourth day of the month Dystrus, which is the ninth before the Kalends of April.

5. Meanwhile, a change in the emperors occurred, and the first of them all in dignity, and the second retired into private life, and public affairs began to be troubled.

6. Shortly after the Roman government became divided against itself, and a cruel war arose among them. And this division, with the troubles which grew out of it, was not settled until peace toward us had been established throughout the entire Roman Empire.

7. For when this peace arose for all, as the daylight after the darkest and most gloomy night, the public affairs of the Roman government were re-established, and became happy and peaceful, and the ancestral good-will toward each other was revived. But we will relate these things more fully at the proper time. Now let us return to the regular course of events.

Chapter IV.

1. Maximinus Cæsar having come at that time into the government, as if to manifest to all the evidences of his reborn enmity against God, and of his impiety, armed himself for persecution against us more vigorously than his predecessors.

2. In consequence, no little confusion arose among all, and they scattered here and there, endeavoring in some way to escape the danger; and there was great commotion everywhere. But what words would suffice for a suitable description of the Divine love and boldness, in confessing God, of the blessed and truly innocent lamb, I refer to the martyr Apphianus,—who presented in the sight of all, before the gates of Cæsarea, a wonderful example of piety toward the only God?

3. He was at that time not twenty years old. He had first spent a long time at Berytus, for the sake of a secular Grecian education, as he belonged to a very wealthy family. It is wonderful to relate how, in such a city, he was superior to youthful passions, and clung to virtue, uncorrupted neither by his bodily vigor nor his young companions; living discreetly, soberly and piously, in accordance with his profession of the Christian doctrine and the life of his teachers.

4. If it is needful to mention his native country, and give honor to it as producing this noble athlete of piety, we will do so with pleasure.

5. The young man came from Pagæ,—if any one is acquainted with the place—a city in Lycia of no mean importance. After his return from his course of study in Berytus, though his father held the first place in his country, he could not bear to live with him and his relatives, as it did not please them to live according to the rules of religion. Therefore, as if he were led by the Divine Spirit, and in accordance with a natural, or rather an inspired and true philosophy, regarding this preferable to what is considered the glory of life, and despising bodily comforts, he secretly left his family. And because of his faith and hope in God, paying no attention to his daily needs, he was led by the Divine Spirit to the city of Cæsarea, where was prepared for him the crown of martyrdom for piety.

6. Abiding with us there, and conferring with us in the Divine Scriptures diligently for a short time, and fitting himself zealously by suitable exercises, he exhibited such an end as would astonish any one should it be seen again.

7. Who, that hears of it, would not justly admire his courage, boldness, constancy, and even more than these the daring deed itself, which evidenced a zeal for religion and a spirit truly superhuman?

8. For in the second attack upon us under Maximinus, in the third year of the persecution, edicts of the tyrant were issued for the first time, commanding that the rulers of the cities should diligently and speedily see to it that all the people offered sacrifices. Throughout the city of Cæsarea, by command of the governor, the heralds were summoning men, women, and children to the temples of the idols, and besides this, the chiliarchs were calling out each one by name from a roll, and an immense crowd of the wicked were rushing together from all quarters. Then this youth fearlessly, while no one was aware of his intentions, eluded both us who lived in the house with him and the whole band of soldiers that surrounded the governor, and rushed up to Urbanus as he was offering libations, and fearlessly seizing him by the right hand, straightway put a stop to his sacrificing, and skillfully and persuasively, with a certain divine inspiration, exhorted him to abandon his delusion, because it was not well to forsake the one and only true God, and sacrifice to idols and demons.

9. It is probable that this was done by the youth through a divine

power which led him forward, and which all but cried aloud in his act, that Christians, who were truly such, were so far from abandoning the religion of the God of the universe which they had once espoused, that they were not only superior to threats and the punishments which followed, but yet bolder to speak with noble and untrammeled tongue, and, if possible, to summon even their persecutors to turn from their ignorance and acknowledge the only true God.

10. Thereupon, he of whom we are speaking, and that instantly, as might have been expected after so bold a deed, was torn by the governor and those who were with him as if by wild beasts. And having endured manfully innumerable blows over his entire body, he was straightway cast into prison.

11. There he was stretched by the tormentor with both his feet in the stocks for a night and a day; and the next day he was brought before the judge. As they endeavored to force him to surrender, he exhibited all constancy under suffering and terrible tortures. His sides were torn, not once, or twice, but many times, to the bones and the very bowels; and he received so many blows on his face and neck that those who for a long time had been well acquainted with him could not recognize his swollen face.

12. But as he would not yield under this treatment, the torturers, as commanded, covered his feet with linen cloths soaked in oil and set them on fire. No word can describe the agonies which the blessed one endured from this. For the fire consumed his flesh and penetrated to his bones, so that the humors of his body were melted and oozed out and dropped down like wax.

13. But as he was not subdued by this, his adversaries being defeated and unable to comprehend his superhuman constancy, cast him again into prison. A third time he was brought before the judge; and having witnessed the same profession, being half dead, he was finally thrown into the depths of the sea.

14. But what happened immediately after this will scarcely be believed by those who did not see it. Although we realize this, yet we must record the event, of which to speak plainly, all the inhabitants of Cæsarea were witnesses. For truly there was no age but beheld this marvelous sight.

15. For as soon as they had cast this truly sacred and thrice-blessed youth into the fathomless depths of the sea, an uncommon commotion and disturbance agitated the sea and all the shore about it, so that the land and the entire city were shaken by it. And at the same time with this wonderful and sudden perturbation, the sea threw out before the gates of the city the body of the divine martyr, as if unable to endure it. Such was the death of the wonderful Apphianus. It occurred on the second day of the month Xanthicus, which is the fourth day before the Nones of April, on the day of preparation.

Chapter V.

1. About the same time, in the city of Tyre, a youth named Ulpianus, after dreadful tortures and most severe scourgings, was enclosed in a raw oxhide, with a dog and with one of those poisonous reptiles, an asp, and cast into the sea. Wherefore I think that we may properly mention him in connection with the martyrdom of Apphianus.

2. Shortly afterwards, Ædesius, a brother of Apphianus, not only in God, but also in the flesh, being a son of the same earthly father, endured sufferings like his, after very many confessions and protracted tortures in bonds, and after he had been sentenced by the governor to the mines in Palestine. He conducted himself through them all in a truly philosophic manner; for he was more highly educated than his brother, and had prosecuted philosophic studies.

3. Finally in the city of Alexandria, when he beheld the judge, who was trying the Christians, offending beyond all bounds, now insulting holy men in various ways, and again consigning women of greatest modesty and even religious virgins to procurers for shameful treatment, he acted like his brother. For as these things seemed insufferable, he went forward with bold resolve, and with his words and deeds overwhelmed the judge with shame and disgrace. After suffering in consequence many forms of torture, he endured a death similar to his brother's, being cast into the sea. But these things, as I have said, happened to him in this way a little later.

Chapter VI.

1. In the fourth year of the persecution against us, on the twelfth day before the Kalends of December, which is the twentieth day of the month Dius, on the day before the Sabbath, while the tyrant Maximinus was present and giving magnificent shows in honor of his birthday, the following event, truly worthy of record, occurred in the city of Cæsarea.

2. As it was an ancient custom to furnish the spectators more splendid shows when the emperors were present than at other times,— new and foreign spectacles taking the place of the customary amusements, such as animals brought from India or Ethiopia or other places, or men who could astonish the beholders with skillful bodily exercises—it was necessary at this time, as the emperor was giving the exhibition, to add to the shows something more wonderful. And what should this be?

3. A witness of our doctrine was brought into the midst and endured the contest for the true and only religion. This was Agapius, who, as we have stated a little above, was, with Thecla, the second to

be thrown to the wild beasts for food. He had also, three times and more, marched with malefactors from the prison to the arena; and every time, after threats from the judge, whether in compassion or in hope that he might change his mind, had been reserved for other conflicts. But the emperor being present, he was brought out at this time, as if he had been appropriately reserved for this occasion, until the very word of the Saviour should be fulfilled in him, which through divine knowledge he declared to his disciples, that they should be brought before kings on account of their testimony unto him.

4. He was taken into the midst of the arena with a certain malefactor who they said was charged with the murder of his master.

5. But this murderer of his master, when he had been cast to the wild beasts, was deemed worthy of compassion and humanity, almost like Barabbas in the time of our Saviour. And the whole theater resounded with shouts and cries of approval, because the murderer was humanely saved by the emperor, and deemed worthy of honor and freedom.

6. But the athlete of religion was first summoned by the tyrant and promised liberty if he would deny his profession. But he testified with a loud voice that, not for any fault, but for the religion of the Creator of the universe, he would readily and with pleasure endure whatever might be inflicted upon him.

7. Having said this, he joined the deed to the word, and rushed to meet a bear which had been let loose against him, surrendering himself most cheerfully to be devoured by him. After this, as he still breathed, he was cast into prison. And living yet one day, stones were bound to his feet, and he was drowned in the depths of the sea. Such was the martyrdom of Agapius.

Chapter VII.

1. Again, in Cæsarea, when the persecution had continued to the fifth year, on the second day of the month Xanthicus, which is the fourth before the Nones of April, on the very Lord's day of our Saviour's resurrection, Theodosia, a virgin from Tyre, a faithful and sedate maiden, not yet eighteen years of age, went up to certain prisoners who were confessing the kingdom of Christ and sitting before the judgment seat, and saluted them, and, as is probable, besought them to remember her when they came before the Lord.

2. Thereupon, as if she had committed a profane and impious act, the soldiers seized her and led her to the governor. And he immediately, like a madman and a wild beast in his anger, tortured her with dreadful and most terrible torments in her sides and breasts, even to the very bones. And as she still breathed, and withal stood with a joyful and beaming countenance, he ordered her thrown into the waves

of the sea. Then passing from her to the other confessors, he condemned all of them to the copper mines in Phæno in Palestine.

3. Afterwards on the fifth of the month Dius, on the Nones of November according to the Romans, in the same city, Silvanus (who at that time was a presbyter and confessor, but who shortly after was honored with the episcopate and died a martyr), and those with him, men who had shown the noblest firmness in behalf of religion, were condemned by him to labor in the same copper mines, command being first given that their ankles be disabled with hot irons.

4. At the same time he delivered to the flames a man who was illustrious through numerous other confessions. This was Domninus, who was well known to all in Palestine for his exceeding fearlessness After this the same judge, who was a cruel contriver of suffering, and an inventor of devices against the doctrine of Christ, planned against the pious punishments that had never been heard of. He condemned three to single pugilistic combat. He delivered to be devoured by wild beasts Auxentius, a grave and holy old man. Others who were in mature life he made eunuchs, and condemned them to the same mines. Yet others, after severe tortures, he cast into prison. Among these was my dearest friend Pamphilus, who was by reason of every virtue the most illustrious of the martyrs in our time.

5. Urbanus first tested him in rhetorical philosophy and learning; and afterwards endeavored to compel him to sacrifice. But as he saw that he refused and in nowise regarded his threats, being exceedingly angry, he ordered him to be tormented with severest tortures.

6. And when the brutal man, after he had almost satiated himself with these tortures by continuous and prolonged scrapings in his sides, was yet covered with shame before all, he put him also with the confessors in prison.

7. But what recompense for his cruelty to the saints, he who thus abused the martyrs of Christ, shall receive from the Divine judgment, may be easily determined from the preludes to it, in which immediately, and not long after his daring cruelties against Pamphilus, while he yet held the government, the Divine judgment came upon him. For thus suddenly, he who but yesterday was judging on the lofty tribunal, guarded by a band of soldiers, and ruling over the whole nation of Palestine, the associate and dearest friend and table companion of the tyrant himself, was stripped in one night, and overwhelmed with disgrace and shame before those who had formerly admired him as if he were himself an emperor; and he appeared cowardly and unmanly, uttering womanish cries and supplications to all the people whom he had ruled. And Maximinus himself, in reliance upon whose favor Urbanus was formerly so arrogantly insolent, as if he loved him exceedingly for his deeds against us, was set as a harsh and most severe judge in this same Cæsarea to pronounce sentence of death

against him, for the great disgrace of the crimes of which he was convicted.

8. Let us say this in passing. A suitable time may come when we shall have leisure to relate the end and the fate of those impious men who especially fought against us, both of Maximinus himself and those with him.

Chapter VIII.

1. Up to the sixth year the storm had been incessantly raging against us. Before this time there had been a very large number of confessors of religion in the so-called Porphyry quarry in Thebais, which gets its name from the stone found there. Of these, one hundred men, lacking three, together with women and infants, were sent to the governor of Palestine. When they confessed the God of the universe and Christ, Firmilianus, who had been sent there as governor in the place of Urbanus, directed, in accordance with the imperial command, that they should be maimed by burning the sinews of the ankles of their left feet, and that their right eyes with the eyelids and pupils should first be cut out, and then destroyed by hot irons to the very roots. And he then sent them to the mines in the province to endure hardships with severe toil and suffering.

2. But it was not sufficient that these only who suffered such miseries should be deprived of their eyes, but those natives of Palestine also, who were mentioned just above as condemned to pugilistic combat, Since they would neither receive food from the royal storehouse nor undergo the necessary preparatory Exercises.

3. Having been brought on this account not only before the overseers, but also before Maximinus himself, and having manifested the noblest persistence in confession by the endurance of hunger and stripes, they received like punishment with those whom we have mentioned, and with them other confessors in the city of Cæsarea.

4. Immediately afterwards others who were gathered to hear the Scriptures read, were seized in Gaza, and some endured the same sufferings in the feet and eyes; but others were afflicted with yet greater torments and with most terrible tortures in the sides.

5. One of these, in body a woman, but in understanding a man, would not endure the threat of fornication, and spoke directly against the tyrant who entrusted the government to such cruel judges. She was first scourged and then raised aloft on the stake, and her sides lacerated.

6. As those appointed for this purpose applied the tortures incessantly and severely at the command of the judge, another, with mind fixed, like the former, on virginity as her aim—a woman who was altogether mean in forth and contemptible in appearance; but, on the other hand, strong in soul, and endowed with an understanding superior

to her body—being unable to bear the merciless and cruel and inhuman deeds, with a boldness beyond that of the combatants famed among the Greeks, cried out to the judge from the midst of the crowd: "And how long will you thus cruelly torture my sister?" But he was greatly enraged, and ordered the woman to be immediately seized.

7. Thereupon she was brought forward and having called herself by the august name of the Saviour, she was first urged by words to sacrifice, and as she refused she was dragged by force to the altar. But her sister continued to maintain her former zeal, and with intrepid and resolute foot kicked the altar, and overturned it with the fire that was on it.

8. Thereupon the judge, enraged like a wild beast, inflicted on her such tortures in her sides as he never had on any one before, striving almost to glut himself with her raw flesh. But when his madness was satiated, he bound them both together, this one and her whom she called sister, and condemned them to death by fire. It is said that the first of these was from the country of Gaza; the other, by name Valentina, was of Cæsarea, and was well known to many.

9. But how can I describe as it deserves the martyrdom which followed, with which the thrice-blessed Paul was honored. He was condemned to death at the same time with them, under one sentence. At the time of his martyrdom, as the executioner was about to cut off his head, he requested a brief respite.

10. This being granted, he first, in a clear and distinct voice, supplicated God in behalf of his fellow-Christians, praying for their pardon, and that freedom might soon be restored to them. Then he asked for the conversion of the Jews to God through Christ; and proceeding in order he requested the same things for the Samaritans, and besought that those Gentiles, who were in error and were ignorant of God, might come to a knowledge of him, and adopt the true religion. Nor did he leave neglected the mixed multitude who were standing around.

11. After all these, oh! great and unspeakable forbearance! he entreated the God of the universe for the judge who had condemned him to death, and for the highest rulers, and also for the one who was about to behead him, in his hearing and that of all present, beseeching that their sin toward him should not be reckoned against them.

12. Having prayed for these things with a loud voice, and having, as one who was dying unjustly, moved almost all to compassion and tears, of his own accord he made himself ready, and submitted his bare neck to the stroke of the sword, and was adorned with divine martyrdom. This took place on the twenty-fifth day of the month Panemus, which is the eighth before the Kalends of August.

13. Such was the end of these persons. But not long after, one hundred and thirty admirable athletes of the confession of Christ, from

the land of Egypt, endured, in Egypt itself, at the command of Maximinus the same afflictions in their eyes and feet with the former persons, and were sent to the above-mentioned mines in Palestine. But some of them were condemned to the mines in Cilicia.

Chapter IX.

1. After such noble acts of the distinguished martyrs of Christ, the flame of persecution lessened, and was quenched, as it were by their sacred blood, and relief and liberty were granted to those who, for Christ's sake, were laboring in the mines of Thebais, and for a little time we were beginning to breath pure air. But by some new impulse, I know not what, he who held the power to persecute was again aroused against the Christians.

2. Immediately letters from Maximinus against us were published everywhere in every province. The governors and the military prefect urged by edicts and letters and public ordinances the magistrates and generals and notaries in all the cities to carry out the imperial decree, which ordered that the altars of the idols should with all speed be rebuilt; and that all men, women, and children, even infants at the breast, should sacrifice and offer oblations; and that with diligence and care they should cause them to taste of the execrable offerings; and that the things for sale in the market should be polluted with libations from the sacrifices; and that guards should be stationed before the baths in order to defile with the abominable sacrifices those who went to wash in them.

3. When these orders were being carried out, our people, as was natural, were at the beginning greatly distressed in mind; and even the unbelieving heathen blamed the severity and the exceeding absurdity of what was done. For these things appeared to them extreme and burdensome. As the heaviest storm impended over all in every quarter, the divine power of our Saviour again infused such boldness into his athletes, that without being drawn on or dragged forward by any one, they spurned the threats.

4. Three of the faithful joining together, rushed on the governor as he was sacrificing to the idols, and cried out to him to cease from his delusion, there being no other God than the Maker and Creator of the universe. When he asked who they were, they confessed boldly that they were Christians.

5. Thereupon Firmilianus, being greatly enraged, sentenced them to capital punishment without inflicting tortures upon them. The name of the eldest of these was Antoninus; of the next, Zebinas, who was a native of Eleutheropolis; and of the third, Germanus. This took place on the thirteenth of the month Dius, the Ides of November?

6. There was associated with them on the same day Ennathas, a

woman from Scythopolis, who was adorned with the chaplet of virginity. She did not indeed do as they had. done, but was dragged by force and brought before the judge.

7. She endured scourgings and cruel insults, which Maxys, a tribune of a neighboring district, without the knowledge of the superior authority, dared to inflict upon her. He was a man worse than his name, sanguinary in other respects, exceedingly harsh, and altogether cruel, and censured by all who knew him. This man stripped the blessed woman of all her clothing, so that she was covered only from her loins to her feet and the rest of her body was bare. And he led her through the entire city of Cæsarea, and regarded it as a great thing to beat her with thongs while she was dragged through all the market-places.

8. After such treatment she manifested the noblest constancy at the judgment seat of the governor himself; and the judge condemned her to be burned alive. He also carried his rage against the pious to a most inhuman length and transgressed the laws of nature, not being ashamed even to deny burial to the lifeless bodies of the sacred men.

9. Thus he ordered the dead to be exposed in the open air as food for wild beasts and to be watched carefully by night and day. For many days a large number of men attended to this savage and barbarous decree. And they looked out from their post of observation, as if it were a matter worthy of care, to see that the dead bodies should not be stolen.

10. And wild beasts and dogs and birds of prey scattered the human limbs here and there, and the whole city was strewed with the entrails and bones of men, so that nothing had ever appeared more dreadful and horrible, even to those who formerly hated us; though they bewailed not so much the calamity of those against whom these things were done, as the outrage against themselves and the common nature of man.

11. For there was to be seen near the gates a spectacle beyond all description and tragic recital; for not only was human flesh devoured in one place, but it was scattered in every place; so that some said that limbs and masses of flesh and parts of entrails were to be seen even within the gates.

12. After these things had continued for many days, a wonderful event occurred. The air was clear and bright and the appearance of the sky most serene. When suddenly throughout the city from the pillars which supported the public porches many drops fell like tears; and the market places and streets, though there was no mist in the air, were moistened with sprinkled water, whence I know not. Then immediately it was reported everywhere that the earth, unable to endure the abomination of these things, had shed tears in a mysterious manner; and that as a rebuke to the relentless and unfeeling nature of men, stones and lifeless wood had wept for what had happened. I know well

that this account may perhaps appear idle and fabulous to those who come after us, but not to those to whom the truth was confirmed at the time.

Chapter X.

1. On the fourteenth day of the following month Appellæus, the nineteenth before the Kalends of January, certain persons from Egypt were again seized by those who examined people passing the gates. They had been sent to minister to the confessors in Cilicia. They received the same sentence as those whom they had gone to help, being mutilated in their eyes and feet. Three of them exhibited in Ascalon, where they were imprisoned, marvelous bravery in the endurance of various kinds of martyrdom. One of them named Ares was condemned to the flames, and the others, called Probus and Elias, were beheaded.

2. On the eleventh day of the month Audynæus, which is the third before the Ides of January, in the same city of Cæsarea, Peter an ascetic, also called Apselamus, from the village of Anea, on the borders of Eleutheropolis, like purest gold, gave noble proof by fire of his faith in the Christ of God. Though the judge and those around him besought him many times to have compassion on himself, and to spare his own youth and bloom, he disregarded them, preferring hope in the God of the universe to all things, even to life itself. A certain Asclepius, supposed to be a bishop of the sect of Marcion, possessed as he thought with zeal for religion, but "not according to knowledge," ended his life on one and the same funeral pyre. These things took place in this manner.

Chapter XI.

1. It is time to describe the great and celebrated spectacle of Pamphilus, a man thrice dear to me, and of those who finished their course with him. They were twelve in all; being counted worthy of apostolic grace and number.

2. Of these the leader and the only one honored with the position of presbyter at Cæsarea, was Pamphilus; a man who through his entire life was celebrated for every virtue, for renouncing and despising the world, for sharing his possessions with the needy, for contempt of earthly hopes, and for philosophic deportment and exercise. He especially excelled all in our time in most sincere devotion to the Divine Scriptures and indefatigable industry in whatever he undertook, and in his helpfulness to his relatives and associates.

3. In a separate treatise on his life, consisting of three books, we have already described the excellence of his virtue. Referring to this work those who delight in such things and desire to know them, let us

now consider the martyrs in order.

4. Second after Pamphilus, Vales, who was honored for his venerable gray hair, entered and versed in the Divine Scriptures, if any one ever was. He had so laid up the memory of them in his heart that he did not need to look at the books if he undertook to repeat any passage of Scripture.

5. The third was Paul from the city of Jamna, who was known among them as most zealous and fervent in spirit. Previous to his martyrdom, he had endured the conflict of confession by cauterization. After these persons had continued in prison for two entire years, the occasion of their martyrdom was a second arrival of Egyptian brethren who suffered with them.

6. They had accompanied the confessors in Cilicia to the mines there and were returning to their homes. At the entrance of the gates of Cæsarea, the guards, who were men of barbarous character, questioned them as to who they were and whence they came. They kept back nothing of the truth, and were seized as malefactors taken in the very act. They were five in number.

7. When brought before the tyrant, being very bold in his presence, they were immediately thrown into prison. On the next day, which was the nineteenth of the month Peritius, according to the Roman reckoning the fourteenth before the Kalends of March, they were brought, according to command, before the judge, with Pamphilus and his associates whom we have mentioned. First, by all kinds of torture, through the invention of strange and various machines, he tested the invincible constancy of the Egyptians.

8. Having practised these cruelties upon the leader of all, he asked him first who he was. He heard in reply the name of some prophet instead of his proper name. For it was their custom, in place of the names of idols given them by their fathers, if they had such, to take other names; so that you would hear them calling themselves Elijah or Jeremiah or Isaiah or Samuel or Daniel, thus showing themselves inwardly true Jews, and the genuine Israel of God, not only in deeds, but in the names which they bore. When Firmilianus had heard some such name from the martyr, and did not understand the force of the word, he asked next the name of his country.

9. But he gave a second answer similar to the former, saying that Jerusalem was his country, meaning that of which Paul says, "Jerusalem which is above is free, which is our mother," and, "Ye are come unto Mount Sion, and unto the city of the living God, the heavenly Jerusalem."

10. This was what he meant; but the judge thinking only of the earth, sought diligently to discover what that city was, and in what part of the world it was situated. And therefore he applied tortures that the truth might be acknowledged. But the man, with his hands twisted

behind his back, and his feet crushed by strange machines, asserted firmly that he had spoken the truth.

11. And being questioned again repeatedly what and where the city was of which he spoke, he said that it was the country of the pious alone, for no others should have a place in it, and that it lay toward the far East and the rising sun.

12. He philosophized about these things according to his own understanding, and was in nowise turned froth them by the tortures with which he was afflicted on every side. And as if he were without flesh or body he seemed insensible of his sufferings. But the judge being perplexed, was impatient, thinking that the Christians were about to establish a city somewhere, inimical and hostile to the Romans. And he inquired much about this, and investigated where that country toward the East was located.

13. But when he had for a long time lacerated the young man with scourgings, and punished him with all sorts of torments, he perceived that his persistence in what he had said could not be changed, and passed against him sentence of death. Such a scene was exhibited by what was done to this man. And having inflicted similar tortures on the others, he sent them away in the same manner.

14. Then being wearied and perceiving that he punished the men in vain, having satiated his desire, he proceeded against Pamphilus and his companions. And having learned that already under former tortures they had manifested an unchangeable zeal for the faith, he asked them if they would now obey. And receiving from every one of them only this one answer, as their last word of confession in martyrdom, he inflicted on them punishment similar to the others.

15. When this had been done, a young man, one of the household servants of Pamphilus, who had been educated in the noble life and instruction of such a man, learning the sentence passed upon his master, cried out from the midst of the crowd asking that their bodies might be buried.

16. Thereupon the judge, not a man, but a wild beast, or if anything more savage than a wild beast, giving no consideration to the young man's age, asked him only the same question. When he learned that he confessed himself a Christian, as if he had been wounded by a dart, swelling with rage, he ordered the tormentors to use their utmost power against him.

17. And when he saw that he refused to sacrifice as commanded, he ordered them to scrape him continually to his very bones and to the inmost recesses of his bowels, not as if he were human flesh but as if he were stones or wood or any lifeless thing. But after long persistence he saw that this was in vain, as the man was speechless and insensible and almost lifeless, his body being worn out by the tortures.

18. But being inflexibly merciless and inhuman, he ordered him to

be committed straightway, as he was, to a slow fire. And before the death of his earthly master, though he had entered later on the conflict, he received release from the body, while those who had been zealous about the others were yet delaying.

19. One could then see. Porphyry, like one who had come off victorious in every conflict, his body covered with dust, but his countenance cheerful, after such sufferings, with courageous and exulting mind, advancing to death. And as if truly filled with the Divine Spirit, covered only with his philosophic robe thrown about him as a cloak, soberly and intelligently he directed his friends as to what he wished, and beckoned to them, preserving still a cheerful countenance even at the stake. But when the fire was kindled at some distance around him in a circle, having inhaled the flame into his mouth, he continued most nobly in silence from that time till his death, after the single word which he uttered when the flame first touched him, and he cried out for the help of Jesus the Son of God. Such was the contest of Porphyry.

20. His death was reported to Pamphilus by a messenger, Seleucus. He was one of the confessors from the army. As the bearer of such a message, he was forthwith deemed worthy of a similar lot. For as soon as he related the death of Porphyry, and had saluted one of the martyrs with a kiss, some of the soldiers seized him and led him to the governor. And he, as if he would hasten him on to be a companion of the former on the way to heaven, commanded that he be put to death immediately.

21. This man was from Cappadocia, and belonged to the select band of soldiers, and had obtained no small honor in those things which are esteemed among the Romans. For in stature and bodily strength, and size and vigor, he far excelled his fellow-soldiers, so that his appearance was matter of common talk, and his whole form was admired on account of its size and symmetrical proportions.

22. At the beginning of the persecution he was prominent in the conflicts of confession, through his patience under scourging. After he left the army he set himself to imitate zealously the religious ascetics, and as if he were their father and guardian he showed himself a bishop and patron of destitute orphans and defenceless widows and of those who were distressed with penury or sickness. It is likely that on this account he was deemed worthy of an extraordinary call to martyrdom by God, who rejoices in such things more than in the smoke and blood of sacrifices.

23. He was the tenth athlete among those whom we have mentioned as meeting their end on one and the same day. On this day, as was fitting, the chief gate was opened, and a ready way of entrance into the kingdom of heaven was given to the martyr Pamphilus and to the others with him.

24. In the footsteps of Seleucus came Theodulus, a grave and pious old man, who belonged to the governor's household, and had been honored by Firmilianus himself more than all the others in his house on account of his age, and because he was a father of the third generation, and also on account of the kindness and most faithful conscientiousness which he had manifested toward him. As he pursued the course of Seleucus when brought before his master, the latter was more angry at him than at those who had preceded him, and condemned him to endure the martyrdom of the Saviour on the cross.

25. As there lacked yet one to fill up the number of the twelve martyrs of whom we have spoken, Julian came to complete it. He had just arrived from abroad, and had not yet entered the gate of the city, when having learned about the martyrs while still on the way, he rushed at once, just as he was, to see them. When he beheld the tabernacles of the saints prone on the ground, being filled with joy, he embraced and kissed them all.

26. The ministers of slaughter straightway seized him as he was doing this and led him to Firmilianus. Acting as was his custom, he condemned him to a slow fire. Thereupon Julian, leaping and exulting, in a loud voice gave thanks to the Lord who had judged him worthy of such things, and was honored with the crown of martyrdom.

27. He was a Cappadocian by birth, and in his manner of life he was most circumspect, faithful and sincere, zealous in all other respects, and animated by the Holy Spirit himself. Such was the company which was thought worthy to enter into martyrdom with Pamphilus.

28. By the command of the impious governor their sacred and truly holy bodies were kept as food for the wild beasts for four days and as many nights. But since, strange to say, through the providential care of God, nothing approached them—neither beast of prey, nor bird, nor dog—they were taken up uninjured, and after suitable preparation were buried in the customary manner.

29. When the report of what had been done to these men was spread in all directions, Adrianus and Eubulus, having come from the so-called country of Manganaea to Cæsarea, to see the remaining confessors, were also asked at the gate the reason for their coming; and having acknowledged the truth, were brought to Firmilianus. But he, as was his custom, without delay inflicted many tortures in their sides, and condemned them to be devoured by wild beasts.

30. After two days, on the fifth of the month Dystrus, the third before the Nones of March, which was regarded as the birthday of the tutelary divinity of Cæsarea, Adrianus was thrown to a lion, and afterwards slain with the sword. But Eubulus, two days later, on the Nones of March, that is, on the seventh of the month Dystrus, when the judge had earnestly entreated him to enjoy by sacrificing that which

was considered freedom among them, preferring a glorious death for religion to transitory life, was made like the other an offering to wild beasts, and as the last of the martyrs in Cæsarea, sealed the list of athletes.

31. It is proper also to relate here, how in a short time the heavenly Providence came upon the impious rulers, together with the tyrants themselves. For that very Firmilianus, who had thus abused the martyrs of Christ, after suffering with the others the severest punishment, was put to death by the sword. Such were the martyrdoms which took place at Cæsarea during the entire period of the persecution.

Chapter XII.

1. I Think it best to pass by all the other events which occurred in the meantime: such as those which happened to the bishops of the churches, when instead of shepherds of the rational flocks of Christ, over which they presided in an unlawful manner, the divine judgment, considering them worthy of such a charge, made them keepers of camels, an irrational beast and very crooked in the structure of its body, or condemned them to have the care of the imperial horses—and I pass by also the insults and disgraces and tortures they endured from the imperial overseers and rulers on account of the sacred vessels and treasures of the Church; and besides these the lust of power on the part of many, the disorderly and unlawful ordinations, and the schisms among the confessors themselves; also the novelties which were zealously devised against the remnants of the Church by the new and factious members, who added innovation after innovation and forced them in unsparingly among the calamities of the persecution, heaping misfortune upon misfortune. I judge it more suitable to shun and avoid the account of these things, as I said at the beginning. But such things as are sober and praiseworthy, according to the sacred word—"and if there be any virtue and praise,"—I consider it most proper to tell and to record, and to present to believing hearers in the history of the admirable martyrs. And after this I think it best to crown the entire work with an account of the peace which has appeared unto us from heaven.

Chapter XIII.

1. The seventh year of our conflict was completed; and the hostile measures which had continued into the eighth year were gradually and quietly becoming less severe. A large number of confessors were collected at the copper mines in Palestine, and were acting with considerable boldness, so far as even to build places of worship. But the ruler of the province, a cruel and wicked man, as his acts against the

martyrs showed, having come there and learned the state of affairs, communicated it to the emperor, writing in accusation whatever he thought best.

2. Thereupon, being appointed superintendent of the mines, he divided the band of confessors as if by a royal decree, and sent some to dwell in Cyprus and others in Lebanon, and he scattered others in different parts of Palestine and ordered them to labor in various works.

3. And, selecting the four who seemed to him to be the leaders, he sent them to the commander of the armies in that section. These were Peleus and Nilus, Egyptian bishops, also a presbyter, and Patermuthius, who was well known among them all for his zeal toward all. The commander of the army demanded of them a denial of religion, and not obtaining this, he condemned them to death by fire.

4. There were others there who had been allotted to dwell in a separate place by themselves—such of the confessors as on account of age or mutilations, or for other bodily infirmities, had been released from service. Silvanus, a bishop from Gaza, presided over them, and set a worthy and genuine example of Christianity.

5. This man having from the first day of the persecution, and throughout its entire continuance, been eminent for his confessions in all sorts of conflicts, had been kept all that time that he might, so to speak, set the final seal upon the whole con-flier in Palestine.

6. There were with him many from Egypt, among whom was John, who surpassed all in our time in the excellence of his memory. He had formerly been deprived of his sight. Nevertheless, on account of his eminence in confession he had with the others suffered the destruction of his foot by cauterization. And although his sight had been destroyed he was subjected to the same burning with fire, the executioners aiming after everything that was merciless and pitiless and cruel and inhuman.

7. Since he was such a man, one would not be so much astonished at his habits and his philosophic life, nor would he seem so wonderful for them, as for the strength of his memory. For he had written whole books of the Divine Scriptures, "not in tables of stone" as the divine apostle says, neither on skins of animals, nor on paper which moths and time destroy, but truly "in fleshy tables of the heart," in a transparent soul and most pure eye of the mind, so that whenever he wished he could repeat, as if from a treasury of words, any portion of the Scripture, whether in the law, or the prophets, or the historical books, or the gospels, or the writings of the apostles.

8. I confess that I was astonished when I first saw the man as he was standing in the midst of a large congregation and repeating portions of the Divine Scripture. While I only heard his voice, I thought that, according to the custom in the meetings, he was reading. But when I came near and perceived what he was doing, and observed all the others standing around him with sound eyes while he was using only

the eyes of his mind, and yet was speaking naturally like some prophet, and far excelling those who were sound in body, it was impossible for me not to glorify God and wonder. And I seemed to see in these deeds evident and strong confirmation of the fact that true manhood consists not in excellence of bodily appearance, but in the soul and understanding alone. For he, with his body mutilated, manifested the superior excellence of the power that was within him.

9. But as to those whom we have mentioned as abiding in a separate place, and attending to their customary duties in fasting and prayer and other exercises, God himself saw fit to give them a salutary issue by extending his right hand in answer to them. The bitter foe, as they were armed against him zealously through their prayers to God, could no longer endure them, and determined to slay and destroy them from off the earth because they troubled him.

10. And God permitted him to accomplish this, that he might not be restrained from the wickedness he desired, and that at the same time they might receive the prizes of their manifold conflicts. Therefore at the command of the most accursed Maximinus, forty, lacking one, were beheaded in one day.

11. These martyrdoms were accomplished in Palestine during eight complete years; and of this description was the persecution in our time. Beginning with the demolition of the churches, it increased greatly as the rulers rose up from time to time against us. In these assaults the multiform and various conflicts of those who wrestled in behalf of religion produced an innumerable multitude of martyrs in every province—in the regions extending from Libya and throughout all Egypt, and Syria, and from the East round about to the district of Illyricum.

12. But the countries beyond these, all Italy and Sicily and Gaul, and the regions toward the setting sun, in Spain, Mauritania, and Africa, suffered the war of persecution during less than two years, and were deemed worthy of a speedier divine visitation and peace; the heavenly Providence sparing the singleness of purpose and faith of those men.

13. For what had never before been recorded in the annals of the Roman government, first took place in our day, contrary to all expectation; for during the persecution in our time the empire was divided into two parts. The brethren dwelling in the part of which we have just spoken enjoyed peace; but those in the other part endured trials without number. But when the divine grace kindly and compassionately manifested its care for us too, then truly our rulers also, those very ones through whom the wars against us had been formerly carried on, changed their minds in a most wonderful manner, and published a recantation; and by favorable edicts and mild decrees concerning us, extinguished the conflagration against us. This

recantation also must be recorded.

Book IX.

Chapter I.

THE PRETENDED RELAXATION.

1. The imperial edict of recantation, which has been quoted above, was posted in all parts of Asia and in the adjoining provinces. After this had been done, Maximinus, the tyrant in the East—a most impious man, if there ever was one, and most hostile to the religion of the God of the universe—being by no means satisfied with its contents, instead of sending the above-quoted decree to the governors under him, gave them verbal commands to relax the war against us.

2. For since he could not in any other way oppose the decision of his superiors, keeping the law which had been already issued secret, and taking care that it might not be made known in the district under him, he gave an unwritten order to his governors that they should relax the persecution against us. They communicated the command to each other in writing.

3. Sabinus, at least, who was honored with the highest official rank among them, communicated the will of the emperor to the provincial governors in a Latin epistle, the translation of which is as follows:

4. "With continuous and most devoted earnestness their Majesties, our most divine masters, the emperors, formerly directed the minds of all men to follow the holy and correct course of life, that those also who seemed to live in a manner foreign to that of the Romans, should render the worship due to the immortal gods. But the obstinacy and most unconquerable determination of some went so far that they could neither be turned back from their purpose by the just reason of the command, nor be intimidated by the impending punishment.

5. Since therefore it has come to pass that by such conduct many have brought themselves into danger, their Majesties, our most powerful masters, the emperors, in the exalted nobility of piety, esteeming it foreign to their Majesties' purpose to bring men into so great danger for such a cause, have commanded their devoted servant, myself, to write to thy wisdom, that if any Christian be found engaging in the worship of his own people, thou shouldst abstain from molesting and endangering him, and shouldst not suppose it necessary to punish any one on this pretext. For it has been proved by the experience of so long a time that they can in no way be persuaded to abandon such obstinate conduct.

6. Therefore it should be thy care to write to the curators and magistrates and district overseers of every city, that they may know that

it is not necessary for them to give further attention to this matter.

7. Thereupon the rulers of the provinces, thinking that the purpose of the things which were written was truly made known to them, declared the imperial will to the curators and magistrates and prefects of the various districts in writing. But they did not limit themselves to writing, but sought more quickly to accomplish the supposed will of the emperor in deeds also. Those whom they had imprisoned on account of their confession of the Deity, they set at liberty, and they released those of them who had been sent to the mines for punishment; for they erroneously supposed that this was the true will of the emperor.

8. And when these things had thus been done, immediately, like a light shining forth in a dark night, one could see in every city congregations gathered and assemblies thronged, and meetings held according to their custom. And every one of the unbelieving heathen was not a little astonished at these things, wondering at so marvelous a transformation, and exclaiming that the God of the Christians was great and alone true.

9. And some of our people, who had faithfully and bravely sustained the conflict of persecution, again became frank and bold toward all; but as many as had been diseased in the faith and had been shaken in their souls by the tempest, strove eagerly for healing, beseeching and imploring the strong to stretch out to them a saving hand, and supplicating God to be merciful unto them.

10. Then also the noble athletes of religion who had been set free from their sufferings in the mines returned to their own homes. Happily and joyfully they passed through every city, full of unspeakable pleasure and of a boldness which cannot be expressed in words.

11. Great crowds of men pursued their journey along the highways and through the market-places, praising God with hymns and psalms. And you might have seen those who a little while before had been driven in bonds from their native countries under a most cruel sentence, returning with bright and joyful faces to their own firesides; so that even they who had formerly thirsted for our blood, when they saw the unexpected wonder, congratulated us on what had taken place.

Chapter II.

THE SUBSEQUENT REVERSE.

1. But the tyrant who, as we have said, ruled over the districts of the Orient, a thorough hater of the good and an enemy of every virtuous person, as he was, could no longer bear this; and indeed he did not permit matters to go on in this way quite six months. Devising all possible means of destroying the peace, he first attempted to restrain us, under a pretext, from meeting in the cemeteries.

2. Then through the agency of some wicked men he sent an embassy to himself against us, inciting the citizens of Antioch to ask from him as a very great favor that he would by no means permit any of the Christians to dwell in their country; and others were secretly induced to do the same thing. The author of all this in Antioch was Theotecnus, a violent and wicked man, who was an impostor, and whose character was foreign to his name. He appears to have been the curator of the city.

Chapter III.

THE NEWLY ERECTED STATUE AT ANTIOCH.

1. After this man had carried on all kinds of war against us and had caused our people to be diligently hunted up in their retreats, as if they were unholy thieves, and had devised every sort of slander and accusation against us, and become the cause of death to vast numbers, he finally erected a statue of Jupiter Philius with certain juggleries and magic rites. And after inventing unholy forms of initiation and ill-omened mysteries in connection with it, and abominable means of purification, he exhibited his jugglery, by oracles which he pretended to utter, even to the emperor; and through a flattery which was pleasing to the ruler he aroused the demon against the Christians and said that the god had given command to expel the Christians as his enemies beyond the confines of the city and the neighboring districts.

Chapter IV.

THE MEMORIALS AGAINST US.

1. The fact that this man, who took the lead in this matter, had succeeded in his purpose was an incitement to all the other officials in the cities under the same government to prepare a similar memorial. And the governors of the provinces perceiving that this was agreeable to the emperor suggested to their subjects that they should do the same.

2. And as the tyrant by a rescript declared himself well pleased with their measures, persecution was kindled anew against us. Priests for the images were then appointed in the cities, and besides them high priests by Maximinus himself. The latter were taken from among those who were most distinguished in public life and had gained celebrity in all the offices which they had filled; and who were imbued, moreover, with great zeal for the service of those whom they worshiped.

3. Indeed, the extraordinary superstition of the emperor, to speak in brief, led all his subjects, both rulers and private citizens, for the sake of gratifying him, to do everything against us, supposing that they

could best show their gratitude to him for the benefits which they had received from him, by plotting murder against us and exhibiting toward us any new signs of malignity.

Chapter V.

THE FORGED ACTS.

1. Having therefore forged Acts of Pilate and our Saviour full of every kind of blasphemy against Christ, they sent them with the emperor's approval to the whole of the empire subject to him, with written commands that they should be openly posted to the view of all in every place, both in country and city, and that the schoolmasters should give them to their scholars, instead of their customary lessons, to be studied and learned by heart.

2. While these things were taking place, another military commander, whom the Romans call Dux, seized some infamous women in the market-place at Damascus in Phœnicia, and by threatening to inflict tortures upon them compelled them to make a written declaration that they had once been Christians and that they were acquainted with their impious deeds—that in their very churches they committed licentious acts; and they uttered as many other slanders against our religion as he wished them to. Having taken down their words in writing, he communicated them to the emperor, who commanded that these documents also should be published in every place and city.

Chapter VI.

THOSE WHO SUFFERED MARTYRDOM AT THIS TIME.

1. Not long afterward, however, this military commander became his own murderer and paid the penalty for his wickedness. But we were obliged again to endure exile and severe persecutions, and the governors in every province were once more terribly stirred up against us; so that even some of those illustrious in the Divine Word were seized and had sentence of death pronounced upon them without mercy. Three of them in the city of Emesa in Phœnicia, having confessed that they were Christians, were thrown as food to the wild beasts. Among them was a bishop Silvanus, a very old man, who had filled his office full forty years.

2. At about the same time Peter also, who presided most illustriously over the parishes in Alexandria, a divine example of a bishop on account of the excellence of his life and his study of the sacred Scriptures, being seized for no cause and quite unexpectedly,

was, as if by command of Maxi-minus, immediately and without explanation, beheaded. With him also many other bishops of Egypt suffered the same fate.

3. And Lucian, a presbyter of the parish at Antioch, and a most excellent man in every respect, temperate in life and famed for his learning in sacred things, was brought to the city of Nicomedia, where at that time the emperor happened to be staying, and after delivering before the ruler an apology for the doctrine which he professed, was committed to prison and put to death.

4. Such trials were brought upon us in a brief time by Maximinus, the enemy of virtue, so that this persecution which was stirred up against us seemed far more cruel than the former.

Chapter VII.

THE DECREE AGAINST US WHICH WAS ENGRAVED ON PILLARS.

1. The memorials against us and copies of the imperial edicts issued in reply to them were engraved and set up on brazen pillars in the midst of the cities,—a course which had never been followed elsewhere. The children in the schools had daily in their mouths the names of Jesus and Pilate, and the Acts which had been forged in wanton insolence.

2. It appears to me necessary to insert here this document of Maximinus which was posted on pillars, in order that there may be made manifest at the same time the boastful and haughty arrogance of the God-hating man, and the sleepless evil-hating divine vengeance upon the impious, which followed close upon him, and under whose pressure he not long afterward took the opposite course in respect to us and confirmed it by written laws. The rescript is in the following words:

3. *Copy of a translation of the rescript of Maximinus in answer to the memorials against us, taken from the pillar in Tyre.* "Now at length the feeble power of the human mind has become able to shake off and to scatter every dark mist of error, which before this besieged the senses of men, who were more miserable than impious, and enveloped them in dark and destructive ignorance; and to perceive that it is governed and established by the beneficent providence of the immortal gods.

4. It passes belief how grateful, how pleasing and how agreeable it is to us, that you have given a most decided proof of your pious resolution; for even before this it was known to every one how much regard and reverence you were paying to the immortal gods, exhibiting not a faith of bare and empty words, but continued and wonderful

exampies of illustrious deeds.

5. Wherefore your city may justly be called a seat and dwelling of the immortal gods. At least, it appears by many signs that it flourishes because of the presence of the celestial gods.

6. Behold, therefore, your city, regardless of all private advantages, and omitting its former petitions in its own behalf, when it perceived that the adherents of that execrable vanity were again beginning to spread, and to start the greatest conflagration—like a neglected and extinguished funeral pile when its brands are rekindled,—immediately resorted to our piety as to a metropolis of all religiousness, asking some remedy and aid.

7. It is evident that the gods have given you this saving mind on account of your faith and piety. "Accordingly that supreme and mightiest Jove, who presides over your illustrious city, who preserves your ancestral gods, your wives and children, your hearths and homes from every destructive pest, has infused into your souls this wholesome resolve; showing and proving how excellent and glorious and salutary it is to observe with the becoming reverence the worship and sacred rites of the immortal gods.

8. For who can be found so ignorant or so devoid of all understanding as not to perceive that it is due to the kindly care of the gods that the earth does not refuse the seed sown in it, nor disappoint the hope of the husbandmen with vain expectation; that impious war is not inevitably fixed upon earth, and wasted bodies dragged down to death under the influence of a corrupted atmosphere; that the sea is not swollen and raised on high by blasts of intemperate winds; that unexpected hurricanes do not burst forth and stir up the destructive tempest; moreover, that the earth, the nourisher and mother of all, is not shaken from its lowest depths with a terrible tremor, and that the mountains upon it do not sink into the opening chasms. No one is ignorant that all these, and evils still worse than these, have oftentimes happened hitherto.

9. And all these misfortunes have taken place on account of the destructive error of the empty vanity of those impious men, when it prevailed in their souls, and, we may almost say, weighed down the whole world with shame."

10. After other words he adds: "Let them look at the standing crops already flourishing with waving heads in the broad fields, and at the meadows glittering with plants and flowers, in response to abundant rains and the restored mildness and softness of the atmosphere.

11. Finally, let all rejoice that the might of the most powerful and terrible Mars has been propitiated by our piety, our sacrifices, and our veneration; and let them on this account enjoy firm and tranquil peace and quiet; and let as many as have wholly abandoned that blind error and delusion and have returned to a right and sound mind rejoice the

more, as those who have been rescued from an unexpected storm or severe disease and are to reap the fruits of I pleasure for the rest of their life.

12. But if they still persist in their execrable vanity, let them, as you have desired, be driven far away from your city and territory, that thus, in accordance with your praiseworthy zeal in this matter, your city, being freed from every pollution and impiety, may, according to its native disposition, attend to the sacred rites of the immortal gods with becoming reverence.

13. But that ye may know how acceptable to us your request respecting this matter has been, and how ready our mind is to confer benefits voluntarily, without memorials and petitions, we permit your devotion to ask whatever great gift ye may desire in return for this your pious disposition.

14. And now ask that this may be done and that ye may receive it; for ye shall obtain it without delay. This, being granted to your city, shall furnish for all time an evidence of reverent piety toward the immortal gods, and of the fact that you have obtained from our benevolence merited prizes for this choice of yours; and it shall be shown to your children and children's children."

15. This was published against us in all the provinces, depriving us of every hope of good, at least from men; so that, according to that divine utterance, "If it were possible, even the elect would have stumbled" at these things.

16. And now indeed, when the hope of most of us was almost extinct, suddenly while those who were to execute against us the above decree had in some places scarcely finished their journey, God, the defender of his own Church, exhibited his heavenly interposition in our behalf, well-nigh stopping the tyrant's boasting against us.

Chapter VIII.

THE MISFORTUNES WHICH HAPPENED IN CONNECTION
WITH THESE THINGS, IN FAMINE, PESTILENCE, AND WAR.

1. The customary rains and showers of the winter season ceased to fall in their wonted abundance upon the earth and an unexpected famine made its appearance, and in addition to this a pestilence, and another severe disease consisting of an ulcer, which on account of its fiery appearance was appropriately called a carbuncle. This, spreading over the whole body, greatly endangered the lives of those who suffered from it; but as it chiefly attacked the eyes, it deprived multitudes of men, women, and children of their sight.

2. In addition to this the tyrant was compelled to go to war with the Armenians, who had been from ancient times friends and allies of the

Romans. As they were also Christians and zealous in their piety toward the Deity, the enemy of God had attempted to compel them to sacrifice to idols and demons, and had thus made friends foes, and allies enemies.

3. All these things suddenly took place at one and the same time, and refuted the tyrant's empty vaunt against the Deity. For he had boasted that, because of his zeal for idols and his hostility against us, neither famine nor pestilence nor war had happened in his time. These things, therefore, coming upon him at once and together, furnished a prelude also of his own destruction.

4. He himself with his forces was defeated in the war with the Armenians, and the rest of the inhabitants of the cities under him were terribly afflicted with famine and pestilence, so that one measure of wheat was sold for twenty-five hundred Attic drachms.

5. Those who died in the cities were innumerable, and those who died in the country and villages were still more. So that the tax lists which formerly included a great rural population were almost entirely wiped out; nearly all being speedily destroyed by famine and pestilence.

6. Some, therefore, desired to dispose of their most precious things to those who were better supplied, in return for the smallest morsel of food, and others, selling their possessions little by little, fell into the last extremity of want. Some, chewing wisps of hay and recklessly eating noxious herbs, undermined and mined their constitutions.

7. And some of the high-born women in the cities, driven by want to shameful extremities, went forth into the market-places to beg, giving evidence of their former liberal culture by the modesty of their appearance and the decency of their apparel.

8. Some, wasted away like ghosts and at the very point of death, stumbled and tottered here and there, and too weak to stand fell down in the middle of the streets; lying stretched out at full length they begged that a small morsel of food might be given them, and with their last gasp they cried out Hunger! having strength only for this most painful cry.

9. But others, who seemed to be better supplied, astonished at the multitude of the beggars, after giving away large quantities, finally became hard and relentless, expecting that they themselves also would soon suffer the same calamities as those who begged. So that in the midst of the market-places and lanes, dead and naked bodies lay unburied for many days, presenting the most lamentable spectacle to those that beheld them.

10. Some also became food for dogs, on which account the survivors began to kill the dogs, lest they should become mad and should go to devouring men.

11. But still worse was the pestilence which consumed entire

houses and families, and especially those whom the famine was not able to destroy because of their abundance of food. Thus men of wealth, rulers and governors and multitudes in office, as if left by the famine on purpose for the pestilence, suffered swift and speedy death. Every place therefore was full of lamentation; in every lane and market-place and street there was nothing else to be seen or heard than tears, with the customary instruments and the voices of the mourners.

12. In this way death, waging war with these two weapons, pestilence and famine, destroyed whole families in a short time, so that one could see two or three dead bodies carried out at once. Such were the rewards of the boasting of Maximinus and of the measures of the cities against us. Then did the evidences of the universal zeal and piety of the Christians become manifest to all the heathen.

13. For they alone in the midst of such ills showed their sympathy and humanity by their deeds. Every day some continued caring for and burying the dead, for there were multitudes who had no one to care for them; others collected in one place those who were afflicted by the famine, throughout the entire city, and gave bread to them all; so that the thing became noised abroad among all men, and they glorified the God of the Christians; and, convinced by the facts themselves, confessed that they alone were truly pious and religious.

15. After these things were thus done, God, the great and celestial defender of the Christians, having revealed in the events which have been described his anger and indignation at all men for the great evils which they had brought upon us, restored to us the bright and gracious sunlight of his providence in our behalf; so that in the deepest darkness a light of peace shone most wonderfully upon us from him, and made it manifest to all that God himself has always been the ruler of our affairs. From time to time indeed he chastens his people and corrects them by his visitations, but again after sufficient chastisement he shows mercy and favor to those who hope in him.

Chapter IX.

THE VICTORY OF THE GOD-BELOVED EMPERORS.

1. Thus when Constantine, whom we have already mentioned as an emperor, born of an emperor, a pious son of a most pious and prudent father, and Licinius, second to him, -two God-beloved emperors, honored alike for their intelligence and their piety—being stirred up against the two most impious tyrants by God, the absolute Ruler and Saviour of all, engaged in formal war against them, with God as their ally, Maxentius was defeated at Rome by Constantine in a remarkable manner, and the tyrant of the East did not long survive him, but met a most shameful death at the hand of Licinius, who had not yet become

insane.

2. Constantine, who was the superior both in dignity and imperial rank, first took compassion upon those who were oppressed at Rome, and having invoked in prayer the God of heaven, and his Word, and Jesus Christ himself, the Saviour of all, as his aid, advanced with his Whole army, proposing to restore to the Romans their ancestral liberty.

3. But Maxentius, putting confidence rather in the arts of sorcery than in the devotion of his subjects, did not dare to go forth beyond the gates of the city, but fortified every place and district and town which was enslaved by him, in the neighborhood of Rome and in all Italy, with an immense multi-rude of troops and with innumerable bands of soldiers. But the emperor, relying upon the assistance of God, attacked the first, second, and third army of the tyrant, and conquered them all; and having advanced through the greater part of Italy, was already very near Rome.

4. Then, that he might not be compelled to wage war with the Romans for the sake of the tyrant, God himself drew the latter, as if bound in chains, some distance without the gates, and confirmed those threats against the impious which had been anciently inscribed in sacred books—disbelieved, indeed, by most as a myth, but believed by the faithful—confirmed them, in a word, by the deed itself to all, both believers and unbelievers, that saw the wonder with their eyes.

5. Thus, as in the time of Moses himself and of the ancient God-beloved race of Hebrews, "he cast Pharaoh's chariots and host into the sea, and overwhelmed his chosen charioteers in the Red Sea, and covered them with the flood," in the same way Maxentius also with his soldiers and body-guards "went down into the depths like a stone," when he fled before the power of God which was with Constantine, and passed through the river which lay in his way, over which he had formed a bridge with boats, and thus prepared the means of his own destruction.

6. In regard to him one might say, "he digged a pit and opened it and fell into the hole which he had made; his labor shall turn upon his own head, and his unrighteousness shall fall upon his own crown."

7. Thus, then, the bridge over the river being broken, the passageway settled down, and immediately the boats with the men disappeared in the depths, and that most impious one himself first of all, then the shield-bearers who were with him, as the divine oracles foretold, "sank like lead in the mighty waters";

8. so that those who obtained the victory from God, if not in words, at least in deeds, like Moses, the great servant of God, and those who were with him, fittingly sang as they had sung against the impious tyrant of old, saying, "Let us sing unto the Lord, for he hath gloriously glorified himself; horse and rider hath he thrown into the sea; a helper and a protector hath he become for my salvation;" and "Who is like

unto thee, O Lord; among the gods, who is like unto thee? glorious in holiness, marvelous in glory, doing wonders."

9. These and the like praises Constantine, by his very deeds, sang to God, the universal Ruler, and Author of his victory, as he entered Rome in triumph. Immediately all the members of the senate and the other most celebrated men, with the whole Roman people, together with children and women, received him as their deliverer, their saviour, and their benefactor, with shining eyes and with their whole souls, with shouts of gladness and unbounded joy.

10. But he, as one possessed of inborn piety toward God, did not exult in the shouts, nor was he elated by the praises; but perceiving that his aid was from God, he immediately commanded that a trophy of the Saviour's passion be put in the hand of his own statue. And when he had placed it, with the saving sign of the cross in its right hand, in the most public place in Rome, he commanded that the following inscription should be engraved upon it in the Roman tongue:

11. "By this salutary sign, the true proof of bravery, I have saved and freed your city from the yoke of the tyrant and moreover, having set at liberty both the senate and the people of Rome, I have restored them to their ancient distinction and splendor."

12. And after this both Constantine himself and with him the Emperor Licinius, who had not yet been seized by that madness into which he later fell, praising God as the author of all their blessings, with one will and mind drew up a full and most complete decree in behalf of the Christians, and sent an account of the wonderful things done for them by God, and of the victory over the tyrant, together with a copy of the decree itself, to Maximinus, who still ruled over the nations of the East and pretended friendship toward them.

13. But he, like a tyrant, was greatly pained by what he learned; but not wishing to seem to yield to others, nor, on the other hand, to suppress that which was commanded, for fear of those who enjoined it, as if on his own authority, he addressed, under compulsion, to the governors under him this first communication in behalf of the Christians, falsely inventing things against himself which had never been done by him.

14. *Copy of a translation of the epistle of the tyrant Maximinus.* "Jovius Maximinus Augustus to Sabinus. I am confident that it is manifest both to thy firmness and to all men that our masters Diocletian and Maximianus, our fathers, when they saw almost all men abandoning the worship of the gods and attaching themselves to the party of the Christians, rightly decreed that all who gave up the worship of those same immortal gods should be recalled by open chastisement and punishment to the worship of the gods.

15. But when I first came to the East under favorable auspices and learned that in some places a great many men who were able to render

public service had been banished by the judges for the above-mentioned cause, I gave command to each of the judges that henceforth none of them should treat the provincials with severity, but that they should rather recall them to the worship of the gods by flattery and exhortations.

16. Then when, in accordance with my command, these orders were obeyed by the judges, it came to pass that none of those who lived in the districts of the East were banished or insulted, but that they were rather brought back to the worship of the gods by the fact that no severity was employed toward them.

17. But afterwards, when I went up last year under good auspices to Nicomedia and sojourned there, citizens of the same city came to me with the images of the gods, earnestly entreating that such a people should by no means be permitted to dwell in their country.

18. But when I learned that many men of the same religion dwelt in those regions, I replied that I gladly thanked them for their request, but that I perceived that it was not proffered by all, and that if, therefore, there were any that persevered in the same superstition, each one had the privilege of doing as he pleased, even if he wished to recognize the worship of the gods.

19. Nevertheless, I considered it necessary to give a friendly answer to the inhabitants of Nicomedia and to the other cities which had so earnestly presented to me the same petition, namely, that no Christians should dwell in their cities—both because this same course had been pursued by all the ancient emperors, and also because it was pleasing to the gods, through whom all men and the government of the state itself endure—and to confirm the request which they presented in behalf of the worship of their deity.

20. Therefore, although before this time, special letters have been sent to thy devotedness, and commands have likewise been given that no harsh measures should be taken against those provincials who desire to follow such a course, but that they should be treated mildly and moderately—nevertheless, in order that they may not suffer insults or extortions from the beneficiaries, or from any others, I have thought meet to remind thy firmness in this epistle also that thou shouldst lead our provincials rather by flatteries and exhortations to recognize the care of the gods.

21. Hence, if any one of his own choice should decide to adopt the worship of the gods, it is fitting that he should be welcomed, but if any should wish to follow their own religion, do thou leave it in their power.

22. Wherefore it behooves thy devotedness to observe that which is committed to thee, and to see that power is given to no one to oppress our provincials with insults and extortions, since, as already written, it is fitting to recall our provincials to the worship of the gods

rather by exhortations and flatteries. But, in order that this command of ours may come to the knowledge of all our provincials, it is incumbent upon thee to proclaim that which has been enjoined, in an edict issued by thyself."

23. Since he was forced to do this by necessity and did not give the command by his own will, he was not regarded by any one as sincere or trustworthy, because he had already shown his unstable and deceitful disposition after his former similar concession.

24. None of our people, therefore, ventured to hold meetings or even to appear in public, because his communication did not cover this, but only commanded to guard against doing us any injury, and did not give orders that we should hold meetings or build churches or perform any of our customary acts.

25. And yet Constantine and Licinius, the advocates of peace and piety, had written him to permit this, and had granted it to all their subjects by edicts and ordinances. But this most impious man did not choose to yield in this matter until, being driven by the divine judgment, he was at last compelled to do it against his will.

Chapter X.

THE OVERTHROW OF THE TYRANTS AND THE WORDS WHICH THEY UTTERED BEFORE THEIR DEATH.

1. The circumstances which drove him to this course were the following. Being no longer able to sustain the magnitude of the government which had been undeservedly committed to him, in consequence of his want of prudence and imperial understanding, he managed affairs in a base manner, and with his mind unreasonably exalted in all things with boastful pride, even toward his colleagues in the empire who were in every respect his superiors, in birth, in training, in education, in worth and intelligence, and, greatest of all, in temperance and piety toward the true God, he began to venture to act audaciously and to arrogate to himself the first rank.

2. Becoming mad in his folly, he broke the treaties which he had made with Licinius and undertook an implacable war. Then in a brief time he threw all things into confusion, and stirred up every city, and having collected his entire force, comprising an immense number of soldiers, he went forth to battle with him, elated by his hopes in demons, whom he supposed to be gods, and by the number of his soldiers.

3. And when he joined battle he was deprived of the oversight of God, and the victory was given to Licinius, who was then ruling, by the one and only God of all.

4. First, the army in which he trusted was destroyed, and as all his

guards abandoned him and left him alone, and fled to the victor, he secretly divested himself as quickly as possible of the imperial garments, which did not fitly belong to him, and in a cowardly and ignoble and unmanly way mingled with the crowd, and then fled, concealing himself in fields and villages. But though he was so careful for his safety, he scarcely escaped the hands of his enemies, revealing by his deeds that the divine oracles are faithful and true, in which it is said,

5. "A king is not saved by a great force, and a giant shall not be saved by the greatness of his strength; a horse is a vain thing for safety, nor shall he be delivered by the greatness of his power. Behold, the eyes of the Lord are upon them that fear him, upon them that hope in his mercy, to deliver their souls from death."

6. Thus the tyrant, covered with shame, went to his own country. And first, in frantic rage, he slew many priests and prophets of the gods whom he had formerly admired, and whose oracles had incited him to undertake the war, as sorcerers and impostors, and besides all as betrayers of his safety. Then having given glory to the God of the Christians and enacted a most full and complete ordinance in behalf of their liberty, he was immediately seized with a mortal disease, and no respite being granted him, departed this life. The law enacted by him was as follows:

7. *Copy of the edict of the tyrant in behalf of the Christians, translated from the man tongue.* "The Emperor Cæsar Caius Valerius Maximinus, Germanicus, Sarmaticus, Plus, Felix, Invictus, Augustus. We believe it manifest that no one is ignorant, but that every man who looks back over the past knows and is conscious that in every way we care continually for the good of our provincials, and wish to furnish them with those things which are of especial advantage to all, and for the common benefit and profit, and whatever contributes to the public welfare and is agreeable to the views of each.

8. When, therefore, before this, it became clear to our mind that under pretext of the command of our parents, the most divine Diocletian and Maximianus, which enjoined that the meetings of the Christians should be abolished, many extortions and spoliations had been practiced by officials; and that those evils were continually increasing, to the detriment of our provincials toward whom we are especially anxious to exercise proper care, and that their possessions were in consequence perishing, letters were sent last year to the governors of each province, in which we decreed that, if any one wished to follow such a practice or to observe this same religion, he should be permitted without hindrance to pursue his purpose and should be impeded and prevented by no one, and that all should have liberty to do without any fear or suspicion that which each preferred.

9. But even now we cannot help perceiving that some of the judges

have mistaken our commands, and have given our people reason to doubt the meaning of our ordinances, and have caused them to proceed too reluctantly to the observance of those religious rites which are pleasing to them.

10. In order, therefore, that in the future every suspicion of fearful doubt may be taken away, we have commanded that this decree be published, so that it may be clear to all that whoever wishes to embrace this sect and religion is permitted to do so by virtue of this grant of ours; and that each one, as he wishes or as is pleasing to him, is permitted to practice this religion which he has chosen to observe according to his custom. It is also granted them to build Lord's houses.

11. But that this grant of ours may be the greater, we have thought good to decree also that if any houses and lands before this time rightfully belonged to the Christians, and by the command of our parents fell into the treasury, or were confiscated by any city—whether they have been sold or presented to any one as a gift—that all these should be restored to their original possessors, the Christians, in order that in this also every one may have knowledge of our piety and care."

12. These are the words of the tyrant which were published not quite a year after the decrees against the Christians engraved by him on pillars. And by him to whom a little before we seemed impious wretches and atheists and destroyers of all life, so that we were not permitted to dwell in any city nor even in country or desert—by him decrees and ordinances were issued in behalf of the Christians, and they who recently had been destroyed by fire and sword, by wild beasts and birds of prey, in the presence of the tyrant himself, and had suffered every species of torture and punishment, and most miserable deaths as atheists and impious wretches, were now acknowledged by him as possessors of religion and were permitted to build churches; and the tyrant himself bore witness and confessed that they had some rights.

13. And having made such confessions, as if he had received some benefit on account of them, he suffered perhaps less than he ought to have suffered, and being smitten by a sudden scourge of God, he perished in the second campaign of the war.

14. But his end was not like that of military chieftains who, while fighting bravely in battle for virtue and friends, often boldly encounter a glorious death; for like an impious enemy of God, while his army was still drawn up in the field, remaining at home and concealing himself, he suffered the punishment which he deserved. For he was smitten with a sudden scourge of God in his whole body, and harassed by terrible pains and torments, he fell prostrate on the ground, wasted by hunger, while all his flesh was dissolved by an invisible and God-sent fire, so that the whole appearance of his frame was changed, and there was left only a kind of image wasted away by length of time to a skeleton of dry bones; so that those who were present could think of his body as

nothing else than the tomb of his soul, which was buried in a body already dead and completely melted away.

15. And as the heat still more violently consumed him in the depths of his marrow, his eyes burst forth, and falling from their sockets left him blind. Thereupon still breathing and making free confession to the Lord, he invoked death, and at last, after acknowledging that he justly suffered these things on account of his violence against Christ, he gave up the ghost.

Chapter XI.

THE FINAL DESTRUCTION OF THE ENEMIES OF RELIGION.

1. Thus when Maximinus, who alone had remained of the enemies of religion and had appeared the worst of them all, was put out of the way, the renovation of the churches from their foundations was begun by the grace of God the Ruler of all, and the word of Christ. shining unto the glory of the God of the universe, obtained greater freedom than before, while the impious enemies of religion were covered with extremest shame and dishonor.

2. For Maximinus himself, being first pronounced by the emperors a common enemy, was declared by public proclamations to be a most impious, execrable, and God-hating tyrant. And of the portraits which had been set up in every city in honor of him or of his children, some were thrown down from their places to the ground, and torn in pieces; while the faces of others were obliterated by daubing them with black paint. And the statues which had been erected to his honor were likewise overthrown and broken, and lay exposed to the laughter and sport of those who wished to insult and abuse them.

3. Then also all the honors of the other enemies of religion were taken away, and all those who sided with Maximinus were slain, especially those who had been honored by him with high offices in reward for their flattery, and had behaved insolently toward our doctrine.

4. Such an one was Peucetius, the dearest of his companions, who had been honored and rewarded by him above all, who had been consul a second and third time, and had been appointed by him chief minister; and Culcianus, who had likewise advanced through every grade of office, and was also celebrated for his numberless executions of Christians in Egypt; and besides these not a few others, by whose agency especially the tyranny of Maximinus had been confirmed and extended.

5. And Theotecnus also was summoned by justice which by no means overlooked his deeds against the Christians. For when the statue had been set up by him at Antioch, he appeared to be in the happiest

state, and was already made a governor by Maximinus.

6. But Licinius, coming down to the city of Antioch, made a search for impostors, and tortured the prophets and priests of the newly erected statue, asking them for what reason they practiced their deception. They, under the stress of torture, were unable longer to conceal the matter, and declared that the whole deceptive mystery had been devised by the art of Theotecnus. Therefore, after meting out to all of them just judgment, he first put Theotecnus himself to death, and then his confederates in the imposture, with the severest possible tortures.

7. To all these were added also the children of Maximinus, whom he had already made sharers in the imperial dignity, by placing their names on tablets and statues. And the relatives of the tyrant, who before had been boastful and had in their pride oppressed all men, suffered the same punishments with those who have been already mentioned, as well as the extremest disgrace. For they had not received instruction, neither did they know and understand the exhortation given in the Holy Word:

8. "Put not your trust in princes, nor in the sons of men, in whom there is no salvation; his spirit shall go forth and return to his earth; in that day all their thoughts perish."

9. The impious ones having been thus removed, the government was preserved firm and undisputed for Constantine and Licinius, to whom it fittingly belonged. They, having first of all cleansed the world of hostility to the Divine Being, conscious of the benefits which he had conferred upon them, showed their love of virtue and of God, and their piety and gratitude to the Deity, by their ordinance in behalf of the Christians.

Book X.

Chapter I.

THE PEACE GRANTED US BY GOD.

1. Thanks for all things be given unto God the Omnipotent Ruler and King of the universe, and the greatest thanks to Jesus Christ the Saviour and Redeemer of our souls, through whom we pray that peace may be always preserved for us firm and undisturbed by external troubles and by troubles of the mind.

2. Since in accordance with thy wishes, my most holy Paulinus, we have added the tenth book of the Church History to those which have preceded, we will inscribe it to thee, proclaiming thee as the seal of the whole work;

3. and we will fitly add in a perfect number the perfect panegyric

upon the restoration of the churches, obeying the Divine Spirit which exhorts us in the following words: "Sing unto the Lord a new song, for he hath done marvelous things. His right hand and his holy arm hath saved him. The Lord hath made known his salvation, his righteousness hath he revealed in the presence of the nations."

4. And in accordance with the utterance which commands us to sing the new song, let us proceed to show that, after those terrible and gloomy spectacles which we have described, we are now permitted to see and celebrate such things as many truly righteous men and martyrs of God before us desired to see upon earth and did not see, and to hear and did not hear.

5. But they, hastening on, obtained far better things, being carried to heaven and the paradise of divine pleasure. But, acknowledging that even these things are greater than we deserve, we have been astonished at the grace manifested by the author of the great gifts, and rightly do we admire him, worshiping him with the whole power of our souls, and testifying to the truth of those recorded utterances, in which it is said,

6. "Come and see the works of the Lord, the wonders which he hath done upon the earth; he removeth wars to the ends of the world, he shall break the bow and snap the spear in sunder, and shall burn the shields with fire." Rejoicing in these things which have been clearly fulfilled in our day, let us proceed with our account.

7. The whole race of God's enemies was destroyed in the manner indicated, and was thus suddenly swept from the sight of men. So that again a divine utterance had its fulfillment: "I have seen the impious highly exalted and raising himself like the cedars of Lebanon and I have passed by, and behold, he was not and I have sought his place, and it could not be found."

8. And finally a bright and splendid day, overshadowed by no cloud, illuminated with beams of heavenly light the churches of Christ throughout the entire world. And not even those without our communion were prevented from sharing in the same blessings, or at least from coming under their influence and enjoying a part of the benefits bestowed upon us by God.

Chapter II.

THE RESTORATION OF THE CHURCHES.

1. All men, then, were freed from the oppression of the tyrants, and being released from the former ills, one in one way and another in another acknowledged the defender of the pious to be the only true God. And we especially who placed our hopes in the Christ of God had unspeakable gladness, and a certain inspired joy bloomed for all of us, when we saw every place which shortly before had been desolated by

the impieties of the tyrants reviving as if from a long and death-fraught pestilence, and temples again rising from their foundations to an immense height, and receiving a splendor far greater than that of the old ones which had been destroyed.

2. But the supreme rulers also confirmed to us still more extensively the munificence of God by repeated ordinances in behalf of the Christians; and personal letters of the emperor were sent to the bishops, with honors and gifts of money. It may not be unfitting to insert these documents, translated from the Roman into the Greek tongue, at the proper place in this book, as in a sacred tablet, that they may remain as a memorial to all who shall come after us.

Chapter III.

THE DEDICATIONS IN EVERY PLACE.

1. After this was seen the sight which had been desired and prayed for by us all; feasts of dedication in the cities and consecrations of the newly built houses of prayer took place, bishops assembled, foreigners came together from abroad, mutual love was exhibited between people and people, the members of Christ's body were united in complete harmony.

2. Then was fulfilled the prophetic utterance which mystically foretold what was to take place: "Bone to bone and joint to joint," and whatever was truly announced in enigmatic expressions in the inspired passage.

3. And there was one energy of the Divine Spirit pervading all the members, and one soul in all, and the same eagerness of faith, and one hymn from all in praise of the Deity. Yea, and perfect services were conducted by the prelates, the sacred rites being solemnized, and the majestic institutions of the Church observed, here with the singing of psalms and with the reading of the words committed to us by God, and there with the performance of divine and mystic services; and the mysterious symbols of the Saviour's passion were dispensed.

4. At the same time people of every age, both male and female, with all the power of the mind gave honor unto God, the author of their benefits, in prayers and thanksgiving, with a joyful mind and soul. And every one of the bishops present, each to the best of his ability, delivered panegyric orations, adding luster to the assembly.

Chapter IV.

PANEGYRIC ON THE SPLENDOR OF AFFAIRS.

1. A Certain one of those of moderate talent, who had composed a discourse, stepped forward in the presence of many pastors who were assembled as if for a church gathering, and while they attended quietly and decently, he addressed himself as follows to one who was in all things a most excellent bishop and beloved of God, through whose zeal the temple in Tyre, which was the most splendid in Phœnicia, had been erected.

2. *Panegyric upon the building of the churches, addressed to Paulinus, Bishop of Tyre.* "Friends and priests of God who are clothed in the sacred gown and adorned with the heavenly crown of glory, the inspired unction and the sacerdotal garment of the Holy Spirit; and thou? oh pride of God's new holy temple, endowed by him with the wisdom of age, and yet exhibiting costly works and deeds of youthful and flourishing virtue, to whom God himself, who embraces the entire world, has granted the distinguished honor of building and renewing this earthly house to Christ, his only begotten and first-born Word, and to his holy and divine bride;—

3. one might call thee a new Beseleel, the architect of a divine tabernacle, or Solomon, king of a new and much better Jerusalem, or also a new Zerubabel, who added a much greater glory than the former to the temple of God;—

4. and you also, oh nurslings of the sacred flock of Christ, habitation of good words, school of wisdom, and august and pious auditory of religion:

5. It was long ago permitted us to raise hymns and songs to God, when we learned from hearing the Divine Scriptures read the marvelous signs of God and the benefits conferred upon men by the Lord's wondrous deeds, being taught to say 'Oh God! we have heard with our ears, our fathers have told us the work which thou didst in their days, in days of old.'

6. But now as we no longer perceive the lofty arm and the celestial right hand of our all-gracious God and universal King by hearsay merely or report, but observe so to speak in very deed and with our own eyes that the declarations recorded long ago are faithful and true, it is permitted us to raise a second hymn of triumph and to sing with loud voice, and say, 'As we have heard, so have we seen; in the city of the Lord of hosts, in the city of our God.'

7. And in what city but in this newly built and God-constructed one, which is a 'church of the living God, a pillar and foundation of the truth,' concerning which also another divine oracle thus proclaims,

'Glorious things have been spoken of thee, oh city of God.' Since the all-gracious God has brought us together to it, through the grace of his Only-Begotten, let every one of those who have been summoned sing with loud voice and say, 'I was glad when they said unto me, we shall go unto the house of the Lord,' and 'Lord, I have loved the beauty of thy house and the place where thy glory dwelleth.'

8. And let us not only one by one, but all together, with one spirit and one soul, honor him and cry aloud, saying, 'Great is the Lord and greatly to be praised in the city of our God, in his holy mountain.' For he is truly great, and great is his house, lofty and spacious and 'comely in beauty above the sons of men.' 'Great is the Lord who alone doeth wonderful things'; 'great is he who doeth great things and things past finding out, glorious and marvelous things which cannot be numbered'; is great is he 'who changeth times and seasons, who exalteth and debaseth kings'; 'who raiseth up the poor from the earth and lifteth up the needy from the dunghill.' 'He hath put clown princes from their thrones and hath exalted them of low degree from the earth. The hungry he hath filled with good things and the arms of the proud he hath broken.'

9. Not only to the faithful, but also to unbelievers, has he confirmed the record of ancient events; he that worketh miracles, he that doeth great things, the Master of all, the Creator of the whole world, the omnipotent, the all-merciful, the one and only God. To him let us sing the new song, supplying in thought, 'To him who alone doeth great wonders: for his mercy endureth forever'; 'To him which smote great kings, and slew famous kings: for his mercy endureth forever'; 'For the Lord remembered us in our low estate and delivered us from our adversaries.'

10. And let us never cease to cry aloud in these words to the Father of the universe. And let us always honor him with our mouth who is the second cause of our benefits, the instructor in divine knowledge, the teacher of the true religion, the destroyer of the impious, the slayer of tyrants, the reformer of life, Jesus, the Saviour of us who were in despair.

11. For he alone, as the only all-gracious Son of an all-gracious Father, in accordance with the purpose of his Father's benevolence, has willingly put on the nature of us who lay prostrate in corruption, and like some excellent physician, who for the sake of saving them that are ill, examines their sufferings, handles their foul sores, and reaps pain for himself from the miseries of another, so us who were not only diseased and afflicted with terrible ulcers and wounds already mortified, but were even lying among the dead, he hath saved for himself from the very jaws of death. For none other of those in heaven had such power as without harm to minister to the salvation of so many.

12. But he alone having reached our deep corruption, he alone having taken upon himself our labors, he alone having suffered the punishments due for our impieties, having recovered us who were not half dead merely, but were already in tombs and sepulchers, and altogether foul and offensive, saves us, both anciently and now, by his beneficent zeal, beyond the expectation of any one, even of ourselves, and imparts liberally of the Father's benefits, he who is the giver of life and light, our great Physician and King and Lord, the Christ of God.

13. For then when the whole human race lay buried in gloomy night and in depths of darkness through the deceitful arts of guilty demons and the power of God-hating spirits, by his simple appearing he loosed once for all the fast-bound cords of our impieties by the rays of his light, even as wax is melted.

14. But when malignant envy and the evil-loving demon wellnigh burst with anger at such grace and kindness, and turned against us all his death-dealing forces, and when, at first, like a dog gone mad which gnashes his teeth at the stones thrown at him, and pours out his rage against his assailants upon the inanimate missiles, he leveled his ferocious madness at the stones of the sanctuaries and at the lifeless material of the houses, and desolated the churches—at least as he supposed—and then emitted terrible hissings and snake-like sounds, now by the threats of impious tyrants, and again by the blasphemous edicts of profane rulers, vomiting forth death, moreover, and infecting with his deleterious and soul-destroying poisons the souls captured by him, and almost slaying them by his death-fraught sacrifices of dead idols, and causing every beast in the form of man and every kind of savage to assault us—

15. then, indeed, the 'Angel of the great Council,' the great Captain of God after the mightiest soldiers of his kingdom had displayed sufficient exercise through patience and endurance in everything, suddenly appeared anew, and blotted out and annihilated his enemies and foes, so that they seemed never to have had even a name.

16. But his friends and relatives he raised to the highest glory, in the presence not only of all men, but also of celestial powers, of sun and moon and stars, and of the whole heaven and earth, so that now, as has never happened before, the supreme rulers, conscious of the honor which they have received from him, spit upon the faces of dead idols, trample upon the unhallowed rites of demons, make sport of the ancient delusion handed down from their fathers, and acknowledge only one God, the common benefactor of all, themselves included. And they confess Christ, the Son of God, universal King of all, and proclaim him Saviour on monuments, imperishably recording in imperial letters, in the midst of the city which rules over the earth, his righteous deeds and his victories over the impious. Thus Jesus Christ our Saviour is the only

one from all eternity who has been acknowledged, even by those highest in the earth, not as a common king among men, but as a trite son of the universal God, and who has been worshiped as very God, and that rightly.

17. For what king that ever lived attained such virtue as to fill the ears and tongues of all men upon earth with his own name? What king, after ordaining such pious and wise laws, has extended them from one end of the earth to the other, so that they are perpetually read in the hearing of all men?

18. Who has abrogated barbarous and savage customs of uncivilized nations by his gentle and most philanthropic laws? Who, being attacked for entire ages by all, has shown such superhuman virtue as to flourish daily, and remain young throughout his life?

19. Who has founded a nation which of old was not even heard of, but which now is not concealed in some comer of the earth, but is spread abroad everywhere under the sun? Who has so fortified his soldiers with the arms of piety that their souls, being firmer than adamant, shine brilliantly in the contests with their opponents?

20. What king prevails to such an extent, and even after death leads on his soldiers, and sets up trophies over his enemies, and fills every place, country and city, Greek and barbarian, with his royal dwellings, even divine temples with their consecrated oblations, like this very temple with its superb adornments and votive offerings, which are themselves so truly great and majestic, worthy of wonder and admiration, and clear signs of the sovereignty of our Saviour? For now, too, 'he spake, and they were made; he commanded, and they were created.' For what was there to resist the nod of the universal King and Governor and Word of God himself?

21. "A special discourse would be needed accurately to survey and explain all this; and also to describe how great the zeal of the laborers is regarded by him who is celebrated as divine, who looks upon the living temple which we all constitute, and surveys the house, composed of living and moving stones, which is well and surely built upon the foundation of the apostles and prophets, the chief cornerstone being Jesus Christ himself, who has been rejected not only by the builders of that ancient building which no longer stands, but also by the builders— evil architects of evil works—of the structure, which is composed of the mass of men and still endures But the Father has approved him both then and now, and has made him the head of the corner of this our common church.

22. Who that beholds this living temple of the living God formed of ourselves—this greatest and truly divine sanctuary, I say, whose inmost shrines are invisible to the multitude and are truly holy and a holy of holies—would venture to declare it? Who is able even to look within the sacred enclosure, except the great High Priest of all, to

whom alone it is permitted to fathom the mysteries of every rational soul?

23. But perhaps it is granted to another, to one only, to be second after him in the same work, namely, to the commander of this army whom the first and great High Priest himself has honored with the second place in this sanctuary, the shepherd of your divine flock who has obtained your people by the allotment and the judgment of the Father, as if he had appointed him his own servant and interpreter, a new Aaron or Melchizedec, made like the Son of God, remaining and continually preserved by him in accordance with the united prayers of all of you.

24. To him therefore alone let it be granted, if not in the first place, at least in the second after the first and greatest High Priest, to observe and supervise the inmost state of your souls—to him who by experience and length of time has accurately proved each one, and who by his zeal and care has disposed you all in pious conduct and doctrine, and is better able than any one else to give an account, adequate to the facts, of those things which he himself has accomplished with the Divine assistance.

25. As to our first and great High Priest, it is said, 'Whatsoever he seeth the Father doing those things likewise the Son also doeth.' So also this one, looking up to him as to the first teacher, with pure eyes of the mind, using as archetypes whatsoever things he seeth him doing, produceth images of them, making them so far as is possible in the same likeness, in nothing inferior to that Beseleel, whom God himself 'filled with the spirit of wisdom and understanding' and with other technical and scientific knowledge, and called to be the maker of the temple constructed after heavenly types given in symbols.

26. Thus this one also bearing in his own soul the image of the whole Christ, the Word, the Wisdom, the Light, has formed this magnificent temple of the highest God, corresponding to the pattern of the greater as a visible to an invisible, it is impossible to say with what greatness of soul, with what wealth and liberality of mind, and with what emulation on the part of all of you, shown in the magnanimity of the contributors who have ambitiously striven in no way to be left behind by him in the execution of the same purpose. And this place— for this deserves to be mentioned first of all—which had been covered with all sorts of rubbish by the artifices of our enemies he did not overlook, nor did he yield to the wickedness of those who had brought about that condition of things, although he might have chosen some other place, for many other sites were available in the city, where he would have had less labor, and been free from trouble.

27. But having first aroused himself to the work, and then strengthened the whole people with zeal, and formed them all into one great body, he fought the first contest. For he thought that this church,

which had been especially besieged by the enemy, which had first suffered and endured the same persecutions with us and for us, like a mother bereft of her children, should rejoice with us in the signal favor of the all-merciful God.

28. For when the Great Shepherd had driven away the wild animals and wolves and every cruel and savage beast, and, as the divine oracles say, 'had broken the jaws of the lions,' he thought good to collect again her children in the same place, and in the most righteous manner he set up the fold of her flock, 'to put to shame the enemy and avenger,' and to refute the impious daring of the enemies of God.

29. And now they are not—the haters of God—for they never were. After they had troubled and been troubled for a little time, they suffered the fitting punishment, and brought themselves and their friends and their relatives to total destruction, so that the declarations inscribed of old in sacred records have been proved true by facts.

30. In these declarations the divine word truly says among other things the following concerning them: 'The wicked have drawn out the sword, they have bent their bow, to slay the righteous in heart; let their sword enter into their own heart and their bows be broken.' And again: 'Their memorial is perished with a sound' and 'their name hast thou blotted out forever and ever'; for when they also were in trouble they 'cried out and there was none to save: unto the Lord, and he heard them not.' But 'their feet were bound together, and they fell, but we have arisen and stand upright.' And that which was announced beforehand in these words, 'O Lord, in thy city thou shalt set at naught their image,'—has been shown to be true to the eyes of all.

31. But having waged war like the giants against God, they died in this way. But she that was desolate and rejected by men received the consummation which we behold in consequence of her patience toward God, so that the prophecy of Isaiah was spoken of her:

32. 'Rejoice, thirsty desert, let the desert rejoice and blossom as the lily, and the desert places shall blossom and be glad.' 'Be strengthened, ye weak hands and feeble knees. Be of good courage, ye feeble-hearted, in your minds; be strong, fear not. Behold our God recompenseth judgment and will recompense, he will come and save us.' 'For,' he says, 'in the wilderness water has broken out, and a pool in thirsty ground, and the dry land shall be watered meadows, and in the thirsty ground there shall be springs of water.'

33. These things which were prophesied long ago have been recorded in sacred books; but no longer are they transmitted to us by hearsay merely, but in facts. This desert, this dry land, this widowed and deserted one, 'whose gates they cut down with axes like wood in a forest, whom they broke down with hatchet and hammer,' whose books also they destroyed, 'burning with fire the sanctuary of God, and profaning unto the ground the habitation of his name,' 'whom all that

passed by upon the way plucked, and whose fences they broke down, whom the boar out of the wood ravaged, and on which the savage wild beast fed,' now by the wonderful power of Christ, when he wills it, has become like a lily. For at that time also she was chastened at his nod as by a careful father; 'for whom the Lord loveth he chasteneth, and scourgeth every son whom he receiveth.'

34. Then after being chastened in a measure, according to the necessities of the case, she is commanded to rejoice anew; and she blossoms as a lily and exhales her divine odor among all men. 'For,' it is said, 'water hath broken out in the wilderness,' the fountain of the saving bath of divine regeneration. And now she, who a little before was a desert, 'has become watered meadows, and springs of water have gushed forth in a thirsty land.' The hands which before were 'weak' have become 'truly strong'; and these works are great and convincing proofs of strong hands. The knees, also, which before were 'feeble and infirm,' recovering their wonted strength, are moving straight forward in the path of divine knowledge, and hastening to the kindred flock of the all-gracious Shepherd.

35. And if there are any whose souls have been stupefied by the threats of the tyrants, not even they are passed by as incurable by the saving Word; but he heals them also and urges them on to receive divine comfort, saying, 'Be ye comforted, ye who are faint-hearted; be ye strengthened, fear not.'

36. This our new and excellent Zerubabel, having heard the word which announced beforehand, that she who had been made a desert on account of God should enjoy these things, after the bitter captivity and the abomination of desolation, did not overlook the dead body; but first of all with prayers and supplications propitiated the Father with the common consent of all of you, and invoking the only one that giveth life to the dead as his ally and fellow-worker, raised her that was fallen, after purifying and freeing her from her ills. And he clothed her not with the ancient garment, but with such an one as he had again learned from the sacred oracles, which say clearly, 'And the latter glory of this house shall be greater than the former.'

37. Thus, enclosing a much larger space, he fortified the outer court with a wall surrounding the whole, which should serve as a most secure bulwark for the entire edifice.

38. And he raised and spread out a great and lofty vestibule toward the rays of the rising sun, and furnished those standing far without the sacred enclosure a full view of those within, almost turning the eyes of those who were strangers to the faith, to the entrances, so that no one could pass by without being impressed by the memory of the former desolation and of the present incredible transformation. His hope was that such an one being impressed by this might be attracted and be induced to enter by the very sight.

39. But when one comes within the gates he does not permit him to enter the sanctuary immediately, with impure and unwashed feet; but leaving as large a space as possible between the temple and the outer entrance, he has surrounded and adorned it with four transverse cloisters, making a quadrangular space with pillars rising on every side, which he has joined with lattice-work screens of wood, rising to a suitable height; and he has left an open space in the middle, so that the sky can be seen, and the free air bright in the rays of the sun.

40. Here he has placed symbols of sacred purifications, setting up fountains opposite the temple which furnish an abundance of water wherewith those who come within the sanctuary may purify themselves. This is the first halting-place of those who enter; and it furnishes at the same time a beautiful and splendid scene to every one, and to those who still need elementary instruction a fitting station.

41. But passing by this spectacle, he has made open entrances to the temple with many other vestibules within, placing three doors on one side, likewise facing the rays of the sun. The one in the middle, adorned with plates of bronze, iron bound, and beautifully embossed, he has made much higher and broader than the others, as if he were making them guards for it as for a queen.

42. In the same way, arranging the number of vestibules for the corridors on each side of the whole temple, he has made above them various openings into the building, for the purpose of admitting more light, adorning them with very fine wood-carving. But the royal house he has furnished with more beautiful and splendid materials, using unstinted liberality in his disbursements.

43. It seems to me superfluous to describe here in detail the length and breadth of the building, its splendor and its majesty surpassing description, and the brilliant appearance of the work, its lofty pinnacles reaching to the heavens, and the costly cedars of Lebanon above them, which the divine oracle has not omitted to mention, saying, 'The trees of the Lord shall rejoice and the cedars of Lebanon which he hath planted.'

44. Why need I now describe the skillful architectural arrangement and the surpassing beauty of each part, when the testimony of the eye renders instruction through the ear superfluous? For when he had thus completed the temple, he provided it with lofty thrones in honor of those who preside, and in addition with seats arranged in proper order throughout the whole building, and finally placed in the middle the holy of holies, the altar, and, that it might be inaccessible to the multitude, enclosed it with wooden lattice-work, accurately wrought with artistic carving, presenting a wonderful sight to the beholders.

45. And not even the pavement was neglected by him; for this too he adorned with beautiful marble of every variety. Then finally he passed on to the parts without the temple, providing spacious exedræ

and buildings on each side, which were joined to the basilica, and communicated with the entrances to the interior of the structure. These were erected by our most peaceful Solomon, the maker of the temple of God, for those who still needed purification and sprinkling by water and the Holy Spirit, so that the prophecy quoted above is no longer a word merely, but a fact; for now it has also come to pass that in truth 'the biter glory of this house is greater than the former.'

46. For it was necessary and fitting that as her shepherd and Lord had once tasted death for her, and after his suffering had changed that vile body which he assumed in her behalf into a splendid and glorious body, leading the very flesh which had been delivered from corruption to incorruption, she too should enjoy the dispensations of the Saviour. For having received from him the promise of much greater things than these, she desires to share uninterruptedly throughout eternity with the choir of the angels of light, in the far greater glory of regeneration, in the resurrection of an incorruptible body, in the palace of God beyond the heavens, with Christ Jesus himself, the universal Benefactor and Saviour.

47. But for the present, she that was formerly widowed and desolate is clothed by the grace of God with these flowers, and is become truly like a lily, as the prophecy says, and having received the bridal garment and the crown of beauty, she is taught by Isaiah to dance, and to present her thank-offerings unto God the King in reverent words.

48. Let us hear her saying, 'My soul shall rejoice in the Lord; for he hath clothed me with a garment of salvation and with a robe of gladness; he hath bedecked me like a bridegroom with a garland, and he hath adorned me like a bride with jewels; and like the earth which bringeth forth her bud, and like a garden which causeth the things that are sown in it to spring forth, thus the Lord God hath caused righteousness and praise to spring forth before all the nations.'

49. In these words she exults. And in similar words the heavenly bridegroom, the Word Jesus Christ himself, answers her. Hear the Lord saying, 'Fear not because thou hast been put to shame, neither be thou confounded because thou hast been rebuked; for thou shalt forget the former shame, and the reproach of thy widowhood shalt thou remember no more.' 'Not as a woman deserted and faint-hearted hath the Lord called thee, nor as a woman hated from her youth, saith thy God. For a small moment have I forsaken thee, but with great mercy will I have mercy upon thee; in a little wrath I hid my face from thee, but with everlasting mercy will I have mercy upon thee, saith the Lord that hath redeemed thee.'

50. 'Awake, awake, thou who hast drunk at the hand of the Lord the cup of his fury; for thou hast drunk the cup of ruin, the vessel of my wrath, and hast drained it. And there was none to console thee of all thy

sons whom thou didst bring forth, and there was none to take thee by the hand.' 'Behold, I have taken out of thine hand the cup of ruin, the vessel of my fury, and thou shalt no longer drink it. And I will put it into the hands of them that have treated thee unjustly and have humbled thee.'

51. 'Awake, awake, put on thy strength, put on thy glory. Shake off the dust and arise. Sit thee down, loose the bands of thy neck.' 'Lift up thine eyes round about and behold thy children gathered together; behold they are gathered together and are come to thee. As I live, saith the Lord, thou shalt clothe thee with them all as with an ornament, and gird thyself with them as with the ornaments of a bride. For thy waste and corrupted and ruined places shall now be too narrow by reason of those that inhabit thee, and they that swallow thee up shall be far from thee.

52. For thy sons whom thou hast lost shall say in thine ears, The place is too narrow for me, give place to me that I may dwell. Then shalt thou say in thine heart, Who hath begotten me these? I am childless and a widow, and who hath brought up these for me? I was left alone, and these, where were they for me?'

53. "These are the things which Isaiah foretold; and which were anciently recorded concerning us in sacred books; and it was necessary that we should sometime learn their truthfulness by their fulfillment.

54. For when the bridegroom, the Word, addressed such language to his own bride, the sacred and holy Church, this bridesman—when she was desolate and lying like a corpse, bereft of hope in the eyes of men—in accordance with the united prayers of all of you, as was proper, stretched out your hands and aroused and raised her up at the command of God, the universal King, and at the manifestation of the power of Jesus Christ; and having raised her he established her as he had learned from the description given in the sacred oracles.

55. This is indeed a very great wonder, passing all admiration, especially to those who attend only to the outward appearance; but more wonderful than wonders are the archetypes and their mental prototypes and divine models; I mean the reproductions of the inspired and rational building in our souls.

56. This the Divine Son himself created after his own image, imparting to it everywhere and in all respects the likeness of God, an incorruptible nature, incorporeal, rational, free from all earthly matter, a being endowed with its own intelligence; and when he had once called her forth from non-existence into existence, he made her a holy spouse, an all-sacred temple for himself and for the Father. This also he clearly declares and confesses in the following words: 'I will dwell in them and will walk in them; and I will be their God, and they shall be my people.' Such is the perfect and purified soul, so made from the beginning as to bear the image of the celestial Word.

57. But when by the envy and zeal of the malignant demon she became, of her own voluntary choice, sensual and a lover of evil, the Deity left her; and as if bereft of a protector, she became an easy prey and readily accessible to those who had long envied her; and being assailed by the batteries and machines of her invisible enemies and spiritual foes, she suffered a terrible fall, so that not one stone of virtue remained upon another in her, but she lay completely dead upon the ground, entirely divested of her natural ideas of God.

58. "But as she, who had been made in the image of God, thus lay prostrate, it was not that wild boar from the forest which we see that despoiled her, but a certain destroying demon and spiritual wild beasts who deceived her with their passions as with the fiery darts of their own wickedness, and burned the truly divine sanctuary of God with fire, and profaned to the ground the tabernacle of his name. Then burying the miserable one with heaps of earth, they destroyed every hope of deliverance.

59. But that divinely bright and saving Word, her protector, after she had suffered the merited punishment for her sins, again restored her, securing the favor of the all-merciful Father.

60. Having won over first the souls of the highest rulers, he purified, through the agency of those most divinely favored princes, the whole earth from all the impious destroyers, and from the terrible and God-hating tyrants themselves. Then bringing out into the light those who were his friends, who had long before been consecrated to him for life, but in the midst, as it were, of a storm of evils, had been concealed under his shelter, he honored them worthily with the great gifts of the Spirit. And again, by means of them, he cleared out and cleaned with spades and mattocks—the admonitory words of doctrine—the souls which a little while before had been covered with filth and burdened with every kind of matter and rubbish of impious ordinances.

61. And when he had made the ground of all your minds clean and clear, he finally committed it to this all-wise and God-beloved Ruler, who, being endowed with judgment and prudence, as well as with other gifts, and being able to examine and discriminate accurately the minds of those committed to his charge, from the first day, so to speak, down to the present, has not ceased to build. Now he has supplied the brilliant gold, again the refined and unalloyed silver, and the precious and costly stones in all of you, so that again is fulfilled for you in facts a sacred and mystic prophecy, which says,

62. 'Behold I make thy stone a carbuncle, and thy foundations of sapphire, and thy battlements of jasper, and thy gates of crystals, and thy wall of chosen stones; and all thy sons shall be taught of God, and thy children shall enjoy complete peace; and in righteousness shall thou be built.'

63. Building therefore in righteousness, be divided the whole

people according to their strength. With some he fortified only the outer enclosure, walling it up with unfeigned faith; such were the great mass of the people who were incapable of bearing a greater structure. Others he permitted to enter the building, commanding them to stand at the door and act as guides for those who should come in; these may be not unfitly compared to the vestibules of the temple. Others he supported by the first pillars which are placed without about the quadrangular hall, initiating them into the first elements of the letter of the four Gospels. Still others he joined together about the basilica on both sides; these are the catechumens who are still advancing and progressing, and are not far separated from the inmost view of divine things granted to the faithful.

64. Taking from among these the pure souls that have been cleansed like gold by divine washing, he then supports them by pillars, much better than those without, made from the inner and mystic teachings of the Scripture, and illumines them by windows.

65. Adorning the whole temple with a great vestibule of the glory of the one universal King and only God, and placing on either side of the authority of the Father Christ, and the Holy Spirit as second lights, he exhibits abundantly and gloriously throughout the entire building the clearness and splendor of the truth of the rest in all its details. And having selected from every quarter the living and moving and well-prepared stones of the souls, he constructs out of them all the great and royal house, splendid and full of light both within and without; for not only soul and understanding, but their body also is made glorious by the blooming ornament of purity and modesty.

66. And in this temple there are also thrones, and a great number of seats and benches, in all those souls in which sit the Holy Spirit's gifts, such as were anciently seen by the sacred apostles, and those who were with them, when there 'appeared unto them tongues parting asunder, like as of fire, and sat upon each one of them.'

67. But in the leader of all it is reasonable to suppose that Christ himself dwells in his fullness, and in those that occupy the second rank after him, in proportion as each is able to contain the power of Christ and of the Holy Spirit. And the souls of some—of those, namely, who are committed to each of them for instruction and care—may be seats for angels.

68. But the great and august and unique altar, what else could this be than the pure holy of holies of the soul of the common priest of all? Standing at the right of it, Jesus himself, the great High Priest of the universe, the Only Begotten of God, receives with bright eye and extended hand the sweet incense from all, and the bloodless and immaterial sacrifices offered in their prayers, and bears them to the heavenly Father and God of the universe. And he himself first worships him, and alone gives to the Father the reverence which is his due,

beseeching him also to continue always kind and propitious to us all.

69. "Such is the great temple which the great Creator of the universe, the Word, has built throughout the entire world, making it an intellectual image upon earth of those things which lie above the vault of heaven, so that throughout the whole creation, including rational beings on earth, his Father might be honored and adored.

70. But the region above the heavens, with the models of earthly things which are there, and the so-called Jerusalem above, and the heavenly Mount of Zion, and the supramundane city of the living God, in which innumerable choirs of angels and the Church of the first born, whose names are written in heaven, praise their Maker and the Supreme Ruler of the universe with hymns of praise unutterable and incomprehensible to us—who that is mortal is able worthily to celebrate this? 'For eye hath not seen nor ear heard, neither have entered into the heart of men those things which God hath prepared for them that love him.'

71. Since we, men, children, and women, small and great, are already in part partakers of these things, let us not cease all together, with one spirit and one soul, to confess and praise the author of such great benefits to us, 'Who for-giveth all our iniquities, who healeth all our diseases, who redeemeth our life from destruction, who crowneth us with mercy and compassion, who satisfieth our desires with good things.' 'For he hath not dealt with us according to our sins, nor rewarded us according to our iniquities;' 'for as far as the east is from the west, so far hath he removed our iniquities from us. Like as a father pitieth his own children, so the Lord pitieth them that fear him.'

72. Rekindling these thoughts in our memories, both now and during all time to come, and contemplating in our mind night and day, in every hour and with every breath, so to speak, the Author and Ruler of the present festival, and of this bright and most splendid day, let us love and adore him with every power of the soul. And now rising, let us beseech him with loud voice to shelter and preserve us to the end in his fold, granting his unbroken and unshaken peace forever, in Christ Jesus our Saviour; through whom be the glory unto him forever and ever. Amen."

Chapter V.

COPIES OF IMPERIAL LAWS.

1. Let us finally subjoin the translations from the Roman tongue of the imperial decrees of Constantine and Licinius.

2. *Copy of imperial decrees translated from the Roman tongue.* "Perceiving long ago that religious liberty ought not to be denied, but that it ought to be granted to the judgment and desire of each individual

to perform his religious duties according to his own choice, we had given orders that every man, Christians as well as others, should preserve the faith of his own sect and religion.

3. But since in that rescript, in which such liberty was granted them, many and various conditions seemed clearly added, some of them, it may be, after a little retired from such observance.

4. When I, Constantine Augustus, and I, Licinius Augustus, came under favorable auspices to Milan and took under consideration everything which pertained to the common weal and prosperity, we resolved among other things, or rather first of all, to make such decrees as seemed in many respects for the benefit of every one; namely, such as should preserve reverence and piety toward the deity. We resolved, that is, to grant both to the Christians and to all men freedom to follow the religion which they choose, that whatever heavenly divinity exists may be propitious to us and to all that live under our government.

5. We have, therefore, determined, with sound and upright purpose, that liberty is to be denied to no one, to choose and to follow the religious observances of the Christians, but that to each one freedom is to be given to devote his mind to that religion which he may think adapted to himself, in order that the Deity may exhibit to us in all things his accustomed care and favor.

6. It was fitting that we should write that this is our pleasure, that those conditions being entirely left out which were contained in our former letter concerning the Christians which was sent to your devotedness, everything that seemed very severe and foreign to our mildness may be annulled, and that now every one who has the same desire to observe the religion of the Christians may do so without molestation.

7. We have resolved to communicate this most fully to thy care, in order that thou mayest know that we have granted to these same Christians freedom and full liberty to observe their own religion.

8. Since this has been granted freely by us to them, thy devotedness perceives that liberty is granted to others also who may wish to follow their own religious observances; it being clearly in accordance with the tranquillity of our times, that each one should have the liberty of choosing and worshiping whatever deity he pleases. This has been done by us in order that we might not seem in any way to discriminate against any rank or religion.

9. And we decree still further in regard to the Christians, that their places, in which they were formerly accustomed to assemble, and concerning which in the former letter sent to thy devotedness a different command was given, if it appear that any have bought them either from our treasury or from any other person, shall be restored to the said Christians, without demanding money or any other equivalent, with no delay or hesitation.

10. If any happen to have received the said places as a gift, they shall restore them as quickly as possible to these same Christians: with the understanding that if those who have bought these places, or those who have received them as a gift, demand anything from our bounty, they may go to the judge of the district, that provision may be made for them by our clemency. All these things are to be granted to the society of Christians by your care immediately and without any delay.

11. And since the said Christians are known to have possessed not only those places in which they were accustomed to assemble, but also other places, belonging not to individuals among them, but to the society as a whole, that is, to the society of Christians, you will command that all these, in virtue of the law which we have above stated, be restored, without any hesitation, to these same Christians; that is, to their society and congregation: the above-mentioned provision being of course observed, that those who restore them without price, as we have before said, may expect indemnification from our bounty.

12. In all these things, for the behoof of the aforesaid society of Christians, you are to use the utmost diligence, to the end that our command may be speedily fulfilled, and that in this also, by our clemency, provision may be made for the common and public tranquillity.

13. For by this means, as we have said before, the divine favor toward us which we have already experienced in many matters will continue sure through all time.

14. And that the terms of this our gracious ordinance may be known to all, it is expected that this which we have written will be published everywhere by you and brought to the knowledge of all, in order that this gracious ordinance of ours may remain unknown to no one."

15. *Copy of another imperial decree which they issued, indicating that the grant was made to the Catholic Church alone.* "Greeting to thee, our most esteemed Anulinus. It is the custom of our benevolence, most esteemed Anulinus, to will that those things which belong of right to another should not only be left unmolested, but should also be restored.

16. Wherefore it is our will that when thou receivest this letter, if any such things belonged to the Catholic Church of the-Christians, in any city or other place, but are now held by citizens or by any others, thou shalt cause them to be restored immediately to the said churches. For we have already determined that those things which these same. churches formerly possessed shall be restored to them.

17. Since therefore thy devotedness perceives that this command of ours is most explicit, do thou make haste to restore to them, as quickly as possible, everything which formerly belonged to the said

churches,—whether gardens or buildings or whatever they may be— that we may learn that thou hast obeyed this decree of ours most carefully. Farewell, our most esteemed and beloved Anulinus."

18. *Copy of an epistle in which the Emperor commands that a synod of bishops be held at Rome in behalf of the unity and concord of the churches.* "Constantine Augustus to Miltiades, bishop of Rome, and to Marcus. Since many such communications have been sent to me by Anulinus, the most illustrious proconsul of Africa, in which it is said that Cæcilianus, bishop of the city of Carthage, has been accused by some of his colleagues in Africa, in many matters; and since it seems to me a very serious thing that in those provinces which Divine Providence has freely entrusted to my devotedness, and in which there is a great population, the multitude are found following the baser course, and dividing, as it were, into two parties, and the bishops are at variance—

19. it has seemed good to me that Cæcilianus himself, with ten of the bishops that appear to accuse him, and with ten others whom he may consider necessary for his defense, should sail to Rome, that there, in the presence of yourselves and of Retecius and Maternus and Marinus, your colleagues, whom I have commanded to hasten to Rome for this purpose, he may be heard, as you may understand to be in accordance with the most holy law.

20. But in order that you may be enabled to have most perfect knowledge of all these things, I have subjoined to my letter copies of the documents sent to me by Anulinus, and have sent them to your above-mentioned colleagues. When your firmness has read these, you will consider in what way the above-mentioned case may be most accurately investigated and justly decided. For it does not escape your diligence that I have such reverence for the legitimate Catholic Church that I do not wish you to leave schism or division in any place. May the divinity of the great God preserve you, most honored sirs, for many years."

21. *Copy of an epistle in which the emperor commands another synod to be held for the purpose of removing all dissensions among the bishops.* "Constantine Augustus to Chrestus, bishop of Syracuse. When some began wickedly and perversely to disagree among themselves in regard to the holy worship and celestial power and Catholic doctrine, wishing to put an end to such disputes among them, I formerly gave command that certain bishops should be sent from Gaul, and that the opposing parties who were contending persistently and incessantly with each other, should be summoned from Africa; that in their presence, and in the presence of the bishop of Rome, the matter which appeared to be causing the disturbance might be examined and decided with all care.

22. But since, as it happens, some, forgetful both of their own

salvation and of the reverence due to the most holy religion, do not even yet bring hostilities to an end, and are unwilling to conform to the judgment already passed, and assert that those who expressed their opinions and decisions were few, or that they had been too hasty and precipitate in giving judgment, before all the things which ought to have been accurately investigated had been examined—on account of all this it has happened that those very ones who ought to hold brotherly and harmonious relations toward each other, are shamefully, or rather abominably, divided among themselves, and give occasion for ridicule to those men whose souls are aliens to this most holy religion. Wherefore it has seemed necessary to me to provide that this dissension, which ought to have ceased after the judgment had been already given by their own voluntary agreement, should now, if possible, be brought to an end by the presence of many.

23. Since, therefore, we have commanded a number of bishops from a great many different places to assemble in the city of Arles, before the kalends of August, we have thought proper to write to thee also that thou shouldst secure from the most illustrious La-tronianus, corrector of Sicily, a public vehicle, and that thou shouldst take with thee two others of the second rank whom thou thyself shalt choose, together with three servants who may serve you on the way, and betake thyself to the above-mentioned place before the appointed day;

24. that by thy firmness, and by the wise unanimity and harmony of the others present, this dispute, which has disgracefully continued until the present time, in consequence of certain shameful strifes, after all has been heard which those have to say who are now at variance with one another, and whom we have likewise commanded to be present, may be settled in accordance with the proper faith, and that brotherly harmony, though it be but gradually, may be restored. May the Almighty God preserve thee in health for many years."

Chapter VI.

COPY OF AN IMPERIAL EPISTLE IN WHICH MONEY IS GRANTED TO THE CHURCHES.

1. "Constantine Augustus to Cæcilianus, bishop of Carthage. Since it is our pleasure that something should be granted in all the provinces of Africa and Numidia and Mauritania to certain ministers of the legitimate and most holy catholic religion, to defray their expenses, I have written to Ursus, the illustrious finance minister of Africa, and have directed him to make provision to pay to thy firmness three thousand folles.

2. Do thou therefore, when thou hast received the above sum of money, command that it be distributed among all those mentioned

above, according to the briefs sent to thee by Hosius.

3. But if thou shouldst find that anything is wanting for the fulfillment of this purpose of mine in regard to all of them, thou shalt demand without hesitation from Heracleides, our treasurer, whatever thou findest to be necessary. For I commanded him when he was present that if thy firmness should ask him for any money, he should see to it that it be paid without delay.

4. And since I have learned that some men of unsettled mind wish to turn the people from the most holy and catholic Church by a certain method of shameful corruption, do thou know that I gave command to Anulinus, the proconsul, and also to Patricius, vicar of the prefects, when they were present, that they should give proper attention not only to other matters but also above all to this, and that they should not overlook such a thing when it happened.

5. Wherefore if thou shouldst see any such men continuing in this madness, do thou without delay go to the above-mentioned judges and report the matter to them; that they may correct them as I commanded them when they were present. The divinity of the great God preserve thee for many years."

Chapter VII.

THE EXEMPTION OF THE CLERGY.

1. *Copy of an epistle in which the emperor commands that the rulers of the churches be exempted from all political duties.* "Greeting to thee, our most esteemed Anulinus. Since it appears from many circumstances that when that religion is despised, in which is preserved the chief reverence for the most holy celestial Power, great dangers are brought upon public affairs; but that when legally adopted and observed it affords the most signal prosperity to the Roman name and remarkable felicity to all the affairs of men, through the divine beneficence—it has seemed good to me, most esteemed Anulinus, that those men who give their services with due sanctity and with constant observance of this law, to the worship of the divine religion, should receive recompense for their labors.

2. Wherefore it is my will that those within the province entrusted to thee, in the catholic Church, over which Cæcilianus presides, who give their services to this holy religion, and who are commonly called clergymen, be entirely exempted from all public duties, that they may not by any error or sacrilegious negligence be drawn away from the service due to the Deity, but may devote themselves without any hindrance to their own law. For it seems that when they show greatest reverence to the Deity, the greatest benefits accrue to the state. Farewell, our most esteemed and beloved Anulinus."

Chapter VIII.

THE SUBSEQUENT WICKEDNESS OF
LICINIUS, AND HIS DEATH.

1. Such blessings did divine and heavenly grace confer upon us through the appearance of our Saviour, and such was the abundance of benefits which prevailed among all men in consequence of the peace which we enjoyed. And thus were our affairs crowned with rejoicings and festivities.

2. But malignant envy, and the demon who loves that which is evil, were not able to bear the sight of these things; and moreover the events that befell the tyrants whom we have already mentioned were not sufficient to bring Licinius to sound reason.

3. For the latter, although his government was prosperous and he was honored with the second rank after the great Emperor Constantine, and was connected with him by the closest ties of marriage, abandoned the imitation of good deeds, and emulated the wickedness of the impious tyrants whose end he had seen with his own eyes, and chose rather to follow their principles than to continue in friendly relations with him who was better than they. Being envious of the common benefactor he waged an impious and most terrible war against him, paying regard neither to laws of nature, nor treaties, nor blood, and giving no thought to covenants.

4. For Constantine, like an all-gracious emperor, giving him evidences of true favor, did not refuse alliance with him, and did not refuse him the illustrious marriage with his sister, but honored him by making him a partaker of the ancestral nobility and the ancient imperial blood, and granted him the right of sharing in the dominion over all as a brother-in-law and co-regent, conferring upon him the government and administration of no less a portion of the Roman provinces than he himself possessed.

5. But Licinius, on the contrary, pursued a course directly opposite to this; forming daily all kinds of plots against his superior, and devising all sorts of mischief, that he might repay his benefactor with evils. At first he attempted to conceal his preparations, and pretended to be a friend, and practiced frequently fraud and deceit, in the hope that he might easily accomplish the desired end.

6. But God was the friend, protector, and guardian of Constantine, and bringing the plots which had been formed in secrecy and darkness to the light, he foiled them. So much virtue does the great armor of piety possess for the warding off of enemies and for the preservation of our own safety. Protected by this, our most divinely favored emperor escaped the multitudinous plots of the abominable man.

7. But when Licinius perceived that his secret preparations by no means progressed according to his mind—for God revealed every plot and wickedness to the God-favored emperor—being no longer able to conceal himself, he undertook an open war.

8. And at the same time that he determined to wage war with Constantine, he also proceeded to join battle with the God of the universe, whom he knew that Constantine worshiped, and began, gently for a time and quietly, to attack his pious subjects, who had never done his government any harm. This he did under the compulsion of his innate wickedness which drove him into terrible blindness.

9. He did not therefore keep before his eyes the memory of those who had persecuted the Christians before him, nor of those whose destroyer and executioner he had been appointed, on account of the impieties which they had committed. But departing from sound reason, being seized, in a word, with insanity, he determined to war against God himself as the ally of Constantine, instead of against the one who was assisted by him.

10. And in the first place, he drove from his house every Christian, thus depriving himself, wretched man, of the prayers which they offered to God in his behalf, which they are accustomed, according to the teaching of their fathers, to offer for all men. Then he commanded that the soldiers in the cities should be cashiered and stripped of their rank unless they chose to sacrifice to the demons. And yet these were small matters when compared with the greater things that followed.

11. Why is it necessary to relate minutely and in detail all that was done by the hater of God, and to recount how this most lawless man invented unlawful laws? He passed an ordinance that no one should exercise humanity toward the sufferers in prison by giving them food, and that none should show mercy to those that were perishing of hunger in bonds; that no one should in any way be kind, or do any good act, even though moved by Nature herself to sympathize with one's neighbors. And this was indeed an openly shameful and most cruel law, calculated to expel all natural kindliness. And in addition to this it was also decreed, as a punishment, that those who showed compassion should suffer the same things with those whom they compassionated; and that those who kindly ministered to the suffering should be thrown into bonds and into prison, and should endure the same punishment with the sufferers. Such were the decrees of Licinius.

12. Why should we recount his innovations in regard to marriage or in regard to the dying—innovations by which he ventured to annul the ancient laws of the Romans which had been well and wisely formed, and to introduce certain barbarous and cruel laws, which were truly unlawful and lawless? He invented, to the detriment of the provinces which were subject to him, innumerable prosecutions, and all sorts of methods of extorting gold and silver. new measurements of

land and injurious exactions from men in the country, who were no longer living, but long since dead.

13. Why is it necessary to speak at length of the banishments which, in addition to these things, this enemy of mankind inflicted upon those who had done no wrong, the expatriations of men of noble birth and high reputation whose young wives he snatched from them and consigned to certain baser fellows of his own, to be shamefully abused by them, and the many married women and virgins upon whom he gratified his passions, although he was in advanced age—why, I say, is it necessary to speak at length of these things, when the excessive wickedness of his last deeds makes the first appear small and of no account?

14. For, finally, he reached such a pitch of madness that he attacked the bishops, supposing that they—as servants of the God over all—would be hostile to his measures. He did not yet proceed against them openly, on account of his fear of his superior, but as before, secretly and craftily, employing the treachery of the governors for the destruction of the most distinguished of them. And the manner of their murder was strange, and such as had never before been heard of.

15. The deeds which he performed at Amaseia and in the other cities of Pontus surpassed every excess of cruelty. Some of the churches of God were again razed to the ground, others were closed, so that none of those accustomed to frequent them could enter them and render the worship due to God.

16. For his evil conscience led him to suppose that prayers were not offered in his behalf; but he was persuaded that we did everything in the interest of the God-beloved emperor, and that we supplicated God for him. Therefore he hastened to turn his fury against us.

17. And then those among the governors who wished to flatter him, perceiving that in doing such things they pleased the impious tyrant, made some of the bishops suffer the penalties customarily inflicted upon criminals, and led away and without any pretext punished like murderers those who had done no wrong. Some now endured a new form of death: having their bodies cut into many pieces with the sword, and after this savage and most horrible spectacle, being thrown into the depths of the sea as food for fishes.

18. Thereupon the worshipers of God again fled, and fields and deserts, forests and mountains, again received the servants of Christ. And when the impious tyrant had thus met with success in these measures, he finally planned to renew the persecution against all.

19. And he would have succeeded in his design, and there would have been nothing to hinder him in the work, had not God, the defender of the lives of his own people, most quickly anticipated that which was about to happen, and caused a great light to shine forth as in the midst of a dark and gloomy night, and raised up a deliverer for leading into

those regions with a lofty arm, his servant, Constantine.

Chapter IX.

THE VICTORY OF CONSTANTINE, AND THE BLESSINGS WHICH UNDER HIM ACCRUED TO THE SUBJECTS OF THE ROMAN EMPIRE.

1. To him, therefore, God granted, from heaven above, the deserved fruit of piety, the trophies of victory over the impious, and he cast the guilty one with all his counselors and friends prostrate at the feet of Constantine.

2. For when Licinius carried his madness to the last extreme, the emperor, the friend of God, thinking that he ought no longer to be tolerated, acting upon the basis of sound judgment, and mingling the firm principles of justice with humanity, gladly determined to come to the protection of those who were oppressed by the tyrant, and undertook, by putting a few destroyers out of the way, to save the greater part of the human race.

3. For when he had formerly exercised humanity alone and had shown mercy to him who was not worthy of sympathy, nothing was accomplished; for Licinius did not renounce his wickedness, but rather increased his fury against the peoples that were subject to him, and there was left to the afflicted no hope of salvation, oppressed as they were by a savage beast.

4. Wherefore, the protector of the virtuous, mingling hatred for evil with love for good, went forth with his son Crispus, a most beneficent prince, and extended a saving right hand to all that were perishing. Both of them, father and son, under the protection, as it were, of God, the universal King, with the Son of God, the Saviour of all, as their leader and ally, drew up their forces on all sides against the enemies of the Deity and won an easy victory; God having prospered them in the battle in all respects according to their wish.

5. Thus, suddenly, and sooner than can be told, those who yesterday and the day before breathed death and threatening were no more, and not even their names were remembered, but their inscriptions and their honors suffered the merited disgrace. And the things which Licinius with his own eyes had seen come upon the former impious tyrants he himself likewise suffered, because he did not receive instruction nor learn wisdom from the chastisements of his neighbors, but followed the same path of impiety which they had trod, and was justly hurled over the same precipice.

6. Thus he lay prostrate. But Constantine, the mightiest victor, adorned with every virtue of piety, together with his son Crispus, a most God-beloved prince, and in all respects like his father, recovered

the East which belonged to them; and they formed one united Roman empire as of old, bringing under their peaceful sway the whole world from the rising of the sun to the opposite quarter, both north and south, even to the extremities of the declining day.

7. All fear therefore of those who had formerly afflicted them was taken away from men, and they celebrated splendid and festive days. Everything was filled with light, and those who before were downcast beheld each other with smiling faces and beaming eyes. With dances and hymns, in city and country, they glorified first of all God the universal King, because they had been thus taught, and then the pious emperor with his God-beloved children.

8. There was oblivion of past evils and forgetfulness of every deed of impiety; there was enjoyment of present benefits and expectation of those yet to come. Edicts full of clemency and laws containing tokens of benevolence and true piety were issued in every place by the victorious emperor.

9. Thus after all tyranny had been purged away, the empire which belonged to them was preserved firm and without a rival for Constantine and his sons alone. And having obliterated the godlessness of their predecessors, recognizing the benefits conferred upon them by God, they exhibited their love of virtue and their love of God, and their piety and gratitude to the Deity, by the deeds which they performed in the sight of all men.

THE END

96253781R00195

Made in the USA
Columbia, SC
23 May 2018